Social Security
in Global Perspective

JOHN DIXON

 PRAEGER

Westport, Connecticut
London

Library of Congress Cataloging-in-Publication Data

Dixon, John E.
    Social Security in global perspective / John Dixon.
        p. cm.
    Includes bibliographical references and index.
    ISBN 0–275–96509–0 (alk. paper)—ISBN 0–275–96510–4 (pbk. : alk. paper)
        1. Social security.   I. Title.
    HD7091.D59   1999
    368.4—dc21   98–41090

British Library Cataloguing in Publication Data is available.

Library of Congress Catalog Card Number: 98–41090
ISBN: 0–275–96509–0
        0–275–96510–4 (pbk.)

First published in 1999

Praeger Publishers, 88 Post Road West, Westport, CT 06881
An imprint of Greenwood Publishing Group, Inc.
www.praeger.com

Printed in the United States of America

The paper used in this book complies with the
Permanent Paper Standard issued by the National
Information Standards Organization (Z39.48–1984).

10 9 8 7 6 5 4 3 2 1

To Dr Jack Wing,
once a colleague for a short time,
now a friend and confidant for life.
For Tina, Piers and Aliki.

Contents

Tables

Preface

This study began in 1985 as a short monograph (Dixon 1986) written during a sabbatical as a Fulbright Scholar-in-Residence at the University of Wisconsin-Milwaukee. It subsequently grew. Its focus is on the diverse array of approaches to social security that is in evidence around the world. Its threefold objectives are: to articulate the values that underpin the global development of social security; to explore global social security patterns, recent developments and future issues; and to assess and rank social security programs and systems. Under comparative-evaluative review are the social security systems in 172 countries.

It is readily acknowledged that a social security system sits in a context that embraces economics, geography, history, political institutions, social structures and processes, and, of course, values and ideology. Deciding whether and how best to contextualize a social security system in a comparative framework is a problem that bedevils comparative scholars. For those masochistic enough to want to take a global perspective it becomes a nightmare: how do you contextualize 172 social security systems? The simple answer is that it cannot be done.

My path to whatever social security enlightenment I have achieved is littered with unpaid intellectual debts. As a lowly postgraduate scholar at the Australian National University (ANU) in the early 1970s I shared a space with Ron Mendelsohn, blissfully unaware at the time of his esteemed position in the comparative social security pantheon. I recall being fascinated by his insights into why Australia has such a distinctive social security system, an issue that was the subject of my research (Dixon 1977, 1978/79, 1981a and 1983). Then followed a stimulating exposure to Jim Cutt (then Professor and Head of the Masters in Administrative Studies Program at the ANU, now at the University of Victoria in Canada), who recruited me to work on an income-support evaluation project (Cutt et all. 1977, Cutt and Dixon 1975 and 1978, Dixon et al. 1984). Jim revealed to me the importance of conceptualizing social security as a system that is, itself, a subsystem of a complex socioeconomic system. My knowledge of the structure and processes of social security — albeit Australian social security (Dixon 1983) — was honed with the very valuable assistance of David Stanton (Australian Department of Social Security).

My first detailed encounter with another social security system came with my research on China in the late 1970s (Dixon 1981b). This line of research brought me into contact with Nelson Chow (University of Hong Kong), one of the first scholars in Asia to embark on comparative social security research (Chow 1975). Nelson made me more sensitive to the importance of understanding that a social security system is molded by a country's ideological and cultural values, both of which determine who the social security winners and losershould be (Chow 1988c).

My next intellectual creditor is Peter Kaim-Caudle (University of Durham), who suggested to me in 1980 that a fertile line of social security research might be found in the idiosyncratic National Provident Funds. How right he was (Dixon 1982, 1985b, 1987a, 1989a, 1989b, 1993, 1996b and 1996c)!

My early forays into international and comparative social security brought me into contact with scholars who were much more comfortable with such intellectual endeavors. Werner Boehm (Rutgers University) was the first, as a result of a visiting professorship appointment at Rutgers. Dick Estes (University of Pennsylvania) was, however, the most influential because of his capacity to conceptualize on a global basis (Estes 1984 and 1988). Without Dick's encouragement in 1985 this study would not even have begun. This intellectual move towards a global perspective was reinforced, soon after, when I met Dalmer Hoskins (then in United States Social Security Administration, now the Director-General of the International Social Security Association); Joe Vigilante (Adelphi University), where I was a Social Development Fellow for a short time; and Brij Mohan (Louisiana State University), with whom I worked for the best part of 10 years producing the *Journal of International and Comparative Social Welfare*.

Having cut my social security teeth on the mavericks — Australia, China and the National Provident Funds — my exposure in the mid-1980s to the social security mainstream of social insurance was ably, but unknowingly, facilitated by Warren McGillivray (then with the International Labor Organisation, now with the International Social Security Association).

My grounding in the global patterns of social security practice came from the Cook's tour of global social welfare provision I took over the next 10 years, with the very able assistance of Hung-shik Kim (then at the Western Australia College of Advanced Education) (Dixon and Kim 1985); Bob Scheurell (University of Wisconsin-Milwaukee) (Dixon and Scheurell 1989, 1990, 1994a and 1994b); David Macarov (Hebrew University of Jerusalem) (Dixon and

Macarov 1992 and 1998); and Bob Magill (University of Wisconsin-Milwaukee) (Dixon and Magill 1997). To each of these coeditors I am deeply indebted because of the insights they shared with me. I must also express my indebtedness to the 50 or so scholars who shared with me their knowledge and insights about national social security systems.

Bob Pinker (London School of Economics), Glen Drover (Dalhousie University) and Stewart MacPherson (Edith Cowan University) have each been a significant intellectual influence. Bob, who gave a quintessential keynote address at a conference I organized in Canberra in 1980, put the idea of social security traditions into my head. Glen and Stewart, who were both at the City University of Hong Kong when I was in Hong Kong in the early-to-mid 1990s, influenced my thinking on social security privatization and the connection between poverty and social security, respectively.

Jimmy Midgley (University of California, Berkeley) has been a source of great support and encouragement, and remains a dominant intellectual influence because of his seminal works on social security in the Third World (Midgley 1984a) and, more recently, on global social welfare (Midgley 1997).

Alex Kouzmin (University of Western Sydney, Nepean), a long-time colleague and friend, gave me insights into neoliberalism and, particularly, the ideological underpinnings of neoclassical economics that forced me to confront its domain assumptions after years of arrogant denial.

I am greatly also indebted to the staff in the United States Social Security Administration's Office of Research and Statistics and in the International Social Security Association who gathered and compiled the national social security profiles that form the information base for this study (US SSA 1996), none of whom I have met, yet. My thanks go Susan Grad and her staff, Alexander Estrin, Barbara Kritzer, Lillian Liu, Concepcion McNeace, Peter Puidak and Joseph Simanis.

I must thank my faithful research assistant for three years in Hong Kong, Mr Raman Athinathan, who, with diligence and an eye for detail, helped me search the enormous literature on comparative social security.

My sincere thanks go to Dr Jack Wing for voluntarily undertaking the tedious task of reading the entire manuscript. He has ensured not only that internal inconsistencies and errors born of gremlins are minimized, but also that both the clarity and readability are maximized.

To my wife, Tina, go my thanks, as usual, for putting up with me throughout the preparation of this manuscript. Without her support and tolerance this book would have taken even longer to complete and would be far less readable.

For any errors of fact and for all opinions and interpretations expressed, I must accept full responsibility.

John Dixon
Plymouth, May 1999

1

Social Security: The Concept, the Strategies and the System

INTRODUCTION

On a global basis social security practices have spread far and wide, well beyond the clique of industrialized countries that dominated the field in the late nineteenth century. As a mechanism for meeting human needs social security has achieved nearly universal acceptance. Access to social security has become a fundamental human right (Perrin 1985) proclaimed in the 1948 Universal Declaration of Human Rights (Articles 22 and 25) adopted by the United Nations General Assembly; in the International Covenant on Economic, Social and Cultural Rights (Article 9); and in numerous national constitutions (as in Australia, Japan and China). This right is, of course, realized in varying degrees in different countries, as determined by their traditions, history, level of socioeconomic development and the prevailing political and social philosophies, which come together to determine who should be the social security winners and losers. It is, perhaps, the adaptability of the social security idea to local conditions and varied cultural traditions that explains its global appeal.

There has been dramatic global expansion in social security throughout the twentieth century. Social security systems were first established in a small group of developed countries — essentially in Europe — in the 30 years before the First World War. Then they emerged in South and North America during the interwar years, only to flood subsequently into the Third World. There they often offered initial coverage to only European expatriates, as in the former French colonies from as early as 1941 (Ejuba 1982: 101–12). This post-Second World War expansion was encouraged by colonial authorities, especially the British and French, who were eager for political and social order and stability and who were frequently willing to replicate, inappropriately, their own systems (Ejuba 1982, Gardner and Judd 1954, Grimal 1978, Hassen 1972, Jenkins 1981, MacPherson 1982, MacPherson and Midgley 1987, Mair 1944, Midgley 1984a, 1984b and 1984c, Moulton 1975, Wicker 1958). The newly independent ex-colonies that emerged after the war found that their colonial social security heritage was reinforced, rather than questioned, by the expert advice they received from international agencies with their penchant for Eurocentric approaches (Midgley 1984a, Perrin 1969a and 1969b).

By the mid-1990s social security programs existed in 172 countries and territories, some 78 percent of all the then-extant countries and territories (see Appendix 1.1). There were thus 49 countries and territories that could not be identified as having a social security system, which does not, of course, necessarily mean that they did not have one. Indeed the United States Social Security Administration (1998) has very recently identified often long-standing social security programs in a number of countries and territories that have not been included in this study (namely, Andorra, Croatia, Guernsey, Jersey (Jersey, Employment and Social Security Review Committee 1995), Liechtenstein and Monaco). Those countries without a known social security program in 1995 fell into three distinct categories: 38 very diverse microcountries and territories (total population: 10 million); seven low-income countries: Bhutan, Cambodia, Eritrea, Guinea-Bissau, Laos, Lesotho and Mozambique (total population: 40 million); three lower-middle-income countries: Angola, Mongolia and Namibia (total population: 14 million); and one high-income country: the United Arab Emirates (population: 2 million) (World Bank 1995a and 1995b). Three recently formed post-socialist countries have inherited social security systems, but program details were not available (Bosnia and Herzegovina, and Croatia (but now see US SSA 1998) from the former Federal People's Republic of Yugoslavia, and Tajikistan from the former Soviet Union) (Ruzica 1992 and 1995, Wiktorow 1992, George 1991). It should also be noted that of the social security systems formally extant in the mid-1990s, some had probably collapsed or had been made largely inoperative because of war (as in, at least, Afghanistan, Azerbaijan, Burundi, Georgia, Iraq, Liberia, Rwanda, Sierra Leone, Somalia, Sudan, Turkmenistan and Yugoslavia (previously, Serbia and Montenegro)), while others had been severely restricted by war, natural disasters or severe economic dislocation (as in, at least, Albania, Armenia, Bulgaria, Ethiopia, Haiti, Kazakhstan, Kyrgyzstan, North Korea, Russia, the Ukraine and Uzbekistan) (Nagel et al. 1997).

THE SOCIAL SECURITY CONCEPT

Social security can usefully be thought of as the product of centuries of effort to provide people with a means of support in the face of individual, social or economic distress. As Mathew (1979b: 71) notes: "Its history is probably as old as the history of man. The quest for survival has prompted people, from the beginning of its existence, to devise ways of protecting itself from the hazards of life."

Definition

Under the rubric of social security falls public measures that provide cash and in-kind benefits upon the occurrence of prescribed contingencies (Igle 1994), namely, lost or inadequate earnings (income replacement or maintenance), and to offset the cost of supporting dependents (income supplementation). The former embraces situations where an individual's earning power *ceases permanently* (due to old age, permanent disability or death); *is interrupted* (by short-term injury or sickness, maternity or loss of employment); *never develops* (due to a physical or intellectual handicap, an emotional disturbance or an inability to gain first employment); *is insufficient to avoid poverty* (due to inadequate work remuneration or inadequately developed personal or vocational skills); and *is exercisable only at an unacceptable social cost* (such as lone parenthood or individual support of elderly parents or handicapped children or siblings). The domains of social security are thus *poverty prevention, poverty alleviation, social compensation* and *income redistribution.*

Boundaries

It must be recognized, of course, that the concept of social security has many blurred boundaries.

Occupational and Personal Plans. In many developed countries, social security coexists with *occupational* and *personal pension* and *savings* plans (Burchardt and Crescentini 1993, Davis 1996, European Commission 1991, Fuery et al. 1988, ISSA 1993b, Littlewood, 1998, OECD 1988 and 1991a, Roberts 1993, Roduit 1994, Turner and Beller 1990, Turner and Dailey 1991, Turner and Watanabe 1995, Voirin 1995). These are voluntary, privately administered, *defined-contribution plans* (which collect prescribed contributions but do not guarantee any defined benefits) or *defined-benefit plans* (which provide defined benefits for the payment of prescribed contributions).

Fiscal Welfare. This has long defined a boundary with social security in most developed countries, where favorable tax treatment, by means of taxable income deduction, tax allowances or refundable tax credits, is given to prescribed categories of taxpayers (particularly families with children, lone-parent families and the aged), so as to reduce their tax liabilities to achieve social security objectives (Brookes 1979, Harris 1977, Messere and Owens 1979, OECD 1977a and 1977b, Surrey 1985).

Mandatory Family Support. Rather more recently, the practice of legislating has created yet another boundary with social security. Some countries require either parents to support their children (as in Australia, New Zealand, the United Kingdom and in some states in the United States), or adult children to support their elderly parents (as in Algeria, Bangladesh, Egypt, China, Iraq, Kuwait, Japan, Jordan, Libya, Mauritius, Oman, Pakistan, Poland, South Africa, Syria, Tunisia and Yemen) (Eekelaar and Pearl 1989, Griffiths et al. 1987, Harding

1994, McDonald and Sorrano 1994).

Social Welfare and Health Services. Adding further to definitional complexity is the lack of consensus on what in-kind benefits and services should be treated as part of social security. Under the aegis of social security, many countries provide healthcare benefits, and a few provide milk, child care and a baby's layette.

Traditional Social Protection. It must also be recognized that in some developing countries both formal and informal social protection mechanisms exist at the village, tribal or family level that interface with state social security programs (Benda-Beckmann et al. 1988, Benda-Beckmann and Benda-Beckmann 1995, Guhan 1994, Hirtz 1988, 1990 and 1995, Zacher 1988). In some countries, formal measures have their origins in antiquity. The Aztec and Inca civilizations in Latin America required local communities to farm communal land to support the elderly, disabled people and the needy without family support (Mesa-Lago 1978: 17–18). Ancient Hindu law in India contained provisions for the care of the needy (Hallen 1967: 4). In the Byzantine empire the Christian virtue of *philanthropia* was enforced (Triseliotis 1977: 6). The practice of *zakat* — alms giving — is one of the five pillars of Islam dating back to the seventh century (Hassen 1965: 6, Mashhour 1998).

SOCIAL SECURITY STRATEGIES

Despite the rich diversity of social security strategies in evidence on a global basis, it is possible to identify the major ones: social insurance, social assistance, social allowances, mandatory public savings, employee liability, mandated occupational pensions and savings, and mandated personal pension and savings (see Table 1.1). All countries have constructed their social security systems by adopting one or more of these strategies. To provide a definition for each strategy that does more than identify its main features is impossible because of the vast array of idiosyncratic adaptions that have been made by countries adopting them.

Social Insurance

This strategy is an *employment-related, contributory approach* to social security, whereby upon the occurrence of prescribed social security contingency, cash benefits are provided to covered employees (typically, those in regular formal employment, but perhaps in only designated industries, occupations or regions, and, perhaps, subject to their earnings being above a minimum earnings floor or below a maximum earnings ceiling) and their dependents or survivors. Eligibility is determined either by the existence of an employment relationship or by satisfying a prescribed minimum period of employment, covered employment or contribution payments.

The cash pensions and benefits paid are usually related to current or past earnings (or perhaps to past contributions paid). They may, however, be paid at a flat rate. They may also be subject to a means test, albeit rarely. In-kind and healthcare benefits are also commonly provided.

Program benefits can be financed from current contribution revenue or from past contribution revenue accumulated, with interest, as reserves. Such revenue is derived from mandatory contributions, usually specified as a percentage of earnings, paid with respect to employees in designated categories (that is, covered employees) generally by the covered employees and their employers (perhaps also by the self-employed and independent farmers). (In some post-socialist countries in transition, where employee contributions are not required, the distinction between social insurance and employer liability measures is rather blurred.) Commonly, a subsidy is provided by the central government, and, considerably less frequently, the regional and local levels of government.

Contributions are paid to publicly supervised funds that are administered either by a public agency under direct government control or by a statutory public body (typically under tripartite management) under government supervision (typically by a ministry or department of social security or social welfare) .

Voluntary coverage may be permitted for designated employee categories or the self-employed.

Voluntary supplementary contributions may be paid by employees alone, by

Social Assistance

This strategy is a *selective-categorical* approach to social security, whereby residents (usually subject to a minimum residency period requirement) or citizens in designated social security beneficiary categories who can also satisfy a means test, receive a flat-rate cash entitlement at a rate that is most commonly uniform, although it can be differentiated (typically according to marital status or even age). Entitlement tapering because of the receipt of income or the ownership of assets is not common. The cash entitlements provided are intended to bring the recipient's total income up to a community-accepted minimum level. Typically, those who can demonstrate that they are in special need by satisfying specific additional eligibility conditions (perhaps including a more stringent asset and/or income test) qualify for supplementary assistance (for dependents) and special-need grants and allowances (typically including rent allowances, educational allowances, clothing allowances, household appliance allowances and travel allowances).

Social assistance is financed entirely from general government revenues, usually at the central government level, although financial contributions from regional and local government levels are not uncommon. Administration is usually by a public agency under direct central government control (typically a ministry or department of social security or social welfare), but occasionally the administration is undertaken at the regional agencies or local government level.

Table 1.1
Social Security Strategies

Social Security Strategy	Primary Social Security Goal	Primary Sources of Funding	Coverage	Primary Benefits Eligibility	Primary Forms of Benefits
Social Assistance	Poverty alleviation	Public revenue	Entire population or designated categories	Domicile Categorical tests Means test	Flat-rate periodic payments In-kind benefits
Social Insurance	Poverty prevention	Contributions from covered employees, their employers, and government	Employees in designated categories and their dependents	Categorical tests Contribution or employment record	Earnings-related or contribution related periodic payments In-kind benefits Healthcare benefits
Social Allowances	Social compensation	Public revenue	Entire population or designated categories	Categorical tests Domicile	Flat-rate periodic payments

Mandatory Public Savings	Poverty prevention	Contributions from covered employees and their employers	Employees in designated categories and their dependents	Categorical tests Past payment of contributions	Lump-sum, perhaps convertible to periodic payments
Employer Liability	Poverty prevention	Designated employers	Employees and their dependents	Current employment	Earning-related periodic payments Lump-sum payments
Mandated Occupational Pension or Savings	Poverty prevention	Contributions from covered employees and their employers	Employees in designated categories and their dependents	Past payment of contributions	Accrued lump-sum payments, periodic payments or defined benefits
Mandated Personal Pension or Savings	Poverty prevention	Contributions from insured individuals	Contributing individuals	Past payment of contributions	Accrued lump-sum payment, periodic payments

Where social assistance constitutes only a supplementary strategy, however, it may be administered by the statutory body responsible for the administration of the dominant social security strategy.

Social Allowances

This strategy is a *universal-categorical approach* to social security, whereby usually flat-rate and uniform cash pensions and benefits are provided to residents (usually subject to a minimum residency period requirement) or citizens in designated categories of presumed need, commonly without reference to their current or past employment experience. Program benefits are financed from general government revenue and administered by a public agency under direct government control (typically a ministry or department of social affairs or social security).

Mandatory Public Savings

This strategy is a *publicly administered, employment-related, compulsory savings (personal capitalization)* approach to social security that involves no risk pooling. The social security institutions — National Provident Funds — have members (or covered employees who are, typically, employees in regular formal employment, but perhaps in only designated industries, occupations or regions, and perhaps subject to their earnings being above a minimum earnings floor or below a maximum earnings ceiling) on whose behalf employers pay them regular contributions (usually defined as a percentage of earnings), part of which are withheld from employees earnings.

The contributions collected are credited to separate accounts maintained for each member. The contribution revenue is invested (usually subject to investment portfolio restrictions that limit or prohibit private sector investment) and members' accounts are credited with interest from the investment return earned.

Members have access to the balance standing in their accounts. They can withdraw it totally (but in some instances only partially) in a lump sum (or perhaps as equivalent value periodic payments or as an annuity, perhaps even an augmented annuity) upon the occurrence of a prescribed social security contingency or some other prescribed event (typically emigration or marriage) or purpose (typically to buy a home (perhaps, alternatively, by providing interest-bearing or interest-free housing loans), to provide healthcare (perhaps, alternatively, as a gratis benefit or as an interest-bearing loan), to cover the cost of various contingencies and social obligations.

The National Provident Funds are statutory public bodies (typically under tripartite management) under government supervision (typically by a ministry or department of labor or treasury), although administration may be by one or more public agencies under direct government control.

Employer Liability

This strategy is an *employment-related, employer-financed* approach to social security that also involves no risk pooling. Employers are required by law, in the event of any prescribed social security contingency, to provide cash benefits (usually earnings-related or in a lump-sum) and, perhaps, healthcare benefits, directly to employees and their dependents or survivors, perhaps after a judicial determination.

Employers may be required to insure against their employment injury liability risks with a public and/or private carrier. (On occasion, the distinction between employer liability and social insurance is blurred where the required public insurance carrier is also responsible for delivering social insurance programs.) Less commonly, only employers unable to establish their financial capacity to meet potential social security liabilities may be required to carry insurance. Alternatively, employers may merely either be encouraged to carry insurance against their employment injury risks, or be given the opportunity to do so with a public carrier.

Regulatory enforcement is by a public agency under direct government control (typically a ministry or department of labor).

Mandated Occupational Pension or Savings

This strategy is a *privately administered* approach to social security that makes membership of mandated occupational pension or savings plans a full substitute for, an optional alternative to, or a complement to, participation in a public social security program. These programs can be either defined-contribution or defined-benefit in form. They are established through collective bargaining, or as part of an employment contract, to provide social security pensions and benefits, whether as lump sums, earnings-related periodic payments or annuities, to their members (employees) and their dependents or survivors. They are financed by employer and employee premiums or savings contributions. They may be administered either by for-profit organizations (such as insurance companies, banks and investment funds) or not-for-profit organizations (such as mutual benefit societies) operating in a competitive market environment, or by trade unions and industry-based umbrella organizations operating in monopoly or contestable market environment. They are invariably subject to governmental regulatory regimes, and may receive favorable tax treatment.

Mandated Personal Pension or Savings

This strategy is a *privately administered* approach to social security that makes membership of mandated personal pension or savings plans a full substitute for, an optional alternative to, or a complement to, participation in a public social security program. These programs can be either defined-contribution or defined-benefit in form. They are established by individuals to provide social security pensions and benefits, whether as lump sums, earnings-related periodic payments or annuities for themselves and their dependents or survivors. They are financed by individual premiums or savings contributions. They may be administered by for-profit organizations (such as insurance companies, banks and investment funds) and by not-for-profit organizations   such as mutual benefit societies) in a competitive market environment. They are subject to governmental regulatory regimes, and they may receive favorable tax treatment.

SOCIAL SECURITY SYSTEM FEATURES

A social security system is made up of one or more social security programs, a method of financing, and a mode of administration, that can be configured to achieve particular social security objectives.

Program Coverage

Social security coverage defines the scope of the protection provided by a social security program (Trenk-Hinterberger 1994) — the covered population — which may be either *universal* or *categorical.*

Universal Coverage. This is where the entire population is protected by a social security program if a prescribed social security contingency occurs.

Categorical Coverage. This is where only certain population categories are protected by a social security program. These categories may be based on *employment* (current or past) or on *specific population characteristics* (such as residency status, age, gender and marital status). Both types of categorization can also be subject to general second-level classifiers. Categorizations based on employment can be further narrowed by exempting employees in designated geographic regions, economic sectors, industry sectors, occupational groups (such as farmers, self-employed, public employees), forms of employment (such as temporary, casual, unpaid or family labor), employer categories (those employing below a minimum number of employees), or earnings categories (those earning below or above an earnings ceiling). Categorization based on population characteristics can be narrowed by exempting individuals on the basis of, for example, their citizenship or residency status, age, gender, social security recipient status, marital status and the adequacy of their voluntary social security provision.

Voluntary coverage can be made available to specific exempt population categories (notably, the self-employed, previously covered employees, uncovered employees in general or in specific exempt industries or occupations, and farmers).

Alternatively, special systems can be made available for exempt categories (notably the self-employed, farmers, farm employees, public employees (including military personnel) and employees in designated industries and occupational groups).

Program Benefit Eligibility

Eligibility criteria determine who, from amongst the covered population, are eligible for social security program benefits. They are used to determine whether social security applicants qualify for a specific benefit entitlement. They can be classified as *categorical, general qualifying* and *means-assessment criteria*.

Categorical Criteria. These are the eligibility criteria that define whether a social security applicant falls within a social security beneficiary category and thus qualifies for a specific benefit entitlement. These requirements are, of course, program-specific, but can include age, gender, marital status, degree of disability, health status, number and type of dependents, and employment status.

General Qualifying Eligibility Criteria. These are the eligibility criteria used to exclude social security applicants who satisfy the categorical criteria from qualifying for a specific benefit because they fail to meet a set of general qualifying requirements. These requirements include minimum periods of residency, employment, employment with the same employer, contribution and waiting (Griffith 1974) because of sickness, disability and unemployment; annual average rate of weekly contributions; maximum payment periods; and residency status.

Means-Assessment Criteria. These are the means-based eligibility criteria used to exclude social security applicants who satisfy the categorical criteria, and perhaps even the general qualifying eligibility criteria, because they cannot demonstrate that they have an insufficient level of income and/or assets. This involves the application of an asset and/or an income test (Dixon and Cutt 1975 and 1976, Dixon 1978/79 and 1983, Moon 1977 and 1979).

An income test comprises an *income disregard limit* (Im), which may be at a standard level or differentiated by marital status; a prescribed uniform or a differentiated *entitlement withdrawal* (claw-back) *rate* for income in excess of the income disregard limit (a); and the *maximum entitlement rate* (Em), which may be at a uniform rate or differentiated by marital status, all of which define an *income cutout threshold*, which is the income limit (Ie) at which any entitlement ceases:

$$Ie = Im + Em/a < max\ Ie,$$

where max Ie is any statutory maximum income cutout threshold.

An asset test comprises an *asset disregard limit* (Am), which may be at standard level or differentiated on the basis of marital status or, perhaps, home ownership; a prescribed uniform or a differentiated *entitlement withdrawal* (claw-back) *rate* for assets in excess of the asset disregard limit (b); the *maximum entitlement rate* (Em), all of which define an *asset cutout threshold*, which is the asset limit (Ae) at which any entitlement ceases:

$$Ae = Am + Em/b < \max Ae,$$

where max Ae is any statutory maximum asset cutout threshold.
If both an income and an asset test apply then:

$$Ie = (Im + Em/a) - b (A - Am) < \max Ie,$$

where A is the value of non-exempt assets owned, and,

$$Ae = Am + (Em - (I - Im))/b < \max Ae,$$

where I is the amount of non-exempt income received.

Clearly, the income or asset cutout thresholds would be higher, other parameters being constant, the smaller the value of assets owned in excess of the asset disregard limit or the income received in excess of the income disregard limit, respectively.

The separate, but interrelated, income and asset tests can be integrated, as happened in Australia between 1960 and 1976, by providing a formula that converts non-exempt assets into an income equivalent, so defining a concept of "means" (M):

$$M = I + c (A - Am),$$

where c is the asset-value income-equivalent coefficient with a value of between zero and one (Dixon 1977).

Hence, given a *"means" disregard limit* (Mm), which has both an income component and an asset-value, income-equivalent component; a prescribed uniform or a differentiated *entitlement withdrawal* (claw-back) *rate* for "means" in excess of the "means" disregard limits (d); and a *maximum entitlement rate* (Em), the *"means" cutout threshold* (Me) can be defined:

$$Me = Mm + Em/a < \max Me.$$

Thus, when the value of non-exempt assets does not exceed the asset disregard limit, then the "means" cutout point defines an income cutout threshold equal to what would have applied if the income and asset tests were administered separately. However, if non-exempt income does not exceed the income disregard limit, then, provided the entitlement withdrawal rate for "means" (d) is greater than the asset-value income equivalent coefficient (c), the "means" cutout threshold defines an asset cutout threshold that exceeds what would have applied if the income and asset tests were administered separately. Hence, the integration of the two elements of a means test in this way effectively liberalizes the asset test without liberalizing the asset disregard limit.

It should be noted that the impact of any means test can also be liberalized or restricted, without changing the income or asset cutout thresholds, by a redefinition of the types of income and assets that fall under the rubric of "income" and "assets" (that is, by changing what are permitted forms of "exempt" income (typically irregular income and cash gifts) and assets (typically the residential home and personal effects)), and by not adequately indexing the disregard limits or maximum entitlements to inflation.

Program Benefits

Cash entitlements can be either *periodic payments* or *lump sums*. They can be augmented by *supplementary, special purpose* and *healthcare benefits*.

Periodic Cash Entitlements. These are cash entitlements dispensed on a regular (weekly or monthly) basis. They can be paid either at a *flat* or a *variable* rate (typically as a proportion of past earnings, past contributions paid, or national average or minimum earnings), set at either a *uniform* or a *differentiated* level (depending, for example, on the number of years over which contributions have been paid, amount of contributions paid, annual average contribution periods, years of covered employment, age and marital status of the recipient, number and type of dependents, the degree of disability suffered, current earnings or assets owned). They can also be subject to minimum and/or maximum payment rates.

Earnings-related entitlements are based on statutory earnings-replacement rates. They can also be subject to minimum and/or maximum earnings requirements (that is, the minimum and/or maximum amount of earnings to which the statutory earnings-replacement rates apply). It should be noted that earnings-related benefit generosity can also be changed, without changing the income-replacement rate, by a redefinition of the types of income that come under the rubric of "income" for the purposes of calculating entitlement rates.

Flat-rate entitlements that are means tested are paid at the maximum entitlement level (Em) either if all eligible beneficiaries receive the same entitlements, because they confront a means testing mechanism that incorporates only statutory cutout thresholds and thus does not taper entitlements, or because they have assets and/or incomes below those thresholds. Those receiving tapered entitlements who have income and/or assets above the threshold limits receive a reduced or partial entitlement (E) determined as follows:

$$E = Em - (a\,(I - Im) + b\,(A - Am)).$$

Clearly, the entitlement generosity can be changed by a redefinition of non-exempt income and assets.

The periodic cash entitlements may be ongoing or they may be subject to a maximum payment period.

They may also be indexed to prices or average earnings.

Lump-sum Cash Entitlements. These can be based on *prescribed contribution rates* (individual capitalization) or on *prescribed benefit rates*, which can be *uniform* or *differentiated* (depending, for example, on past earnings, contribution period, degree of disability and age). There can also be minimum payment rates specified. Lump-sum payments can also be made convertible to periodic payments or annuities.

Supplementary Cash Benefits. These are paid, perhaps subject to satisfying a tailored means test, with respect to dependents, including dependent spouse, children (typically subject to an age limit unless disabled), and dependent adult parents, siblings, other relatives and even non-family members.

Special Need Benefits. These are provided, perhaps subject to satisfying a tailored means test, as cash or in-kind benefits to those who can demonstrate a special need (such as disabled people's need for constant attendance) or who incur specified expenses (such as funeral costs).

Healthcare Benefits. Medical and/or hospital care may be provided by the *social security institution* (either directly or under contract by the public and/or private health services sectors), by the *public healthcare system,* by *employers directly*; or by *national health insurance* (using either public or private carriers).

Program Entitlement Expenditure Targeting

Social security program entitlements can be targeted within a social security category on particular population categories — *categorical targeting* (or "pseudo-targeting" (Bolderson and Mabbett 1996: 4) or "positive selectivism" in Titmussian terms (Titmuss 1976: 134), see also Titmuss 1974) — or on particular income or means groups — *income or means targeting.* (Alcock 1996, Bolderson and Mabbett 1996, Corden 1983, Graham 1984, Kanbur and Besley 1992, Lipton and Ravaillion 1993, Morgan 1992).

Categorical Targeting. This uses of *categorical* and/or *general qualifying eligibility criteria* to achieve the desired proportion of beneficiaries within a particular target population group (horizontal target efficiency considerations — the extent to which the targeted population group should be assisted) by increasing their share of social security program entitlement expenditure at the expense of other population categories (vertical target efficiency considerations — the extent to which benefits should be confined to the targeted group) (Weisbrod 1970). Categorical target efficiency is the degree to which this is achieved.

Income or Means Targeting. This uses the *means-assessment criteria* and/or *benefit calculation formula* to achieve a desired degree of support to those below specified asset and/or income thresholds within an eligible social security program category (horizontal target efficiency considerations) by increasing their share of the entitlement expenditure at the expense of higher income or "means" groups (vertical target efficiency considerations). Two forms of income or means targeting can be identified: *poverty targeting* (or "negative selectivism" in Titmussian terms (Titmuss 1976: 134)), as defined by a poverty threshold (Cutt et al. 1977, Saunders 1991, Millar 1988, Oorschot and Schell 1989); and *affluence targeting*, as defined by an affluence threshold (Cutt et al. 1977).

Poverty Targeting. This concentrates a social security program's entitlement expenditure on those deemed to be "poor" because they are under or only marginally above a poverty threshold. Such targeting can be achieved in three ways.

First, those outside the poverty target group can be excluded from benefit eligibility by the specification of statutory asset and/or income cutout thresholds at the poverty or near-poverty thresholds. Second, a set of statutory asset and/or income disregard levels and appropriate withdrawal rates can be defined to concentrate benefit expenditure on those in poverty — the poor — whilst providing varying degrees of support to those beyond the poverty threshold by means of entitlement tapering. Finally, benefit entitlement eligibility can be restricted over time by not adjusting statutory benefit entitlement cutout points or disregard limits in line with inflation, thereby concentrating benefit entitlement expenditure increasingly on those in or near poverty.

The impact of poverty targeting tactics can be measured by means of Beckerman's (1979) indicators of *poverty-reduction efficiency* (the proportion of benefit expenditure that goes towards reducing the pre-transfer aggregate poverty gap) and *poverty-reduction effectiveness* (the proportional reduction of the pre-transfer aggregate poverty gap caused by benefit expenditure).

Affluence Targeting. This ensures that those deemed to be "affluent" because they are above an affluence threshold receive a reduced share of any social security program entailment expenditure. Such targeting can be achieved in five ways. First, those beyond the designated affluence asset and/or income thresholds can be excluded from benefit eligibility by the specification of statutory asset and/or income cutout thresholds at the affluence threshold limits. Second, a set of asset and/or income disregard levels and appropriate withdrawal rates can be defined to concentrate benefit entitlement expenditure on those with assets and/or income below the affluence threshold, whilst providing some support to those in varying degrees of marginal affluence by means of entitlement tapering. Third, those deemed to be affluent because of particular forms of assets or income can be exclude from benefit entitlement only by deeming those forms of assets and/or income to be non-exempt when determining statutory disregard limits asset and/or cutout thresholds. Fourth, benefit eligibility can be restricted by using the income tax system to claw-back entitlements, or by making them subject to income tax (perhaps with a surcharge) once a prescribed taxable income threshold is breached. Finally, earnings-related entitlements can be restricted by specifying a maximum entitlement rate or a statutory earnings-replacement rate that is subject to a maximum earnings requirement for those beyond the affluence threshold.

The impact of these tactics can be measured by two indicators: *affluence-delimiting efficiency* (the proportion of benefit entitlement expenditure that is withdrawn from the pre-transfer aggregate affluence margin — the sum of all pre-transfer incomes of those above an affluence threshold and the affluence threshold itself (Cutt et al. 1977); and *affluence-targeting effectiveness* (the proportional reduction of the pre-transfer aggregate affluence margin caused by the withdrawal of benefit entitlement expenditure).

Financing

There are various ways by which social security programs can be financed. A distinction can be drawn between social security programs that are financed by *contributory* or *non-contributory* funding methods (ILO 1984a, ISSA 1979, Thompson 1996).

Contributory Funding. This method of funding defined-benefit programs covers a spectrum from the *annual assessment* (or pay-as-you-go)*method* to the *fully funded method*. Indeed, the former may be adjusted to incorporate a degree of reserve accumulation (to accommodate, for example, anticipated demographic trends), while the latter may benefit from a degree of pay-as-you-go funding (to reduce, for example, risk exposure to anticipated inflation rates).

Under the annual assessment method, current revenue (social security contributions, effectively payroll tax revenue) must match current outlays (entitlement expenditure plus administrative costs and contingency reserve allocations). Thus for any program, the required payroll tax (t) is (from MacKellar and McGreevey 1997: 15):

$$t = R*D,$$

where R is the replacement ratio (entitlements as a proportion of average earnings); and D is the dependency ratio (recipients as a proportion of contributors).

Of the many approaches to fully funding social security programs, the most commonly used are the *general average premium method* (whereby the contribution rate is determined by equating the present value of contributions of existing insured persons and future entrants, plus future interest earnings and any government subsidies, to the present value of all benefit expenditure commitments with respect to existing members and future entrants, plus projected administrative costs and any contingency reserve requirements); and the *scaled premium method* (whereby the contribution rate is set initially at a lower rate than that required by the general average premium method but subsequently increased to ensure that during a stipulated period of equilibrium (typically between 10 and 20 years) the annual contributions plus interest derived from the accumulated reserves are sufficient to meet the expenditure commitments).

Revenue is derived from a variety of sources. These include mandatory contributions paid with respect to *covered employees* (all or designated employees). These can be specified as either a *flat rate*, which can be either *uniform* or *differentiated* (depending on, for example, wage, industry or occupational categories or age), or a *percentage of earnings* (typically total emoluments received, including overtime payments, regular supplementary allowances and any bonuses paid), either on the basis of *actual earnings* or *earnings categories*.. They can be subject to a *contribution ceiling* (the maximum amount of earnings to which the contribution rate applies) or *floor* (the minimum amount of earnings to which the contribution rate applies). These contributions are usually paid by *covered employees* and their *employers* (invariably as a tax deductible business expense). The division of responsibility between the employer and covered employee for the payment of the total social security contribution — the *statutory contribution incidence* — is defined in the enabling legislation.

The distinction between *statutory contribution incidence* and *economic incidence* (how the actual social security contribution cost burden is finally distributed allowing for the behavioral responses of both employers and covered employees to the payment of contributions) is an important one for the impact social security contributions may have on the distribution of income; on inflation, through their effect on total labor and commodity costs; and on unemployment, through their effect on the structure of employment and on factor substitution (the substitution of capital for labor in the production process) (see, for example, Euzeby 1995). Employers can seek to shift their statutory contribution burden either forward towards consumers by imposing compensatory commodity price increases over time (their ability to do this depends on the sensitivity of end-user demand to commodity price changes) or backward towards covered employees by seeking compensatory wage reductions over time (their ability to do this depends on the degree of competition in the labor market and their relative market dominance). Covered employees can, alternatively, seek to shift their statutory contribution burden either forward towards employers, by demanding compensatory wage increases over time (their ability to do this depends on their relative labor market dominance) or backward towards government, by demanding compensating social wage increases in the form of tax-financed government services and benefits (their ability to do this depends on their relative political influence).

With respect to employment-injury benefit financing, contributions can also vary *according to the risks* to which various insured-person categories are exposed, as determined for each risk class or industry class (based on the frequency and the severity of the risk appropriate to each such class, perhaps moderated by an experience rating determined with reference to past accident experience and to the accident prevention measures taken).

Government subsidies may be provided in a variety of forms: *deficit funding, an annual subvention, a proportion of contributions collected, administrative cost subsidies, the proceeds of earmarked tax and surcharge impositions* (such as taxes on pharmaceutical advertising, alcohol and tobacco, and surcharges on accident insurance premiums), or *specific subsidies for specific target groups.* Such subsidies may be provided by the central, regional and local levels of government. Governments can also act as a guarantor for the financial viability of contributory social security systems. The precise form of subsidy provided (from which can be identified who are the actual — as distinct from intended — recipients of government subsidization) and its method of financing (from which can be identified who are the actual carriers of the cost burden of government subsidization) are significant determinants of the impact that a social security system has on the distribution of income, inflation, unemployment and economic growth. Earmarked commodity or income taxes potentially permit a specific transfer of income from one or more targeted population categories to targeted social security recipients, although the chosen tax instrument's economic incidence may well distort the desired outcomes of this income redistribution process.

Non-contributory Funding. This method of funding takes two forms: *exclusive government funding* and *exclusive employer funding.*

Exclusive government funding applies when social security programs are financed entirely by governments, usually at the central level but possibly at the regional and local levels, as part of a governmental budgeting process. Increased or new social security program expenditure can thus be financed by reducing outlays on other government programs, by increasing the productivity of existing revenue sources (by widening the tax bases or by increasing tax rates), by introducing new tax instruments, by increasing budgetary deficits financed from public borrowings, or even by reducing budget surpluses. Each of these alternative methods of financing defines the population categories upon whom the social security cost burden is intended to fall, although efforts to shift this cost burden towards other population categories — perhaps even social security recipients themselves — may well distort the desired outcomes of this income redistribution process.

Exclusive employer funding applies when employers have exclusive responsibility for the direct provision of social security benefits. They may be required to insure against their social security risks with a public or private carrier. Of course, employers can seek to minimize their social security cost burden by seeking to shift their statutory social security cost burden either forwards towards consumers or backwards towards employees, which may well distort the desired outcomes of this employer-employee income redistribution.

Administration

The administration of social security systems can be in the hands of *the public sector, the non-government sector,* or both.

The Public Sector. Administrative responsibility may rest with *public* agencies under direct government control or with *statutory public bodies* (typically under bipartite or tripartite management) under the general supervision of a ministry, department or even a supervisory committee. The administrative arrangements may be centralized or decentralized, involving either decentralized administrative units attached to the social security organization or the contracting out of services to other central public agencies, to lower-level government agencies, to non-government agencies, or to the private sector, including employers.

The Non-Government Sector. Administration responsibility may rest with either *for-profit* organizations (such as insurance companies, banks and investment funds) or *not-for-profit* organizations (such as mutual benefit societies, labor unions and industry-based umbrella organizations), subject to a governmental regulatory regime enforced by a ministry or department.

CONCLUSION

The social norms that mold and infiltrate a society's perceptions of social security are the result of an accumulation of preferences regarding the respective roles of the individual, the family, the clan, the tribe and the nation-state generated by people as they shape their specific society. The institution of social security has always had a past to reflect on — its genesis being mutual aid and philanthropic organizations— and a future to ponder. Indeed, social security's future has always been chiseled from its past by the practice known to public administration as disjointed incrementalism, the practice of making small changes in policy in a rather desultory manner. Throughout the last century this has involved the transplanting of essentially nineteenth-century European values and the adoption of contemporary administrative and financial practices.

APPENDIX 1.1: PRIMARY SOCIAL SECURITY STRATEGIES BY PROGRAM THROUGHOUT THE WORLD, 1995

Region/Country	Social Security Programs:											
	Old-age	Disability	Death	Sickness	Maternity	Temp. Employment-related Disbility	Perm. Employment-related Disability	Employment-related Suvivors'	Unemployment	Family	Child	Health
NORTH AFRICA												
ALGERIA	A	A	A	A	A	A	A	A				A
EGYPT	A	A	A	A	A	A	A	A	A			A
LIBYA	A	A	A	D	D	D	D	A	D			A
MOROCCO	A	A	A	A	A	D	D	D			A	D
SUDAN	A	A	A	D	D	D	D	D				I
TUNISIA	A	A	A	A	A	D	D	D	B	A	A	A

WEST AFRICA

BENIN	A	A	A	D	A	A	A		A	D
BURKINA FASO	A	A	A	A	A	A	A		A	A
CAMEROON	A	A	A	D	A	A	A		A	A
CAPE VERDE	A	A	A	A	A	A	A	A	A	A
CÔTE D'IVOIRE	A	A	A	A	A	A	A		A	A
EQUATORIAL GUINEA	A	A	A	A	A	A	A		A	A
GABON	A	A	A	D	A	A	A		A	A
GAMBIA, THE	E	E	E	A		D	D			I
GHANA	A	A	A	A		D	D			D
GUINEA	A	A	A	A	A	A	A		A	A
LIBERIA	A	A	A	A		A	A			A
MALI	A	A	A	D	A	A	A		A	A

	1	2	3	4	5	6	7	8	9	10
MAURITANIA	A	A	A		A	A	A	A	A	A
NIGER	A	A	A	D	A	A	A	A	A	A
NIGERIA	A	A	A	D	D	D	D	D		I
SÃO TOMÉ AND PRINCIPE	A	A	A	A	A	A		A		I
SENEGAL	A	A	A		A	A	A	A	A	J
SIERRA LEONE						D	D	D		D
TOGO	A	A	A	D	A	A	A	A	A	A
MIDDLE AFRICA										
CENTRAL AFRICAN REP.	A	A	A	D	A	A	A	A	A	A
CHAD	A	A	A	D	A	A	A	A	A	A
CONGO	A	A	A	D	A	A	A	A	A	A
ZAIRE	A	A	A	D	D	A	A	A	A	A

EAST AFRICA

BURUNDI	A	A	A	D	D	A	A	A			D	1
ETHIOPIA	A	A	A	D	D	D	D	D				1
KENYA	E	E	E	D	D	D	D	D				J
MADAGASCAR	A	A	A	D	A	A	A	A		A		A
MALAWI						D	D	D				1
MAURITIUS	C	C	C	D	D	A	A	A	B			I
RWANDA	A	A	A	D	D	A	A	A				A
SEYCHELLES	A	A	A	A	A	A	A					I
SOMALIA						A	A	A				I
TANZANIA	E	E	E			D	D	D	D			I
UGANDA	E	E	E	D	D	D	D	D				I
ZAMBIA	E	E	E	D	D	D	D	D	E			I

23

SOUTHERN AFRICA

BOTSWANA	B	B	B	D	D	D	D	D	D	D		D
SOUTH AFRICA		B	E	A	A	D	D	D	D	A		I
SWAZILAND	E	E	E			D	D	D	D			D
ZIMBABWE	A	A	A	D	D	D	D	D	D			I

CENTRAL ASIA

ARMENIA	A	A	A	A	A	A	A	A	A	A	C C	I
AZERBAIJAN										A		I
GEORGIA	A	A	A	A	A	A	A	A	A	A		I
KAZAKHSTAN	A	A	A		A	A	A	A	A			I
KYRGYZSTAN	A	A	A	A	A	A	A	A	A	A	B	I
TURKMENISTAN	A	A	A	A	A	A	A	A	A	A		I
UZBEKISTAN	A	A	A	A	A	A	A	A	A	A		I

EAST ASIA

CHINA	A	A	A	A	A	D	D	D	A	D
HONG KONG	B	C		D	D	D	D	D	B	I
JAPAN	A	A	A	A	A	A	A	A	A	J
KOREA, NORTH	D			D	A	A	A	A		I
KOREA, SOUTH	A	A	A			D	D	D	A	J
MACAU	A	A	A			A			A	I
TAIWAN	A	A	A	A	A	A	A	A	A	J

SOUTH ASIA

AFGHANISTAN	A	A		A	A	F	F	F		I
BANGLADESH			D	D	D	D	D	D	D	I
INDIA	E	E	E	A	A	A	A	A	D	A
MYANMAR			A	A	A	D	D	D	D	A

NEPAL	E	E	E			D	D	D	E		I
PAKISTAN	A	A	A	A	A	A	A	A	D		A
SRI LANKA	E	E	E		D	D	D	D	E	B	I
SOUTH-EAST ASIA											
INDONESIA	E	E	E			A	A	A			A
MALAYSIA	E	A	A			A	A	A			I
PHILIPPINES	A	A	A	A	A	A	A	A			A
SINGAPORE	E	E	E	D	D	D	D	D			E
THAILAND	A	A		A	A	D	D	D			A
VIETNAM	A	A	A	A	A	A	A	A			A
AUSTRALASIA											
AUSTRALIA	B	B	B	B	D	D	D	D	B	C	J
NEW ZEALAND	C	B	B	B	B	A	A	A	B	B	I

WESTERN EUROPE

AUSTRIA	A	A	A	A	A	A	A	A		C	A
BELGIUM	A	A	A	A	D	D	D	A		A	A
CYPRUS	A	A	A	A	A	A	A	A		C	I
DENMARK	B	B	C	C	C	D	D	A	C	C	I
FINLAND	C	C	A	A	D	D	D	B	C	C	A
FRANCE	A	A	A	A	A	A	A	A	A	A	A
GERMANY	A	A	A	A	D	D	D	A		C	A
GREECE	A	A	A	A	A	A	A	A		A	A
ICELAND	C	C	C	C	A	A	A	A		#	I
IRELAND	A	A	A	A	A	A	A	A	B	C	I
ITALY	A	A	A	A	A	A	A	A		A	A
LUXEMBOURG	A	A	A	A	A	A	A	C		A	A

MALTA	A	A	A	A	D	A	A	A	A	A	A	A	A	B	A	I
NETHERLANDS	A	A	A	A	A	A	A	A	A	A	A	A			C	A
NORWAY	C	C	A	A	A	A	A	A	A	A	A	A			C	A
PORTUGAL	A	A	A	A	A	D	D	A	A	A	A	A			A	I
SPAIN	A	A	A	A	A	A	A	A	A	A	A	A			A	A
SWEDEN	C	C	A	A	A	A	A	A	C	A	A	A			C	I
SWITZERLAND	A	A	A	A	A	D	D	A	A	A	A	A			A	A
UNITED KINGDOM	A	A	D	D	A	A	A	A	A	A	A	A			C	I

EASTERN EUROPE

ALBANIA	A	A	A	A	A	A	A	A	A	A	A				C	J
BELARUS	A	A	A	A	A	A	A	A	A	A	A	A			A	I
BULGARIA	A	A	A	A	A	A	A	A	A	A	A	A	A	A	A	I
CZECH REP.	A	A	A	A	A	A	A	A	A	A	A	A	A	A	A	I

	1	2	3	4	5	6	7	8	9	10	11	12
ESTONIA	A	A	A	A	A	A	A	A	C		C	I
HUNGARY	A	A	A	A	A	A	A	A	A		C	I
LATVIA	A	A	A	A	A	A	A	A	A		C	I
LITHUANIA	A	A	A	A	A	A	A	A	A	B		I
MOLDOVA	A	A	A	A		A	A	A	A	A		I
POLAND	A	A	A	A	A	A	A	A	A	B	B	A
ROMANIA	A	A	A	A	A	A	A	A	A		C	I
RUSSIA	A	A	A	A	A	A	A	A	A		C	J
SLOVAKIA	A	A	A	A	A	A	A	A	C		B	J
SLOVENIA	A	A	A	A	A	A	A	A	A		B	A
UKRAINE	A	A	A	A	A	A	A	A	A		A	I
YUGOSLAVIA	A	A	A	A	A	A	A	A	A		A	A

NORTH AMERICA

	C									#	
CANADA	A	A	A A	A	D	D	D	A			J
UNITED STATES	A	A	A A	A	D	D	D	A	B		I

CENTRAL AMERICA

	C									#	
BELIZE	A	A	A A	A	A	A	A				I
COSTA RICA	A	A	A A	A	D	D	D		A		A
EL SALVADOR	A	A	A A	A	A	A	A				A
GUATEMALA	A	A	A A	A	A	A	A	F			A
HONDURAS	A	A	A A	A	A	A	A	D			A
MEXICO	A	A	A A	A	A	A	A	D			A
NICARAGUA	A	A	A A	A	A	A	A			A	I
PANAMA	A	A	A A	A	D	D	D				A

CARIBBEAN

	C									#	
ANTIGUA-BARBUDA	A	A	A A	A							I

30

BAHAMAS	A	A	A	A	A	A	A	A		I
BARBADOS	A	A	A	A	A	A	A	A		I
BERMUDA	A	A	A			D	D	D	A	J
BRIT. VIRGIN ISLANDS	A	A	A	A	A	A	A	A		A
CUBA	A	A	A	A	A	A	A	A		I
DOMINICA	A	A	A	A	A	D	D	D		I
DOMINICAN REP.	A	A	A	A	A	A	A	A		A
GRENADA	A	A	A	A	A					I
HAITI	A	A	A			A	A	A		A
JAMAICA	A	A	A		D	A	A	A		I
MONTSERRAT	E	E	E							I
ST KITTS AND NEVIS	A	A	A	A	A	A	A	A		I

ST LUCIA	A	A	A	A	A	A	A	A				I
ST VINCENT AND THE GRENADINES	A	A	A	A	A	D	D	D				I
TRINIDAD AND TOBAGO	A	A	A	A	A	A	A	A				I
SOUTH AMERICA												
ARGENTINA	A	A	A	A	A	D	D	A	A	A	A	A
BOLIVIA	A	A	A	A	A	A	A	A	D	A	D	A
BRAZIL	A	A	A	A	A	A	A	A	B	A	A	A
CHILE	G	G	A	A	A	A	A	A	C	C	C	I
COLOMBIA	A	A	A	A	A	A	A	A	F	A	A	A
ECUADOR	A	A	A	A	A	A	A	A	A		A	A
GUYANA	A	A	A	A	A	A	A	A				I
PARAGUAY	A	A	A	A	A	A	A	A	D		D	A
PERU	G	G	A	A	A	A	A	A				A

SURINAM	A	A									I
URUGUAY	A	A	A	A	D	D	A	A	A	A	A
VENEZUELA	A	A	A	A	A	A	A	A			A
MIDDLE EAST											
BAHRAIN	A	A	A	A	A	A	A				I
IRAN	A	A	A	A	A	A	A	A	A	D	A
IRAQ	A	A	A	A	A	A	A	A			A
ISRAEL	A	A	D	A	A	A	A	A	A	A	A
JORDAN	A	A	A	D	A	A	A	D			I
KUWAIT	A	A	A	A	A	A					I
LEBANON	A	A	A	A	A	A	A	A	A	A	A
OMAN	A	A	A	A	A	A					I
SAUDI ARABIA	A	A	D	A	A	A	A				I

33

SYRIA	A	A	A		A	A	A				I
TURKEY	A	A	A	A	A	A	A	D	D		A
YEMEN	A	A	A		A	A	A				I
PACIFIC ISLANDS											
COOK ISLANDS	C	B	A							C	I
FIJI	E	E	E		D	D	D				I
KIRIBATI	E	E	E		D	D	D				I
MARSHALL ISLANDS	A	A	A								I
MICRONESIA	A	A	A								I
NAURU	B	B	B		D					C	I
PALAU	A	A	A								I
PAPUA NEW GUINEA	E	E	E		D	D	D				I
SOLOMON ISLANDS	E	E	E		D	D	D	D	D		I

TUVALU	E	E				I
VANUATU	E	E				I
WESTERN SAMOA	E	E	D	D	D	I

Sources: US SSA 1996, Dixon 1989b, Kim 1992, Hui and Fung 1994

Notation:
A Social Insurance;
B Social Assistance
C Social Allowances
D Employer Liability Measure
E National Provident Fund
F Mandated Personal Savings Program
G Mandated Personal Pension Program
H Mandated Occupational Pension Program
I Public Health System
J National Health Insurance System

APPENDIX 1.2:   THE DATA BASE

Unless otherwise stated, social security system features described throughout this book come from the United States Social Security Administration's series *Social Security Programs Throughout the World*, which was first published in 1937, and has since been published biennially. The 1995 edition is the primary database used (US SSA 1996); other sources when used have been cited. Changes in the description of social security design features have been taken to reflect design changes. The design feature reported in this series are, according to the US SSA (1996: v), based on

laws and regulations in force at the beginning of 1995, or the last date for which information has been received.

Much of the information used in this report was received through the Annual Survey on Developments and Trends conducted by the International Social Security Association (ISSA) under the sponsorship of the United States Social Security Administration. . . .

Other sources include official publications, periodicals, and other documents received from social security institutions, foreign embassies, or the Law Library of the Library of Congress. Information transmitted by Labor Attaches and Labor Reporting Officers or American Embassies abroad has been invaluable. Other important sources of information include the International Labor Office and other international organizations such as the Permanent Inter-American Social Security Committee, the Organization for Economic Co-operation and Development, the European Communities, the World Bank, the International Monetary Fund, the Inter-American Development Bank, as well as foreign social security officials, and social security experts in the United States.

This information source is unique in both its scope — global — and its content — program specific — although it is not without its blemishes.

Certain benefits and programs included fail to meet the definitional requirements to be classified here as social security measures. This applies to the public employment earnings and voluntary supplementary pensions in the Seychelles and to child-care agencies in Mexico. Some voluntary insurance measures have, with the passage of time, become de facto social security programs, as with the voluntary unemployment insurance in Denmark and Finland, where it is state subsidized, and in Sweden, where it is temporarily deficit-funded; and voluntary sickness insurance in Switzerland, where it attracts special government subsidies. Where these measures coexist with public programs, as they do in Finland and Sweden, they are deemed to be supplementary social insurance strategies. Moreover, some social security systems provide social benefits that fall outside the scope of social security. The Philippines' social security institutions, for example, make available educational and housing loans to their recipients (Gerdes and Pehrson 1998: 198). National Provident Funds commonly give their members withdrawal rights in the event of emigration and marriage, to permit the purchase of housing and real estate, property insurance, or to meet the cost of children's education, healthcare or natural disasters; or loan rights to permit the purchase of housing and real estate or to meet the cost of social obligations or to buy capital items (Dixon 1989b: 34–37). These have been ignored because they relate to broader social objectives that are beyond the scope of this study.

The provision of only death benefits to employment-related survivors in Guatemala and to general survivors in Hong Kong is deemed not to constitute a social security program and so it has been incorporated into family benefit programs.

The United States Social Security Administration's treatment of social assistance, especially supplementary assistance programs, is perfunctory for, at its own admission, such programs are only "generally noted, but no details concerning it are given" (US SSA 1996: vii). Thus, it is not surprising that supplementary social assistance programs are identified variously as income-tested benefits (Libya) or allowance (Austria), means-tested allowances (Bahamas, Brazil and Belgium) or income support (Israel), non-contributory schemes for the needy aged (Liberia), means-tested social pensions (Czech Republic and Italy) and special systems for the indigent (Gabon and Nicaragua). Additional information about supplementary social assistance programs has been drawn from other cited sources (notably, Ferrera 1989, Gough et al. 1996, Macarov 1987, Malloy 1979, Midgley 1984b and 1984c, Seeleib-Kaiser 1995, Soeda 1990).

The United States Social Security Administration's treatment of mandated occupational or personal pension or savings programs is also perfunctory (in the cases of Bolivia, Côte d'Ivoire, France, Switzerland, United Kingdom and Venezuela) or non-existent (Australia). In Finland, "statutory earnings-related pension plans" are deemed to constitute a mandated occupational pension program on the basis that both employers and employees contribute and that the carriers include private sector organizations. The "private termination indemnity program" in Colombia is deemed to be a mandated personal savings program, as it is administered by the private sector. Similarly, Guatemala's compulsory savings approach to unemployment provision is designated a mandated personal savings program because it involves "savings accounts" into which employees must contribute. Contextual information on these programs has been drawn from other cited sources (notably Mesa-Lago 1991a, Price 1994, Dixon and Scheurell 1990).

The United States Social Security Administration's treatment of social insurance measures is rather confusing at times. Social security measures classified as "employment-related" (30 countries) or "compulsory insurance systems" (10 countries), "pension schemes" (The Gambia) or not classified at all (Cape Verde) have been re-classified as social insurance measures when employer contributions are paid to a separate social security agency. Employment-injury programs in Ethiopia constitute social insurance rather than employer liability measures, because they are funded from social insurance pension contributions, while in Sudan they are employer liability measures rather than social insurance, because they require employers to insure their employment injury risks with private insurance company (see also US SSA 1992 and 1994). Sickness and maternity programs in Bangladesh are employer liability measures, rather than social insurance, because employers are required to pay the "total cost." Unemployment programs in Hungary, Slovenia and Yugoslavia are all social insurance measures, not social assistance, because they are contributory and not means tested, whereas in Slovakia the unemployment program is a social allowance measure, not social insurance measure, as it is neither non-contributory nor means-tested. Social security programs that require only employee contributions to a public agency but where employers are obliged to reimburse employees for part of that contribution (the Netherlands and Slovenia) are deemed to be social insurance. Social security programs with two-tier benefits sometimes cause definitional dilemmas. Where basic and complementary benefits are integrated and where the social security program is explicitly classified as "social insurance" it has been treated as a social insurance program, even though the delivery of the complementary benefits is by non-governmental carriers — such as "joint employer-employee bodies" (the Netherlands) or "pension funds" (Iceland). Healthcare benefits programs have been included under the rubric of social insurance where they are the only form of social security benefit offered in the event of sickness and/or maternity (Indonesia and Gabon) and/or where the contributions are collected by a social security administrative agency, which differentiates them from health insurance systems, where health insurance agencies collect the contributions and arrange service delivery or cost reimbursement.

The United States Social Security Administration's treatment of social allowance measures is also a little confusing at times. Family allowances in Albania are more appropriately classified as social allowances, rather than employment-related, given that the government pays the whole cost. Child allowances in Austria are classified as a social allowance measure because it is tax-financed, even though one of the revenue sources is a payroll tax paid by employers. The unemployment program in Luxembourg is a social allowance, rather than a social insurance measure, because it is explicitly financed by an income tax surcharge — a solidarity tax. Unemployment programs are social allowances in Chile, even though coverage is restricted to employed persons, and in Estonia, because they are entirely funded by government and not means-tested. The special pensions paid in Egypt to all those who fail to qualify for a social insurance pension must also be considered a social allowance measure. Bermuda's non-contributory disability pensions are deemed to be a social allowance, because they are not means-tested.

The United States Social Security Administration's treatment of employer liability measures is also somewhat confusing at times. The family allowance programs in Bolivia and Iran have been re-classified as employer liability measures, rather than employment-related programs, given that the employer pays the "total cost." China's post-socialist transitional arrangements with respect to old-age, disability, survivors', sickness and maternity benefit programs have been classified as social insurance, rather than as employer liability measures, as they all require contributions from both employees and employers. Contextual information on these programs has been drawn from other cited sources (notably Dixon 1987c, Dixon and Scheurell 1989 and 1990, Dixon and Macarov 1992).

The United States Social Security Administration's treatment of National Provident Funds is also very incomplete necessitating the drawing of information from other cited sources (notably, Dixon 1989b and 1996c).

2

Social Security's Traditions

INTRODUCTION

Since the early sixteenth century, traditions have evolved that promote and enforce patterns of belief, prejudices and preconceptions about social security and its winners and losers. Twentieth-century social security practices are the progeny of nineteenth-century traditions, sired by a growing state welfare paternalism that blossomed after the First World War. It is possible to identify seven social security traditions, each of which has had a significant, sometimes a profound, impact on global social security practices. Some are an offshoot of another tradition; others are reactions against an earlier tradition; all are, however, intimately interconnected (Dixon 1986 and 1995b).

THE EUROPEAN POOR LAW TRADITION

Much has been written about the secularization of poor relief in Europe from early in the sixteenth century, concomitant with the emergence of the nation-state and with the growing acceptance of the moral precepts of Martin Luther, John Calvin and those who followed in their footsteps (Dolgoff and Feldstein 1984, Scheweinitz 1943, Swaan 1988, Tierney 1959, Trattner 1974). The social security milieu for 300 years can be characterized by the English Poor Law Acts of 1598 and 1601, which, as Sidney and Beatrice Webb (1927: 63) commented, contained little that was new, merely redrafting various halting and confused statutes of past years [going back as early as 928 (Scheweinitz 1943: 38) and especially the English Statutes of Labourers, 1349 and 1351 (Midgley 1984c: 20)] into one [law] that was drastic and direct, explicit in its commands and practically enforceable.

The Elizabethan Poor Laws, which were the product of experience in continental Europe as well as England, had no truck with mendicants and vagrants, who had long been the focus of harsh punitive sanctions to limit their mobility, so as to create local pools of unemployed labor to hold down wage demands. These statutes sought to inhibit the evils of crime, begging, insobriety, vandalism, destitution and prostitution. Thus, they insisted upon the categorization of the poor into those who were deserving of poor relief (in Elizabethan terms, those who were poor by impotency (orphans, the aged, lame and blind, and those with long-term diseases such as leprosy and dropsy) or by casualty (wounded soldiers, "decayed" householders or those "visited by grievous disease"); and those who were not deserving (again, in Elizabethan terms, the able bodied "rioter who consumeth all," the vagabond who "will abide in no place," and the idle, "as the strumpet and others" (quoted in Webb and Webb 1927: 49). Adherence to the work ethic and to the principle of individual responsibility (Goodin and Schmidtz 1998, Midwinter 1994) was de rigueur. Equally importantly, it required that poor relief had to be financed from a compulsory tax, rather than from charitable donations that fulfilled a religious obligation and promised a reward beyond the grave.

The social security strategy embodied in the Poor Laws required local governments to appoint a Poor Law overseer, to levy an earmarked poor-law tax on property owners, to provide poor relief to the incapacitated, to set the able-bodied to work, and to punish vagrants and beggars. Those who were poor because of "acts of God" — the "deserving" — received society's grudging protection. Those who were poor because of their personal attributes or because of the inherent problems of the society in which they lived — the "undeserving" — received only society's contempt. Incarcerating applicants for poor relief in residential facilities — indoor relief — or even jail reflected an increasingly punitive social attitude to the poor, especially the able-bodied, undeserving poor (Young and Ashton 1956).

Public relief has always been a strategy designed to ameliorate absolute poverty (see, for example, Booth 1892). To paupers it was a mere palliative against excessive suffering — just enough to postpone death. To the taxpayers, however, even a palliative must be constrained by an adherence to an ethic that held as sacrosanct the proposition that hard work, self-denial and self-discipline would provide serenity, if not happiness, in this life and ensure spiritual progress towards and in the next. Indeed, the sleep of the burgeoning middle class was, no doubt, made considerably easier by the comforting thought that poverty was both inevitable and morally culpable. The proposition that poverty was the self-inflicted lot of the poor made it clear that what the poor needed more than other people's money was "remoralization" by proselytizing moralists. After all, would it not be sinful to subvert God's will by mitigating poverty? The good intentions of the Poor Law taxpayers — the losers — were forever under threat by the moral turpitude of the poor — the gainers, with their perfidious expectations — which must have provided solid moral grounds for minimizing any income redistribution. The containment and, indeed, the repression of pauperism were thus perceived to be both morally right and highly desirable; to all but the poor! In essence, the poor had no right to relief, and they lost their personal reputation, their personal freedom, and their political freedom (Marshall 1975: 26).

The moralistic Poor Law tradition, itself a legacy of some 300 years of Poor Law experience, has had an indelible impact on both the idea and the form of social security.

Impact on the Idea of Social Security

The Poor Law experience, by focusing on the morality of the poor, has substantiated and propagated the belief that poverty is the fault of the poor, achieved over time by the convenient use of anecdotal evidence. Thus, social security strategies designed to assist the poor have become viewed as a necessary evil. Ideally, people should be independent, healthy and well adjusted, and thus able to engage in work (alternatively, see Neulinger 1990). It is recognized, of course, that some people will fail to achieve a minimum acceptable standard of living, and may thereby create a real or potential public menace by becoming a focus for political dissent, by creating a health hazard or by representing a moral or aesthetic defect of the existing social order (Swaan 1988). Social security is, therefore, seen as a mechanism that keeps society's failures above an acceptable level of subsistence, to ensure that they do not remain a real or potential public threat. In essence, the use of social security to mitigate the lot of the poor is frowned upon. Indeed, to suggest that social security should seek to achieve vertical income redistribution objectives would be anathema within this tradition, even though social security programs may vertically redistribute income depending on both the progressivity of the methods of financing and the poverty and affluence target efficiencies achieved.

Another facet of this tradition is that "need" per se does not generate a "right" to social security; it merely justifies "public charity" (Marshall 1965). The corollary is, of course, that its legacy, the selective-categorical approach to social security, must always be a form of "public charity." The selectivist tactic, with its implied stigma of deterrence, is considered incompatible with any idea of social rights.

Impact on the Form of Social Security

The European Poor Law tradition has cast an inordinately long intertemporal shadow over social security. This tradition has raised to the realms of mythology the belief that a selective-categorical approach must have deterrence as its objective, because it excludes would-be recipients on the basis of "subjective" appraisals, and stigma as its outcome, irrespective of the administrative processes used, for to have it any other way would be to "waste" public money on the "undeserving" (Dixon 1994, Ginneken et al. 1979, Midgley 1984a, 1984b, 1984c, and 1993, Stitt 1994). This is the once much-cherished principle of "less eligibility," a principle espoused by the 1832 English Commission on the Poor Law when it insisted that the poor relief recipient "shall not be made really or apparently so eligible as the situation of the independent labourer of the lowest class" (UK 1832: 13). Stigmatization and inhuman workhouse conditions were its consequences, for only those tactics would definitely ensure that the poor relief recipients had a standard of living worse than that of the poorest worker (Fraser 1973). This principle was embodied in the English Poor Law Amendment Act of 1834 and has undoubtedly become the ghost that still haunts social assistance (Dixon 1995b, Leibfried 1979, Macarov 1981, Tasssel 1995).

The Poor Law tradition insists upon an adherence to the work ethic, which holds that hard work, self-denial and self-discipline, along with a steadfast and vigorous pursuit of one's calling, provide serenity and ensures spiritual progress. Thus, it insists upon the attachment of work tests and wage stops to social security strategies aimed at the employable (Macarov 1981 and 1993, also Chester 1977). Moreover, it instills an administrative preoccupation with the search for real and imagined malingerers in every social security nook and cranny. This preoccupation is not surprising when work is seen as the panacea for man's intransigent welfare maladies (Macarov 1980, 1981 and 1993).

Legacy

Countries that established social assistance programs usually drew heavily either on their own Poor Law experience (as with Denmark (1891) (Petersen 1990), New Zealand (1898) (Castles 1985, Uttley 1989), Australia (1900–08) (Dixon 1977, 1978/79, 1981a and 1983, Kewley 1972, McCallum 1989), the United Kingdom (1908) (Deakin 1982, Keithley 1989), Ireland (1908), Iceland (1909), the Netherlands (1913) (Roebroek 1989), Canada (1927) (Bellamy and Irving 1989, Guest 1985), South Africa (1928) (McKendrick and Dudas 1987), Jamaica (1937), Trinidad and Tobago (1939) and Mauritius (1951) (Joynathsing 1987)); or on the English, Australian or New Zealand Old Age Pension Acts (as with Uruguay (1919), Barbados (1937), Zimbabwe (1936) (Kaseke 1995 and 1998), Guyana (1944), Cyprus (1953) (Triseliotis 1977), India (first in Uttar Pradesh (1957) (Chowdhry 1985, Hallen 1967), the Cook Islands (1966) (Tuavera 1985), Nauru (1967) and Hong Kong (1971) (Chan 1996, Chow 1985a)) (see also Flora and Heidenheimer 1981, Kaim-Caudle 1973, Mendelsohn 1954, Mesa-Lago 1978, Midgley 1984b and 1984c, Simey 1946, Swaan 1988). Over the years, however, poverty amelioration has gradually replaced deterrence as the overriding policy focus in those countries where social assistance remains the dominant form of social security (Australia (Cox 1998, Carney 1994, Castles 1996), the Cook Islands, Nauru and New Zealand (Castles 1996, Uttley 1989)). For these countries, the burden of European Poor Law tradition has been lifted from their shoulders. As Esping-Andersen (1996c: 263) remarks in the Australian context: "The Australian approach suggests that if the net is very wide and if eligibility is assessed via innocuous tax returns rather than stigmatizing means-tests, selectivity can be both efficient and legitimate." To a lesser degree, the legacy of the European Poor Law tradition is even less pronounced in those countries where social assistance, while not dominant overall, is the dominant strategy in at least one social security branch (namely, Brazil (Leite 1990, Malloy 1979), Denmark, Finland, France (Spicker 1998), Hong Kong (Chow 1985b, MacPherson 1998, Lee 1994), Ireland (Callen and Nolan 1998), Kyrgyzstan, Lithuania, Malta (Tabone 1998), Mauritius (Joynathsing 1987), Poland (Les 1992, Stoesz and Lusk 1995), Slovakia, Slovenia, South Africa (McKendrick and Dudas 1987), Sri Lanka (Jayasuriya et al. 1985), Tunisia and the United States) (Magill 1989, Midgley and Livermore 1998)).

Yet remnants of this tradition still survive where social assistance has only ever acted as a residualist income maintenance safety net, either by design or by benign neglect, for those who either fall through the dominant poverty prevention net (because of maximum benefit payment periods) or who entirely miss it (because of restrictive coverage and/or eligibility criteria) (MacPherson 1994, Midgley 1984a, 1984b, and 1984c, Tang 1996a). In all, 49 countries provide supplementary social assistance programs, notably throughout most of Western Europe (see for example, Dixon and Scheurell 1989, George 1973, Gough et al. 1996), much of post-socialist Eastern Europe (Dixon and Macarov 1992), North America (Dixon and Scheurell 1987) and even in Africa (Dixon 1987c), the Middle East (Dixon 1987d), Latin America (Dixon and Scheurell 1990, Mesa-Lago 1978) and Asia (Dixon and Chow 1992, Dixon and Kim 1985, Soeda 1990).

The development of social security over the last 100 years has buried the worst excesses of the Poor Law mentality — although the ghost of "less eligibility" still haunts social security policy and administration — along with the legitimacy of social security's poverty alleviation goal, although its exorcism would seem to be in process.

THE MASTER-SERVANT TRADITION

Where a person, on his own responsibility for his own profit, sets in motion agencies which create risk for others, he should be civilly responsible for the consequences of what he does — Herbert Henry Asquith, 1906 (cited in Schwedtman and Emery 1911: 5).

The then British prime minister's statement embodies a legal principle that has been made sacrosanct by both common law and the passage of time. The idea that employers have some legal responsibility to protect the welfare of their employees, which dates back to Roman law, has its modern roots in the patriarchal tradition of medieval feudal landlordism (Higuchi 1970: 7). Its legal origin lies in the common law of negligence, or tort liability, implicit in which was the assumption of "fault" — "no liability without fault" was the catchphrase. When judicially interpreted in nineteenth-century Europe, this meant employer exemptibility rather than responsibility.

A common-law relationship between employers and their employees evolved in Europe and elsewhere over the centuries. It placed legal obligations on both employers and employees as an implied employment contract. One of those obligations required employers to provide their employees with a safe place to work. In the nineteenth century employees could seek, through the courts, full compensation from their employers for any employment injury they suffered, provided they could prove that the employer alone was responsible for it. The burden of proof for establishing the employer's negligence fell, however, upon the employee. Indeed, the employer had only to defend against the accusations of negligence. In this legal setting, the employee faced three legal hurdles (Armstrong 1932: 232–33). The first was the contributory negligence doctrine, under which if the employee had been negligent to any, even trivial, degree, regardless of the extent of the employer's negligence, then the employer had not acted negligently. The second was the fellow servants or common employment doctrine, under which if could be shown that injury resulted from negligence of a fellow worker, then the employer had not acted negligently. The third was the presumption of risk doctrine — *volenti non fit injuria* — under which if the injury was due to an inherent hazard of the job, about which the employee had, or should have had, prior knowledge, then the employer had not acted negligently. This unholy trinity of common-law doctrines, which so effectively protected the employer against claims of negligence, long dominated the common-law employer liability system throughout Europe, the British empire (Commonwealth) and North America.

The juxtaposition of an increasing humanitarian public and political concern with the inequities of the common-law approach to employer liability, and the growing concern within the business community about the escalation and unpredictability of industrial injury costs, led, from the 1840s, to the gradual introduction, throughout Europe and elsewhere, of legislation that defined the statutory obligations of employers in the event of employment-related injuries. One of the first was the English Fatal Accidents Act of 1846. Such statutes tentatively introduced remedies for certain defects and hardships arising from common law by modifying, extending or just defining common-law obligations, most notably the abolition of the defense of common employment, the mitigation of the harsh defense of contributory negligence and the inclusion of a remedy for close relatives of a deceased employment-injury victim. This codification process culminated, in the 1880s and 1890s, in the emergence of workers' compensation laws, which were initially designed to supplement rather than replace common law and statutory employer liability measures (Armstrong 1932). This new body of law articulated a new legal principle of "occupational risk" — liability without fault — which made the employer fully responsible for the cost of employment-related injuries and deaths (ILO 1936: 26–8). As Higuchi (1970: 111) explains:

Under legislation based on the principle of occupational risk, an employer . . . is regarded as the ultimate cause of employment-related injuries and is liable for the payment of compensation . . . , whether their occurrence is attributable to his negligence or the worker's and even where there has been no fault at all.

Employers, by accepting full responsibility for employment injuries, found that their employment-injury costs became a known and predictable business cost, not only because the required income-replacement and/or lump-sum compensation payments were limited by statute, but also because employees usually had to forfeit their common-law remedy rights. This principle has, however, been recently challenged in one post socialist country — Latvia — where additional benefits are paid by employers if they are deemed to be at fault.

The legalistic master-servant tradition, with its emphasis on the employer-employee relationship, has strongly influenced both the idea and the form of social security.

Impact on the Idea of Social Security

By making employers responsible for the cost of employment-related injuries, common law and subsequent statutory provisions have created the quiddity of the master-servant tradition; the employer has been cast in a social security role. This has had three significant ramifications. First, the employer has been identified as an appropriate source of funding for social security strategies. Initially this was restricted to only negligent employers meeting the cost of employment-related injuries, but by the end of the nineteenth century the net was considerably widened by the substitution of the legal principle of "occupational risk" for that of "fault." Moreover, as the twentieth century progressed the concept of employer liability was gradually extended to embrace other, mainly short-term, social security contingencies, often as a precursor to the adoption of the social insurance strategy. In some socialist countries, most notably China, it was even the preferred social security strategy for the long-term contingencies of old age, invalidity and death (Dixon 1981b, 1981c, 1984, 1985a and 1992b). Second, the use of social security strategies to redistribute income from employers to employees has become legitimate, initially because industrial accidents were recognized as one of the inevitable hazards of industrialization, and so their cost should legitimately be carried by employers. The gradual widening of the employer's social security responsibilities throughout the twentieth century has merely been a reflection of how societies favorably view this type of income redistribution (Melling 1991). Third, the idea that the cost of work injuries was a legitimate cost of production has its origins in this tradition. This blossomed into the view that employer contributions should be seen as a legitimate production cost rather than charity.

The master-servant tradition has fostered the proposition that recipients of employer-financed social security benefits are not receiving charity but rather employment-related benefits as a matter of legal right. This has contributed to a shift in the focus of social security away from poverty amelioration towards poverty prevention. Indeed, in many countries, as if to reinforce this, employment-injury programs are embedded in labor laws rather than in social security or social welfare statutes. Once ensconced in the public mind, this view has survived, untarnished by the worldwide trend towards greater government subsidies for such benefits. This legalistic social security tradition has thus thrust legitimacy upon poverty prevention as a social security objective, while the poverty mitigation objective still languishes in the moral quagmire of the Poor Law tradition.

The master-servant tradition moved social security from the welfare domain of the Poor Law tradition, dominated by the social reformers, and more recently, social and behavioral scientists, to a legalistic domain, dominated by lawyers and the judiciary. These domains have quite different conceptual frameworks and lexicons and thus very little in common. This legacy still survives.

Impact on the Form of Social Security

The master-servant tradition created a global social security elite, namely, employment-related injury victims (Higuchi 1970 and 1985, Leite 1995, Spielmeyer 1965). As Higuchi (1970: 111) has noted:

an element of reparation still remains in the benefits payable under legislation based on the principle of occupational risk, and this element appears to have contributed towards the realization of different levels of social security benefits according to the origin of the accident or disease.

Yet, as Beveridge (UK 1942: 38) remarked:

If a workman loses his leg in an accident, his needs are the same whether the accident occurred in a factory or in the street; if he is killed, the needs of his widow and other dependents are the same however the death occurred.

Legacy

Workers' compensation programs constituted the foundation of social security systems in 17 countries prior to the First World War (Finland and Norway (1895); Austria and Czechoslovakia (1897); Ireland and the United Kingdom (1897); Denmark, France and Italy (1898); Belgium and Russia (1903); Canada (first province) and the United States (first state) (1908) (Day 1989, Guest 1985), Japan and Peru (1911); and Rumania and Ukraine (1912). Their subsequent adoption elsewhere over the ensuing decades means that they now exist in 47 countries.

Employer liability measures have, as the twentieth century has progressed, been extended well beyond employment-injury programs and now constitute a significant primary social security strategy for the contingencies of sickness (30 countries), maternity (24 countries), unemployment (12 countries) and old-age (1 country), as well as for the provision of family benefits (5 countries). Indeed, employer liability programs can be found in 115 countries, and they are especially important in Africa (Gruat 1990).

Reflecting that employers have become a preferred source of social security finance, only two countries with social security systems (Afghanistan and Surinam) do not require employers either to pay a social security contribution or to provide directly some form of social security provision.

The ghost that has been raised is, of course, the employers' burgeoning social security statutory cost burden. The desirability of exorcising this ghost, however, has, in recent years, begun to take root.

THE OCCUPATIONAL PROVIDENT FUND TRADITION

This is essentially a British colonial tradition with its roots in nineteenth-century industrial welfare paternalism. The names Robert Owen and Titus Salt are synonymous with the beginning of this movement. It began as the reaction of a few humanitarian employers to the shocking working conditions prevailing during the early-to-mid nineteenth-century English Industrial Revolution in factories so aptly denounced by William Blake as "Satanic Mills." This humanitarianism, however, was initially strongly tinged with paternalism, which was built upon a philanthropic sense of charity and a moral responsibility for character building. What may have begun as humanitarian paternalism, however, soon became an act of enlightened employer self-interest, as employers searched for ways to reduce the costs of employment-related injuries and to promote industrial efficiency and harmony. Occupational provident funds were thus established by individual employers seeking to provide a means by which their provident employees could be protected against old age, disability and death.

The idea of employer humanitarian paternalism tinged with self-interest soon moved to the British colonies, where it came under the patronage of colonial authorities. Expatriate employers, especially those involved in private plantations, mining enterprises and railways, were commonly among the first to establish provident funds. State railways on the Indian subcontinent and in British colonial Africa, for example, created a variety of provident funds for their workers and staff in the 1880s and 1890s (see, for example, Riebenack 1905: 118–26). Initially, provident fund membership was restricted to expatriate staff, but membership was gradually extended to permanent local staff, typically on a less generous basis.

By the middle years of the twentieth century these occupational provident funds were peppered throughout the British empire and elsewhere (Pilch and Wood 1960: 18–19). They provided a useful social and institutional heritage upon which National Provident Funds could be built.

Impact on the Idea of Social Security

The occupational provident fund tradition advances the proposition that social security protection could be provided by means of mandatory savings, without risk pooling, which means no income transfer amongst individuals. This proposition has a curious corollary: National Provident Fund members identify their account balances as "their" compulsory savings, and tend to claim proprietary rights over them (see, for example, Lall 1986). This brings into question whether these social security savings should be accessible. If "social security" is defined narrowly (as income maintenance, support or supplementation) then interim access must be prohibited. If, alternatively, it is defined to include "quality-of-life" dimensions, then such access is justifiable. This brings into focus the libertarian principle that individuals are the best judges of their own well-being. National Provident Funds do not sit comfortably in the social security arena.

National Provident Funds have achieved a significant level of popularity in their host communities. Members see them as financial institutions accumulating "their" savings, which have, over time, become more readily accessible to them, due to the introduction of interim quality-of-life withdrawal and borrowing rights (notably for healthcare, housing, education, marriage and social obligations). Singapore, for example, takes a particularly liberal view toward National Provident Fund members' accessing the balance standing in their accounts (Bradley 1994, Chan 1994, Chow 1981 and 1985a, Kalirajan and Wiboonchutikula 1986, Robinson 1984). Indeed, these quality-of-life outcomes would seem to be much valued by members, who appear all-too-willing to trade-off social security protection in their later life. Employers see National Provident Funds as the means by which their legal obligation for their employees' welfare can be fulfilled at a known, modest and stable cost. Government sees them as a self-help vehicle for the provision of affordable basic social security protection, which, as a bi-product, also facilitates both quality-of-life improvements and increases in public savings. As publicly managed institutions, they are required to hold a large proportion of their investment portfolios in government and semi-government securities, which means the rate of return they can offer their members is determined by their host governments, which see them as a reliable source of relatively cheap public finance. When the real rate of interest on their members' accounts becomes negative then they confront a dilemma that cannot be easily resolved.

Impact on the Form of Social Security

National Provident Funds began appearing after the Second World War in the newly emerging countries of: *Asia* — Indonesia (1951), Malaysia (1952) (Amin

1980, Sushama 1985, Tracy 1995), India (1952) (Coal Mines Provident Fund, India 1986, Chowdhry 1985, Sarma 1979) (1952), Singapore (1953) (Asher 1991, Bradley 1994, Central Provident Fund Study Group 1986, Chan 1994, Kalirajan and Wiboonchutikula 1986, Ramesh 1992), Sri Lanka (1958) (Jayasuriya et al. 1985) and Nepal (1962); *the Middle East* — Egypt (1955) (Kashef 1989) and Iraq (1956); *Africa* — Nigeria (1961) (Aire 1974, Sanda 1987), Tanzania (1964) (Mallya and Mwankanye 1987), Ghana (1965) (Asamoah and Nortey 1987, Ofori 1976), Kenya (1965) (Gethaiga and Williams 1987), Zambia (1965) (Brooks and Nyirenda 1987, Godfrey 1974a and 1974b), Uganda (1967), the Seychelles (1971), Swaziland (1974) and The Gambia (1982); *the Pacific Islands* — Fiji (1966), Western Samoa (1972), the Solomon Islands (1976), Kiribati (1977), Papua New Guinea (1981), Tuvalu and Vanuatu (1986); and *the Caribbean* (Gobin 1977) — St Kitts and Nevis (1968), Dominica, St Lucia, St Vincent and the Grenadines (1970) and Montserrat (1972).

Legacy

The legacy of the occupational provident fund tradition is the existence of 20 National Provident Funds in Asia, Africa, and the Caribbean (Dixon 1982, 1985b, 1987a, 1989a, 1989b, 1993, 1996b and 1996c).

The ghost that haunts National Provident Funds is the willingness of their host communities to trade-off social security objectives for social and economic objectives. It can be exorcised only by the political recognition of the primacy of their social security goals, which may well encourage their conversion into social insurance programs, as has happened in 10 countries (Egypt (1964), Iraq (1971), Dominica (1975), St Kitts and Nevis (1977), St Lucia (1978), the Seychelles (1979) (Lay-Sion 1977), St Vincent and the Grenadines (1986), The Gambia (1987), Ghana (1991) and Nigeria (1994)).

THE INSURANCE TRADITION

The insurance tradition evolved in Europe towards the end of the nineteenth century, as a reaction to its Poor Law experience, in a setting where private insurance practices had reached a high level of sophistication (Pfeffer and Klock 1974). Insurance has its origins in antiquity as a commercial technique for reducing the inevitable fear and anxiety experienced by people whose lives are fraught with uncertainty. Indeed the *raison d'être* of insurance has always been to reduce uncertainty. There are four key insurance concepts: *peril*, the contingency or the event to be insured against; *risk*, the probability of the event occurring; *risk pooling*, the sharing of risks; and *indemnity*, the restoration of the insured to the same economic condition they were in prior to the insured event happening. Thus, according to Pfeffer (1956: 53):

Insurance is a device for the reduction of uncertainty of the one party, called the insured, through the transfer of particular risk to another party, called the insurer, who offers restoration, at least in part, of economic losses suffered by the insured.

Insurance is also a device for the voluntary redistribution of a society's resources; it takes a little from many, while giving larger amounts to a few.

The insurance tradition has two key value premises: personal responsibility and mutual aid (Armstrong 1932). Personal responsibility is the sense that individuals have a responsibility to provide for themselves and their families and that they are accountable for their actions, or lack of them. This is firmly within the spirit of *bourgeois* liberalism, that progeny of the Enlightenment which holds that individuals have both rights and duties, and should be responsible for their own success or failure, prosperity and welfare (O'Brien and Penna 1998). Liberalism, as a social philosophy, emphasizes the virtues of individualism and the abhorrence of government (Bentham [1789] 1970, Mills [1859] 1977). It spawned the nineteenth-century laissez-faire economic philosophy, with its presumption of the supremacy of the market-place, based on an adherence to the values of individualistic utilitarianism, which fitted so comfortably with the prevailing social and economic milieu (Bromely 1990, Frey 1984). Together, liberal and laissez-fair philosophies reinforced the Social Darwinists' assertion that the person who is rewarded deserves the reward (Dolgoff and Feldstein 1984: 77). Mutual aid, which is predicated upon helping and being helped, is, according to Macarov (1978: 43), "one of the oldest and most ubiquitous motives for meeting human needs" (see also Tierney 1959, Schweinitz 1943). Mutual benefit organizations — essentially burial societies, friendly societies and life insurance societies — have their origins in sixteenth-century Spain and Portugal (Mesa-Lago 1978), but blossomed in the last half of the nineteenth century throughout Europe (Baernreither 1883, Bruce 1966, Hutchins 1993, Linden 1993 and 1996), Australia (Knibbs 1910) and Latin America (Mesa-Lago 1978, Toso 1993) and subsequently elsewhere (see for example, Dasgupta 1993, Ingleson 1993). They were perceived as a concrete means by which people could express their mutual dependence and concern for one another, and as a vehicle for the promotion of solidarity, although their effectiveness as a form of voluntary social security was severely limited because of shortsightedness and competing expenditure demands (see, for example, Dreyfus 1993, Dumont 1993, Knibbs 1910).

The private insurance model has three basic postulates: individual equity, voluntary participation and the contractual right to economic restitution guaranteed by full funding. Its commercial preoccupation with actuarial soundness provided the means by which social security could be re-conceptualized as an economic activity obeying market forces, rather than as a non-market, charitable activity. It permitted the economist's dichotomous distinction between social security's efficiency role (redistributing income and thus consumption over the life cycle) and its equity role (redistributing income amongst income groups)

(Barr 1989 and 1992). This permitted the relegation to the realms of secondary importance issues relating to equity, which, by their very nature, are non-cognitive and thus not susceptible to empirical or rational testing.

The proposition that private insurance can, by means of risk pooling, indemnify individuals overcome by an insurable peril has a certain superficial confluence with the view that self-help through mutual aid should be the main method used to solve social security maladies. Indeed, making long-term pension insurance mandatory has overcome the problem of inadequate voluntary precautionary savings due to insurance market failure caused by shortsightedness (attaching high discount rates to post-retirement consumption), by adverse selection (the propensity of individuals to underinsure if they perceive the insurance risk to be low) and by imperfect information (creating uncertainty about the long-term solvency of and rate of return on available savings instruments).

By the middle decades of the nineteenth century, insurance practices had become quite sophisticated. The tontines that operated in seventeenth-century France, Holland and England, which were primitive insurance devices for the provision of survivors' benefits, had given way to term insurance, whole-of-life insurance, endowment insurance and annuity insurance (Pfeffer and Klock 1974: 19). Moreover, insurance had become substantially scientific, in large part due to the development of actuarial science. As Pfeffer and Klock (1974: 314) remark:

Where the actuary in the eighteenth century was proficient in mortality and simple probabilities, by the turn of the twentieth century he was conversant with most phases of the insurance business as we know it today.

This expertise was available to the late nineteenth-century architects of social security.

Impact on the Idea of Social Security

The insurance tradition has had an oppressive impact on the conceptualization of social security in the twentieth century, mainly because it offered an alternative to the draconian Poor Laws. The word "insurance" conjured up images of security, respectability and virtuous providence. In the language of social security, insurance concepts replaced Poor Law concepts: "needs" became "contingencies," "deserving beneficiaries" became "the insured," and "poor taxes" became "contributions." In short, social security moved from being a welfare concept to being an insurance concept. This reconceptualization of social security, which began in the last quarter of the nineteenth century, developed along two competing lines.

The first line followed the Bismarckian conservative-paternalistic principles embodied in the German social insurance statutes of the 1880s (Kolb 1989). These enactments were more concerned with resolving the *arbeiterfrage* — the workers' question — to emasculate threats to the German social order. They have their origin in a vibrant and thriving nineteenth-century mutual benefit system that provided practical manifestation of the growing sense of solidarity — the doublebinding of the individual to the society and society to the individual (Moulton 1984, Olsson et al. 1993). The Bismarckian approach limited coverage to specific occupations, made entitlement dependent upon past contribution history and provided earnings-related entitlements administered by quasi-government institutions (Muller 1993). It adopted the solidarity concept of the "contract of generations," whereby, through insurance, "the younger generation of workers provides a financial guarantee for the old age of parents and grandparents" (Muller 1989: 90–91) and drew upon the principle of subsidiarity — first the individual, then the family and the community, only then the state (Andersen 1992: 19–20). These principles dominated the idea of social insurance up to the Second World War and remain the dominant influence in most of continental Europe (Castellino 1982, Ferrera 1989, Hennock 1987, Kohler and Zacher 1982, Kolb 1989) and throughout much of the Third World (Midgley 1984a).

The second line followed from the Beveridgian reform-liberal principles embodied in the Beveridge blueprint for the United Kingdom's post war Welfare State (Beveridge 1944 and 1945, UK 1942). This blueprint for "freedom from fear and want," a mission that Winston Churchill and Franklin D. Roosevelt jointly proclaimed in the Atlantic Charter of 1942, was intended to prevent the United Kingdom from returning to the inequities of the past, by ensuring three citizenship rights: the right to live without war and the fear of war; the right to work and earn; and the right to "an income sufficient for honourable subsistence and the maintenance of one's dependents when for any reason one was unable to earn a living" (Beveridge 1945: 11). Beveridge has been characterized by some as a reluctant socialist but an enthusiastic collectivist who drew strength from the interventionist economic arguments of John Maynard Keynes, and who envisioned a form of capitalism that was at one and the same time both more humane and more productive than in the past (Abel-Smith 1992a, Atkinson 1987, Diamond 1977, Keynes 1936, Wilson and Wilson 1993). He thus advocated a form of social security that emphasized comprehensiveness of scope, universality of coverage, eligibility as a right earned by the payment of contributions, and the adequacy of flat-rate benefits, with the state assuming a significant financial responsibility, as an efficient facilitator of inter-generational transfers, designed "to be equitable to insured persons and to avoid hardship to insured persons of small means or any disturbance to production" (Recommendation No. 67) (Abel-Smith 1992a, Alcock 1996, George 1968, Baldwin 1992, George and Wilding 1976 and 1985, Hills et al. 1994, Marsh 1950, Marshall 1975, Perrin 1992, Pinker 1979, Veit-Wilson 1992). As Keithly (1989: 309) elaborates:

'Cradle-to-grave' provisions would tackle want (through income maintenance), disease (health services), squalor (housing programmes), ignorance (education) and idleness (full employment policies). Schemes would cover all contingencies and groups on the basis of citizenship, without occupational or income differentiation. Cash benefits would be flat-rate and adequate for subsistence, but above that level individuals should be encouraged to make private provision.

The international appeal of these Beveridgian principles was that they challenged the prevailing wisdom of both classical economic theory and Marxist theory that social welfare and a market economy were incompatible: "Security can be combined with freedom and enterprise and responsibility for one's own welfare" (UK 1942: 166, see also Baldwin 1992). These principles were embodied in the International Labor Organization's wartime Income Security and Medical Care Recommendations (Nos. 67 and 69 of 1944) (ILO 1944). They have also come to dominate social insurance policy and practice in other parts of Europe, notably Denmark, Ireland (Callen and Nolan 1998), the Netherlands (Roebroek 1993), as well selected Third World countries, most notably Mauritius (Joynathsing 1987) and the Seychelles (Lay-Sion 1977).

The insurance tradition has radically changed the way social security is viewed. First, the focus of social security has moved from poverty mitigation — ministering to the poverty crises that lack of prevention causes — to poverty prevention, which is hardly surprising, given that the intent of insurance is indemnity following the occurrence of a peril. The unfortunate corollary of this is, of course, that social security strategies designed to achieve other objectives are perceived by those imbued with this tradition as in some way inferior, perhaps even spurious; after all, social security should be concerned with scientifically insurable hazards, not moral issues.

Second, the insurance tradition insists that social security's concern moves from the poor to the potentially poor. It identifies a range of biological and health perils that might result in the loss or interruption of earning power — old age, invalidity, death or sickness — to which it adds the perils of job loss, child bearing and child raising, to define a set of "socially insurable" contingencies. Those in poverty because their earning power never developed, because they are unable to earn an adequate wage or because to work causes unacceptable social costs, do not fit into the social security framework built upon the social insurance tradition.

Third, the insurance tradition, with its admiration for risk pooling and individual equity, has embraced as a social security objective horizontal income redistribution (from those in work earning a regular income, to those who are not) rather than vertical income redistribution (between different income groups). The effect of social security risk pooling, however, may be vertical income redistribution, depending on the universality of coverage, benefit generosity and chosen method of finance, but that is rarely its intent (George 1973).

Fourth, the insurance tradition has added yet another track along which social security has developed in the twentieth century: "socially insurable" contingencies have become the domain of actuaries and their methodologies. Their perspectives are, of course, quite different to those viewing social security from the legal or welfare tracks. Each has developed its own conceptual frameworks, analytical tools and thus language, making communication between them problematic.

Finally, the insurance tradition, with its roots in the contractual rights of the insured, has removed stigma from the receipt of social security benefits by making them an earned right. It has given contributory social security a legitimacy that tax-financed strategies have long struggled to achieve.

Impact on the Form of Social Security

The bequest of the insurance tradition to social security is social insurance, with its inclination towards earnings-related benefits, connoting restitution, and a penchant for employee contributions and minimum contribution periods. Over a hundred or more years it has been transformed from the nineteenth-century social security deviant to the twentieth-century cynosure; so becoming the ne plus ultra of social security, before its recent fall from grace began.

It has become evident that social insurance is unable to solve all social security maladies. The consequence has been the development of a social security mélange; a pot-pourri of social insurance, social assistance and, in some instances, even employer liability and fiscal welfare strategies, each designed to achieve different — perhaps even conflicting — social security objectives. These mosaics, designed to accommodate the inadequacies of social insurance, have complicated both social security administration and finance. Moreover, social security recipients are categorized according to which form of social security they receive. Ignominy is the sine qua none of those who fall through the social insurance safety net, because, perhaps, they fail to meet minimum requirements with respect to contribution periods or maximum benefit periods, or those who miss the net entirely because their social security needs are not the result of socially insurable contingencies.

Legacy

Some European countries, eager to forestall any feared social or political instability, took immediately to the idea of social insurance, which promised to keep their burgeoning and politically potent middle classes out of poverty, while, at the same time, providing a mechanism to exert industrial and political control over the working classes (see Flora and Alber 1981a and 1981b, Flora and Heidenheimer 1981, Gordon 1963, Kaim-Caudle 1973). Social insurance emerged first in Bismarck's Germany (1883–89) (Muller 1989), subsequently, over the next 25 years, spreading to Austria (1888) (Hofmeister 1982), Czechoslovakia (1888) (Czechoslovakia 1992), Sweden (1891) (Olsson 1989), Hungary (1891) (Hegyesi et al. 1992), Denmark (1892) (Goldman and Hollman 1936), Belgium (1894), Argentina (1904) (Queiro-Tajali 1990), France (1905), Norway

(1906) (Forsund 1989), Ireland (1911), the United Kingdom (1911) (Keithly 1989), Luxembourg (1911), Armenia and Romania (1912), and Cuba (1913) (Mesa-Lago and Roca 1990 and 1992). Social insurance then gradually spread throughout the rest of Western Europe, into South America (Mesa-Lago 1978), beginning with Brazil (1923) (Leite 1990, Malloy 1979) and Chile (1924) (Borzutzky 1983 and 1990), and then to United States (1936) (Skidmore 1995, Lockhart 1991). During the Second World War, it moved into Central America, beginning with Costa Rica and Panama (1941), and into Asia (Dixon and Chow 1992), beginning with Japan (1941) (Anderson 1987 and 1993, Goodman and Peng 1996, Ichien 1995, Takahashi and Someya 1985, Takahashi 1997, Takayama 1982). After the war it began to blossom in Africa (Dixon 1987c, Kessler 1966, Moulton 1975), beginning with Equatorial Guinea (1947); in the Caribbean (Gobin 1977), beginning with the Dominican Republic (1947); and in the Middle East (Dixon 1987b), beginning with Turkey (1949) (Danisoglu 1987). It almost entirely bypassed the remote Pacific Islands (Dixon and Chow 1992), the notable exception being the then Trust Territories of the Pacific Islands (1967). The social insurance model has thus long been the internationally dominant social security strategy (ILO 1953b). It has now been adopted by 148 countries for at least one of their social security programs.

Social insurance's employment-based coverage ensures, however, that its efforts are targeted at keeping employees, most notably those in regular full-time employment, out of poverty, which makes it irrelevant to the needs of most people in most countries (Midgley 1984a, Schulz 1992). In most developed countries, nevertheless, social insurance has achieved both universality of full-time employment coverage — at the neglect of those outside the workforce or in atypical forms of employment, notably women — and a level of benefit generosity that ensures that the middle class remains out of poverty. These achievements have occurred because governments have been willing to provide ongoing and ever-increasing, social insurance subsidies. This juxtaposition has contrived to create unrealistic community expectations about the appropriate levels of social insurance coverage, income-replacement rates and contribution rates that can, and, indeed, should be achieved (see, for example, Goodin 1990). This gave rise to the ghost of burgeoning government cost burdens, which now actively haunts both Europe and the Americas, although its exorcism has also begun. In most developing countries, in contrast, social insurance has not been able successfully to meet the twin challenges of penetrating the rural workforce or protecting the middle class from even the worst excesses of unemployment and/or inflation (Iyer 1993, Jenkins 1993). These are the ghosts of irrelevancy and inadequacy that haunt developing countries, but their exorcism has also begun.

THE MARXIST-LENINIST-STALINIST TRADITION

The Marxist-Leninist-Stalinist tradition in social security is yet another reaction to the European Poor Law experience. Marx saw the Poor Laws as a demeaning palliation, a vehicle designed by the *bourgeoisie* to reinforce the existing class structure by perpetuating inequalities through the *lumpenproletariat*, that morally contemptible, politically dangerous urban mass of deprived human depravity, comprising

thieves and criminals of all kinds, living on the crumbs of society, people without a definite trade, vagabonds, *gens san feu et sans aveu* . . . discharged soldiers, discharged jailbirds, escaped galley slaves, swindlers, mountebanks, *lazzaroni*, pickpockets, tricksters, gamblers, *maquereaux*, brothel keepers, porters, literati, organgrinders, ragpickers, knife grinders, tinkers, beggars . . . this scum, offal, refuse of all classes (Marx [1851] 1962: 295).

The inevitable socialist revolution that he envisioned would, of course, obliterate this vestige of capitalism (O'Brien and Penna 1998). His robust cosmology predicted an egalitarian future society in which every member would have an equal share in future abundance and an equal opportunity to contribute to that prosperity (Dixon and Kim 1992, Elliot 1987, George and Manning 1980, Machan 1988). According to Yudin (196–: 7–8), it would be a transfigured society that

is most of all distinguished by its high level of development of the productive forces, by the soundness of its material and technical bases. Relations of production are more mature here [than under its harbinger, socialism] . . . the class divisions in society disappear with the withering away of the distinction between the working class and the peasants and the intellectuals. This is inseparably bound up with the elimination of the important distinction between mental and manual labour.

Labour becomes a prime necessity of all members of society and the socialist principle of distribution according to work gives way to the communist principle of distribution according to need. This leads to the eradication of all remnants of inequality based on property.

Marx, however, said very little about the precise nature of the society that would emerge from the ruins of capitalism, but he did, rather simplistically, suggest that there would be "a fund for people unable to work, etc. in short for what today [1875] comes under so-called poor relief" (Marx 1970: 31). This public consumption fund, Marx argued, should be financed by deductions from the total value of production before the payment of earnings, but its administration was left to the imagination. Indeed, it was left to Lenin to articulate the guiding principles of social security under socialism.

Lenin's conceptualization of social security was somewhat more sophisticated and strongly and positively influenced by the early European experience with social insurance. He envisioned cradle-to-grave protection by means of a broad-based labor insurance system, with universal employment coverage and

complete income replacement, financed by employers and the state, but administered by insured workers themselves on a territorial basis (George and Manning
1980: 33).

Stalin made two Machiavellian contributions to this trinal tradition (Dixon
1981b). The first was to fuse social security to work discipline and incentives,
thereby ensuring that social security contributed to economic development by
rewarding work effort and punishing perceived malingerers. The underlying psychological premise was that it is only through work that a person's nature can
be transformed to be compatible with that required for the coming egalitarian
communist society. As the Commissioner of Labor in the USSR in the late
1920s so eloquently and aptly expressed it (cited in Dixon 1981b: 7), social security became:

a weapon in the struggle to attach workers to their enterprises and strike hard at loaf-
ers, malingerers, and disorganizers of work. At the centre of . . . social insurance
work must be care for the worker who has been actively wrestling with the fulfillment
of the industrial financial plan and work norms.

Stalin's second contribution was to make political and ideological confor-
mity a prerequisite for the receipt of social security benefits, thereby consolidat-
ing socialism.

Social security under this tradition may be likened to putting a patch on the
status quo in the pious hope that an ideal society would ultimately emerge, as a
matter of dialectical inevitability. Thus, social security became a means to a set
of ideological ends rather than an end in itself.

Impact on the Idea of Social Security

This tradition held certain social security propositions to be sacrosanct. First,
that social security should be integral part of a socialist society and should be a
practical manifestation of class solidarity (Rimlinger 1971: 255). Second, non-
contributory social security should be a fundamental right of all loyal and hard-
working socialists and their families. Third, social security should not have the
intention of equalizing the earnings of those who make different work contributions; that would be contrary to the socialist distribution principle of "from each
according to their ability; to each according to their labor." Rather, as Mikul'shii
(1975: 40) has noted, social security benefits should rather

promote the resolution of the problem of securing more consistent observance of the
principle of distribution according to labor. They serve as the main instrument that
makes it possible to combine the policy of preserving, or if necessary, somewhat
increasing wage differentiation, depending on the quality and quantity of labor, while
reducing such discrepancies in per capita income levels of families that are caused by
differences in the ratio of workers to dependents in the family.

Thus, under this tradition social security has the legitimate role of reinforcing and widening wage inequalities. Fourth, social security should not be made available to anyone capable of self-support through work. To provide supplementary assistance to low-income earners or to pledge support to those overtaken by a misfortune beyond their control is to foster the work spirit. To support the employable unemployed would be to deter them from working. The plight of the unemployable — the halt, the lame and the blind — is a cause of consternation for those conditioned by this tradition. When work is seen as the panacea for people's intransigent welfare maladies, what of those unable to work?

Impact on the Form of Social Security

The Marxist-Leninist-Stalinist tradition introduced a set of new dimensions to social security practice in the twentieth century. First, socialist trade unions gained a prominent role in the administration of social security, ostensibly to implement Lenin's call for workers' management of social security, but, in the Stalinist tradition, also to promote labor discipline and productivity by directly relating the receipt of social security benefits to work history, work performance and work attitude, which would not have been possible with more remote bureaucratic forms of administration. Second, eligibility for social security benefit entitlements became dependent, in part, on the political attitudes and activities of the applicant. Preferential and special social security treatment was given to those who worked to consolidate socialism — trade unionists and "model" workers — while those "deprived of their political or civil rights" — political dissidents and non-conformists — had to be disqualified. Third, both individual eligibility and the generosity of the benefits provided depended upon past work histories (see George and Manning 1980: 39–40). Thus, not only did eligibility depend on the satisfaction of work tests, in the form of minimum employment periods, even minimum employment periods with the same employer, but also benefit entitlements sometimes varied with the length of aggregate or continuous employment periods.

Under the aegis of the Marxist-Leninist-Stalinist tradition social insurance became an anamorphic form of the authentic model that has its roots firmly in the insurance tradition.

Legacy

Out of this tradition emerged a social insurance variant, first developed in the Soviet Union (1922) (Wiktorow 1992), that became the model adopted, with variations, in the socialist countries that emerged after the Second World War, either by introducing this variant as the first form of social insurance (as in Albania (1947)) or by modifying existing social security systems (Dixon 1981b,

Dixon and Macarov 1992). This has created the specter of overburdened state enterprises making cradle-to-grave social security provisions for their workers. Now this manifestation of the ghost of burgeoning employer statutory cost burdens has come to haunt the 27 post-socialist countries, 24 of which can be found in Eastern Europe and Central Asia (Deacon and Szalai 1990, Standing 1996, Voirin 1993, Zukowski 1994), as well as China (Dixon 1981b and 1992b, Chow 1988b and 1995), Vietnam and Cuba (Mesa-Lago and Roca 1992).

THE STATE WELFARE PATERNALISM TRADITION

This tradition has as its guiding principle that the abrogation of individual freedom by the state in the name of benevolence is justified (Dworkin 1981, Klienig 1984). State welfare paternalism is justified by reasons referring exclusively to "good," "happiness," "need," "well-being," and "interests" of the person whose liberty is restricted, as interpreted by those exercising freedom-diminishing authority (Dworkin 1971, Goodin 1982, Sugden 1982, Weale 1978). It stands in contradistinction to libertarian principles:

if . . . government uses its coercive powers to ensure that men are given what some expert thinks they need . . . people thus can no longer exercise any choice in some of the most important matters of their lives, such as health, employment, housing, and provision for old age, but must accept decisions made for them by appointed authority on the basis of its evaluation of their need. . . (Hayek 1960: 261, see also Brennan and Friedman 1981, Friedman 1970, Mill 1859, Seldon 1957 and 1998)

Interestingly, perhaps one of the most enduring libertarian icons, Adam Smith, believed fervently that liberty, as ensured by just laws, and security for all people were the ultimate objectives of all human endeavor and countenanced government intervention to improve the life chances of the disadvantaged and to improve the lot of the poor (Rothschild 1995a and 1995b).

State welfare paternalism has two distinct, but entwined, modalities: social stability and social progress. The social stability mode has its roots in the Poor Law experience, is the manifestation of a societal reluctance to abandon totally libertarian principles, and thus retains a certain empathy with the residual welfare paradigm. It seeks only to humanize the face of capitalism, to disarm its critics. The social progress mode seeks to remove what Freud (1951: 44) has described as "the social sources of our distress" by the use state intervention, perhaps in a "series of fits of conscience," as Bruce (1966: 259) suggests, to promote social cohesion, integration and inclusion, and so progress towards a free, equal and more secure society. In such a milieu, exemplified by the Welfare State, citizenship guarantees every individual a secure lifestyle (Marshall 1964 and 1965), with a minimum degree of insecurity, and the wherewithal for him or her to develop to the greatest possible extent as an individual and as a member of society (Alber 1988a, Allardt 1987, Baldwin 1990a and 1990b, Barry 1998, Briggs

1965). Robert Henry Cox (1998:5) sums it up admirably:

The welfare state establishes and enforces national standards of social rights. These rights are expressed through a variety of programs, but primarily through social security. The realization of national standards fits best with a centralized view of state capacities, and technical application of knowledge to problem solving. Finally, when properly functioning, the welfare state will bring out the best in human nature.

This places the Welfare State firmly within the Titmussian institutional-redistributive paradigm and thus the antithesis of the Poor Law tradition (Titmuss 1974).

Indeed the Welfare State, the appeal of which has spread well beyond its European origins (Pinch 1996), is the embodiment of its altruistic sentiment that people are entitled to social security protection as a right of nation-state citizenship (Marshall 1965, see also Allardt 1987, Ashford 1986b and 1987, Briggs 1965, Bruce 1966, Bryson 1992, Esping-Andersen 1990, Leonard 1997, Macarov 1978, Mishra 1984 and 1987, Rieger and Liebfried 1998, Titmuss 1976). It is, moreover, arguably the most significant set of social institutions developed in the twentieth century, albeit one that has within it the seeds of its own potential destruction — the vicious spiral of growing welfare dependency, increasing state control, deepening poverty and, arguably, the emergence of an intractable underclass (Mead 1986 and 1996, Murray 1984 and 1991) — and that has legitimated calls for what Ferge (1996) describes as the "individualisation of the social." As Mohan (1996: 1), insightfully remarks:

The Industrial Revolution that unleashed mass production, colonial and, eventually, global economy, left individuals in a society that seems to have lost its soul. The rise and fall of the Welfare State have been monumental twentieth century events.

The intellectual antecedents of the state welfare paternalism tradition can be found in romanticism (evoking a sentimental melancholy for the dignity and rights of the individual), humanism (evoking the ultimate ethical premise of the greatest happiness for the greatest number), and functionalism (evoking the need to ensure a society's survival, stability and well-being) (Jones 1974, Lamount 1965, Pinker 1983).

Romanticism, a literary concept with sociopolitical overtones, has a concern for individual rights as its focal point. In the context of welfare, it is, according to Pinker (1983: 8), a "preoccupation with the recovery or the preservation of self-respect." It strives to recover man's lost innocence from the oppression of an alienating society. It seeks to preserve the established order, which is deeply rooted in tradition, and social institutions against the threat of inevitable modernity. Progress means that the individual becomes a total human being (Jones 1974: 260).

Humanism has as its essential conviction that there is a common responsibility of all people for everyone's well-being. It recognizes the inevitability of interdependence and thus the need for mutual respect. Society, moreover, is obliged to provide the conditions necessary for the fullest possible development of each individual. Social justice is, then, the progressive realization of equality.

Functionalism has its focus on survival, stability and the well-being of society. Thus, according to Schenk and Schenk (1981: 17) "welfare services to individuals contribute to the well-being of society, because welfare services aim to ensure that each person is an adequately functioning member of society."
In this perspective there is no conflict between the interest of society and those of the individual; what is good for one must be good for the other (Poloma 1979: 28).

Impact on the Idea of Social Security

The way a society views state welfare paternalism influences its perception of social security. Clearly, ipso facto, it justifies the quintessential quiddity of social security — the financing of social security benefits by the state — which now takes place in 113 countries. Yet what society views as acceptable forms and degrees of state paternalism has a profound impact on its perceptions of acceptable forms of social security.

Countries adopting social insurance in the closing decades of the nineteenth century exhibited a strong tradition of state paternalism — notably Germany (Muller 1989, Muller 1993), Austria (Hofmeister 1982), Czechoslovakia, Sweden (Heckscher 1994, Olsson 1989), Hungary and Belgium (see also Rimlinger 1971). Indeed, the convenient marriage of the insurance and the social stability mode of the state paternalism traditions molded those societies' views on social security.

In contrast, countries adopting social assistance strategies around the turn of the twentieth century — notably New Zealand and Australia — did so, in part, because the idea of compulsory insurance was considered socially and morally objectionable (see, for example, Davidson 1989, Dixon 1977, Mendelsohn 1954). In these societies paternalistic social security intervention by the state was accepted only with considerable reluctance; libertarian principles could be stretched only so far. Thus the Poor Law tradition and social stability mode of the state paternalism traditions came together to engender in those societies a desire and the courage to transform the much-maligned Poor Law strategy into a dignified and humane social security strategy.

As the twentieth century progressed, the idea of state paternalism became more acceptable. Old ties to libertarian principles had been weakened by economic, social and political circumstances. The social progress mode of the state paternalism tradition began to take root. Its impact on social security came through the acceptance of Beveridgian social security principles. The need for greater state welfare paternalism became both more conspicuous and more addictive after the Second World War. This had a catalytic effect on the adoption of social security strategies around the world. In 1940 only 57 countries could be identified as having any social security programs; by 1983 145 countries could be so identified (US SSA 1984: x); by 1995 the number of countries had reached 172. It has also promoted the advancement of social security towards universality of coverage, and the payment of more generous benefits. Indeed, the pinnacle of social security aspirations under this tradition is the universal-general strategy of universal demogrants, or basic income grants, paid to every resident irrespective of their income, their citizenship or their employment participation (Collins 1990, Parijs 1992, Offe 1996, Purdy 1994, see also Kingson 1994).

Impact on the Form of Social Security

The state welfare paternalism tradition has incubated the only novel form of social security to emerge in the twentieth century; universal social allowances. They were first introduced in New Zealand (1938) as an old-age allowance (Davidson 1989, Uttley 1989). Their major impetus, however, came when child allowances were introduced during and just after the Second World War in Australia (1941) (Kewley 1972, Weatherly 1994), Canada (1944) (Bellemy and Irving 1989, Wolley et al. 1996), Ireland (1944), Romania (1944), Soviet Union (1944) (Wiktorow 1992), the United Kingdom (1945) (Keithley 1989), Norway (1946) (Forsund 1989), Iceland (1946), Sweden (1947) (Olsson 1989, Wilson 1979), and Austria and Finland (1948). Their introduction was the product of economic and political pragmatism; they represented the embodiment of all that is important to those committed to the social progress mode of this tradition (see Bolderson and Mabbett 1991, Esping-Andersen and Korpi 1987, Flora and Alber 1981a; Heckscher 1984; Kaim-Caudle 1973, Mendelsohn 1954, Watts 1987).

As social allowances constitute an expression of the common responsibility of all people for the welfare of others and acknowledge the dignity of the individual, they stand in stark contrast to demeaning social assistance. Thus for most of the second half of the twentieth century they have been the *desideratum* of social security.

Social allowances are, of course, the progeny of affluence, and thus a luxury that few developing countries can afford.

Legacy

One manifest legacy of this tradition is the adoption of social allowance programs by 38 largely developed countries, including Hong Kong (1973) (Chow 1985b), and a few developing countries, most notably Mauritius (1976) (Joynathsing 1987).

The state paternalism tradition has both legitimated and made achievable the Welfare State aspirations of those seeking to improve society by means of state intervention. The very idea that social security expenditure is a desirable form of public expenditure that is socially and politically acceptable in most countries is its major legacy. The prospect of burgeoning government cost burdens is the specter born of this tradition. Scandinavian countries, with their penchant for social allowances, in particular, are grappling with this ghost (Andersen 1993, Olsson 1990, Olsson et al. 1993, Stephens 1995 and 1996, Backman and Sharma 1998).

THE MARKETIZATION TRADITION

The marketization tradition emerged as a reaction to the state welfare paternalism tradition, drawing strength from the spirit of liberalism, emphasizing the virtues of the marketplace. At its heart is myth of the marketplace (Engler 1995), posited by its adherents as being "morally right and economically efficient" as an impersonal distributor of a society's resources (Muller 1994: 46).

This tradition advances the proposition that individuals should, in their self-interest, fend for themselves in the face of social security risks. They should not depend on governments for cradle-to-grave protection that bloats public social security budgets — the legacy of the largess inspired by the state welfare paternalism tradition. This brings into focus a rebalancing of the equity and efficiency dimensions of social security. The marketization tradition draws support from neoclassical economic theory, which is, of course, at its neoliberal heart.

Neoclassical economics embraces the philosophical position that truth and knowledge are attainable through a priori reasoning — neopositivism — (Kolakowski 1972). Neoclassical economists are satisfied only with "objective" and "empirically verifiable" knowledge and are dismissive of normative concerns. They postulate a worldview based on a set of reductionist premises that permit logico-deductive conclusions to be drawn about scarcity and efficiency, the elegant cornerstone of which is the Pareto efficiency principle: that a society's welfare will be enhanced if, at any time, an individual can be made better off without reducing the well-being of another individual. Subsumed under this efficiency principle are conceptualizations of "productive" or "technical" efficiency (that is, configurations of resource utilization patterns that maximize production) and of "exchange" efficiency (that is, configurations of consumption patterns that maximize utility or satisfaction), which, together, determine an array of Pareto-efficient resource-consumption configurations ("economic" efficiency). From this Pareto efficiency paradigm the following axiomatic propositions can be derived:

- that provided any loss in economic well-being experienced by some members of a society is more than offset by gains in the economic well-being achieved by other members, then that society's welfare — as the simple aggregation of its members' economic well-being — is improved;
- that, in the Hobbesian tradition, individuals are the best judge of their own

well-being; and
- that individuals are rational, desirous, calculating, consistent and self-interested with a known and consistently ordered set of preferences that allows them to allocate their scarce resources to maximize their well-being, on the basis that they have complete and certain knowledge of, and the ability to compute, the consequences of alternative diverse and heterogeneous courses of action.

Neoclassical economists, ever conscious of their need to be objective, represent the world they seek to understand and improve as a reductionist model, invariably cast in mathematical terms, based on a set of axioms that are so self-evidently correct that they could not possibly be otherwise. Neoclassical economics presumes that the underlying order of a complicated system can be expressed in mathematical form and can be understood by applying logico-deductive reasoning to the behavior of its constituent parts. It is extraordinarily difficult to prove the correctness of neoclassical economic theory, with its syllogistic arguments. Empirical testing is problematic (Eusepi 1987, Ormerod 1998, Polanyi 1957, Robinson 1977, Wisman 1978 and 1979), for it can always be argued that "*ceteris* was not *paribus*," and cannot be depended upon "to distinguish economic truth from economic falsehood" (Wisman 1980: 137–38, also 1987: 96). As Guitton has noted (1987: 33), economists are "engaged chiefly in improving the rationality [logicality] of their theory much more than knowing whether these theories conform to the reality of the present world." Rigor is everything; relevance is nothing, which is why neopositivist syllogistic economic arguments and positivist presumptions are sacrosanct, although barren. Neoclassical economic theory is highly resistant to basic change, despite the dubiousness of its presuppositions. It is as if, as theory, neoclassical economic is too mathematically elegant to be wrong.

Because their intellectual traditions have grown so wealthy, so cognitively arrogant, neoclassical economists seem to lack the interest in undertaking the reflexive analysis needed to gain a critical self-awareness of the epistemological commitment embodied in their "domain assumptions" — those unverified and unrecognized assumptions about the nature of man and society (Gouldner 1970: 70) — and of the "metaphysical pathos in which the theory comes packaged" (Gouldner 1955: 498). Thus they refuse to verify their assumptions according to the dictates of the "scientific method" — that no statement is meaningful unless verified. Neoclassical economists are unable to recognize, let alone acknowledge, the dramatic, if not Socratic, irony of their meta-empirical speculations, which are interesting enough to provoke further comment, but which do not move them towards unveiling universal truths that are shrouded in clouds of unknowing. They would even deny the appropriateness to neoclassical economics of Kahn's (1974: 489) proposition that "the mill of science grinds only when hypotheses and data are in continuous and abrasive contact." As Torgerson (1986: 40) observes:

It becomes apparent that the narrow, positivist conception of reason has fostered an intellectual style which is insensitive to its own nature and context — which is, in a word, irrational.

Deane (cited in Fitzgerald 1990: 24) expresses the view, somewhat cynically, that,

economists study complex economic systems by constructing drastically simplified models of economic behaviour, based on incompletely verified time and space evidence, in order to derive partially intuitive judgments about the past and future consequences of changes in the social and political context of economic activity.

In essence, neoclassical economics applies "instrumentality (means-ends) mode of rationality" and is thus concerned with the relationship between "means" and "ends," having no bearing on the choice of "ends" beyond presuming that the Pareto efficiency principle is an unexceptionable, even almost indisputable, ethical proposition because, in the words of Buchanan (1959: 125) "it is one which requires a minimum of premises and one that should command wide assent." Thus, neoclassical economists are preoccupied with determining allocatively efficient means for arriving at exogenously determined goals, within an economic system conceptualized as being independent of, rather than integrated into, the total social fabric, preferring to exile the issue of what those goals should be, and how they might best be changed, to the domain of the unscientific. This is done because goals involve values, which, by their very nature are non-cognitive and thus not susceptible to empirical or rational testing, hence they involve, in Friedman's (1953: 5) words, "differences about which men can only ultimately fight." Values are thus eschewed by economists, who consider them to be beyond the scope of rational discourse (Coates 1964, Robinson 1977). Claims to value neutrality are supported by the assumption that behavior reveals preferences, but as Thurow (1984: 217) cogently observes:

Revealed preferences . . . is just a fancy way of saying that individuals do what individuals do, and whatever they do, economists will call it "utility maximization." Whether individuals buy good X or good Y, they are still rational individual utility maximizers. By definition, there is no such thing as an individual who does not maximize his utility. But, if a theory can never be wrong, it has no content. It is merely a tautology.

The fundamental ideological underpinning of this neoliberal perspective is a set of beliefs that claim legitimacy by drawing heavily upon Adam Smith's *Wealth of Nations* (1776) infused with the interpretations of the Austrian school of economic thought (Gretschmann 1991: 47–67). At its heart is the idealized and stylized marketplace. It must be acknowledged, of course, the marketplace has shown itself to be an efficient producer of income and wealth, but it has also revealed its capacity to produce distributional inequities (see, for example, Dixon 1992a). Yet is posited as an efficient and impersonal distributor of society's resources, a belief held, despite the reality of market failure, because of the inherent imperfections of democracy (Arrow 1963 and 1976); and the inherent limitations of government supply and policy implementation (Weimer and Vining 1992: 131–38, Wolf 1979). The pursuit for the most "efficient" means of achieving exogenous socioeconomic goals is often ruthless, sometimes stultifying, and occasionally heartless, but it is always pragmatic and, to the neoclassical economist, a disinterested and value-free exercise (O'Brien 1981, Georgiou 1973). In such a policy milieu "efficiency" invariably defines what ought to be adopted as public policy. As Fay (1975: 50) concludes, "Efficiency becomes the criterion by virtue of which the merits of various political measures will be assessed." The ideological pendulum has swung too far; by making market forces such an act of faith, anything done in its name cannot be questioned.

The inevitable neoclassical presumption — ideological prejudice — is, in the classical Benthamite tradition (Bentham [1789] 1970), that the public sector is bloated, inefficient, wasteful, and thus not giving value for money, because the absence of any automatic disciplining mechanism permits rent-seeking behavior (Tullock and Eller 1994) by bureaucrats, their clients and the politicians who govern them, perhaps even with a Machiavellian flair (Gilman et al. 1993, Terrell 1993). Premised on a set of simplistic notions of bureaucratic behavior, and theories about democracy, principal-agent relationships, transaction costs, property rights and government failure (see, for example, Arrow 1963 and 1976, Coarse 1937, Williamson 1985, Bryson and Ring 1990, Weimer and Vining 1992; but also Self 1993), there emerges a concern about "opportunism" in public administration. Self-serving, even deceitful and dishonest behavior by bureaucrats contrives with the equally self-serving behavior by politicians and voters to develop expenditure programs that distribute benefits to maximize voter support, financed by tax mechanisms that spread the cost across the entire population. It certainly seems that the neoclassical economist is unable to proceed without assuming a rational agent seeking to find an optimal means to a well-defined end (Dixon et al. 1998). It would seem that for the neoclassical economist, acolytes of ash cloth coupled with the obligatory hirsute appendage constitute accepted dress. Such dress, it could be argued, is inappropriate, perhaps even somewhat incongruous. "like finding Falstaff dressed in a bikini!" (with apologies to Panitach as quoted by Metcalfe and McQuillan (1979: 268). The outcome is these neoclassical presumptions and prejudices is a predisposition towards opposing state provision. They invariably favor privatization (Donahue 1989; Gormley 1994) — "the shifting of a [government] function, either in whole or in part, from the public sector to the private sector" (Butler 1991:17); marketization (Salamon 1993) — the creation by statute of a marketplace (by means of, mandatory private sector provision) to achieve public policy goals; or, at the very least, the adoption of policy instruments that cause least "market distortion" (Howlett and Ramesh 1993). This redrawing of the boundaries around the public sphere does not, however, mean the retreat of the state (see, for example, Dixon 1988, Dixon and Kouzmin 1994, Dixon, et al. 1995, Kouzmin and Dixon 1993), for even neoclassical economists accept that the public regulation of private economic activity may be justified if there is market failure. Others would, of course, go further (see, for example, Majone 1994).

Neoliberals, of course, also accept, quite uncritically, the public choice explanation of the development of social security in terms of vote-maximization behavior by politicians and benefit-maximization behavior by voters (Bridges 1978, Browning 1975, Verbon 1988, Velthoven and Winden 1985). They have a deep suspicion of populist democracy and the proposition that the will of the people should be sovereign. Riker (1982: 238) has pronounced that government does not and cannot know what the people want. Neoliberals present a broad presumption that individual decision-making is preferred to collective decision-making. Thus they advocate that the boundaries around state intervention must be redrawn more tightly; the state must thus retreat to create market opportunities for commercial exploitation. As Cerney (1990: 230) notes, the state itself is having to "act increasingly like a market player, shaping its policies to promote, control and maximize returns from market forces in an international setting."

It is as if private managerial authority is, without doubt, legitimate, while government authority is a malevolent burden (Rowlands 1990: 267). Harris and Seldon (1979: 23) captured the spirit of this malevolence when they remarked: "The Welfare State has gradually changed from the expression of compassion to an instrument of political repression unequaled in British history and in other Western industrial societies."

Of the neoliberal reform agenda, Cerney (cited in Kouzmin et al. 1997: 19) has observed: "The central policy objective has been to shift public policy from the 'social goal' to the 'economic goal'; from a 'welfare state' to 'the competitive state'" (see also Rieger and Leibfried 1998).

Neoliberalism, with its penchant for economic models and actuarial predictions and its specious epistemological dualism of objectivism-subjectivism, is disdainful of irrational values discourse, because it involves abhorrent "subjective" judgments. Instead, it prefers to conceptualize social security as a set of purely technical issues. This allows efficiency considerations, essentially supply-side preoccupations, to be stressed and kept well separated from the down-played equity considerations (see, for example, Reichlin and Siconolfi 1996; but see also LeGrand 1990). Kingson and Williamson (1997: 30) make the pertinent observation:

There is a disturbing tendency in public discourse to reduce social security discussions to mere accounting exercises on the financial costs of the [social security] program, overlooking its value as a source of national social cohesion and as an expression of the obligations of all to each member of the national community, especially those at greatest risk.

Yet neoliberalism does embody a set of politically conservative values (O'Brien and Penna 1998), the principal tenets of which in the social security context are: individual and family responsibility, personal choice, dignity based on contractual relationships, fair returns and economic efficiency. These are, of course, fundamental to neoliberalism's analytical premises and presumptions, which are taken to be axiomatic, requiring no justification. It is as if the economic efficiency of social security systems is all that matters (Kotlikoff 1989, Ippolito 1986).

Perhaps efficiency is what matters to the politically influential business lobbies, for which it has become the informing ideology in the face of the perceived threats and challenges of the expanding global marketplace (see, for example, European Commission 1994). These lobbies plead that more needs to be done to enhance their "international competitiveness," irrespective of what government has already done. For legitimacy, they draw upon the economic metaphors of "free trade," "open-market economy" and "level playing field" of "comparative advantage" and the "division of labor," which are all premised on the principles first espoused by Adam Smith and David Ricardo and which are founded on the crucial assumption that "capital and labor are completely free to move between industries within a specific society, but not across national boundaries (they are not internationally mobile)" (Kouzmin and Korac-Kakabadse 1997: 146–47). These presumptions and assumptions have, however, lost much of its validity over the last 200 years, with the emergence of the information age that permits an allocative emphasis on competitive advantage. Business lobbies advocate cuts in their statutory social security cost burden, not to mention other tax burdens, even though they may well have shifted that burden forward on to consumers or backward on to employees. The rather doubtful assumption made is that by reducing labor costs production costs would be reduced (the extent of any such cost savings would, of course, depend on the labor intensity of the production processes involved). This would lower domestic-currency commodity prices and thus increase domestic or export demand, at the expense of foreign competitors (given, of course, that the domestic-currency price reductions achieved are not offset by counteracting exchange rate variations, that end users respond to the price reductions by increasing their demand, and that this market penetration pricing strategy does not induce strategic responses from competitors).

Perhaps efficiency is also what matters to politicians, who evince concern about the predicted economic and fiscal consequences of the so-called moral hazards — the adverse behavioral responses that may be induced by social security systems, notably, work and savings disincentives, family formation and dissolution, and completed family size. The importance of the interaction between social security and human behavior is indisputable (Kaim-Caudle 1993). Underlying this importance is the proposition that it may be socially and politically unacceptable to operate social security measures that give people assistance but, at the same time, create a set of disincentives that gives rise to a *dependency trap* (the unwillingness of social security recipients to avoid dependency on social security benefits through employment or past savings) or a *poverty trap* (the inability of social security recipients to leave poverty through employment or past savings). It also acknowledges that material well-being is primarily determined by the growth in absolute incomes not by income redistribution. What is disputable, however, is the economist's behavioral response presumptions (LeGrand 1996), which are based on the proposition that an individual's behavior, and the institutions and practices that arise from it, can ultimately be attributed to causal considerations derived from deductive reductionist economic theory (Barr 1992, Diamond 1977) that assumes rational maximizing behavior, and presumes, if not ignores, prevailing commodity, labor and capital market realities.

Whether, or to what extent, social security recipients who are capable of contributing to the total labor supply reduce their work effort upon the receipt of entitlements is undoubtedly an issue of social security policy relevance (Atkinson and Morgensen 1993, Atkinson and Rein 1993, Cain and Watts 1973, Dixon et al. 1984, Keeley et al. 1978, Whiteford 1980). Clearly, the cost of social security programs over time depends somewhat on the extent to which either the transfer from welfare to work is discouraged or the transfer from work to welfare is encouraged. Moreover, the political acceptability of a particular social security program similarly depends, at least in part, on this work-disincentive effect. Finally, the impact of social security on inflation, unemployment and economic growth depends, in part, on its effect on the supply of labor over time.

Given their rational maximizing behavior assumptions, economists hypothesize that cash entitlements reduce labor supply because of the distortions they cause to the work-leisure decisions if an acceptable level of total current income can be gained from social security benefits with little or no earned income. Under these circumstances, rational social security recipients capable of work would not enter or re-enter the workforce (as with, for example, first job seekers or previously dependent widows); would totally withdraw from the workforce (for example, by taking early retirement (Parnes 1983, Stagner 1978, Thompson, 1998) or by being designated as disabled); would partially withdraw from the workforce by engaging in continuous part-time or discontinuous full-time employment (as with, for example, the unemployed and lone parents); or would temporarily withdraw from work — absenteeism — (as with sickness beneficiaries) (Weaver 1994). The economists' presumption, akin to that made by McGregor's (1960) Theory X managers, is that people inherently dislike work and, whenever possible, will avoid it.

Undoubtedly the work-leisure decision nexus is complex, involving social security, economic, psychological, health and social dimensions (Boaz 1989, Goodwin 1972, Reimers and Honig 1996). Indeed, many factors determine whether an individual works or not, including the nature of social security programs available (including the generosity of entitlements, the nature of any means tests and work tests applied, the nature of any minimum employment or contribution period requirements attached, and the latitude given to interpreting categorical requirements); the state of the labor market (the availability of suitable full-time or part-time work); the need to meet personal psychological needs (such as, physiological, safety, love, esteem and self-actualization (Maslow 1954); perceived health status; perceived family responsibilities; attitudes towards risk and the ability to borrow. Neoclassical economic theory notwithstanding, there is no comprehensive social theory that integrates all the factors that impinge on an individual's work-leisure decision. Thus, the extent to which individuals adjust their work effort after receiving social security benefits remains an empirical question which has yet to be definitively answered (Thompson 1998), although much deductive analysis has been done on the basis of a priori premises and ceteris paribus presumptions (see, for example, Cameron 1972: 141–50, Creedy 1994, US Congress 1974, Krueger and Pischke 1992, Lampman 1978, Snower 1995, Stock and Wise 1990, World Bank 1994).

Whether, or to what extent, social security diminishes savings by distorting individual savings decisions is also of social security policy relevance because of its macroeconomic ramifications. The conventional economic wisdom is that the payment of social security contributions significantly reduces other forms of savings (see, for example, Feldstein 1996) and that social security measures reduce an individual's propensity to save by reducing the precautionary savings motivation. But as Pechman, Arron and Taussig (1968: 183) argued long ago, social security "may well provide an incentive for individuals to save more; with major hazards already covered, other savings goals may appear 'within reach.'" (see also Ciggno and Rosati 1996, Munnell 1974, Feldstein 1974 and 1996, Thompson 1998).

Undoubtedly the savings-consumption decision nexus is complex involving social security, economic, social and psychological dimensions. Indeed, many factors determine an individual's savings propensity, including the nature of current and expected future social security programs (including the perceived generosity of current and expected future benefit entitlements, the nature of any income and asset tests currently applied, the risk that coverage or eligibility requirements will be made more stringent, or that benefit rates or formulas will be made less generous); the level of current disposable income, expected future disposable income stream; current and expected future consumption and savings needs (as determined by, for example, family composition, lifestyle aspirations and preferences, and attitudes towards risk and uncertainty). Again, neoclassical economic theory notwithstanding, there is no comprehensive social theory that integrates all the factors that impinge on an individual's savings decisions. Thus the extent to which individuals adjust their savings behavior in the light of social security remains yet another empirical question awaiting a definitive answer, although, again, much deductive analysis has been done (see, for example, Artus

1994, Bernheim and Leven 1989, Butare 1994, Gutierrez 1990, Kotlikoff 1987, Leimer and Richardson 1992, Munnell 1974, World Bank 1994).

MacKellar and McGreevey (1997: 3) sum up the neoliberal perspective on social security most perceptively:

The trade-off in social security policy is between addressing genuine market failures and redistributing income from savers to those clever enough to evade personal responsibility for saving. The disincentives to the labor supply and the erosion of economic efficiency that result from over-expansion of social security systems seriously impair macroeconomic performance.

Emerging from the deductive reasoning of neoclassical economic theory, with its a priori premises and ceteris paribus presumptions, is an advocacy of incentive-driven social security policies aimed at the goals of promoting economic efficiency, promoting individual responsibility and promoting family solidarity.

Impact on the Idea of Social Security

Neoliberals seek to shift the prevailing social security paradigm from *community solidarity* (the acceptance of public responsibility for social security provision so as to enhance social cohesion, integration and inclusion) to *marketization, individualization* and/or *familialization*.

Marketization leads to the creation by statute of a market in which the delivery of social security benefits or administrative services takes place to achieve public policy goals. The policy outcome sought is to divest government or employers of social security responsibilities, either partially or completely.

Individualization is the partial or complete shifting of a governmental social security responsibility towards individuals. This can be achieved by the imposition of statutory obligations upon them (perhaps by introducing employer social security contributions) or by the renunciation of a statutory responsibility (perhaps by withdrawing unemployment benefits from individuals in particular population categories, so forcing them to be more active job seekers in the labor market). The policy outcomes sought are to achieve fairer returns; to minimize economic distortions, especially in the labor market, caused by adverse selection and moral hazards; and to reduce public outlays.

Familialization is the partial or complete shifting of a governmental social security responsibility to the family — and to women as unpaid care givers. This can be achieved by the imposition of statutory obligations on families (perhaps by making mandatory family support for particular population categories, typically the aged and children), or the renunciation of a statutory responsibility (perhaps by withdrawing benefit entitlement from individuals in particular population categories, such as the adolescent first job seekers or adolescent unmarried mothers, or by withdrawing special needs benefits from the most vulnerable, such as the frail elderly or disabled people), so forcing families to step into the breach. The policy outcomes sought are to promote family solidarity and to reduce public outlays.

This paradigmatic shift is intended to move the social security debate away from issues of social justice, social inclusion and equality of opportunity towards issues related to the technical realignment of boundaries that demarcate public-private, public-employer, public-individual and public-family responsibilities for social security, especially regarding funding. This re-orientation overlooks, as Kingson and Williamson (1996: 30) correctly note, social security's intangible "value as a source of national social cohesion and as an expression of the obligations of all to each member of the national community, especially those at greatest risk."

Reflecting on market-driven social security systems, Maydell (1994: 506) ponders:

one question that should be asked is whether [such] a system will guarantee the safety of the long-term capital investment for old age and whether it can achieve a measure of equality between the weak and the strong.

At risk are the weak and vulnerable — the poor, the sick and the unemployed — because they are inherently bad insurance risks, which, of commercial necessity, must be culled from the good and profitable risks wherever possible. Only the latter are a good business opportunity. If good risks can be distinguished from bad, why should the former cross-subsidize the latter at the expense of paying higher premiums? This, of course, may become the basis for a clarion call for government subsidies. Thus, those who are most vulnerable and most in need confront the prospect of paying contributions they can ill afford or even becoming the new underclass of the uninsurables — if they are excluded from the social security protection available to others — because the insurance risks are being spread across a narrower risk spectrum to minimize contributions and/or to maximize profits (see, for example, Burchardt and Hills 1997). After all, vertical income redistribution is not a function of the laissez-faire marketplace; it is a task for the state.

The marketization tradition propagates the view that the marketplace can deliver social security outcomes more cost-efficiently or even more cost-effectively than the public sector. Cynics, however, might be tempted to conclude, as Silburn (1998: 244) does, that "[t]he mantra of the unregulated free market forces may act as little more than ideological cover for sectional advantage and, at the extreme, of unbridled corporate greed."

Adherents to the marketization tradition advocate that responsibility for the collection of contributions and the payment of entitlements could be contracted out, even if the state continues to set the priorities for the investment of public social security reserves. Such investment portfolio priorities could still be set in the context of prevailing political attitudes towards the appropriate socioeconomic role of social security institutions, and articulated as constraints specified in its enabling legislation, and/or as the institutional arrangements surrounding the investment decision-making process. Alternatively, responsibility of the management of the investment of social security reserves could be contracted out, in the hope that it would achieve a higher real rate of return on those funds, although perhaps at the cost of increased risk (see, for example, World Bank 1994, Mitchell and Zeldes 1996) even if the state wishes to continue collecting contributions and paying out cash entitlements. Private sector involvement in investment portfolio management offers, according to those imbued with the values of the marketization tradition, the promise of greater domestic capital market depth and liquidity (Crespo 1994), not to mention a lowering of the cost of capital, provided any regulatory regimes imposed on the private sector are liberal in the range of permitted financial instruments and conservative in permitting international investments (Holzmann 1996, Montas 1983).

Impact on the Form of Social Security

The market-driven panaceas proffered under the rubric of marketization take four forms.

Service contracting out occurs when the delivery of specific administrative and other services undertaken by a public social security agency is contracted out to service providers operating in a market environment (such service might relate to healthcare, investment portfolio management, or the administration of benefit payments, benefit advise provision or work testing).

Complementary benefit privatization occurs when government creates a market for the provision of complementary social security cash entitlements to supplement those provided by public social security programs. This is achieved either by permitting non-governmental organizations to compete with the public provision of mandatory complementary social security benefits or by obligating employers and/or individuals to purchase complementary social security benefits in a market environment.

Coverage privatization occurs when government creates a market for the provision of primary social security benefits comparable to those publicly provided. This is achieved by permitting non-governmental organizations either to compete with public provision (contracting out) or to replace public provision by obligating designated or all employers and/or individuals to purchase primary social security benefits in a market environment.

Coverage marketization occurs by the statutory creation of a market in which employers and/or individuals are obligated to purchase primary social security benefits, thereby avoiding the use of public provision to meet a new social security need or shifting the contribution cost burden from employers to employees.

Market-driven social security initiatives can be categorized according to the degree of competition they introduce. *Competitive marketization* occurs when non-governmental providers deliver optional or mandated social security services (such as administrative services or the provision of employment-injury insurance) or benefits (such as statutorily defined benefits or benefits based on personal capitalization) in a competitive or at least a contestable market environment. *Partially competitive marketization* occurs when non-governmental organizations deliver optional social security services or benefits (such as optional benefits in a particular industry or occupational group) in only competition with a public social security agency. These stand in contradistinction to *non-competitive marketization*, whereby non-governmental organizations are statutorily granted the exclusive right to deliver social security services or benefits (such as the mandatory complementary social security cash entitlements to a particular industry or occupational group) as a regulated monopolist.

As governments have, throughout the twentieth century, sought to create markets for particular services related to the provision of social security outcomes, the involvement of non-governmental organizations has taken many forms. Many governments, especially before the Second World War, created a regulated workers' compensation insurance market by obligating employers to carry insurance against their employment-related injury, disease and death risks. Over time, however, the popularity of this form of marketization has declined, because of the transformation of many workers' compensation programs into social insurance programs and the emergence of public insurance carriers, for in only 29 countries are employers still required to carry private workers' compensation insurance, although in seven countries the carrier can be either private or public.

The practice of contracting out aspects of social security service delivery to the non-governmental organizations is quite widespread. In the tiny Cook Islands the entire social security system is administered by an insurance company (Tuavera 1985). Healthcare service contracting out happens in 35 countries.

Legacy

The marketization tradition has acquired a cult status over the last 15 or so years, feeding on the neoconservative reaction to what is seen as the uneconomic excesses of the state welfare paternalism tradition. Its major legacy is the market provision of social security benefits that are in lieu of, as a replacement for, or as a complement to public (and also employer) provision in 27 countries (Horlick 1987, Voirin 1995).

The mandating of occupational pension plans as an optional social security strategy dates back to the 1950s. The contracting out of old-age, disability and survivors' program coverage to mandated occupational pension programs was first permitted in Greece (1951) (Knightley 1994) and Japan (1954) (Ichien 1995) and, subsequently, in the United Kingdom (1988) (Creedy and Disney 1988,

Culverhouse 1990, Keithly 1989, Kritzer 1994). The use of such programs to provide mandatory complementary (supplementary) benefits in relation to long-term contingencies first occurred in Finland (1961) and France (1960s) (Morgenstern 1994) — where accumulated pension entitlement rights reflect past contribution revenue collected — and, somewhat later, in Bolivia (1972), Côte d'Ivoire (1976) (Bakayoko and Ehouman 1987), Switzerland (1985) (Roduit 1994) and Venezuela (1990) (see also Campbell 1994a, ISSA 1993b, Reynaud 1995, Rosa 1982).

The mandating of occupational savings plans as an optional social security strategy also has a history dating back to the early 1950s. Coverage contracting out to mandated occupational savings programs began when the first National Provident Funds exempted from their coverage covered employees in equivalent occupational savings plans (Dixon 1989b). This first occurred in Malaysia (1951),and then India (1952), Singapore (1953), Sri Lanka (1958), followed by Fiji (1966), Zambia (1973), the Solomon Islands (1976), Papua New Guinea (1980) and Vanuatu (1987). The use of occupational savings plans to provide mandatory complementary (supplementary) benefits in relation to the long-term contingencies has occurred in Australia (1988) (Price 1994), Venezuela (1990) and Mexico (1992) (Ceniceros 1997, Cross 1994. (Hong Kong as legislated to establish a mandatory occupational savings program (Cross 1994, Dixon 1995a) (1998)).

Replacing public provision with mandated personal pension programs first began in the early 1980s in Chile (1981) (Borzutzky 1983 and 1990, Castaneda 1992, Castillo 1993, Diamond and Valdes-Prieto 1994, Gillion and Bonilla 1992, Kritzer 1996b, Pinera 1995–96, Vittas and Iglesias (1992) and then in Peru (1991) (Kritzer 1995, Estrin 1992), in both countries with respect to their long-term contingency insurance programs. Coverage contracting out to such programs also began in Chile (1981), from its sickness and maternity insurance program; and was subsequently adopted in the United Kingdom (1988), from its old-age, disability and survivors' insurance programs (Disney and Whitehouse 1992, Kritzer 1994), in Peru (1991), from both its old-age, disability and survivors' insurance programs and its sickness and maternity programs (Estrin 1992), and then in Argentina (1994) and Colombia (1994) (Perez 1990, Tiano and Alchini 1994), from their old-age, disability and survivors' programs (see also Gluski 1994, ILO 1994, Queisser 1988, Ryser 1992, Santamaria 1992). (Uruguay plans to follow suit (Kritzer 1996a).) Colombia (1995) also permits contracting out from its social insurance healthcare benefit program into individual healthcare plans (Tiano and Alchini 1994).

Mandated personal saving programs have also been used as a replacement for employer-liability measures in Afghanistan (1987), for all three of its employment-injury programs, soon followed by Colombia (1991), for its unemployment program. Guatemala (1991) adopted this strategy when first addressing the need for an unemployment program without recourse to public provision (Keyes

1990).

This legacy could well give rise to a new social security ghost — ironically, the specter of government subsidies. It should be noted that Argentina, Chile (Borzutzky 1983 and 1990, Castaneda 1992) and Colombia already subsidize their personal pension plan systems to guarantee a minimum pension rate (see also Queisser 1995). Subsidization could emerge under two sets of circumstances.

First, pressures for government subsidies to be paid to mandated defined-contribution programs would build up if their achieved levels of accumulated savings (or equivalent annuities) are so inadequate, or so much below community expectations, as to be unacceptable. Because defined-contribution programs place the burden of the risk of asset value variations on their members (covered employees), then members' interests may not be congruent with those of the plan administrators and investment fund managers. The cost of any financial mismanagement or malfeasance is carried by members, unless the government acts as a guarantor, which might, of course, only encourage greater risk taking by commission-driven investment fund managers. The cost of not minimizing administrative charges is also carried by members, unless government provides some form of administrative subsidy, which might encourage inefficiency. The cost of unpaid contributions from insolvent employers is, furthermore, carried by members, unless government subsidizes this group, which might encourage voluntary insolvency by employers as an acceptable way of avoiding their social security obligations. Making mandatory the membership of what were previously voluntary defined-contribution programs thus places a responsibility on government to design and administer an appropriate regulatory regime in order to reconcile the inherent tensions generated by using profit-making organizations to deliver social security outcomes, so as to ensure both their long-term solvency and the adequacy of their benefits (Daykin 1995, Dixon 1995a). As Wright (1992: 1031) observes "welfare and profit-maximisation are not good bedfellows." The required regulatory regimes must embody both structural regulations (which determine which actors may engage in what activities) and conduct regulation (which are concerned with how the actors should behave). They must also be designed and administered so as to minimize the threat of asymmetrical information (the regulated actors distorting or withholding the information needed by regulators to regulate effectively) and the risk of agency capture (the regulated actors manipulating the regulators (by, perhaps, strategic agenda setting or compromise bargaining) to achieve their ends) (Bernstein 1955, Majone 1994, Wright 1992). Any failure to do so may well encourage the government subsidization ghost to come and haunt offending governments.

Second, pressures for government subsidies to mandated defined-benefit programs would emerge with any diminution of the profitability (or financial viability) of such programs. Such subsidies, of course, may be initially politically more acceptable to enacting, endorsing or even merely permitting either in-

creases in the employee and/or employer contribution rates or decreases in benefit generosity. Such subsidized programs may, eventually, even become cheaper
than reintegrating their covered employees back into the public social security
system. With any such subsidization, however, comes the prospect of efficiency
distortions, which may well overshadow any efficiency benefits gained. In these
circumstances, the government subsidization ghost will come to haunt countries
as they confront the prospect of a fragmented, inefficient and costly social security system.

CONCLUSION

Since the sixteenth century social security has been evolving both as an idea
and as an institution (Schweinitz 1943). The way a society views social security
and its underlying dominant values is, then, a crucial factor in the evolution of
social security within that society, or even on a global basis (Ashford 1986a and
1986b, Gough 1979). The dominant values have, over time, promoted and enforced patterns of beliefs, prejudices and preconceptions about social security's
gainers and losers. They have, in essence, molded the broad contours of the
building blocks that the social security technocrats have sculpted and adorned to
construct their systems. The result has been that most countries have constructed
income-maintenance safety nets that sought to keep their burgeoning middle
classes out of poverty. Social security has thus, unfortunately, been irrelevant to
the human needs of most people, especially those most in need, in most countries for most of the twentieth century.

3

Global Overview of Social Security Practices: Patterns and Recent Developments

INTRODUCTION

The global pattern of social security provision in the mid-1990s is the product of the historical, social, economic and political forces that have determined the nature of national social security systems. While the tapestry of global social security provision is rich in diversity and idiosyncrasies, explored in subsequent chapters, it is possible to identify the major threads — the patterns of social security strategy and branch coverage — and the major changes that have taken place in recent years.

GLOBAL PATTERNS OF SOCIAL SECURITY PROVISION: 1995

Global Social Security Strategy Coverage

The global application of social security strategies in 1995 is shown in Table 3.1.

Social Insurance. Social security has long been dominated by the social insurance strategy. Only 24 countries have never at any time adopted the social insurance strategy for at least one social security branch, including Australia and Hong Kong as the only developed countries. On a geographical basis, social insurance is prevalent throughout Western and Eastern Europe, North and Latin America, and the Middle East. In Africa it is dominant except in East and South Africa. In Asia it is dominant except in South Asia. Its penetration into Australasia and the Pacific Islands is minimal. Social insurance is also the dominant strategy for the long-term contingencies of old age, invalidity and death. A few countries use social insurance to supplement their dominant social security strategy for a particular contingency (notably, Finland, The Gambia and Mauritius).

Table 3.1
The Global Application of Social Security Strategies, 1995

Number of Countries with at least one Social Security Strategy:													
	Social Insurance		Social Assistance		Social Allowance		Mandatory Public Savings		Employee Liability		Mandated Occupational Plans (1)		Mandated Personal Plans (2)
	No.	(%)	No.	(%)	No.	(%)	No.	(%)	No.	(%)	No.	(%)	No. (%)
WESTERN EUROPE													
	20	(14)	14	(25)	13	(36)			15	(13)	3	(38)	
(% Countries)	(100)		(70)		(65)				(75)		(15)		
EASTERN EUROPE													
	16	(11)	11	(20)	10	(28)			11	(10)			
(% Countries)	(100)		(69)		(63)				(69)				

NORTH AMERICA	2 (1)	2 (4)	1 (3)		2 (1)		
(% Countries)	(100)	(100)	(50)		(100)		
LATIN AMERICA	35 (24)	7 (13)	2 (6)	1 (5)	19 (17)	3 (8)	4 (11)
(% countries)	(97)	(19)	(6)	(3)	(53)	(38)	(80)
AFRICA	37 (25)	9 (16)	2 (6)	6 (30)	39 (34)	1 (2)	
(% countries)	(82)	(20)	(4)	(13)	(87)	(12)	
MIDDLE EAST	12 (8)	2 (4)			8 (7)		
(% countries)	(100)	(17)			(67)		

ASIA	21 (14)	7 (13)	3 (8)	6 (30)	14 (12)		1 (20)
(% countries)	(78)	(26)	(11)	(22)	(52)		(4)
AUSTRAL-ASIA	1 (1)	2 (4)	2 (6)	0 (0)	1 (7)	1 (12)	
(% countries)	(50)	(100)	(100)	(0)	(50)	(50)	
PACIFIC ISLANDS	4 (3)	2 (4)	3 (8)	7 (35)	6 (5)		
(% countries)	(33)	(17)	(25)	(58)	(50)		
WORLD	148 (100)	56 (100)	38 (100)	20 (100)	115 (100)	8 (100)	5 (100)
(% countries)	(86)	(33)	(22)	(12)	(67)	(5)	(3)

Sources: US SSA 1996, Dixon 1989b, Kim 1992, Hui and Fung 1994.

Notes: (1) Excludes the 12 countries that permit contracting out to equivalent occupational plans.
(2) Excludes the four countries that permit contracting out to equivalent personal plans.

Social Assistance. Where the social assistance strategy has been adopted it acts primarily as a safety net for those who fall through, or miss, the dominant socialsecurity strategy net. It plays this role in Western Europe, Eastern Europe, North America, and, to a far lesser extent but still significantly, in Africa (notably North and Southern Africa), Asia (notably Centraland East Asia) and Latin America (notably Central America). It has been adopted as the dominant social security strategy in only Australia, the Cook Islands, Hong Kong, New Zealand and Nauru, although it is used as the dominant strategy for at least one social security branch in Brazil, Denmark, Finland, France, Ireland, Kyrgyzstan, Lithuania, Malta, Mauritius, Poland, Slovakia, Slovenia, South Africa, Sri Lanka, Tunisia, the United States.

Social Allowances. Most social allowance programs operate in Europe, where they have been widely adopted. This strategy plays a significant supplementary role for some contingencies in Australasia and North America, and in Asia (notably Central Asia). It is the dominant form of social security in Denmark, Finland, Iceland, Norway and Sweden.

Employer Liability. Employer liability measures have proved to be a resilient and remarkably adaptable social security strategy. Globally, they are the second most frequently adopted form of social security. It is the most frequently adopted strategy in Africa, and it plays a dominant secondary role elsewhere, especially in relations to employment injury, sickness, maternity and unemployment contingencies, with the conspicuous exception, on a sub-regional basis, of Central Asia. It plays a dominant role in Bangladesh, Botswana, Malawi, North Korea and Sierra Leone.

Mandatory Public Savings. National Provident Funds have also proved to be a resilient form of social security. They are quite evenly distributed amongst the regions of the Pacific Islands, Asia (especially in South and South-East Asia) and Africa (especially in East and Southern Africa), with a small presence in the Caribbean. They are dominant in only Montserrat and Nepal.

Mandated Occupational Pension and Savings. Most of the small number of mandated occupational pension and savings programs operate in West Europe and South America, where they play a supporting role, as they do in Australia, Japan and Côte d'Ivoire.

Mandated Personal Pension and Savings. Most of the even smaller number of mandated personal pension and savings programs (7 countries) are concentrated in South America, where they play a significant role in Chile and Peru. They play a minor role in Afghanistan, Colombia and Guatemala.

Social Security Branch Coverage

Table 3.2 gives the global pattern of social security branch coverage in 1995.

Old-Age, Invalidity and Survivors' Programs. These three long-term contingency programs constitute the most commonly adopted social security programs. Of the 172 countries with social security systems only seven do not offer any of these programs (Azerbaijan, Bangladesh, Botswana, Malawi (whichis planning to do so in 2001 (Estrin 1996)), Myanmar, Sierra Leone and Somalia). Some countries offer only old-age programs (North Korea and Surinam) or disability programs (Thailand) or both, but not the survivors' programs (Afghanistan, Hong Kong and Macau).

Sickness and Maternity Programs. Most countries with social security systems have adopted sickness and maternity programs, with the latter being rather more popular (135 as compared with 129 countries).

Although the patterns of global distribution of sickness and maternity programs are broadly similar, there are geographical differences. The Pacific Islands region is the only one where maternity allowances have not taken root, although sickness programs have done so, albeit to only a very limited degree. Neither program has been widely adopted in the Middle East. On a sub-regional basis, maternity programs have been relatively more widely adopted than sickness programs in West Africa and in South Asia, as compared with, respectively, Africa and Asia as a whole. In Latin America both programs are relatively less popular in the Caribbean.

Employment-Injury Programs. These programs are only marginally less popular than the three long-term contingency programs. The geographical regions where employment-injury programs have not been almost universally adopted are the Pacific Islands and, to a lesser degree, the Caribbean. Indeed, only 12 countries do not offer one or more employment-injury programs (Azerbaijan, Antigua-Barbuda, the Cook Islands, Micronesia, Grenada, Kuwait, the Marshall Islands, Montserrat, Palau, Surinam, Tuvalu and Vanuatu). Some countries, however, offer only temporary employment-related disability programs (São Tomé and Principe and Nauru), only permanent employment-related disability programs (Macau) or both but not the employment-related survivors' programs (Guatemala, St Lucia and the Seychelles).

Unemployment Programs. Just under half of the world's social security systems provide unemployment programs. While they are universally offered throughout Europe, North America and Australasia, they are almost non-existent in the Pacific Islands, quite inconspicuous in Africa (indeed, non-existent in West and Middle Africa) and only marginally more conspicuous in Latin America (with the notable exception of South America) and the Middle East.

Family Support Programs. Somewhat less than half of the world's social security systems contain programs that offer support to families with child or adult dependents or with particular compositions. Child benefit programs are, by far, the more popular (74 as compared with 24 countries). Indeed, only seven countries operate family benefit programs in isolation (Costa Rica, Hong Kong, Lithuania, Mauritius, Moldova, Sri Lanka and the United States).

Child benefit programs are almost universally offered throughout Europe and in both Australasian countries. They are, however, non-existent in North America, and most inconspicuous in the Asia (indeed, they are non-existent in South-East Asia) and the Pacific Islands, and only marginally more conspicuous in the Middle East. They are somewhat more evident in Latin America (where they are most prevalent in South America). They are, however, rather more popular in Africa (being universally provided in Middle and West Africa).

Family benefit programs are spread thinly across most regions outside Europe, Australasia and North America, but are non-existent in the Pacific Islands.

Healthcare Benefit Programs. Most countries do not have an integrated health and social security system (see Appendix 1.1). The use of public heath systems to provide healthcare services to social security recipients and their families commonly occurs (86 countries). Indeed, social security systems per se provide only health services in a minority of countries (75 countries). The provision of health service benefits by social security systems is most evident in Latin America (except, conspicuously, in the Caribbean), Western Europe and Africa (with the notable exception of East Africa). Health insurance arrangements operate in 11 countries (Abel-Smith 1992b, Glasser 1988, Ku 1998, Vogel 1990).

Social Security Financing

The overwhelming majority of extant social security systems (165 countries) require covered employees and their employers to pay contributions for at least one primary or supplementary benefit, of which only three countries a specify flat-rate contribution rate (Bermuda, Denmark (where the rate is reduced if less than fully employed) and Macau). Only seven countries have exclusively non-contributory systems, five of which have only employer-financed programs (Bangladesh, Botswana, Malawi, North Korea and Sierra Leone), with the remaining two countries (Nauru and Hong Kong) having both government-financed and employer-financed programs. A little over one-third of all social security systems receive no government funding support (62 countries), half of which are in Africa. The regions with the highest proportion of countries not subsidizing their social security systems are the Pacific Islands (75 percent), Africa (69 percent) and the Caribbean (63 percent).

Government Funding. Government financing of social security programs takes place in 110 countries. Indeed, 36 countries deficit finance one or more social security programs, half of which are post socialist countries in transition, with the highest country incidence can be found in Central Asia (86 percent), Eastern Europe (63 percent) and Europe (40 percent).

Total Contribution Rates. On a global basis, the average total social security contribution is 22 percent of payroll (see Appendix 3.1). The geographic regions with significantly above-average total contribution rates are Eastern Europe (39 percent of payroll), Central Asia (35 percent), Western Europe (34 percent), North Africa (29 percent) and South America (26 percent), while re-

Table 3.2
The Global Pattern of Social Security Branch Coverage, 1995

Number of Countries with at least one Social Security Strategy:

	Old Age		Disability		Survivors		Sickness		Maternity		Employment Injury		Unemployment		Family Support	
	Nno	.(%)	No.	(%)	No.	(%)	No.	(%)	No.	(%)	No.	(%)	No.	(%)	No.	(%)
WESTERN EUROPE																
	20	(12)	20	(12)	20	(13)	20	(16)	20	(15)	20	(13)	20	(25)	19	(23)
(% Countries)	(100)		(100)		(100)		(100)		(100)		(100)		(100)		(95)	
EASTERN EUROPE																
	16	(10)	16	(10)	16	(10)	15	(12)	15	(11)	16	(10)	16	(20)	16	(20)
(% Countries)	(100)		(100)		(100)		(94)		(94)		(100)		(100)		(100)	

NORTH AMERICA							
2 (1)	2 (1)	2 (1)	2 (2)	2 (2)	2 (1)	2 (3)	1 (1)
(% Countries) (100)	(100)	(100)	(100)	(100)	(100)	(100)	(50)
LATIN AMERICA							
36 (22)	35 (21)	35 (22)	31 (24)	32 (24)	32 (20)	12 (15)	10 (12)
(% Countries) (100)	(97)	(97)	(86)	(89)	(89)	(33)	(28)
AFRICA							
41 (25)	41 (25)	41 (26)	32 (25)	38 (28)	45 (28)	8 (10)	23 (28)
(% Countries) (91)	(91)	(91)	(71)	(84)	(100)	(18)	(51)
MIDDLE EAST							
12 (7)	12 (7)	12 (8)	6 (5)	6 (5)	11 (7)	4 (5)	3 (4)
(% Countries) (100)	(100)	(100)	(50)	(50)	(92)	(33)	(25)

	ASIA							
ASIA	23 (14)	23 (14)	19 (12)	19 (15)	20 (15)	26 (16)	15 (19)	5 (4)
(% Countries)	(85)	(85)	(70)	(70)	(74)	(96)	(56)	(19)
AUSTRAL-ASIA	2 (1)	2 (1)	2 (1)	2 (2)	2 (1)	2 (1)	2 (3)	2 (2)
(% Countries)	(100)	(100)	(100)	(100)	(100)	(100)	(100)	(100)
PACIFIC ISLANDS	12 (7)	12 (7)	12 (8)	2 (2)		6 (4)	1 (1)	2 (2)
(% Countries)	(100)	(100)	(100)	(17)		(50)	(8)	(17)
WORLD	164 (100)	163 (100)	159 (100)	129 (100)	135 (100)	159 (100)	80 (100)	81 (100)
(% Countries)	(95)	(95)	(92)	(75)	(78)	(92)	(47)	(47)

Sources: US SSA 1996, Dixon 1989b, Kim 1992, Hui and Fung 1994.

gions with significantly below-average total contribution rates include the Pacific Islands (8 percent) and Southern Africa and the Caribbean (9 percent). The country with the distinction of having the highest total contribution rate is Italy (63 percent of payroll).

Employer Contribution Rates. On a global basis, the average employer social security contribution is 16 percent of payroll. The geographic regions with significantly above-average total contribution rates are Eastern Europe and Central Asia (33 percent) and Western Europe (22 percent), whilst regions with significantly below-average employer contribution rates include Southern Africa and the Pacific Islands (4 percent) and the Caribbean (6 percent). The country with the distinction of having the highest employer contribution rate is Hungary (49 percent).

Globally, the average employer statutory contribution incidence is 69 percent. The regions with significantly above-average employer share are Central Asia (97 percent), Eastern Europe (85 percent) rate) and West Africa (80 percent), while the regions with significantly below-average employer shares are Southern Africa (50 percent), the Pacific Islands (52 percent), South America (54 percent), North America (55 percent) and South Asia (56 percent).

Employee Contribution Rates. On a global basis, the average employee social security contribution is 6 percent of payroll. The highest employee contribution rates can be found in Western Europe and South America (11 percent), while the country with the highest employee contribution rate is the Netherlands (30 percent of earnings, after adjusting for the earnings supplementation paid by employers to compensate for part of the employees' long-term contingency contributions). At the other extreme are 16 countries, largely in post-socialist Eastern Europe and Central Asia, where employer contribution rates have been set at a token rate of 1 percent of earnings or less.

Globally, the average employee statutory contribution incidence is 31 percent. The regions with significantly significantly above-average employee share are Southern Africa (50 percent), the Pacific Islands (48 percent), South America (46 percent), North America (45 percent) and South Asia (44 percent), while those with significantly below-average employee share are Central Asia (3 percent), Eastern Europe (15 percent) and West Africa (20 percent).

Social Security Administration

Social security administration is overwhelmingly a central government responsibility (see Chapter 8). Regional governments play a role in only 15 countries — almost half of which have federal political systems — while local governments do so in only 10 countries, half of which are in Western Europe. The involvement of all three levels of government is rare.

The most common public mode of social security administration is the independent public agency (109 countries), although departments of state are often used (69 countries) to administer at least one social security program. The use of specialized sub-agencies within a public agency to the administration of at least one social security program is also not uncommon (46 countries). All these public agencies form part of a ministerial portfolio.

RECENT DEVELOPMENTS IN SOCIAL SECURITY PRACTICES: 1985–1995

The decade from 1985 to 1995 saw much systemic, programmatic and financial change to social security systems around the world, as countries sought to address newly identified or acknowledged social security needs and issues. In so doing they have sought to exorcise one or more of the social security ghosts of irrelevancy, inadequacy, conflicting objectives and burgeoning of cost burdens.

New Systems Established: 1985–1995

The number of countries that can be identified as having at least one social security program increased from 153 in 1985 to 172 countries in 1995. Most of this increase is attributable to the formation of 17 new nation-states, each with an inherited social security system, following the disintegration of the Trust Territory of the Pacific Islands (from 1986), the Soviet Union (George 1991, Wiktorow 1992) (1990–91), Yugoslavia (Ruzica 1992 and 1995) (1992) and Czechoslovakia (Czechoslovakia 1992) (1995), offset by the reintegration of East and West Germany (1990). Three countries are known to have established new social security systems (Vanuatu (1987), Yemen (1988) and Macau.

Vanuatu decided to establish a National Provident Fund to provide old-age, disability and survivors' benefits.

Yemen choose the social insurance strategy, initially only to provide lump-sum old-age, disability and survivors' benefits, but subsequently extended to provide employment-related injuries benefits (1991).

Macau adopted the social insurance strategy to provide old-age, disability, unemployment and limited employment-related injuries benefits, as well as medical services (Hui and Fung 1994, Ramasamy and Hartono 1992).

New Branches Established: 1985–1995

Twenty-nine developing and post-socialist countries decided to extend their social security systems by introducing new social security branches (see Table 3.3), reflecting their desire to meet previously unmet social security needs and so exorcise the ghost of irrelevance. Unemployment was, undoubtedly, the most common new branch established, albeit almost exclusively in post-socialist Eastern Europe and Asia, by countries facing economic dislocation caused by market reforms. New branches were also established in a small array of countries in Europe (4 family support branches), Asia (3 old-age, disability and survivors'

Table   3.3

New   Social   Security   Branches   Introduced: 1985–1995

Branch/Country	Year	Social Security Strategy Adopted:			
		Social Insurance	Social Assistance	Social Allowances	Mandated Personal Savings
UNEMPLOYMENT					
ALBANIA	1993	1			
ARMENIA (1)	1991	1			
AZERBAIJAN	1991	1			
BELARUS (1)	1993	1			
BULGARIA (1)	1989	1			
CHINA	1986	1			
CZECH REPUBLIC	1994			1	
ESTONIA	1991			1	
GEORGIA (1)	1993	1			
GUATEMALA	1991				1
KYRGYZSTAN (1)	1991	1			
LATVIA	1991			1	
LITHUANIA (1)	1991		1		
MOLDOVA	1992	1			
POLAND (1)	1991	1			
ROMANIA	1991	1			
SLOVAKIA	1991	1			
SLOVENIA (1)	1991			1	
TURKMENISTAN	1991	1			
UZBEKISTAN	1991	1			
YUGOSLAVIA	1990	1			
SUBTOTAL		**1 5**	**1**	**4**	**1**
OLD-AGE, DISABILITY AND DEATH					
AFGHANISTAN	1987	1			
KOREA, SOUTH	1988	1			
THAILAND (2)	1990	1			
ZIMBABWE	1993	1			
SUBTOTAL		**4**			
SICKNESS AND MATERNITY					
ST VINCENT AND THE GRENADINES	1986	1			

SUBTOTAL	**1**				

EMPLOYMENT
INJURY

BRIT. VIRGIN	1994	1			
ISLANDS					
SUBTOTAL	**1**				

FAMILY
ALLOWANCES

ALBANIA	1992			1	
LATVIA	1990			1	
LITHUANIA	1991		1		
SRI LANKA	1990		1		
CYPRUS	1987			1	
SUBTOTAL			**2**	**3**	
TOTAL	**2 1**	**3**	**7**	**1**

Sources: US SSA 1986, 1988, 1990, 1992, 1994 and 1996.

Notes: (1) An earlier unemployment program had been abolished.
          (2) Disability and survivors' programs only. An old-age program was
          introduced in 1998.

branches and 1 family support branch), the Caribbean (a sickness and maternity branch and an employment-related injuries branch), Central America (an unemployment branch) and Africa (an old-age, disability and survivors' branch) (Kaseke 1995, Singhakowin 1994). Thailand (1990) has enacted legislation to establish an old-age branch implemented in 1998 (Raviwongse and Thodtankun 1996, Singhakowin 1994).

Strategy Transformations: 1985–1995

Seventeen countries decided to adopt a new social security strategy with respect to one or more of their existing social security branches (see Table 3.4). National Provident Funds were transformed into social insurance systems in four countries, thereby exorcising their ghost of conflicting objectives. Many countries sought to appease their particular manifestation of the ghost of burgeoning cost burdens by transforming some of their social security branches, thereby shifting the statutory cost burden incidence. Seven countries, most notably China (Chow 1988b and 1995, Dixon 1992, Song and Chu 1997), replaced their employer liability programs by social insurance programs, thereby shifting some of the statutory cost burden on to employees. Family benefit insurance programs were converted into a social allowance program in the Netherlands

(1988) and into a social assistance program in Poland (1994), in both cases transferring the statutory contribution cost burden from employers and employees to government. Peru (1991) and Colombia (1994) fully privatized the coverage of a social security branch, which transferred the statutory contribution cost burden from employers and government to employees. Canada (1992) (Shewell 1998) and Iceland (1993) replaced their universal family benefit programs with fiscal welfare measures, thereby reducing government outlays but increasing tax expenditures (Brookes 1979, Surrey 1985, Wolley et al. 1996).

Marketization: 1985–1995

Social security provision was marketized to varying degrees in 10 countries. This took three forms: coverage marketization, coverage privatization and complementary benefit privatization.

Coverage Marketization. Guatemala (1991) created a mandated personal savings program to provide unemployment benefits for the first time. The substitution of mandated personal saving programs for employer-liability programs occurred in Afghanistan (1987), for all three of its employment-injury programs, and in Colombia (1991), for its unemployment program.

Coverage Privatization. Vanuatu (1987) contracted out its old-age, disability and survivors' insurance program coverage to mandated occupational savings plans. The United Kingdom (1988), contracted-out its old-age, disability and survivors'insurance program coverage to mandated occupational and personal pension plans. Argentina (1994) and Colombia (1994) both contracted out their old-age, disability and survivors' programs to mandated personal pension plans. Peru (1991) contracted out its sickness and maternity insurance program coverage to mandated personal healthcare plans, while Colombia (1995) also contracted out its public medical care program coverage to private healthcare plans. Peru (1991) also followed Chile by replacing its long-term contingencies insurance programs with a mandated personal savings program.

Complementary Benefit Privatization. The mandating of occupational pension plans to provide complementary benefits for the long-term contingencies occurred in Switzerland (1985) and in Venezuela (1990). The mandating of occupational savings plans to provide complementary benefits for long-term contingencies has occurred in Australia (1988), Venezuela (1990) and Mexico (1992).

Program Coverage and Eligibility Changes: 1985–1995

Fifteen countries extended program coverage or liberalized eligibility criteria, suggesting that placating the ghost of inadequacy may be more important for them than reaching a rapprochement with the ghost of burgeoning cost burdens.

Extensions of social security program coverage, particularly with respect to

Table 3.4
Social Security Strategy Changes: 1985–1995

Branch/Country	Year	Transformed From	To
OLD-AGE, DISABILITY			
AND SURVIVORS'			
CHINA (1)	1986	EL	SI
GAMBIA	1987	NPF	SI
GHANA	1991	NPF	SI
NIGERIA	1994	NPF	SI
PERU	1991	SI	MPP
ST VINCENT AND THE GRENADINES	1986	NPF	SI
SICKNESS			
CHINA (1)	1986	EL	SI
ISRAEL	1995	EL	SI
MATERNITY			
CHINA (1)	1986	EL	SI
EMPLOYMENT INJURY			
ST KITTS AND NEVIS	1986	EL	SI
SEYCHELLES	1987	EL	SI
UNEMPLOYMENT			
ARGENTINA	1991	EL	SI
COLOMBIA	1991	EL	MPS
IRAN	1987	EL	SI
VENEZUELA	1989	EL	SI
FAMILY ALLOWANCES			
CANADA	1992	SAL	FISC
ICELAND	1993	SAL	FISC
NETHERLANDS	1988	SI	SAL
POLAND	1994	SI	SA

Sources: US SSA 1986, 1988, 1990, 1992, 1994 and 1996.

Note: (1) State ownership of enterprises confuses the public-employer boundary.

Notations:

EL Employer Liability	SAL Social Allowances
SI Social Insurance	MPP Mandated Personal Pensions
SA Social Assistance	MPS Mandated Personal Savings.

old-age, disability and survivors' programs occurred in eleven countries (see Table 3.5). Eligibility criteria were liberalized in five countries over the same period. The Seychelles (1987) reduced its minimum residency period requirement for old-age, disability and survivors' benefits. Belgium (1989) reduced its minimum employment period for unemployment benefits. Luxembourg (1987) and São Tomé and Principe (1990) reduced their required minimum contribution period for old-age, disability and survivors' benefits, as did Portugal (1989) for its unemployment benefits.

Globally, the mollifying the ghost of burgeoning cost burdens may be more important than pacifying the ghost of irrelevance as 33 countries took steps to tighten program eligibility criteria, thereby reducing current or future social security costs.

The retirement age was increased, or was scheduled to be increased, in 22 countries, mostly in Europe (Royers and Russell 1995), North and South America and Australasia (see Table 3.6). In some instances these retirement age adjustments related to only women, perhaps to achieve gender equality (Simanis 1994, US, SSA, SSB 1991).

Minimum contribution period requirement increases were implemented, or were scheduled to be implemented, in 14 predominantly developed countries (see Table 3.7).

The minimum employment period requirement for unemployment benefits was increased by over 150 percent in Hungary (1990) (Hegyesi et al. 1992).

The degree of disability required for permanent disability benefits was doubled in Ecuador (1988).

An income test on family benefits was imposed in Slovakia (1994).

Greece (1992) imposed a minimum age of 65 (rather than a minimum contribution period) on the payment of death benefits to those starting employment after 1993.

Benefit Provision Changes: 1985–1995

Forty-eight countries enhanced the generosity of at least one of their social security programs, while only 19 countries are known to have done the reverse, suggesting, again, perhaps, that, globally, placating the ghost of inadequacy may be more important than reaching a rapprochement with the ghost of burgeoning cost burdens.

New benefits were introduced in 24 countries (see Table 3.8), although benefits targeting the elderly and families were abolished entirely in eight countries.

Social allowances for those ineligible for old-age, disability and survivors' insurance benefits were introduced by eight post-socialist countries in Eastern Europe and Central Asia. Pre-pensions for older unemployed workers were duced. in six European countries (Schmahl 1989), while Brazil introduced income- test-

Table   3.5
Social   Security   Coverage   Extension: 1985–1995

Branch/Country	Year	Nature of Coverage Extension
OLD-AGE,		
DISABILITY AND		
SURVIVORS'		
BRAZIL	1991	Extended to rural workers.
CHINA	1986	Extended to contract workers.
FINLAND	1990	Widowers covered.
PORTUGAL	1985	Extended to rural workers.
	1989	Voluntary coverage extended to anyone not previously covered.
SOUTH AFRICA	1993	Differential race criteria abolished.
SWEDEN	1995	Minimum earnings requirement reduced by 20 per cent.
SICKNESS		
AND MATERNITY		
CHINA	1986	Extended to contract workers.
KOREA, SOUTH (1)	1988	Gradually extended to all employees.
EMPLOYMENT		
INJURY		
CHINA	1986	Extended to contract workers.
SAUDI ARABIA	1988	Minimum-sized firms reduced from 20 to 10 employees.
UNEMPLOYMENT		
ARGENTINA	1991	Coverage extended to all employees.
FAMILY		
ALLOWANCES		
HUNGARY	1993	First child covered.
JAPAN	1992	First and second children covered.

Sources: US SSA 1986, 1988, 1990, 1992, 1994 and 1996.

Note: (1) Only medical benefits provided.

Table 3.6

Retirement Age Increases Initiated: 1985–1995

Country	Year Initiated	Old Retirement Age: Male	Female	New Retirement Age: Male	Female	Year of Completion
ARGENTINA	1995	62	57	65	60	2001
AUSTRALIA	1995		60		65	2013
BELGIUM	1990		60		65	1990
COLOMBIA	1994	60	55	62	57	2014
ESTONIA	1994	60	55	65	60	2003
GERMANY	1994	63	60	65	65	2012
GHANA (3)	1991	55	50	60	60	1991
GREECE (2)	1993		60		65	1993
HUNGARY	1994		56		60	2003
ITALY	1995	61	56	65	60	2003/2012
JAPAN	1985	60	55	65	65	1985
LITHUANIA (4)	1990	60	55	62	60	1990
NEW ZEALAND	1994	62	62	65	65	2001
PANAMA	1995	60	55	62	57	1995
PERU (3)	1991	60	55	65	60	1991
PORTUGAL	1994	65	65	68	68	1999
SLOVENIA (2)	1990	60	55	63	58	1990
TURKEY (1)	1990	55	50	60	55	1990
UGANDA	1985	50	45	55	55	1985
UNITED KINGDOM	1994		60		65	2000
UNITED STATES	2003	65	65	67	67	2027
ZAIRE	1994	59	59	63	60	1994

Sources: US SSA 1986, 1988, 1990, 1992, 1994 and 1996.

Note: (1) Retirement age flexible between 60 and 65 for both men and women
(2) Applies to new covered employees since year of initiation.
(3) Change introduced with branch transformation.
(4) Change follows introduction of new system with disintegration of the USSR.

ed unemployment benefits. Specific benefits targeting the family were introduced in seven, mainly developed, countries. Health insurance programs were introduced in Russia (Yakushev 1991) and Taiwan (Lin 1991). Benefit generosity, of

Table 3.7

Minimum Contribution Period Increases: 1985–1995

Branch/Country	Year	From:	To:	Comments
OLD-AGE, DISABILITY AND SURVIVORS'				
BAHRAIN	1994	120 months	180 months	women only
FRANCE	1994	150 qtrs	160 qtrs	by 2023, applies to old-age program only
GREECE	1994	No details		applies to disability program only
HUNGARY	1994	10 years	15 years	early retirees after 1993
ITALY	1992	15 years	18 years	by 2001, applies to old-age program only
JAMAICA	1990	156 weeks	351 weeks	applies to old-age program only
JAPAN	1985	20 Years	25 years	
MALI	1986	3 years	10 years	
POLAND	1991	15/20 years	29/25 years	differential rates by gender
SPAIN	1985	10 years	15 years	
SICKNESS				
GERMANY	1994	None	5 years	applies to long-term benefits only
IRELAND	1986	156 weeks	260 weeks	applies to long term benefits only
UNEMPLOYMENT				
BELGIUM	1994	75 days	312 days	in last 18 months
NETHERLANDS	1987	130 days	26 weeks	in last year
SPAIN	1992	6 months	1 year	in last 6 years

Sources: US SSA 1986, 1988, 1990, 1992, 1994 and 1996.

course, is affected by changes in maximum benefits payment periods, income-replacement rates and benefit-rate formulae. The maximum benefit payment periods were reduced for employment-injury benefits in Nigeria (1989), São Tomé and Principe (1990), but increased in the Seychelles (1987); and reduced for unemployment benefits in Uruguay (1990), but increased in Sweden (1994) for older unemployed workers. Income-replacement rates were increased for one or more benefits in 13 mostly developing countries: for old-age, disability and survivors' benefits in Ecuador (1994), Guinea (1994) and Hungary (1988); for employment-related injuries benefits in Ghana (1987), Romania (1994), St Lucia (1991) and São Tomé and Principe (1990); for unemployment benefits in Hungary (1994) and Portugal (1989); and for sickness and maternity benefits in Morocco (1992), Portugal (1988), Russia (1992), the Seychelles (1989) and St Lu-

Table 3.8

New Social Security Benefits Introduced: 1985–1995

Branch/Country   Year Benefit Introduced

OLD-AGE,
DISABILITY
AND SURVIVORS'

BELARUS	1993	Universal social pension for those not qualified for social insurance.
DENMARK	1986	Prepensions for older workers.
FINLAND	1986	Prepensions for older workers.
ICELAND	1993	Prepensions for older workers.
IRELAND	1993	Prepensions for older workers.
KAZAKHSTAN	1991	Universal social pension for those not qualified for social insurance.
KYRGYZSTAN	1990	Universal social pension for those not qualified for social insurance.
MOLDOVA	1990	Universal social pension for those not qualified for social insurance.
NICARAGUA	1987	Assistance to the indigent.
RUSSIA	1990	Universal social pension for those not qualified for social insurance.
	1991	Prepensions for older workers.
TURKMENISTAN	1991	Universal social pension for those not qualified for social insurance.
UKRAINE	1992	Universal social pension for those not qualified for social insurance.
	1992	Prepensions for older workers.
UZBEKISTAN	1994	Universal social pension for those not qualified for social insurance.

SICKNESS
AND MATERNITY

ISRAEL	1993	Multiple birth allowances.
ISRAEL	1995	Health care.
RUSSIA	1995	Health insurance introduction began.

TAIWAN	1995	National health insurance.
EMPLOYMENT INJURY		
AFGHANISTAN	1987	Temporary disability benefits.
UNEMPLOYMENT		
BRAZIL	1990	Means-tested unemployment benefits.
FAMILY ALLOWANCES		
AUSTRALIA	1986	Means-tested homeless youth allowance.
FRANCE	1986	Child care benefit
HONG KONG	1995	Means-tested, flat-rate lone-parent allowance.
IRELAND	1990	Income-tested lone-parent allowances.
LUXEMBOURG	1986	Flat-rate school reentry allowance.
	1988	Flat-rate education allowance. Adoption leave.
MALTA	1988	Income-tested, flat-rate handicapped child and parental allowances.
	1989	Flat-rate family bonus.
NEW ZEALAND	1985	Income-tested family support benefit.

Sources: US SSA 1986, 1988, 1990, 1992, 1994 and 1996.

cia (1990). Income-replacement rates were reduced in six countries: for old-age, disability and survivors' benefits in Russia (1991) and São Tomé and Princip (1990); for employment-injury benefits in Russia (1992); for unemployment benefits in Canada (1993) and the Netherlands (1986); and for sickness and maternity benefits in the Netherlands (1986), Poland (1991) and Sweden (1991). Earnings-related benefits were replaced in Mexico (1992), by specified minimum wage multiples for old-age, disability and survivors' benefits; in Romania (1992), by a flat rate benefit for family allowance; and in Poland (1991), by a specified proportion of average national earnings for old-age and disability benefit. Earnings-related benefits were adopted in Bulgaria (1989) and Italy (1988), both replacing flat-rate unemployment benefits. Zaire (1991) and Russia (1992) both replaced their flat rate family allowances with a rate tied to minimum earnings. Argentina (1993) introduced a two-tier old-age pension. France (1992) modified its average earnings base by extending the highest income years to be considered from 10 to 25 years.

Financing Changes: 1985–1995

How best to redistribute the growing social security cost burden amongst taxpayers, employees and employers has been an important social security policy agenda confronted by many countries eager to reduce the burden of burgeoning costs.

Government Funding Changes. Government expenditure on social security certainly increased between 1985 and 1995 in all developed and most developing countries that directly provided or subsidized the provision of social security programs (Iyer 1993, Maydell 1994). Some countries, however, sought to reduce the growth in such expenditure by reducing program coverage, restricting benefit eligibility, providing less generous benefits, or improving target efficiency. New Zealand (1986), for example, sought to reduce its government expenditure on universal old-age pension by imposing a de facto claw-back mechanism, involving the imposition of an additional tax surcharge on any income received by pensioners above prescribed income disregard limits.

Four developing countries (Cape Verde (1992), Côte d'Ivoire (1988), Central African Republic (1986) and the Congo (1992)) decided to abolish government contributions to their social insurance programs. In contrast, government funding was introduced by four countries (Afghanistan (1987), Pakistan (1986), Panama (1986) and Singapore (1986)).

Total Contribution Rate Changes. The average total contribution rate, globally, in countries with contributory social security systems increased from 17 percent of earnings in 1985 to 22 percent in 1995, an increase of 28 percent (see Appendix 3.1). Indeed, 83 countries increased their total contribution rates, most significantly in the post-socialist countries of Central Asia (+497 percent) and Eastern Europe (averaging 120 percent). Twenty countries, however, decided over the same period to reduce their total contribution rates over the last decade, most significantly in Zaire (–55 percent), Nigeria (–38 percent), Luxembourg and South Korea (–29 percent), Ireland (–21 percent) and Norway (–20 percent).

Employer Contribution Rate Changes. Rhetoric about the need to reduce employers' social security burden has increased in vehemence since the mid-1980s (World Bank 1994). Yet only Afghanistan (1987) decided to abolish its small, one-time lump-sum employer contributions, albeit at the cost of introducing government funding. Globally, however, the employer social security contribution rates rose markedly between 1985 and 1995.

In absolute terms, employers, globally, have faced a 32 percent increase in their average social security contributions between 1985 and 1995 (increasing from 12 percent of payroll in 1985 to 16 percent in 1995). This occurred because 77 countries decided to increase their employer contributions over this period, whilst only 26 countries decided to reduce them. Employer contribution rates were increased most significantly in the post-socialist countries in Central Asia (+477 percent) and Eastern Europe (+144 percent). Employer contribution rates were, however, decreased most significantly in South Korea (–48 percent) and

Peru (–43 percent).

Globally, the employers' share of total social security contributions, however, marginally decreased, on average, from 71 percent in 1985 to 69 percent in 1995 (–3 percent). The most dramatic employer share reductions (other than in countries that introduced employee contributions for the first time) can be found in Peru (–56 percent), Slovenia (–49 percent), Israel (–35 percent) and Romania (–31 percent). The greatest employer share increases occurred in Yugoslavia (100 percent), The Gambia (+50 percent) and Nigeria, Uganda and South Africa (+33 percent).

Employee Contribution Rate Changes. Rhetoric about the need for employees to accept greater responsibility for their future social security needs has also gathered momentum since the mid-1980s (World Bank 1994). Quite against this rhetorical trend, The Gambia (1987) alone decided to abolish its employee social security contributions. Indeed, globally, the employee social security contribution rate did very significantly increase between 1985 and 1995.

In absolute terms, employee contribution rates, on average, rose, globally, between 1985 and 1995 by 18 percent (from 5 percent of earnings in 1985 to 6 percent in 1995). This occurred because 48 countries increased their employee contribution rates, and only 15 countries decided to reduce them, while a further 29 countries decided to introduce generally very modest employee contributions. Employee contributions were increased most dramatically in post-socialist Eastern Europe (+155 percent) and East Asia (+101 percent). They were most significantly reduced in Nigeria (–58 percent), Luxembourg (–44 percent) and Ireland (–30 percent). Employee contributions were introduced largely by postsocialist countries in Central Asia and Eastern Europe (in the early 1990s).

Globally, the employees' share of total social security contributions increased, on average, from 29 percent in 1985 to 31 percent in 1995 (+7 percent). The most dramatic employee share increases (other than in countries that introduced employee contributions for the first time) can be found in Peru (+274 percent), Israel (+153 percent), Taiwan (+120 percent) and South Korea (+99 percent), while the greatest employee share reductions occurred in Brazil (–41 percent), Switzerland (–39 percent), Nigeria and Uganda (–33 percent) and Iceland (–31 percent).

CONCLUSION

The tapestry of global social security provision is rich in diversity at the program level. At the strategy level, however, social insurance has become dominant. Few mavericks exist; Australia and Chile stand out. Overwhelmingly, social security systems require covered employees and their employers to pay contributions towards their cost. On a global basis, the average total social security contribution in 1995 was 22 percent of payroll, with the employer contributing just above two-thirds and the employee just under one-third. Social security is predominantly a central government responsibility, delivered through an independent public agency.

The decade between 1985 and 1995 saw much systemic, programmatic and financial change to social security systems around the world. Evidently, many countries sought to address newly identified or acknowledged social security needs. In so doing they sought to exorcise one or more of the social security ghost of irrelevancy, inadequacy, conflicting objectives and burgeoning of cost burdens. While none of these ghosts dominate the global social security reform agenda, they all continue to haunt, thus demanding placation.

APPENDIX 3.1:   **SOCIAL SECURITY CONTRIBUTION RATES: 1985 AND 1995**

Region/Country	Total Rate 1995	Total Rate 1985	Employee Rate 1995	Employee Rate 1985	Employer Rate 1995	Employer Rate 1985
NORTH AFRICA						
ALGERIA	29.00	29.00	5.00	5.00	24.00	24.00
EGYPT	50.00	35.00	15.00	11.00	35.00	24.00
LIBYA	13.93	6.50	4.13	2.13	9.80	4.38
MOROCCO	19.84	15.70	3.48	1.90	16.36	13.80
SUDAN	36.00	14.00	12.00	5.00	24.00	9.00
TUNISIA	27.75	28.75	6.25	6.25	21.50	22.50
AVERAGE	**29.42**	**21.49**	**7.64**	**5.21**	**21.78**	**16.28**
WEST AFRICA						
BENIN	23.00	21.50	3.60	3.60	19.40	17.90
BURKINA FASO	23.00	23.00	4.50	4.50	18.50	18.50
BURUNDI	12.50	7.50	4.00	3.00	8.50	4.50
CAMEROON	19.00	15.63	2.80	2.80	16.20	12.83
CAPE VERDE	21.00	23.00	7.00	7.00	14.00	16.00
CÔTE D'IVOIRE	14.50	12.00	1.60	1.20	12.90	10.80
EQUATORIAL GUINEA	26.00		4.50		21.50	
GABON	22.60	20.00	2.50	2.00	20.10	18.00
GAMBIA, THE	19.00	15.00		5.00	19.00	10.00
GHANA	17.50	17.50	5.00	5.00	12.50	12.50
GUINEA	23.00	12.00	5.00	3.20	18.00	8.80
LIBERIA	7.75	7.75	3.00	3.00	4.75	4.75
MALI	23.00	16.50	3.60	1.60	19.40	14.90
MAURITANIA	16.00	17.00	1.00	1.00	15.00	16.00
NIGER	17.00	17.00	1.60	1.60	15.40	15.40
NIGERIA	7.50	12.00	2.50	6.00	5.00	6.00
SÃO TOMÉ AND PRINCIPE	10.00	10.00	4.00	4.00	6.00	6.00
SENEGAL	30.00	23.00	7.80	6.20	22.20	16.80
SIERRA LEONE						
TOGO	18.00	20.50	2.40	2.40	15.60	18.10
AVERAGE	**18.44**	**15.31**	**3.49**	**3.32**	**14.94**	**11.99**
MIDDLE AFRICA						
CENTRAL AFRICAN REP.	20.00	20.00	2.00	2.00	18.00	18.00
CHAD	14.50	14.50	2.00	2.00	12.50	12.50
CONGO	16.23	18.48	2.40	2.60	13.83	15.88
ZAIRE	11.00	24.20	3.50	3.00	7.50	21.20
AVERAGE	**15.43**	**19.30**	**2.48**	**2.40**	**12.96**	**16.90**
EAST AFRICA						
ETHIOPIA	10.00		4.00		6.00	
KENYA	10.00	10.00	5.00	5.00	5.00	5.00

MADAGASCAR	14.00	14.00	1.00	1.00	13.00	13.00
MALAWI						
MAURITIUS	9.00	9.00	3.00	3.00	6.00	6.00
RWANDA	8.00	8.00	3.00	3.00	5.00	5.00
SEYCHELLES	25.00	25.00	5.00	5.00	20.00	20.00
SOMALIA	7.00	6.00			7.00	6.00
TANZANIA	20.00	10.00	10.00	5.00	10.00	5.00
UGANDA	15.00	10.00	5.00	5.00	10.00	5.00
ZAMBIA	10.00	10.00	5.00	5.00	5.00	5.00
AVERAGE	**12.80**	**10.20**	**4.10**	**3.20**	**8.70**	**7.00**
SOUTHERN AFRICA						
BOTSWANA						
SOUTH AFRICA	2.00	0.80	1.00	0.50	1.00	0.30
SWAZILAND	10.00	10.00	5.00	5.00	5.00	5.00
ZIMBABWE	6.00		3.00		3.00	
AVERAGE	**9.00**	**5.40**	**4.50**	**2.75**	**4.50**	**2.65**
CENTRAL ASIA						
ARMENIA	41.00	6.70	1.00		40.00	6.70
AZERBAIJAN (1)	2.00	6.70			2.00	6.70
GEORGIA	41.00	6.70	1.00		40.00	6.70
KAZAKHSTAN	38.00	6.70	1.00		37.00	6.70
KYRGYZSTAN	43.50	6.70	3.00		40.50	6.70
TURKMENISTAN	40.00	6.70	1.00		39.00	6.70
UZBEKISTAN	36.50	6.70	1.00		35.50	6.70
AVERAGE	**34.57**	**6.70**	**1.14**		**33.43**	
EAST ASIA						
CHINA	37.00		6.00		31.00	
HONG KONG						
JAPAN	33.11	26.85	12.75	10.95	20.36	15.90
KOREA, SOUTH	9.30	13.04	3.90	2.75	5.40	10.29
KOREA, NORTH						
TAIWAN	18.75	7.51	7.68	1.40	11.08	6.11
AVERAGE	**24.54**	**11.85**	**7.58**	**3.78**	**16.96**	**8.08**
SOUTH ASIA						
AFGHANISTAN	4.00	1.00	4.00	1.00		
BANGLADESH						
INDIA	26.15	24.75	11.50	8.50	14.65	16.25
MYANMAR	4.00		1.50		2.50	
NEPAL	20.00	20.00	10.00	10.00	10.00	10.00
PAKISTAN	12.00	7.00			12.00	7.00
SRI LANKA	23.25	23.25	8.00	8.00	15.25	15.25
AVERAGE	**14.90**	**12.67**	**5.83**	**4.58**	**9.07**	**8.08**
SOUTH-EAST ASIA						
INDONESIA	13.74	7.70	2.00	1.20	11.74	6.50
MALAYSIA	24.25	21.75	10.50	9.00	13.75	12.75

PHILIPPINES	11.50	12.30	4.58	3.70	6.92	8.60
SINGAPORE	40.00	45.00	20.00	20.00	20.00	25.00
THAILAND	5.00	2.15	1.50		3.50	2.15
VIETNAM	20.00		5.00		15.00	
AVERAGE	**19.08**	**14.82**	**7.26**	**5.65**	**11.82**	**9.17**

AUSTRALASIA

AUSTRALIA (1)

NEW ZEALAND	2.65	0.71	0.80		1.85	0.71
AVERAGE	**2.65**	**0.71**	**0.80**		**1.85**	**0.71**

WESTERN EUROPE

AUSTRIA	42.50	43.65	17.20	15.55	25.30	28.10
BELGIUM	40.36	39.81	13.07	12.07	27.29	27.74
CYPRUS	12.60	12.00	6.30	6.00	6.30	6.00
DENMARK						
FINLAND	32.10	21.65	8.85	3.75	23.25	17.90
FRANCE	57.73	52.33	19.92	14.72	37.81	37.61
GERMANY	42.54	36.20	20.55	16.65	21.99	19.55
GREECE	31.85	26.00	10.62	9.00	21.23	17.00
ICELAND	27.00	9.25	4.00	2.00	23.00	7.25
IRELAND	19.95	25.10	7.75	11.00	12.20	14.10
ITALY	62.96	52.06	15.34	8.30	47.62	43.76
LUXEMBOURG	31.00	43.76	12.50	22.15	18.50	21.61
MALTA	18.30	16.60	8.30	8.30	10.00	8.30
NETHERLANDS	55.90	62.85	30.25	38.50	25.65	24.35
NORWAY	22.00	27.50	7.80	10.70	14.20	16.80
PORTUGAL	37.75	36.50	11.00	11.50	26.75	25.00
SPAIN	38.30	37.30	6.30	5.90	32.00	31.40
SWEDEN	27.88	31.35	2.95		24.93	31.35
SWITZERLAND	22.55	12.00	5.70	5.00	16.85	7.00
UNITED KINGDOM	19.20	14.73	9.00	7.00	10.20	7.73
AVERAGE	**33.81**	**31.61**	**11.44**	**10.95**	**22.37**	**20.66**

EASTERN EUROPE

ALBANIA	42.50		10.00		32.50	
BELARUS	19.05	6.70	1.00		18.05	6.70
BULGARIA	42.00	30.00			42.00	30.00
CZECH REP	47.30	20.00	12.05		35.25	20.00
ESTONIA	20.00	6.70			20.00	6.70
HUNGARY	60.50	33.00	11.50	9.00	49.00	24.00
LATVIA	38.00	6.70	1.00		37.00	6.70
LITHUANIA	24.00	6.70	1.00		23.00	6.70
MOLDOVA	39.00	6.70	1.00		38.00	6.70
POLAND	48.00	43.00			48.00	43.00
ROMANIA	31.00	16.00	1.00		30.00	16.00
RUSSIA	40.00	6.70	1.00		39.00	6.70
SLOVAKIA	36.00	20.00	11.00		25.00	20.00
SLOVENIA	45.80	6.70	22.60		23.20	6.70

UKRAINE	41.00	6.70	1.00		40.00	6.70
YUGOSLAVIA	56.20	41.41	28.10	31.16	28.10	10.25
AVERAGE	**39.40**	**16.06**	**6.39**	**2.51**	**33.01**	**13.55**
NORTH AMERICA						
CANADA	12.60	9.24	5.70	4.15	6.90	5.09
UNITED STATES	22.58	21.40	9.95	8.25	12.63	13.15
AVERAGE	**17.59**	**15.32**	**7.83**	**6.20**	**9.77**	**9.12**
CENTRAL AMERICA						
BELIZE						
COSTA RICA	27.00	27.00	8.00	8.00	19.00	19.00
EL SALVADOR	13.50	11.75	4.00	3.50	9.50	8.25
GUATEMALA	14.50	14.50	4.50	4.50	10.00	10.00
HONDURAS	10.50	10.50	3.50	3.50	7.00	7.00
MEXICO	24.71	15.07	5.15	3.75	19.56	11.32
NICARAGUA	15.00	15.00	4.00	4.00	11.00	11.00
PANAMA	19.70	20.20	7.25	7.75	12.45	12.45
AVERAGE	**17.84**	**16.29**	**5.20**	**5.00**	**12.64**	**11.29**
CARIBBEAN						
ANTIGUA-BARBUDA	13.00	10.50	5.50	5.50	7.50	5.00
BAHAMAS	8.80	8.80	3.40	3.40	5.40	5.40
BARBADOS	10.95	10.25	4.73	5.00	6.22	5.25
BERMUDA						
BRITISH VIRGIN ISLANDS	8.50		4.00		4.50	
CUBA	10.00	10.00			10.00	10.00
DOMINICA	9.75	8.00	3.00	3.00	6.75	5.00
DOMINICAN REP.	12.50	12.50	2.50	2.50	10.00	10.00
GRENADA	8.00	8.00	4.00	4.00	4.00	4.00
HAITI	9.00	9.00	3.00	3.00	6.00	6.00
JAMAICA	5.00	5.00	2.50	2.50	2.50	2.50
MONTSERRAT	10.00	10.00	5.00	5.00	5.00	5.00
ST KITTS AND NEVIS	11.00	11.00	5.00	5.00	6.00	6.00
ST LUCIA	10.00	10.00	5.00	5.00	5.00	5.00
ST VINCENT AND THE GRENADINES	5.50	5.50	2.50	2.50	3.00	3.00
TRINIDAD AND TOBAGO	8.40	8.40	2.80	2.80	5.60	5.60
AVERAGE	**9.36**	**8.46**	**3.53**	**3.28**	**5.83**	**5.18**
SOUTH AMERICA						
ARGENTINA	45.40	39.00	15.00	15.00	30.40	24.00
BOLIVIA	23.50	23.50	6.00	3.50	17.50	20.00
BRAZIL	38.80	22.90	9.00	9.00	29.80	13.90
CHILE	24.30	23.74	20.00	19.29	4.30	4.45
COLOMBIA	32.70	20.86	7.13	3.83	25.58	17.03
ECUADOR	17.60	18.55	8.00	8.35	9.60	10.20
GUYANA	12.45	12.50	4.40	4.90	8.05	7.60
PARAGUAY	22.50	26.00	9.50	9.50	13.00	16.50

PERU	28.60	14.60	22.00	3.00	6.60	11.60
SURINAM	2.00	2.00	2.00	2.00		
URUGUAY	40.50	38.50	16.00	17.50	24.50	21.00
VENEZUELA	24.82	12.00	8.07	4.00	16.75	8.00
AVERAGE	**26.10**	**21.18**	**10.59**	**9.08**	**15.51**	**14.03**
MIDDLE EAST						
BAHRAIN	15.00	18.00	5.00	7.00	10.00	11.00
IRAN	30.00	27.00	7.00	7.00	23.00	20.00
IRAQ	17.00	17.00	5.00	5.00	12.00	12.00
ISRAEL	16.49	15.70	9.56	3.60	6.93	12.10
JORDAN	15.00	15.00	5.00	5.00	10.00	10.00
KUWAIT	15.00	15.00	5.00	5.00	10.00	10.00
LEBANON	34.50	25.00	3.00	1.50	31.50	23.50
OMAN	14.00		5.00		9.00	
SAUDI ARABIA	15.00	15.00	5.00	5.00	10.00	10.00
SYRIA	24.00	23.00	7.00	7.00	17.00	16.00
TURKEY	34.75	34.75	14.00	14.00	20.75	20.75
YEMEN	19.00		6.00		13.00	
AVERAGE	**20.81**	**17.12**	**6.38**	**5.01**	**14.43**	**12.11**
PACIFIC ISLANDS						
COOK ISLANDS						
FIJI	14.00	14.00	7.00	7.00	7.00	7.00
KIRIBATI	10.00	10.00	5.00	5.00	5.00	5.00
NAURU						
MARSHALL ISLANDS	10.00	4.00	5.00	2.00	5.00	2.00
MICRONESIA	8.00	4.00	4.00	2.00	4.00	2.00
PALAU	8.00	4.00	4.00	2.00	4.00	2.00
PAPUA NEW GUINEA	12.00	12.00	5.00	5.00	7.00	7.00
SOLOMON ISLANDS	12.50	12.50	5.00	5.00	7.50	7.50
TUVALU	10.00	10.00	5.00	5.00	5.00	5.00
VANUATU	6.00		3.00		3.00	
WESTERN SAMOA	11.00	10.00	5.00	5.00	6.00	5.00
AVERAGE	**8.46**	**8.05**	**4.00**	**3.80**	**4.46**	**4.25**
WORLD						
AVERAGE	**22.09**	**17.27**	**6.11**	**5.17**	**15.98**	**12.10**

Sources: US SSA 1986 and 1996.
Note: (1) Incomplete information.

4

Employment Injury

INTRODUCTION

Employment-injury programs cater to the consequences of employment-related accidents or disease. Under their aegis come the provision of support in the event of immediate but temporary incapacity for work, residual disablement or death. They constitute not only the oldest but also the fastest spreading branch of social security globally.

Employment-injury legislation defining the statutory obligations of employer in the event of an employment injury began emerging in Europe in the 1840s, culminating 40 years later in the enactment of no-fault employment-injury programs covering workers in hazardous industries (ILO 1984b: 45–46). The first country to do this was Germany in 1884 (Kaim-Caudle 1973). Czecho-slovakia and Austria followed suit in 1887. By the turn of the century, 11 European countries had introduced such programs. The practice then spread throughout most of Western Europe into Eastern Europe and further abroad; to Australia (first state 1902), New Zealand, Canada (first province) and the United States (federal employees only) (1908), Japan, El Salvador and Peru (injury only) (1911), and South Africa (1914). By the beginning of the First World War, 32 countries had established one or more employment-injury programs. By the end of the Second World War, that number had more than tripled to 102 countries. By 1995 the number had grown to 160 countries.

Overwhelmingly, countries with an employment-injury branch have programs embracing temporary and permanent disability as well as survivorhood in the event of employment-related death. Macau, however, covers only permanent disabilities, while São Tomé and Principe and Nauru cover only temporary disabilities. Guatemala, the Seychelles and St Lucia restrict themselves to temporary and permanent disability programs.

Employment-injury programs are integrated into other social security programs in only a few countries. The Netherlands and Turkey provide employment-injury benefits under their sickness, disability and survivors' programs, although Turkey imposes an additional contribution liability on employers for these benefits. Distinctively, New Zealand and Switzerland have made employment injury part of a more comprehensive accident program (Higuchi 1985, Uttley 1989 and 1993). A further 34 predominantly post-socialist countries have integrated at least one of their employment-injury programs into their sickness, disability and survivor's programs, most frequently into survivor's programs. For the purposes of international comparison, however, employment-injury provisions are treated as separate social security programs in these countries.

PRIMARY AND SUPPLEMENTARY STRATEGIES ADOPTED

Of the 160 countries with an employment-injury program, an overwhelming 110 countries have adopted social insurance as their primary strategy for all their employment-injury programs, while 47 countries use employer liability (workers' compensation) programs. Afghanistan has, distinctively, chosen the mandated personal savings strategy for all three of its employment-injury programs, involving employer-administered compensation funds. Some countries have adopted different strategies for different employment-injury programs. Denmark uses the employer liability strategy for its permanent disability and survivors' programs, supplemented by a temporary disability allowance program that is integrated into its general sickness allowance program. Libya uses the social insurance strategy for its long-term programs, supplemented by the employer liability strategy for its temporary disability program. Portugal has adopted employer liability measures to deal with employment-related injuries, supplemented by a social insurance program for employment-related diseases. Once a primary strategy has been chosen, strategy change has been uncommon.

Only 36 countries have changed their primary employment injury social security strategy, while Libya did so only for its employment-related disability program. These changes have mainly involved the transformation of employer liability measures into social insurance (33 countries), invariably without the imposition of employee contributions, and have mainly been made in Africa and Asia. Afghanistan replaced its employer liability measures with a mandated personal savings program. Less common has been the adoption of a supplementary strategy to meet social security objectives not attainable by the primary strategy (22 countries).

Supplementary strategies have been adopted for the temporary disability contingency in 22 countries. Nineteen countries have done so to extend their primary strategy coverage, overwhelmingly by means of employer liability measures, although Libya and Portugal both use social insurance for this purpose, and Hong Kong uses social assistance as the safety net for those ineligible for primary benefits. Only Latvia, Lithuania and Trinidad and Tobago use employer liability measures to provide additional benefits.

Five countries have adopted supplementary strategies for the permanent disability contingency. They mainly provide additional benefits by means of employer liability (Latvia and Trinidad and Tobago) and mandated occupational pensions (Bolivia). Coverage extension is the focus of supplementary strategies in Pakistan (a restricted workers' compensation program) and Portugal (a social insurance program). With regard to the death contingency, supplementary survivors' programs exist in four countries, again mainly to augment benefits by means of employer liability measures (Estonia, Latvia and Trinidad and Tobago). Coverage extension is the focus in only Pakistan, achieved by means of restricted workers' compensation.

PRIMARY SOCIAL SECURITY STRATEGY COVERAGE

In all countries the coverage of all employment-injury programs includes those in paid formal employment. Coverage is extended in some countries, however, to include those outside the workforce, namely to students (28 countries, mainly in Africa and Eastern Europe), children in kindergartens (Germany), juvenile court wards (Algeria) and medical and vocational rehabilitees (Algeria). A few countries use employment-injury programs to protect unpaid workers, namely, social welfare volunteers (Algeria, Cape Verde and France) and prison or convict workers (Algeria, Madagascar and Niger).

Employment Coverage

Covered employees generally include farm employees (excluded in only 33 countries, most notably in the Middle East and Asia). Earnings are generally not considered a barrier to coverage. High-income employees (variously defined) are excluded in only 13 countries. Low-income employees are excluded in only Guyana. Covered employees, however, generally exclude the self-employed (included in only 27 countries, most conspicuously in Western and Eastern Europe), farmers (included in only 10 countries, largely in Eastern Europe), immigrant workers (included in only Israel and Saudi Arabia). Non-manual workers are excluded in only the Dominican Republic and Italy (unless engaged in dangerous work), while family workers and/or domestic workers are excluded in 45 countries, particularly in the Pacific Islands, the Middle East and Latin America. Furthermore, employment coverage is incomplete in some developing countries, with coverage gaps existing on an enterprise-size basis (13 countries), a geographical basis (7 countries), an occupational-group basis (6 countries) and an industry basis (6 countries). Chile and Greece permit coverage contracting out of their employment-injury programs to equivalent occupational plans.

Voluntary coverage is commonly unavailable. Where voluntary access is granted, however, it is given to the self-employed (8 countries), to employees otherwise ineligible for coverage (4 countries), to farm employees (Japan) and to small and communal farmers (Mexico).

Special systems for particular population categories are more common. They are most common for public employees (43 countries), although they have also been established for employees in designated occupation groups (10 countries) or industries (4 countries) and for farm employees (China, France and Turkey), the self-employed (France and Gabon), students (China and Luxembourg) and farmers (Finland and France).

PRIMARY SOCIAL SECURITY STRATEGY ELIGIBILITY

Employment-Related Disability Programs

Categorical Criteria. The categorical criteria that define the eligible employment-related disability categories are the cause and degree of disability suffered.

All countries, except Portugal, Macau and Nauru, consider those medically certified to be suffering from employment-related injuries or diseases to be eligible under their primary strategy. Those with employment-related illnesses are dealt with in Portugal by means of a subsidiary strategy, while they are ineligible in Nauru. Those suffering from a temporary employment-related injury are ineligible in Macau. Other eligible categories in some countries include persons who were disabled in childhood and who would otherwise have entered the workforce at age 16 years (New Zealand) and road accident victims (Western Samoa).

What constitutes an employment-related injury is typically the result of an accident occurring during working hours, including perhaps, commuting accidents. What constitutes an employment-related disease is typically determined by reference to a statutory list of prescribed diseases that are presumed to be attributable to an employment-related cause. It is the standard applied to the disability criteria that defines the minimum degree of disability and so determines eligibility for temporary and permanent disability program cash entitlements at the maximum level. For temporary disability benefit eligibility, the categorical criterion in most countries is a medically determined total employment-related disability, as only 11 countries include the partially disabled as an eligible category. For permanent disability benefit eligibility, the categorical criterion is a medically determined disability that results in a permanent or expected long-term reduction of an individual's earning capacity. Some countries specify a minimum earnings loss of up to 15 percent (46 countries), of between 15 and 49 percent (19 countries) or of between 50 and 75 percent (18 countries), which is a significantly more liberal standard than that applied to general disability programs (see Chapter 5). Typically, unlike general disability programs, the partially disabled (that is, those with a degree of disability below that required to qualify for a cash entitlement at the maximum level) do constitute an eligible population category (for they are excluded only in Greece, Macau and Yugoslavia).

General Qualifying Eligibility Criteria. These are attached to employment-related temporary and permanent disability programs in relatively few countries. Where they are, the requirements are modest, in stark contrast to those attached to general disability programs, and relate to minimum periods of disability, contribution and employment; and to maximum payment periods.

Minimum disability period requirements are the most frequently specified general eligibility criteria (66 countries). The most frequently prescribed period is three-to-five days (48 countries), with 12 countries setting a longer period during which, except for Burundi, temporary disability benefits are provided under supplementary social security strategies.

Maximum payment periods for temporary disability entitlements are not uncommon (61 countries) — typically between one and two years (36 countries) or longer (10 countries) and perhaps with the possibility of extension on medical grounds (6 countries) — after which either eligibility ceases unless permanent disability is certified. Less commonly, a maximum payment period is specified for permanent disability entitlements (as in Bangladesh (1 year), the Dominican Republic (160 weeks), Equatorial Guinea (48 months) and Thailand (15 years)).

Minimum contribution periods are generally specified in only Malta (1 week) and the Philippines (1 month) and only with respect to occupational diseases in Ecuador (26 weeks, with at least 8 weeks in the 6 months prior to the onset of the illness) and Nicaragua (6 months in the last year).

Only Ghana specifies a minimum employment period (6 months) under its employer liability program.

Means-Assessment Criteria. No country uses means-based eligibility criteria to exclude applicants who satisfy the categorical criteria from qualifying for employment-related temporary and permanent disability program benefits.

Employment-Related Survivors' Program

Categorical Criteria. The categorical criteria that determine the eligible deceased and survivor categories relate to both the deceased and his or her survivors.

Employment-related survivors' programs make eligibility contingent upon the deceased dying as a result of an injury or illness caused by employment-related accident or disease, although Western Samoa has broadened its program to include death by road accident.

A complex array of categorical criteria determines the benefit eligibility of survivors, who are prioritized by closeness of their relationship to the deceased and by their degree of dependency on the deceased. In all countries eligible survivor categories fall into four groups: surviving spouses, surviving children, other surviving family members, and other surviving dependents. The nomination of survivor beneficiaries is very much the exception, whether by the deceased (only Afghanistan) and by the courts (only Fiji, Nigeria and the Solomon Islands).

Surviving spouses can, clearly, include both widows and widowers and in all countries except Denmark, remarriage results in exclusion from these eligible survivor categories. Widows per se are an eligible survivor category in 100 countries, which is almost double the frequency under general survivors' programs. In stark contrast to general survivors' programs, relatively few countries require widows to meet one or more additional categorical criteria, namely to be: a dependent of the deceased (36 countries); responsible for dependent children or pregnant (13 countries, largely in Eastern Europe); disabled (13 countries); above a minimum age of between 30 and 45 (7 countries) or of between 50 and 60 (5 countries); of pensionable age (3 countries); out of employment (4 countries); or able to satisfy a minimum marriage or cohabitation period (5 years in Sweden, alternatively having mutual children under age 12). In some countries eligibility is extended to cohabitants (9 countries), divorcees who have no other income (5 countries), de facto wives (5 countries), multiple widows (Algeria, Cape Verde and Saudi Arabia) and widows unable to work full time (Sweden) or earning below a minimum income (Bahamas). Widowers are excluded as an eligible survivor category in only nine countries, about half the frequency under general survivors' programs. Widowers per se, however, are an eligible survivor category in only 34 countries, marginally more than under general survivors' programs. In most countries widowers are required to meet one or more additional categorical criteria, namely to be: disabled and a dependent on the deceased (58 countries); dependent on the deceased (32 countries); with dependent children (7 countries); above a minimum age of between 35 and 45 (2 countries) or between 50 and 65 (6 countries); or of a pensionable age (5 countries).

Orphaned dependent children (variously defined) are a universal eligible survivor category. In the Netherlands, however, surviving children of only one deceased parent are excluded from this category unless they are also either students or disabled. Eligibility is extended to fetuses in Cape Verde. Three countries limit eligibility to a maximum number of orphans: the Philippines (the 5 youngest under age 21) and Belgium and Israel (the first 3). Dependency upon the deceased is not a categorical requirement in seven post-socialist countries, six of which do not even specify an eligibility cut-off age. Indeed, as under general survivors' programs, the age at which eligibility ends for a child who is neither disabled nor a student varies markedly. The most frequent cut-off age is 16 (73 countries). Older cut-off ages of between 17 and 22 are specified in 60 countries. Cut-off ages below 16 are specified in only 12 countries, with the youngest age being 14 (5 countries). Students continue to qualify beyond the specified cut-off age in 98 countries, of which 85 countries set an age limit of 21 or over (up to 26 in the Czech Republic and Slovakia), with the remaining 13 countries specifying a cut-off age of either 20 (6 countries) or 18 (7 countries). Similarly, disabled children continue to qualify in 76 countries, of which 60 set no age limit, 11 specify an age limit of between 18 and 21, and five countries set a higher cut-off age (up to 26 in the Czech Republic and Slovakia). Unmarried daughters regain eligibility at a cut-in age of 45 in Spain, but only under certain conditions.

Other eligible family-member survivor categories are designated in 109 countries, which is considerably higher that the frequency for general survivors' programs, are dependent parents (109 countries), dependent siblings (58 countries), dependent grandparents (64 countries), dependent grandchildren (35 countries), non-dependent family members (Japan) and partially dependent family members (Bermuda).

Other eligible non-family-member survivor categories sometimes designated are dependent non-family members (Mauritius, and St Vincent and the Grenadines under certain conditions) and the deceased's carer (Luxembourg).

General Qualifying Eligibility Criteria. The attachment of general qualifying eligibility criteria to employment-related survivors' programs is very much the exception, unlike general survivors' programs. Apart from requiring the deceased to be a resident at the time of death, which all countries do, no country specifies any minimum residency requirements. Minimum contribution period requirements are specified in only Malta (1 week) and the Philippines (1 month), while only Ghana specifies a minimum employment period requirement (6 months) under its employer liability program.

A maximum payment period requirement, beyond which benefit eligibility ceases, is specified in 16 countries — the shortest duration being 52 weeks (Jamaica) — of which eight then require widows to satisfy other categorical criteria for continuation of eligibility. Alternatively, maximum aggregate payment limits are specified for both temporary and permanent disability entitlements in Australia, for permanent and survivors' entitlements in Argentina, and for permanent disability entitlements in only the Dominican Republic.

Means-Assessment Criteria. No country uses means-based eligibility criteria to exclude applicants who satisfy the categorical criteria from qualifying for employment-related survivors' program benefits.

PRIMARY SOCIAL SECURITY STRATEGY BENEFITS

Cash Entitlements

Cash entitlements under employment-injury programs take a variety of forms. Earnings-related pensions are typically provided under temporary disability programs (150 countries) and permanent disability programs (124 countries), with their conversion to a lump sum permitted only in Haiti, Malaysia (in part only), Mauritius (only with respect to workers aged between 52 and 60) and Thailand. They are also the most frequently specified benefit form under survivors' programs (71 countries), with their conversion to a lump sum permitted in only Indonesia and Thailand. Lump-sum benefits are dispensed under survivors' programs (27 countries); under permanent disability programs (23 countries), with conversion to periodic payments permitted in only Guatemala; and under temporary disability programs (only Afghanistan, Ethiopia and Nauru). Flat-rate pensions are even less popular, whether under temporary disability programs (6 countries, notably including Iceland, Ireland and the United Kingdom); under permanent disability programs (11 countries); or under survivors' programs (9 countries, of which 7 are in Western Europe, although Malta and Papua New Guinea do provide flat-rate orphans' pensions).

The relating of employment-related survivors' benefits in aggregate to the deceased's benefit or benefit entitlement at the time of death is, in contrast to general survivors' programs, less frequent (46 countries). Of those countries that do so, 36 countries distribute the entire benefit or entitlement, while six countries distribute less (as low as 75 percent) and four countries distribute more (up to 140 percent in India). The distribution of this aggregate benefit amongst eligible beneficiaries is generally determined by the enabling legislation (123 countries), with the nomination of distributional share entitlements being very much the exception, whether by the deceased (Afghanistan) or by the courts (Australia, Fiji, Nigeria and the Solomon Islands).

Cash entitlements in some countries vary in accordance with designated parameters, namely: period of employment disability, under temporary disability programs (22 countries) and under permanent disability programs (Australia); previous employment-injury entitlements paid, under survivors' programs (9 countries) and under permanent disability programs (Botswana and St Vincent and the Grenadines); degree of disability, under temporary disability programs (10 countries); past earnings categories, under permanent disability programs (Zimbabwe, Zambia and Papua New Guinea), under survivors' programs (Bangladesh, Papua New Guinea and Sri Lanka) and under temporary disability programs (Zambia and Zimbabwe); age at which disability occurs, under permanent disability programs (Finland, Hong Kong, Lebanon and Singapore); age at which death occurs, under survivors' programs (Hong Kong and Israel); length of contribution period, under permanent disability (Hungary, Iran, and Libya); degree of dependency, under survivors' programs (Papua New Guinea and Zambia); length of employment, under permanent disability programs (Cuba); residual earning capacity, under permanent disability programs (Portugal); and whether cause of death due to employment accident or disease, under survivors' programs (Algeria).

Entitlement tapering because of the receipt of other income is very rare, for it happens only with respect to survivors' entitlements under Germany's employer liability program (where an income disregard limit and an entitlement withdrawal rate are specified) and under Malta's social insurance program (applied to only employed eligible orphans, where an entitlement withdrawal rate applies, subject to the combined income not exceeding the minimum wage).

Specifying limits on cash entitlements is common. Maximum cash entitlement rates are specified under temporary disability programs (34 countries), under permanent disability programs (48 countries) and under survivors' programs (93 countries). Minimum cash entitlement rates are rather less frequently specified under temporary disability (20 countries) and under survivors' programs (9 countries), but marginally more frequently specified under permanent disability programs (53 countries). Similarly, under all three employment-injury programs, maximum earnings rates for the calculation of earnings-related cash entitlements are specified in 36 countries, with minimum rates being specified in only nine countries.

The distribution of maximum income-replacement rates varies amongst employment-injury programs. Under temporary disability programs the rate distribution is: 50–70 percent (67 countries), 70–85 percent (46 countries) and over 85 percent (37 countries, all specifying 100 percent). Under permanent disability programs the rate distribution is: 50–70 percent (43 countries), 70–85 percent (50 countries) and over 85 percent (31 countries, of which 23 specify 100 percent). Under survivors' programs the rate distribution is: under 50 percent (China, depending on the number of dependent children), 50–70 percent (16 countries), 70–85 percent (39 countries) and over 85 percent (15 countries, all specifying 100 percent).

Uniquely, New Zealand pays an age-related, flat-rate pension to persons not in the workforce because of a disability suffered in childhood.

Those who are partially disabled receive different forms of benefits under temporary and permanent disability programs. Where they are eligible for temporary disability entitlements (11 countries), they receive pro-rata pensions. Where they are eligible for permanent disability entitlements (155 countries) they most frequently receive pro-rata pensions (79 countries), but other forms of entitlement are paid: lump-sum payments (29 countries), variable pensions (24 countries), uniform flat-rate pensions (21 countries) or earnings-loss equivalence (Australia and the United States where, alternatively, in the case of a scheduled injury, the payment can be at the full rate for a shorter period). Those who are partially but permanently disabled receive a reduced earnings allowance in the United Kingdom if they are able to work at any job. If their degree of permanent disability is below that required for a partial disability entitlement, in many countries they still receive support (61 countries), typically a lump-sum payment (60 countries), sometimes related to the specific injury suffered (as in Australia).

The payment of grants to partial dependents under survivors' programs occurs in only nine countries, seven of which are in Africa, the others being Iceland and Bermuda.

Settlement payments are infrequently paid. Gabon makes a lump-sum settlement upon the survivors who were dependent upon the deceased, provided there are no qualified survivors. In the they are also paid for similarly placed sisters and daughters in Saudi Arabia. Ireland provides flat-rate unemployability allowances to those suffering a permanent disability who are ineligible for a disability pension but who are permanently incapable of work.

Most temporary disability, permanent disability and survivors' programs that provide periodic payments do not regularly adjust them in line with inflation. Those that do, however, do so overwhelmingly on an ad hoc basis. Only six countries make inflationary adjustments to their temporary disability pensions. Rather more do so under their permanent disability programs (29 countries) and their survivors' programs (29 countries).

Gratuities and an array of other relatively minor additional cash entitlements are also provided under some temporary disability programs (3 countries), permanent disability programs (15 countries) and survivors' programs (25 countries).

Supplementary Cash Benefits

These are paid for dependents in only a small minority of countries under temporary disability programs (11 countries, seven of which are in Western Europe) and under survivors' programs (6 countries), although rather more commonly under permanent disability programs (25 countries).

Special Need Benefits

Disabled people with presumed needs are given additional support in many countries. Supplementary assistance is given to those who are temporarily disabled in Belgium, Norway (contingent upon the medical nature and degree of injury) and Cost Rica (as housing grants). Additional support is more readily given to the permanently disabled who require constant attendance (92 countries), who have lasting injuries (Switzerland) or who are in need of social rehabilitation (New Zealand).

Survivors' programs are rather more forthcoming with special need benefits. Grants to cover funeral costs are paid as funeral grants (113 countries) or survivor grants (21 countries). Supplementary benefits are commonly provided to full or double orphans (62 countries) or for disabled orphans (Dominica). Supplementary benefits are also provided by some countries to aged widows (7 countries, 5 of which are in Western Europe) and to disabled widows (Egypt, Israel and Portugal).

CONCLUSION

The indemnifying of victims of employment-related injury under the common law of negligence (tort action) had a long history before the emergence of social security in the last quarter of the nineteenth century. Because the rise of the negligence principle broadly coincided with nineteenth-century industrialization, it began to seem reasonable — especially to employers — that the state should limit the extent to which they must compensate employment-injury victims. Ultimately, the common-law remedies were withdrawn, thus withdrawing the employment-injury victims right to seek full restitution, replaced by the no-fault legal principle. This laid the foundations upon which the employment-injury branch has developed throughout the twentieth century. Employees suffering an employment injury or their survivors have been given near-restitution benefits as a sacrosanct matter of right, irrespective of their means or their employment or contribution records.

The global popularity of employment-injury programs is very evident. The idea that there should be a constrained transfer of resources from employers to employees when an employment injury or death occurred was readily accepted from the latter part of the nineteenth century as the basis for a social security initiative, frequently the first of many. It still remains so in many countries. More countries, however, have shifted the cost burden from the perceived slim shoulders of the employer to the broad shoulders of the community, by establishing appropriate social insurance mechanisms, while only Afghanistan has dared to shift the cost burden to employees.

Employment-injury programs have generally remained separate from other related social security programs in most countries. This practice, as Kaim-Caudle (1973: 102) has pointed out, "makes it less expensive to provide adequate compensation for the relatively small number of persons who suffer industrial injuries than it is to provide for all who are incapacitated."

The 1974 Woodhouse Inquiry into Australia's approach to employment-injury compensation and rehabilitation is indicative of an all embracing vision of reform (Australia 1974: 139):

a universal and comprehensive scheme designed to alleviate the problems of persons afflicted by any physical or mental incapacity that has a significant and adverse effect upon the quality of their lives. Its essential purpose will be to provide a form of social insurance in respect to life and limb during the whole 24 hours of every day.

Relatively few countries have sought radical change in the underlying philosophy of their employer-injury programs. The Netherlands has for two decades fully integrated its employment-injury programs into its general sickness, disability and survivors' programs. Partial integration is, however, rather more common, predominantly in post-socialist countries, which have integrated at least one of their employment-injury programs — most frequently their survivors' program — into other social security branches. New Zealand and Switzerland have, alternatively, chosen a somewhat different path by integrating their employment-injury programs into a comprehensive accident program. Western Samoa has taken a step in that direction with its inclusion of road accident victims under its employment-injury program.

Employment-injury programs have generally created a social security elite, a group of recipients who have come to expect near-restitution of damages caused by employment-related accident or disease. To those protected by these programs they offer a definite respite from poverty; to those suffering general injuries they are a reminder of the unequal treatment given to injured and sick people with identical losses, for the protection proffered is differentiated on the basis of the cause rather than the consequences of an injury.

5

Old Age, Invalidity and Death

INTRODUCTION

Debate on the desirability of establishing social security programs addressing the long-term contingencies — old age, disability and survivorship — began in Europe in the 1880s, but quickly moved to the Antipodes in the early 1890s and then to Latin America a decade later. Germany led the way in 1889, when it developed the first social insurance strategy to provide support to the aged, disabled people and survivors (Kohler and Zacher 1982). The social insurance strategy was picked up a decade later by Belgium (1900, for old-age and survivors' programs only) and then by Czechoslovakia (1906, for salaried employees only), Austria (1909, for salaried employees only), France (1910), Luxembourg (1911, for wage earners only), Romania (1912) and Sweden (1913). Social insurance almost simultaneously established a toe-hold — covering only special occupational groups — in Latin America through Argentina (1904) (Queiro-Tajali 1990) and Cuba (1913) (Mesa-Lago and Roca 1992).

In contradistinction, Denmark opted for the social assistance strategy in 1891, so becoming the second country to establish long-term contingency programs (Petersen 1990). This development strongly influenced the direction of the social security debate in the Antipodes, where the old-age pension debate in the 1890s was robust and very much favoring social assistance. New Zealand established old-age and survivors' assistance programs in 1898, with Australia following close on its heels with its old-age and disability assistance programs from 1900 (initially in three colonies, then federally in 1908) (Dixon 1977, Kewley 1972, New Zealand 1970, Uttley 1989). The Danish model also guided the emergence of social assistance programs for long-term contingencies in Denmark's then territory, Iceland (1909). The adjacent United Kingdom (1908) and its then territory, Ireland (1908), also adopted old-age and disability assistance programs (Kaim-Caudle 1973), while the neighboring Netherlands (1913) adopted a disability assistance program (Roebroek 1989).

By the beginning of the First World War, 18 countries had established some form of social security targeting the aged, disabled people and/or survivors. Some countries that quite quickly followed Germany in taking old-age social security initiatives were, however, tardy in introducing either disability programs, notably Denmark (1921), New Zealand (1924, blindness pensions only, and 1936) and Belgium (1944) or survivors' programs (notably the United Kingdom (1925), Ireland (1935)) and Australia (1942).

The years up to the end of the Second World War saw a further 34 countries join this group. These included most of the remaining parts of Western Europe, with three exceptions, as well as North America, namely Canada (some states during the First World War and federally in 1927) (Shewell 1998, Guest 1985) and the United States (some states in the 1920s and federally in 1935) (Day 1989); Eastern Europe, beginning with the Soviet Union (1922) (Dixon and Macarov 1992); South America, beginning with Brazil (1923, for railway employees only) (Leite 1990); Central America, initially in Costa Rica and Panama (1941) followed closely by Mexico (1943) (Mesa-Lago 1978); and Africa, initially in South Africa (1928) (McKendrick and Dudas 1987).

Since the Second World War, there has been a proliferation of long-term contingency programs. They were established by the three remaining West European countries: Switzerland (1948), which established its first long-term contingency insurance program more than 20 years after a constitutional amendment permitted the creation of old-age and survivors' insurance programs (Janssen and Muller 1982), a delay caused by its reluctance to challenge its long tradition of voluntary insurance (Kohler and Zacher 1982); Cyprus (1956), which simultaneously established all three long-term insurance programs; and Malta (1956), which first established old-age and survivors' insurance programs and then waited nine years before introducing its disability insurance program (1965). They were also established by the vast majority of Third World countries, including some of the most of the poorest. Thus, by 1995, 164 countries had one or more such programs.

OLD-AGE PROGRAMS

Primary and Supplementary Strategies Adopted

While most of the 164 countries with old-age programs have adopted social insurance as their primary strategy (128 countries), some use National Provident Funds (20 countries) and a few have adopted other strategies. A small cluster of nine countries had chosen social allowances (all five Scandinavian countries, Canada, New Zealand and, most surprisingly, Mauritius and the Cook Islands). An even smaller cohort have chosen social assistance (Australia, Hong Kong, Nauru and South Africa). The two real mavericks are Chile and Peru, both with mandated personal pensions. North Korea remains the only country with an employer liability measure (Kim 1992). Strategy changes have not been common.

Only 30 countries have changed their primary old-age social security strategy; Egypt has done so twice. The most common changes have involved the substitution of social insurance for National Provident Funds (10 countries), for social assistance (the Netherlands, the United Kingdom, Ireland and 4 former British colonies in Latin America) and for employer liability measures (China and Vietnam). There has also been a limited replacement of social insurance by social allowances (4 Scandinavian countries and Mauritius) or by mandated personal pensions (Chile and Peru). Social assistance has been replaced by social allowances (Canada, Denmark and New Zealand) and by a National Provident Fund (Egypt). More common has been the adoption of a supplementary strategy to meet social security objectives not attainable by the primary strategy.

Fifty-four countries have coupled their primary old-age social security strategy with one or more supplementary strategies. This has been done in order to cater to the needy aged who are ineligible for benefits under the primary strategy, using social assistance (25 countries); to supplement primary strategy benefits, using either social insurance (7 countries) or mandated personal and occupational pension and savings (9 countries); and/or to extend coverage, using social allowances (13 countries), social insurance (The Gambia), or employer liability measures (Colombia).

Primary Social Security Strategy Coverage

Given the predominance of the employment-based social security strategies it is not surprising to find that the coverage of most old-age programs is restricted to those in paid formal employment, the obvious exceptions being the 13 countries that have adopted social allowances and social assistance as their primary strategy.

Employment Coverage. Covered employees, generally, include farm employees (excluded in only 38 countries, most notably in the Middle East). Earnings are generally not considered a barrier to coverage. High-income employees (variously defined) are excluded in only Austria, the Dominican Republic, India and Switzerland. Low-income employees (variously defined) are, however, excluded in 12 countries, most conspicuously in the Pacific Islands and Asia. Covered employees, however, generally exclude the self-employed (included in only 57 countries, with their exclusion most conspicuous in Africa and Asia). Furthermore, employment coverage is incomplete in some developing countries, with coverage gaps existing on an enterprise-size basis (15 countries), a geographical basis (7 countries) and an occupational-group basis (5 countries).

Voluntary coverage is not commonly available. Where voluntary access is granted, however, it is given to the self-employed (22 countries), to employees otherwise ineligible for coverage (19 countries), to previously covered employees who leave covered employment (12 countries) and to farm employees and farmers (4 countries).

Special systems for particular population categories are not uncommon. Special systems have commonly been established for public employees (85 countries), for designated occupation groups (36 countries) and, less commonly, for the self-employed (10 countries), farmers (10 countries), farm employees (8 countries) and employees in designated industries (4 countries).

Primary Social Security Strategy Eligibility

Categorical Criteria. Age and employment status are the two criteria that define the eligible old-age categories.

The most frequent minimum eligibility age for men is between 60 and 64 (90 countries) and between 55 and 59 for women (76 countries), with the vast majority of countries falling within the age ranges of 60 to 69 for men (127 countries) and 55 to 64 for women (132 countries). At the extremes, the lowest minimum eligibility age range for men is 45 to 49 (6 countries) and the same for women (11 countries); and the highest for men is 65 to 69 (37 countries) and the same for women (21 countries). The minimum eligibility age range for men and women is most frequently the same, with women's being lower than men's in only 68 countries. In most countries, the minimum eligibility age range is lower than the life expectancy at birth for men (124 countries) and for women (124 countries).

Compulsory retirement is not the norm. Compulsory retirement either from all gainful employment or from covered employment is required in only 50 and 26 countries, respectively. Poland only requires partial retirement, and Germany permits retirement with a part pension, where the amount of allowable earnings is determined by the amount of pension sought. Indeed, 30 countries encourage the deferment of retirement by providing larger cash entitlements to those who postpone their retirement.

Early retirement is an option for at least some covered employees in most countries with employment-related strategies. It is available to all covered employees in 47 countries, to designated covered employees in 42 countries, and to covered employees in hazardous industries in 37 countries. Eighteen post-socialist countries grant early retirement rights to women with children (various numbers and ages defined), while in Lebanon women can qualify for a contribution-related retirement benefit by leaving employment during their first year of marriage. Early retirement is available to those living in unhealthy regions in Iran or ecologically disastrous regions in Kazakhstan, Turkmenistan and Uzbekistan. In Egypt early retirement is available to those earning over a minimum monthly income, subject to them being able to satisfy a minimum contribution period requirement that is double that otherwise required for eligibility.

General Qualifying Eligibility Criteria. The general qualifying criteria used to exclude applicants who satisfy the categorical criteria from qualifying for old-age program benefits relate to minimum periods of contribution, covered employment and residency periods, as well as to residency status.

Of the 151 countries with employment-related old-age programs, most specify minimum contribution period requirements (115 countries), although a few specify minimum employment period requirements (6 post-socialist countries). The most frequently specified minimum contribution period requirement is between 11 and 20 years (50 countries), although periods of less than 10 years is only marginally less popular (45 countries), while periods of more than 20 years can be found (20 countries, most if which are post socialist (14 countries), as well as, among others, the Netherlands (49 years for a full pension) and Argentina (30 years) and Japan (25 years). The contribution period sometimes includes credit years for bringing up children (Poland) and for marriage to an insured employee (Japan). Dwarfs and the blind have to satisfy a reduced minimum contribution period requirement in Latvia. In Israel the minimum contribution period requirements are waived entirely for insured women who are widowed, divorced, deserted, married to an uninsured husband or unmarried and aged 55 or over at the time of immigration.

Minimum residency period requirements apply in most countries that have adopted social assistance and social allowance as their primary social security strategy, the exceptions being Norway (requiring, instead, a minimum covered employment period of 3 years, but 40 years for a full pension) and Nauru. The most frequently specified minimum residency period is 10 years and under (11 countries, including the Seychelles (5 years) and Surinam (10 years), both of which, however, use this as an alternative to attaching either minimum contribution period or minimum employment period requirements to their social insurance strategy). The social allowance program in Mauritius specifies a minimum residency period of 12 years for nationals (otherwise 15 years after age 40), while Canada, Denmark, Finland and Iceland all specify a mammoth 40 years for a full pension.

Residency at the time of application is a universal requirement, but 29 countries permit recipients to live abroad.

Means-Assessment Criteria. The means-based eligibility criteria used to exclude applicants who satisfy the categorical criteria from qualifying for old-age program benefits are income and asset tests.

Means testing is uncommon. An income test applies in the four countries that have adopted social assistance as their primary social security strategy, where it is specified as an income disregard limit with an attendant entitlement withdrawal rate (Australia (except for the blind), Hong Kong, Nauru and South Africa). It is attached to some social insurance programs as a statutory maximum income cutout threshold (Bahamas, Malta (applicable only until age 65) and the Philippines (applicable only until age 65)), and to others as an income disregard limit with an attendant entitlement withdrawal rate (Israel and the United States (applicable only until age 70)). New Zealand operates a de facto income test through its income taxation system, as it imposes an additional income tax surcharge (a de facto entitlement withdrawal rate) on superannuation recipients' non-pension incomes above a set of exemption limits (de facto income disregard limits). An asset test has also been attached to all social assistance programs.

Primary Social Security Strategy Benefits

Cash Entitlements. Cash entitlements under old-age programs take a variety of forms. Earnings-related pensions are provided in 110 countries. Flat-rate pensions are provided by all 13 social assistance and social allowance programs and by 12 countries with social insurance programs (most notably Ireland, Japan, Luxembourg, the Netherlands, Switzerland and the United Kingdom, as well as the Seychelles). Lump-sum benefits are dispensed by all 20 National Provident Funds, under a few social insurance programs (Taiwan, Lebanon and Yemen) and under North Korea's employer liability program. These are occasionally made convertible by the National Provident Funds into annuities (4 countries) or periodic payments (5 countries). Pensions that are minimum-wage-related are paid under Mexico's social insurance program, or that are average-wage-related are provided under Israel's social insurance program. Contribution-based entitlements are paid in Jamaica, while Chile and Peru have adopted the individual capitalization approach.

Cash entitlements typically vary directly with the number of years over which contributions have been paid (136 countries) and, less frequently, with years of covered employment (Cuba, Norway and Romania), with the annual average number of weeks of contributions paid (Bermuda and Jamaica), or with years of residency (Canada, Denmark, Finland and Iceland).

Entitlement tapering because of the receipt of other income and ownership of assets is uncommon. Non-pension income derived by beneficiaries is taken into consideration not only under the four social assistance programs but also under social insurance programs in Georgia (applicable only if pensioner remains in gainful employment) and under social allowance program in Iceland (based only on partner's income). Assets acquired by beneficiaries are only considered under the four social assistance programs.

Specifying limits on cash entitlements is common. Minimum and maximum cash entitlement rates are specified in 93 countries and 75 countries, respectively. Moreover, while minimum earnings rates for the calculation of earnings-related cash entitlements are specified in only 10 countries, maximum earnings rates are specified in 45 countries.

The distribution of maximum income-replacement rates is: under 50 percent (Senegal (40 percent) and Haiti (33 percent)); 50-85 percent (93 countries), over 85 percent (15 countries, with Afghanistan and China notably specifying up to 100 percent).

Most old-age pensions are not regularly adjusted in line with inflation. Of the 67 countries that do make periodic pension adjustments, 41 do so on an ad hoc basis, with a further 18 making annual adjustments and only eight making quarterly or biannual adjustments. Greece, uniquely, adjusts its pensions in line with civil service pension adjustments.

Gratuities and an array of other relatively minor additional cash entitlements are provided in 60 countries.

In almost half of the social insurance programs, those who fail to satisfy the general qualifying criteria receive a settlement, typically as lump-sum payments (54 countries), although pro-rata pensions are paid (6 countries) as are means-tested allowances (France)).

Supplementary Cash Benefits. These are paid for dependents in only a minority of countries (41 countries). The most frequently paid are adult dependent allowances (38 countries) and child dependent allowances (32 countries). They are most commonly granted in Australasia and Western Europe, where they may be subject to a separate income test, as in Australia, France, Iceland (where it applies to only the extra supplementary assistance granted under specified conditions), New Zealand (where it applies to only married couples seeking the full married pension rate), Norway and Sweden.

Special Need Benefits. Those aged with presumed special needs receive additional support in some countries. The frail aged are so supported in 21 countries, of which 15 provide constant attendance allowances and eight provide supplementary cash entitlements. Australia provides rental assistance, a remote area supplement and a telephone allowance. Mauritius, uniquely, provides a lump-sum centenarian grant.

DISABILITY PROGRAMS

Primary and Supplementary Strategies Adopted

Social security support in the event of disability (variously defined) is provided in 163 countries. (Only Thailand does so without having an old-age program; North Korea and Surinam do not do so, despite having an old-age program.) An overwhelming 130 countries have adopted social insurance as their primary strategy, while 19 countries use National Provident Funds (the exception being Malaysia). Social allowances have been adopted by six countries (Finland, Hong Kong, Iceland, Mauritius, Norway and Sweden), as has social assistance (Australia, the Cook Islands, Denmark, Nauru, New Zealand and South Africa). The two mavericks are, again, Chile and Peru (both with mandated personal pension programs). In Hong Kong separate public programs exist for injuries due to criminal or law enforcement action, traffic accidents and natural disasters (MacPherson 1998). Once a primary strategy has been chosen, change has been uncommon, but that which did occur (in 26 countries) broadly replicated the pattern with respect to old-age programs. The adoption of a supplementary strategy has been rather more common (47 countries), and the pattern of provision is, again, broadly similar to that for the aged: to cater to the needy who are ineligible for benefits under the primary strategy using social assistance

(20 countries); to supplement benefits using social insurance (Finland, Mauritius, Norway and Sweden) or mandated personal and occupational pensions and savings (Australia, Bolivia, Côte d'Ivoire, Mexico, Switzerland and Venezuela); and/or to extend coverage using social allowances (13 countries), employer liability measures (Colombia and Pakistan), a National Provident Fund (Malaysia) or social insurance (The Gambia).

Primary Social Security Strategy Coverage

Except for the 12 countries that have adopted social allowances and social assistance as their primary strategy, the coverage of most disability programs is restricted to those in employment.

Employment Coverage. As with old-age programs, coverage in most countries is universal amongst those in paid formal employment and the patterns of inclusions, exclusions, voluntary access and special systems are essentially the same as that for old-age programs. Generally, farm employees are included (excluded in 39 countries), as are both high- and low-income employees (variously defined) (excluded in only 5 and 11 countries respectively), while the self-employed are generally excluded (included in only 47 countries). Furthermore, employment coverage is incomplete in some developing countries, with coverage gaps existing on an enterprise-size basis (16 countries), a geographical basis (7 countries), an occupational-group basis (5 countries) and an industry basis (4 countries).

Voluntary coverage is uncommon, most frequently made available to the self-employed (22 countries) and to employees otherwise ineligible for coverage (19 countries), as well as to previously covered employees who leave covered employment (12 countries), farm employees (3 countries) and farmers (4 countries).

Special systems are most common for public employees (85 countries) and for designated occupation groups (37 countries), as well as, far less commonly, for the self-employed (10 countries), farmers (10 countries), farm employees (7 countries) and employees in designated industries (3 countries).

Primary Social Security Strategy Eligibility

Categorical Criteria. A disability is the product of a functional limitation caused by an impairment that arises from an accident, an illness or a congenital condition (Berkowitz 1981: 4–8, see also Nagi 1979, Marshaw 1979). The degree of disability is the categorical criterion for disability programs. In this context, distinctions can be drawn between three disability concepts (ILO 1984b: 74, also ILO 1981): *physical disability*, the loss of a body part or diminished physical or mental function, irrespective of the economic or occupational consequences of that loss); *employment-related disability*, the earnings loss resulting from an inability to continue in previous occupation; and *general disability*, the earnings loss resulting from an inability to take up any employment. The adoption of one categorical criterion is most common, but the application of two or more criteria does happen.

The most frequently adopted categorical criterion is general disability (148 countries), although some countries have adopted the employment-related disability criterion (15 countries), albeit with some variations on "previous occupation" (in Fiji ("work in covered employment"), in Finland, Libya , Malta and the Netherlands ("suitable" work or occupation); in Poland, Romania and São Tomé and Principe ("usual" or "regular" work or profession); and in Luxembourg and Nicaragua ("similar" occupation).

The standard applied to the general and employment-related disability criteria defines the minimum degree of disability required to be eligible for a disability program cash entitlement at the maximum level. The categorical criterion in most countries require a medically determined disability that produces a permanent or expected long-term reduction of an individual's earning capacity of, typically, between 50 and 70 percent (53 countries) or between 71 and 99 percent (48 countries). Bolivia's practice is to judge earnings capacity loss by reference to a comparable, but healthy, worker who is in the same region. The more stringent standard of total and permanent inability to work applies in 61 countries. At the other extreme, Australia requires only that a 20 percent level of impairment results in an inability to work full-time for full earnings for the foreseeable future. It should be noted that, typically, a partial disability (that is, a degree of disability below that required to qualify for a cash entitlement at the maximum level) does not result in benefit eligibility, for this is permitted in only 55 countries. The partially disabled are permitted to continue working while in receipt of a disability pension in Mexico (albeit in different employment).

Only seven countries — four of which operate disability assistance programs — have also adopted the physical disability criterion. The most frequently identified physical impairments are blindness (Albania, Australia, New Zealand and South Africa), severe mutilation (Albania) and profound deafness (Hong Kong). Israel makes a disabled wife eligible if she has a 50 percent level of medical disability.

General Qualifying Eligibility Criteria. The general qualifying criteria used to exclude applicants who satisfy the categorical criteria from qualifying for disability program benefits are typically minimum periods of disability, contribution, covered employment and residency, as well as residency status, minimum age and maximum payment period requirements.

Of the 151 countries with contributory disability programs, most specify minimum contribution period requirements (111 countries), but a few identify, alternatively, minimum employment period requirements (4 countries). The most frequently specified minimum contribution period requirement is between one and five years (74 countries), which is at least half the duration most frequently required for old-age program eligibility. Indeed shorter minimum contribution requirements are specified in 21 countries. Only Haiti specifies a minimum contribution above 10 years (up to 20 years). In 16 countries the minimum contribution period requirements are waived if the disability is caused by a general accident.

Minimum residency period requirements apply in nine of the 12 countries that have adopted either the social assistance or social allowance strategy. The exceptions are Australia (unless the disability occurred before arrival in Australia, in which case it is 10 years), the Cook Islands and Nauru. This residency requirement typically falls within the range of two-to-five years (6 countries), although Hong Kong's is only one year, while New Zealand's is 10 years. Residency at the time of application is a universal requirement, and only five countries permit recipients to live abroad.

Minimum age requirements (between 45 and 55) are specified in four African countries.

Minimum disability period requirements are specified in the Central African Republic (6 months) and Bermuda (1 year).

A maximum payment period — beyond which benefit eligibility ceases — is specified in Thailand (15 years).

Means-Assessment Criteria. The means-based eligibility criteria used to exclude applicants who satisfy the categorical criteria from qualifying for disability program benefits are income and asset tests.

Means testing is uncommon. An income test applies in the six countries that have adopted the social assistance strategy either in the form of an income disregard limit with an attendant entitlement withdrawal rate (Australia, the Cook Islands, Hong Kong, Nauru and South Africa) or as a statutory maximum income cutout threshold (Denmark). An income test has been attached to social insurance programs in Italy and the Seychelles, both also as statutory maximum income cutout thresholds. An assets test is attached to all social assistance programs except in Denmark.

Primary Social Security Strategy Benefits

Cash Entitlements. Cash entitlements under disability programs take a variety of forms. Earnings-related pensions are provided in 110 countries. Flat-rate pensions are provided by all 12 social assistance and social allowance programs and by 12 countries with social insurance programs (most notably, Ireland, Japan, Luxembourg, the Netherlands, Switzerland and the United Kingdom, as well as the Seychelles). Lump-sum benefits are dispensed by all 19 National Provident Funds, by a few social insurance programs (Taiwan, Lebanon, Vietnam, Yemen) and Zimbabwe, and by an employer liability program (North Korea). These are occasionally made convertible by the National Provident Funds to annuities (4 countries) or periodic payments (5 countries). Pensions that are minimum-wage-related are paid under Mexico's social insurance program, or that are average-wage-related are granted under Israel's social insurance program. Contribution-based entitlements are paid in only Jamaica, although Chile and Peru have adopted the individual capitalization approach.

Cash entitlements typically vary directly with the number of years that contributions have been paid (136 countries). A variation occurs in the 11 African countries that increase cash entitlements by converting the gap between the age at which a disability occurred and retirement age into equivalent years of contribution, at the ratio of 2:1. Considerably less commonly, cash entitlements vary with years of covered employment (Cuba, Norway and Romania) and with the annual average number of weeks of contributions paid (Bermuda and Jamaica).

Entitlement tapering because of the receipt of other income and assets is somewhat less common, but still only marginal, under disability programs, as compared with old-age programs. Non-pension income derived by beneficiaries is taken into consideration under five of the six social assistance programs (the exception being Denmark); under the Seychelles' social insurance program (for partial disability benefits only); and under Iceland's social allowance program (based only on partner's income). Assets acquired by beneficiaries are only considered under the five social assistance programs that taper entitlements.

Specifying limits on cash entitlements is not at all uncommon. Minimum and maximum cash entitlement rates are specified in 77 countries and 51 countries, respectively. Moreover, while minimum earnings rates for the calculation of earnings-related cash entitlements are specified in only 10 countries, maximum earnings rates are specified in 45 countries.

The distribution of maximum income-replacement rates is: under 50 percent (14 countries): 50–85 percent (86 countries); and over 85 percent (8 countries).

Of the 55 countries that provide partial disability benefits, 31 countries provide a uniform rate pension (irrespective of degree of disability), 17 countries provide pro-rata benefits (depending on the degree of disability) and seven countries make lump-sum payments.

Most disability pensions are not regularly adjusted in line with inflation. Of the 66 countries that do make inflation adjustments, 36 do so on an ad hoc basis, with a further 19 countries making annual adjustments and only 11 countries making quarterly or biannual adjustments.

Gratuities and an array of other relatively minor additional cash entitlements are provided in 67 countries.

Those who fail to satisfy the general qualifying criteria attached to social insurance programs most frequently receive a disability lump-sum settlement payment (29 countries), although other modes of settlement payments include: pro-rata pension based on years of coverage (19 countries) or a means-tested allowance (France). It should be noted that the frequency of disability settlements is about half that of old-age settlements.

Supplementary Cash Benefits. These are paid for dependents in a minority of 48 countries. The most frequently paid are child dependent allowances (45 countries, including 10 mostly European countries that only provide such allowances to disabled children) and adult dependent allowances (33 countries), again most common only Europe.

Special Need Benefits. Disabled people with presumed needs are given additional support in many countries. These include a constant attendance allowance for those needing constant care (68 countries) and a disability allowance for those permanently disabled (to varying degrees) (9 countries). Finally, those disabled beneficiaries with disabled children receive additional child allowances in seven countries.

SURVIVORS' PROGRAMS

Primary and Supplementary Strategies Adopted

Social security support for survivors of those who die of general causes is provided in 159 countries. (The countries that have old-age and/or disability programs that do not do so are Afghanistan, Hong Kong, Macau, North Korea, Surinam and Thailand.). An overwhelming 128 countries have adopted social insurance as their primary strategy, while 19 countries use National Provident Funds (the exception being Malaysia). Social allowances have been adopted by five countries (Finland, Iceland, Mauritius, Norway and Sweden) as has social assistance (Australia, Denmark, Nauru, New Zealand and South Africa). The two mavericks are, yet again, Chile and Peru (both with mandated personal pensions). Strategy change has been uncommon. Where it did occur (25 countries), the patterns broadly replicated the pattern with respect to old-age and disability programs. The adoption of a supplementary strategy has been rather more common (39 countries), although less prevalent than for either old-age or disability programs. The pattern of supplementary provision is broadly similar to that for the aged and disabled: to cater to the needy aged who are ineligible for benefits under the primary strategy using social assistance (18 countries); to supplement benefits using social insurance (7 countries) or mandated occupational pensions and savings (5 countries) and/or to extend coverage using social allowances (8 post-socialist countries), employer liability measures (Colombia and Pakistan), social insurance (The Gambia) and a National Provident Fund (Malaysia).

Primary Social Security Strategy Coverage

As with old-age and disability programs, the coverage of most disability programs is restricted to those in employment, the exceptions being the 10 countries that have adopted social allowances and social assistance as their primary strategy.

Employment Coverage. As with old-age and disability programs, coverage in most countries is universal amongst those in paid formal employment, and the patterns of inclusions, exclusions, voluntary access and special systems are essentially the same. Generally included are farm employees (excluded in only 37 countries) and both high- and low-income employees (variously defined) (5 and 11 countries, respectively). Generally excluded are the self-employed (included in only 47 countries). Employment coverage is, moreover, incomplete in some developing countries, with coverage gaps existing on an enterprise-size basis (15 countries), a geographical basis (7 countries), an occupational-group basis (5 countries) and an industry basis (4 countries).

Voluntary coverage is uncommon, and most frequently made available to the self-employed (22 countries) and to employees otherwise ineligible for coverage (20 countries) but also, less commonly, to previously covered employees who leave covered employment (12 countries), farm employees (3 countries) and farmers (4 countries).

Special systems are most common for public employees (82 countries) and for designated occupation groups (36 countries), but also, less commonly, for the self-employed (10 countries), farmers (10 countries), farm employees (7 countries) and employees in designated industries (3 countries).

Primary Social Security Strategy Eligibility

Categorical Criteria. The criteria that define the eligible survivor categories relate to both the deceased and his or her survivors.

Survivors' programs make eligibility contingent upon the deceased at the time of death falling into one of a number of categories, most frequently, pensioners (or persons eligible for a pension) (111 countries) or employees (59 countries). Some countries have very restrictive categorical criteria: the deceased must have been at the time of death a pensioners (Sudan and Nigeria), or an insured person either over the retirement age (Cape Verde and the Seychelles) or below age 72 (Ghana). Survivors' benefits are sometimes payable for a deceased dependent spouse or child of an insured person (Tunisia) or for a missing person (Cyprus).

Survivors' programs have, globally, adopted a complex array of categorical criteria to determine the benefit eligibility of survivors. These criteria reflect the rich diversity of family life-styles and values that go well beyond the archetypal family structure prevalent in those countries that first established survivors' programs, namely:

a pattern of family life in which the married women stayed at home, undertook the household tasks and cared for the children, while the husband and father was the provider, the breadwinner (ILO 1984b: 67).

In most instances, the eligible survivor categories specified in the enabling legislation fall into three groups: surviving spouses, surviving children and other surviving family members, although nomination by the deceased occurs in 21 countries — all countries with National Provident Funds and the social insurance programs in Ghana and Malaysia.

Surviving spouses can, clearly, include both widows and widowers. Widows per se are an eligible survivor category in only 55 countries. In most countries, widows are required to meet one or more additional categorical criteria, namely to be: with dependent children (35 countries); disabled over a specified age (34 countries); above a minimum age of between 30 and 45 (15 countries) or between 50 and 60 (26 countries); of a pensionable age (3 countries); dependent on the deceased (15 countries); able to satisfy a minimum marriage period (12 countries); out of employment (13 countries); of a working age and unable to work more than half-time (Denmark); or incapable of gainful employment (Bahamas). In some countries eligibility is extended to divorcees who have no other income (7 countries), de facto wives (5 countries) and deserted wives (4 countries), as well as multiple widows (9 countries). Widowers per se are an eligible survivor category in only 29 countries. In most countries, widowers are required to meet one or more additional categorical criteria, namely to be: disabled and dependent on the deceased (48 countries); dependent on deceased (24 countries); with dependent children (18 countries); above a minimum age of between 35 and 45 (6 countries) or between 50 and 65 (14 countries); or of a pensionable age (6 countries). Only in 17 countries do widowers not constitute an eligible survivor category.

Orphaned dependent children (variously defined) are a universal eligible survivor category. In 10 countries, however, surviving children of one deceased parent are ineligible. Libya has the distinction of being the only country to make female orphans ineligible. Eligibility is, however, extended to surviving illegitimate children in Chile and to surviving adopted children in Uruguay. The Philippines limits eligibility to the five youngest orphaned children. Dependency upon the deceased is not a categorical requirement in seven post-socialist countries, six of which do not specify an eligibility cut-off age. Indeed, the age at which eligibility ends for a child who is neither disabled nor a student (including an apprentice) varies markedly. The most frequent cut-off age is 16 (73 countries), although many countries specify an age between 17 and 22 (59 countries). The oldest cut-off age is 26 (Kuwait); the youngest is 12 (Morocco). In all, only 16 countries specify cut-off ages below 16. Students continue to qualify beyond the specified cut-off age in 94 countries, of which 79 set an age limit over 18 (up to 28 in Kuwait), with the remaining 15 countries specifying 18 as the cut-off age. Similarly, disabled children continue to qualify in 70 countries, of which 61 set no age limit, seven specify an age limit of between 18 and 21, with even higher cut-off ages applying in Syria (24) and Slovakia (26). Daughters without other means of support also retain or regain their eligibility after the specified cut-off age in 11 countries, of which eight in the Middle Eastern and North Africa set no cut-off age limit, while the remaining three countries specify cut-in ages: Spain and Uruguay (45, and only under specified circumstances) and Costa Rica (55).

Other surviving family members who were dependent on the deceased constitute eligible survivor categories in 69 countries, including dependent parents (69 countries), dependent siblings (38 countries), dependent grandparents (22 countries) and dependent grandchildren (12 countries).

General Qualifying Eligibility Criteria. In all countries, the deceased at the time of death, and perhaps the applicants — the eligible survivors — are required to satisfy one or more general qualifying criteria, typically relating to residency status and to minimum periods of residency and contribution.

All countries require that the deceased was a resident at the time of death. Only Finland specifies a minimum residency period for the deceased (3 years before death if a citizen, otherwise 5 years). Only in Australia are applicants not required to be a resident at the time of death, but they must satisfy a minimum residency period of five continuous years before they are allowed to lodge a survivors' benefit application. A minimum residency period requirement applies to social allowance applicants in Finland (1 year prior to death if a citizen, otherwise 5 years) and in Iceland and Sweden (both 3 years prior to death); to social assistance applicants in New Zealand (3-to-5 years); and to social insurance applicants in the Seychelles (5 years). The only countries that permit recipients to live abroad are Australia, Cyprus, Norway and Portugal.

Of the 147 countries with employment-related survivors' programs, 111 specify that the deceased must have satisfied the minimum contribution period requirement for an old-age cash entitlement. Eighteen countries specify a minimum requirement of between one and five years, with the shortest being the Dominican Republic (only 20 weeks' contributions in the last year); a further six countries specify a minimum requirement of over five years. In Iran and Venezuela the minimum contribution period requirements are waived if death is caused by a general accident. Bulgaria is the only country to specify a minimum employment period requirement (5 years if aged over 25, otherwise 3 years), one which is well below that set for old-age cash entitlements

A maximum payment period — beyond which benefit eligibility ceases — is specified in the Seychelles (1 year).

Means-Assessment Criteria. Means testing is common for survivors' programs. An income test applies in the five countries that have adopted social assistance either as an income disregard threshold with an attendant entitlement withdrawal rate (Australia, Nauru, New Zealand and South Africa). or as a statutory maximum income cutout point (Denmark). Income tests have also been attached to social allowance program in a variety of countries: Norway, as a spouse's income disregard threshold with an attendant entitlement withdrawal rate; Luxembourg, Malta and the Seychelles, as a statutory maximum income cutout point; Jordan, as an entitlement withdrawal rate; and the Marshall Islands, Micronesia and Palau, as an income disregard threshold with an attendant entitlement withdrawal rate. An asset test is attached to all social assistance programs except in Denmark.

Primary Social Security Strategy Benefits

Cash Entitlements. Cash entitlements under survivors' programs are determined quite distinctively in comparison with old-age and disability cash entitlements. Ninety-eight countries relate the survivors' benefits in aggregate to the deceased's benefit or benefit entitlement at the time of death; 71 of these countries permit the entire benefit or entitlement to be distributed amongst the eligible survivors, a further 21 countries distribute between 75 and 99 percent of the benefit or entitlement, while in only six countries is the distributable proportion less than 75 percent (most notably in France (52 percent) and Canada (60 percent)). The distribution of this aggregate benefit amongst eligible beneficiaries is generally determined by the enabling legislation (114 countries), although it can be by nomination by the deceased (21 countries). Lump-sum benefits are dispensed by 27 countries (including all 19 National Provident Funds, and under 8 social insurance programs), although they are occasionally made convertible by the National Provident Funds into annuities (5 countries) or periodic payments (5 countries). Flat-rate pensions are paid to widows or widowers under all 10 social assistance and social allowance programs and by nine countries with social insurance programs (most notably, Ireland, the Netherlands and the United Kingdom) and to orphans (15 countries, 9 of which are in Western Europe). Survivors' cash entitlements linked to the deceased's earnings at the time of death are payable in only 14 countries, nine of which are post socialist, with the most frequently specified maximum income-replacement rates being over 85 percent (9 countries) and the remaining five countries specifying rates of between 50 and 85 percent. Pensions that are average-wage-related are granted under Israel's social insurance program.

Cash entitlements, in contradistinction to those distributed under old-age and disability programs, do not typically vary directly with the number of years that contributions have been paid (occurs in only 18 countries); with the annual average number of weeks of contributions paid (Bermuda, Ireland and Jamaica only); with the surviving spouse's age (Costa Rica, The Gambia, Germany and the United Kingdom only); with the period of widowhood (Finland, Germany, Iceland and Sweden only); with length of marriage (Luxembourg only); or with the deceased's years of residency (Finland only).

Entitlement tapering because of the receipt of other income and assets is somewhat less common, as compared with old-age programs, but quite marginal. Non-pension income derived by beneficiaries is taken into consideration under five of the six social assistance programs, the exception being Denmark; under Norway's social allowance programs (partner's income only); and under social insurance programs in Israel (for widowers only), Jordan, the Marshall Islands, Micronesia and Palau). Assets acquired by beneficiaries are only considered under three social assistance programs (Australia, New Zealand and South Africa).

Specifying limits on cash entitlements is also relatively uncommon. Minimum and maximum cash entitlement rates are specified in only 38 countries and 17 countries, respectively. Minimum and maximum earnings rates for the calculation of earnings-related cash entitlements are similarly uncommon, being specified in only 10 countries and 45 countries, respectively.

Temporary survivors' pensions are granted in 22 countries for a specific maximum period of time — up to five years — after which, except in the Seychelles, the continued receipt of cash benefits depends on satisfying the categorical criteria attached to other benefits available to surviving spouses (namely age, age at widowhood, marital status, child rearing responsibilities, age of children, working capacity and employment status).

As with old-age and disability pensions, most survivors' pensions are not regularly adjusted in line with inflation. Of the 62 countries that do make inflation adjustments, 33 countries do so on an ad hoc basis, a further 19 countries make annual adjustments, and only 10 countries make quarterly or biannual adjustments; but monthly adjustments in Slovenia.

Additional benefits are commonly provided: funeral grants (71 countries), gratuities and an array of other relatively minor additional cash entitlements (50 countries), death grants (22 countries) and remarriage grants (6 countries).

Those who fail to satisfy the general qualifying criteria attached to social insurance programs most frequently receive a survivors' lump-sum settlement payment (41 countries) or, less commonly, a pro-rata pension based on the deceased's years of coverage (6 countries). It should be noted that survivors' settlements are about the same frequency as disability settlements, both of which are about half that of old-age settlements.

Supplementary Cash Benefits. These are paid for dependents other than widows or widowers in 84 countries. The most frequently paid is a full (or double) orphan's allowance (80 countries), while eight countries also provide children's allowances separate from any entitlements under child allowance programs.

Special Need Benefits. Disabled orphans receive additional allowances in six countries

CONCLUSION

Long-term social security contingencies have been addressed in most countries by the adoption of the social insurance strategy. There is a high degree of program stability and design feature commonality amongst countries adopting the same social security strategy. Systemic change has not been common, although that which has occurred has been dominated by the conversion of National Provident Funds into social insurance programs.

The cross-fertilization of strategies has also not been common. Neither the income testing of social insurance programs nor the provision of flat-rate benefits by social insurance programs happens to any great extent. The Seychelles in this context, however, offers a distinctive model for Third World countries to explore.

Few instances of innovative, or even distinctive, practices can be identified. Mandated personal and occupational pension and savings programs have achieved barely a global toe-hold, so they remain very much the exception. The Chilean model has not yet taken the social security world by storm, but it does loom large. Social assistance is typically cast in the role of providing a safety net for those who miss or fall through the employment-based social security net and has thus not achieved popularity as a primary strategy outside a few countries. The Australian model, however, is worthy of greater scrutiny by those countries seeking to improve their income or means target efficiency. Social allowances remain the domain of the rich few, with the conspicuous exception of Mauritius, although the Scandinavian model is under threat at home.

Long-term social security programs mostly cater to the needs of those in paid employment by providing most benefits to those able to remain in covered employment for most of their working lives. To those protected they offer a potential respite from poverty; to most people in most countries, however, they are, unfortunately, merely an irrelevancy.

6

Unemployment, Sickness, Maternity and Health Care

INTRODUCTION

Although each of the contingencies of sickness, maternity and unemployment is distinctive, what they do have in common is that they cause a short-term interruption to the flow of earned income. The social security needs that these contingencies create were, throughout the nineteenth century, dealt with in Europe by means of mutual aid and co-operative societies. In the United Kingdom, for example, these institutions had developed, by the 1840s, to the point where "a central government authority had been established to register them and to supervise their activities" (Midgley 1984a: 95). By the turn of the century they had some six million members (Midgley 1984a: 95). Similarly, trade unions were providing their members with unemployment relief in many parts of Europe (ILO 1984b: 83–4). In the United Kingdom such relief was, according to Kaim-Caudle (1973: 205), "on a substantial scale." These voluntary insurance initiatives were the European precursor to the social security legislation initially enacted in the 1880s.

Social security protection in the face of short-term contingencies has its origins in Bismarckian Germany, where the first sickness insurance program was established in 1883. The idea quickly spread to Austria and Czechoslovakia (1888). During the early 1890s such programs had been established in Sweden and Hungary (1891), Denmark (1892) and Belgium (1894). By the outbreak of the First World War, 16 countries — all European except for Armenia (1912) — had adopted sickness and/or maternity programs, while the first countries to establish an unemployment program were France (1905), followed by Norway (1906), Denmark (1907) and the United Kingdom and Ireland (1911).

From this modest beginning, sickness and maternity programs steadily expanded their global coverage, generally in tandem with one another. Italy, however, is an early conspicuous exception, for it established its maternity program in 1912, some 31 years before it introduced a general sickness program in 1943.

By 1945, 67 countries had set up sickness and/or maternity programs, almost double the number that had established unemployment programs (35 countries). Most of these countries were mainly in Europe, North America and Australasia, although a foot-hold was established in Latin America — Brazil (1923) and Chile ((1924) — and toe-holds in Asia — Armenia (1912) and Kyrgyzstan (as part of the Soviet Union) (1922) — and, towards the end of the period, in Africa — South Africa (1937).

It was also during the interwar years that the social assistance strategy came into play, first in New Zealand for its unemployment program (1930) and then for its sickness program (1938), soon followed by Australia (1944, both programs).

The post-Second World War years saw a somewhat slower expansion of sickness and maternity programs (an additional 62 countries) but a faster expansion of unemployment programs (an additional 45 countries). Interestingly, some West European countries were slow to introduce sickness and maternity programs (most notably Finland (1963) with its long tradition of voluntarism). By 1995, 129 countries had sickness programs, marginally less than the 135 countries that had maternity programs, but considerably more than the 80 countries that had unemployment programs.

While most countries that have maternity programs also have sickness programs, nine countries only have maternity programs (6 of which are in Africa) and three countries only have sickness programs (Saudi Arabia (1969), Kiribati (1976) and Nauru (1956)).

UNEMPLOYMENT PROGRAMS

Primary and Supplementary Strategies Adopted

Most of the 80 countries with unemployment programs have adopted social insurance as their primary strategy (51 countries), followed by employer liability measures (12 countries), social assistance (Australia, Brazil, Finland, Hong Kong, Mauritius, New Zealand, Sri Lanka and Tunisia), social allowances (Chile, Estonia, Luxembourg, Slovakia and Sweden), National Provident Funds (Nepal and Zambia) and mandated personal savings (Colombia and Guatemala). Strategy change has been rare.

The strategy changes that have occurred have involved the replacement either by social insurance of social allowances (Sweden and Luxembourg) or of social assistance (Finland); or by employer liability measures of social insurance (Venezuela), of social assistance (Brazil), or of mandated personal savings (Colombia). The adoption of supplementary social security strategies, however, has been rather more common.

The adoption of supplementary social security strategies has occurred in 22 countries. This has involved the use of social assistance to support those in need who fall through the primary social security net (11 countries, 8 of which are in

Western Europe). Some countries supplement unemployment benefits by requiring employers to provide separation or severance pay (Argentina (construction industry only), Brazil, Colombia and Venezuela), although the same outcome has been achieved by means of voluntary unemployment insurance (Finland), social insurance prepensions (Mexico) or National Provident Fund account interim withdrawals (Tanzania and India). Using a supplementary strategy to extend coverage only occurs in a few countries, by means of voluntary unemployment insurance (Sweden), an initial employer-provided three-month earnings-related job search allowance (Russia) and an employer-provided three-month severance pay (the Ukraine).

Primary Social Security Strategy Coverage

The coverage of unemployment programs in all countries is available to all or most of those in paid formal employment, although coverage is extended by some countries to all residents of working age (variously defined but typically 16 years to the minimum age for old-age program eligibility) (21 countries, including 15 post-socialist countries). Interestingly, this broader coverage does not apply to social assistance programs in Brazil, Finland, Sri Lanka and Tunisia, for all restrict coverage to those in employment.

Employment Coverage. Covered employees, generally, include farm employees (excluded in only 13 countries, most notably in the Middle East and, to a lesser degree, Asia). Earnings are generally not considered a barrier to coverage. High-income employees are excluded in only South Africa, while low-income employees (variously defined) are excluded in Austria, Canada and the United Kingdom. Covered employees, however, generally exclude the self-employed (except in Denmark and farmers (except in Australia, New Zealand, and Mauritius. Employment coverage is, however, incomplete in some developing countries, with coverage gaps existing on an industry basis (Bangladesh, China, Nepal and Uruguay), an occupational-group basis (China, Macau and Nepal), an enterprise-size basis (Pakistan) and a geographical basis (Iran).

Voluntary coverage is rare: it occurs in only Japan (for employees in agriculture, forestry and fisheries) and Nepal (for employees in organizations with 10 or more employees).

Special systems for particular population categories are a little more common: for employees in designated industries (Austria, Belgium, Spain and the United States), for employees in designated occupations (France, Greece and Japan) and for farm employees (China and Spain).

Primary Social Security Strategy Eligibility

Categorical Criteria. The categorical criteria that determine the categories into which applicants must fit to gain unemployment benefits are being of working age but without gainful employment, and define three eligible unemployed categories: those suffering a loss of employment (all countries), those seeking their first job (22 countries) and those seeking to re-enter the workforce (15 countries).

General Qualifying Eligibility Criteria. A variety of general qualifying criteria is attached to unemployment programs in all countries, the most stringent being attached to the 63 unemployment insurance, unemployment assistance and unemployment allowance programs. These criteria typically relate to the cause of unemployment; to the willingness to seek work and to work; to minimum periods of employment, contribution, residency and unemployment; and to maximum payment periods.

Unemployment program eligibility in all countries requires that the causes of the job loss be beyond the control of the unemployed person. Thus, voluntarily leaving a job disqualifies a person from unemployment program eligibility in 36 countries — including all 12 employer liability programs — and incurs a waiting period penalty in a further 13 countries. Similarly, some countries disqualify an unemployed person if he or she loses a job because he or she was either "discharged for misconduct" (18 countries, largely in Western Europe (6 countries) and post-socialist Eastern Europe or central Asia (5 countries) or engaged "in a labor dispute" (8 countries, 5 of which are in Western Europe). A waiting period penalty is incurred under these circumstances in a further 13 and 10 countries respectively, again largely in Europe.

That an unemployed person must be available for, and willing to seek, work is another general qualifying criterion applied in most countries. Registering as an unemployed person with an appropriate administrative agency, involving regular, periodic reporting, are requirements in 52 countries. Disqualification can also occur because an unemployed person refuses either to take "suitable" work (14 countries, largely in Western Europe) or "any" work (in 9 post-socialist countries). Alternatively, a waiting period penalty is incurred if a person refuses "suitable" work (11 countries) or if a person refuses "any" work (3 countries), again largely in Europe. Refusing training, in some instances, also results in either disqualification (in 9 countries, 6 of which are post-socialist) or an extended waiting period (in 11 countries, again, largely in Europe).

Minimum unemployment or waiting period requirements are sometimes specified (25 countries). The most frequently prescribed period is three-to-eight days (16 countries), with the remainder setting a longer period (in New Zealand, benefits can be withheld for up to 10 weeks, depending on previous earnings). During this waiting period only Russia and the Ukraine provide cash unemployment entitlements under supplementary social security strategies.

Maximum payment periods for unemployment entitlements are specified in 57 countries: 12 weeks and under (4 countries), 13–26 weeks (22 countries), 27–39 weeks (6 countries), 40–52 (13 countries) and over 52 weeks (12 countries). The maximum payment period is extendible in 25 countries on a discretionary basis (as in South Africa), if designated contribution period requirements are met; or according to the age of the unemployed person (Italy). No maximum payment period is attached to unemployment assistance programs in Australia, Finland, Hong Kong and New Zealand or to unemployment insurance programs in Ireland (which provides a flat-rate entitlement) and Latvia (which provides an entitlement related to minimum earnings). Some countries specify maximum payment periods for first job seekers (12 countries, 10 of which designate 26 weeks) and/or for those reentering the workforce (9 countries, 7 of which designate 26 weeks).

Minimum contribution periods are also commonly specified (28 countries): typically, a year or less (23 countries), occasionally longer (5 countries), up to three years (Tunisia).

Minimum employment period requirements are specified in 20 countries, most frequently set at under six months (11 countries), sometimes longer (9 countries), and up to four years (Hungary). Employment with the same employer is required for a minimum period in Tanzania (3 months), Jordan (6 months) and Botswana (60 months).

Minimum residency period requirement of one year is attached to unemployment assistance programs in Hong Kong and New Zealand.

Minimum earnings requirements are specified in Norway and the United States (most states).

To be eligible for unemployment benefits in Mauritius and Tunisia the unemployed person must have dependents, while in Iceland he or she must be a trade union member.

Means-Assessment Criteria. The imposition of income tests applies not only to the seven countries with unemployment assistance programs, but also to unemployment insurance programs in six post-socialist countries and in Uruguay (for designated forms of income only). Asset tests have been attached to all unemployment assistance programs except in New Zealand.

Primary Social Security Strategy Benefits

Cash Entitlements. Cash entitlements under unemployment programs take three forms. Earnings-related entitlements are the most common (43 countries), typically under unemployment insurance programs, but also under Brazil's unemployment assistance program, Luxembourg's and Slovakia's social allowance programs, and Bangladesh's employer-liability program. Flat-rate entitlements are paid not only under most unemployment assistance and allowance programs (8 countries), but also under some unemployment insurance programs (9 countries, most notably in Iceland, Ireland and the United Kingdom). Lump-sum entitlements are the dominant payment mode under employer liability programs, under the National Provident Funds and under mandated personal savings programs (in total, 16 countries). It also the practice under Ecuador's unemployment insurance program. Relating entitlements to average wages occurs under

Poland's unemployment insurance program; and relating them to minimum wages occurs under Latvia's unemployment insurance program and under Tunisia's unemployment assistance program.

The distribution of maximum income-replacement rates is: under 50 percent (Austria (40–50 percent according to 120 wage categories), Greece (40 percent for wage earners and 50 percent for salary earners), South Africa (45 percent) and Italy (20 percent)); 50–75 percent (37 countries); and over 75 percent (Denmark (90 percent) and Luxembourg (80 percent)).

Unemployment insurance entitlements sometimes vary inversely with the period of unemployment (13, overwhelmingly, European countries) and the age of unemployed (6 countries) and directly with the period of employment (6 predominantly European countries) or years of contributions paid (5 countries).

Employer-provided lump-sum termination indemnity is usually directly related to the length of service (17 countries).

Entitlement tapering because of the receipt of assets and/or non-pension income is distinctly uncommon. Both assets and income are considered under unemployment assistance programs in Australia and Hong Kong, but only income is considered in New Zealand) and under Luxembourg's unemployment insurance program (cohabitant's income only).

Specifying limits on cash entitlements is considerably more common. Maximum and minimum cash entitlement rates are specified in 30 countries and 22 countries, respectively. Moreover, maximum earnings rates for benefit calculation purposes apply in 11 countries (7 of which are in Western Europe). No country specifies a minimum earnings rate for benefit calculation purposes.

First-time job seekers receive flat-rate entitlements in 21 countries (of which 7 are post-socialist and 6 are in Western Europe) and a flat-rate grant in Estonia.

Those seeking to reenter the workforce receive flat-rate entitlements in 16, mostly post-socialist, countries.

The partially unemployed receive proportional wage supplements in Bulgaria, Italy, Spain and Switzerland.

Prepensions are paid to the older unemployed within an age range just below the eligible age for old-age program entitlements (variously defined) in six European countries. These prepensions are paid at a rate higher than the old-age entitlement in Austria and Belgium and at a lower rate in Denmark.

Training allowances are paid under unemployment programs in nine countries.

Cost of living adjustment mechanisms apply in only four countries, three of which are post socialist.

Gratuities and an array of other relatively minor additional cash entitlements are provided in 17 countries.

Supplementary Cash Benefits. These are paid for dependents in 27 countries as dependent spouse allowances (17 countries, of which 10 are in Europe) and child dependent allowances (24 countries, of which 16 are in Europe). Only the

United Kingdom and the Ukraine income test their supplementary cash benefits. *Special Need Benefits*. Additional support is given to those who choose to relocate geographically to gain employment in Australia, Austria, Japan and Norway. Remote area and rental assistance supplements are also provided in Australia.

SICKNESS PROGRAMS

Primary and Supplementary Strategies Adopted

Of the 129 countries that have sickness programs, most have adopted social insurance (93 countries), the rest have largely chosen the employer liability measures (30 countries, of which 22 are in Africa. The only countries to adopt social assistance are Australia, New Zealand and Nauru. Only Denmark and Iceland have chosen social allowances. Kiribati uses its National Provident Fund to provide sickness benefits. Changes in strategy have been very rare.

Perhaps the most innovative strategy changes have occurred in Chile (1981) and Peru (1991), where public and private systems coexist to give a choice. The only other strategy changes made have involved the replacement by social allowances of social insurance (Denmark and Iceland), by social insurance of employer liability measures (Afghanistan and China), and by social insurance of a National Provident Fund (Iraq).

The adoption of supplementary social security strategies, however, has been rather more common, having occurred in 29 countries. This has predominantly involved the use of employer liability measures to extend coverage by requiring employers to provide employee sickness benefits during the waiting period before the primary strategy comes into effect (23 countries), although this has also been achieved by the use of social insurance in Libya (by providing long-term sickness benefits after eligibility for employer-provided benefits ceases) and the United Kingdom (by extending coverage to those who entirely miss the employer-liability net). Social assistance also acts as the safety net for those ineligible for a primary benefit (Bahamas, Hong Kong and Trinidad and Tobago). Using a supplementary strategy to augment the primary strategy benefits does occur to a very limited extent. Employers are occasionally required to pay sick employees directly the difference between their cash sickness insurance entitlements and their earnings (Cape Verde (from the 4th to 19th day of sickness), Greece (during the initial month of sickness) and the Seychelles (for the initial 2 months of sickness)).

Primary Social Security Strategy Coverage

The coverage of sickness programs in all countries is available to all or most of those in paid formal employment, although coverage is sometimes extended to those not in employment, namely, to the unemployed (18 countries, of which

8 are in Europe and 6 are in Asia) and to students (10 countries, of which 9 are post-socialist and the other being Finland).

Employment Coverage. Covered employees, generally, include farm employees (excluded in only 18 countries, most notably in the Middle East and, to a lesser degree, Asia). Earnings are generally not considered a barrier to coverage. High-income employees (variously defined) are generally included (excluded in only 7 countries), as are low-income employees (variously defined) (excluded in only 6 countries). Covered employees, however, generally exclude the self-employed (included in only 33 countries, most conspicuously in Europe and Latin America) and farmers (included in only 9 countries, a majority of which are in Eastern Europe). Employment coverage is, however, incomplete in some developing countries, with coverage gaps existing on an enterprise-size basis (8 countries), a geographical basis (8 countries), an industry basis (6 countries) and an occupational-group basis (3 countries).

Voluntary coverage is not commonly available. Where voluntary access is granted, however, it is given to employees otherwise ineligible for coverage (10 countries), to the self-employed (7 countries), to previously covered employees (4 countries), to farmers (Nicaragua) and to housewives (Peru).

Special systems for particular population categories are rather more common. They exist in some countries for public employees (26 countries), employees in designated industries (14 countries) and occupational groups (13 countries) and farm employees (6 countries); and for farmers (6 countries), the self-employed (4 countries), the unemployed (Norway (for the temporarily unemployed only) and the Dominican Republic (contingent upon previous contribution record)), and students (Brazil).

Primary Social Security Strategy Eligibility

Categorical Criteria. The categorical criterion attached to sickness programs is the existence of a medical condition that is not attributable to employment and that renders covered individuals temporarily but totally incapable of engaging in their usual gainful activity. This requires the certification by a medical practitioner not only of the nature of the incapacitating medical condition but also of the medical need for the sufferer to be absent from his or her usual gainful activity.

General Qualifying Eligibility Criteria. General qualifying criteria are attached to sickness programs in most countries but the requirements are generally quite modest and relate to minimum periods of sickness, contribution, employment and residency; as well as to maximum payment periods.

Maximum payment periods for sickness entitlements are specified in 100 countries: under one month (21 countries), one-to-six months (38 countries), six months to a year (4 countries), one-to-two years (33 countries) and over two years (Algeria (3 years), Cape Verde (3 years) and Portugal (1,095 days)). Some countries permit their statutory maximum payment periods to be extended on medical grounds (32 countries). Argentina doubles the maximum payment period if sickness beneficiaries have dependents. Libya extends the period over which sickness entitlements are paid by transferring those certified to be suffering from a long-term illness to a long-term sickness insurance program after their eligibility for employer-provided benefits ceases. Portugal automatically converts sickness beneficiaries into disability pensioners when their eligibility ceases. Vietnam extends its maximum payment period if an illness requiring approved hospitalization occurs. Both Argentina and Vietnam grant longer payment periods if minimum contribution requirements are met.

Minimum sickness period requirements are also frequently specified (71 countries). The most frequently prescribed period is one-to-five days (48 countries), with the remainder (25 countries) setting a longer period (up to 10 weeks in Austria for wage earners and 12 weeks for salary earners). During this waiting period cash sickness entitlements are sometimes be provided under supplementary social security strategies (23 countries, including Austria). In Iceland, uniquely, the social allowance payment waiting period is 15 days, without any form of statutory gap coverage, and even then it is paid only if the incapacity has lasted at least 21 days and if income from voluntary gap coverage has lapsed. The Philippines waives its minimum sickness period requirement if the medical condition results from an acute disease or injury.

Minimum contribution periods are also quite widely specified (59 countries): generally, one-to-six months (50 countries), although some countries specify a longer period (six months to a year (7 countries)), while a shorter period is specified in France (200 hours of paid employment in the last month) and Norway (14 days). This requirement is occasionally waived if the medical condition is caused by an accident (Guinea, Morocco and Peru) or if it is an infectious disease (Guinea).

Minimum employment period requirements are specified under the employer liability programs adopted in Hong Kong (1 month continuous), the United States (up to 20 weeks and/or minimum level of insured wages, depending on state) and Singapore (1 year).

Minimum residency period requirements of up to one year apply under sickness assistance and allowance programs in Denmark, Iceland, Nauru and New Zealand, as well as under Taiwan's sickness insurance program.

Residency at the time of application is a universal requirement.

Means-Assessment Criteria. All three social assistance programs in Australia, New Zealand and Nauru specify income and asset tests, with Nauru additionally specifying that married working women qualify only if they are not receiving support from their husbands.

Primary Social Security Strategy Benefits

Cash Entitlements. Cash entitlements under sickness programs take three
forms: earnings-related benefits (118 countries), flat-rate benefits (10 countries,
including all 5 social assistance and social allowance programs and under social
insurance programs in India, Ireland, Malta, the Seychelles and Switzerland), and
lump-sum benefits (Kiribati). Only in India do the flat-rate entitlements vary
(directly) with wage class.

The distribution of maximum income-replacement rates is: under 50 percent
(South Africa (45 percent)); 50–75 percent (63 countries); and over 75 percent
(54 countries, including full restitution in 21 countries, of which 14 are in Africa).

Earning-related cash entitlements sometimes vary with the number of years
of contributions paid (17 mostly post socialist countries), the period of sickness
(17 predominantly European countries) and/or the years of covered employment
(only Argentina and Vietnam).

Entitlement tapering because of the receipt of other assets and/or non-benefit
income is distinctly uncommon, occurring in only Australia (for both assets and
income) and in New Zealand (for income only).

In Sweden sickness benefits are taxable.

Specifying limits on cash entitlement is far more common. Maximum and
minimum cash entitlement rates are specified in 20 and 16 countries, respectively. Moreover, while minimum earnings rates for the calculation of earnings-
related cash entitlements are specified in only eight countries, maximum earnings rates are specified in 23 countries.

The flat-rate sickness entitlements are adjusted in line with inflation only in
Australia (on a biannual basis).

Gratuities are provided in Albania, Australia, Brazil and Iceland.

Supplementary Cash Benefits. These are paid with respect to dependents in a
very few countries: spouse's allowances (9 countries, largely in Western Europe
and Australasia, but also Iran and the Seychelles) and child dependent allowance
(8 countries, again largely in Western Europe as well as New Zealand and the
Seychelles).

Special Need Benefits. Additional support is given to sufferers of chronic or
designated illnesses (10 countries), to those forced to change their employment
(income compensation) (Albania), and to those in remote areas (Australia).

MATERNITY PROGRAMS

Primary and Supplementary Strategies Adopted

Most of the 135 countries with maternity programs have adopted the social
insurance strategy (108 countries), while rest have chosen, most commonly,
employer liability measures (24 countries, mainly in Africa and Asia), with
Denmark and Iceland opting for social allowances and New Zealand preferring

social assistance. A change of social security strategy has, as with sickness programs, been rare.

Chile (1981) and Peru (1991), innovatively, decided that public and private systems should coexist to give a choice. The only other changes mirrored those that occurred to sickness programs: the transformation of employer liability measures into social insurance (Afghanistan and China), of social insurance into social allowances (Denmark and Iceland) and of a National Provident Fund into social insurance (Iraq). The adoption of supplementary social security strategies, however, has been rather less common than for the sickness contingency.

The adoption of supplementary social security strategies has occurred in only 21 countries. This has involved the use of supplementary strategies to augment benefits (11 countries) either by requiring employers to pay pregnant employees directly the difference between their cash maternity insurance entitlements and their earnings (10 countries, of which 9 are in Africa) or by permitting interim withdrawals from National Provident Fund accounts (Zambia). Alternatively, coverage extension by means of a supplementary strategy has also been adopted (9 countries). This has been achieved by requiring employers to pay maternity benefits to pregnant employees who are ineligible for maternity insurance benefits (Honduras, India and Madagascar) or who must satisfy a waiting period before the primary strategy comes into effect (Lebanon). A few countries have extended coverage either by means of a supplementary social insurance program for employees who are ineligible for employer-provided maternity leave (Malta and the United Kingdom) or who belong to specific ineligible population categories — the self-employed (Libya) or domestic workers (Jamaica), or by means of a social assistance program for those with limited working capacity (Hong Kong) or the indigent (Trinidad and Tobago).

Primary Social Security Strategy Coverage

The coverage of maternity programs in all countries except New Zealand includes all or most females in paid formal employment. New Zealand restricts the coverage of its maternity assistance program to single women. Thirteen countries, however, have extended coverage to one or more additional female population categories, namely: female students (10 countries, of which 9 are post-socialist, the other being Finland), female unemployed (Belarus, the Ukraine and Uruguay), covered employees' wives (Côte d'Ivoire and Uruguay), female employees leaving employment who were covered during the last year (Japan) and all female residents outside the workforce (Iceland).

Employment Coverage. Covered female employees, generally, include farm employees (excluded in only 18 countries, mainly in the Middle East and, to a lesser degree, Asia). Earnings are generally not considered a barrier to coverage. High-income employees (variously defined) are excluded in only five countries (Dominican Republic (applies to only white-collar workers), Germany (applies to only the self-employed), India, Pakistan and South Africa), while low-income employees (variously defined) are excluded in only four countries (Austria, Guyana, Norway and the United Kingdom). Covered employees, however, generally exclude the self-employed (for they are included in only 30 countries, most conspicuously in Europe and Latin America) and farmers (included in only 6 countries, a majority of which are in Eastern Europe). Employment coverage is, however, incomplete in some developing countries, with coverage gaps existing on an industry basis (8 countries), a geographical basis (8 countries), an enterprise-size basis (6 countries) and an occupational-group basis (3 countries).

Voluntary coverage is not commonly available. Where voluntary access is granted, however, it is given to employees otherwise ineligible for coverage (9 countries), to the self-employed (6 countries), to previously covered employees (5 countries) and to farmers (Nicaragua (ranchers only)).

Special systems for particular population categories are rather more common. They exist in some countries for public employees (26 countries), designated occupational groups (16 countries), farm employees (6 countries), farmers (6 countries), the self-employed (4 countries) and employees in designated industries (the United States).

Primary Social Security Strategy Eligibility

Categorical Criteria. The categorical criteria that define the eligible categories under maternity programs relate to pregnancy, as certified by a medical practitioner, and to the designated person responsible for post-natal child care. The eligible population categories are pregnant female employees (133 countries); fathers, but in only the event of the mother dying during or immediately after child birth (9 countries); pregnant single women (Czech Republic, New Zealand, Norway and Poland); grandparents, but only with the mother's agreement (Bulgaria); and pregnant female residents (Iceland). Some countries have extended their eligible categories to include: persons adopting a child (9 countries, including Finland, France, Luxembourg and Norway), to women who miscarry (Brazil and Vietnam) and to women aborting a pregnancy (China).

General Qualifying Eligibility Criteria. General qualifying criteria are attached to maternity programs in most countries but the requirements are generally modest and relate to minimum periods of contribution, employment and residency before the commencement of pregnancy; and to the maximum number of confinements and to minimum age.

Minimum contribution periods are also quite commonly specified (62 countries): one-to-six months (36 countries) or six months to a year (25 countries), while Algeria requires, alternatively, nine days' or 60 hours' contributions in the last three months, or 36 days' contributions in the last 12 months.

Minimum employment period requirements before commencement of pregnancy are rather less common: three months or less (6 countries), four-to-six months (10 countries), six months to a year (4 countries).

Minimum residency period requirements of up to one year apply in all countries that have adopted social assistance and social allowance as their primary social security strategy.

A minimum age of 16 years is specified in New Zealand.

A maximum number of confinements applies in three countries: Singapore and Thailand (2) and Hong Kong (3).

Means-Assessment Criteria. New Zealand's maternity assistance program specifies an income test, as does Japan's maternity insurance program.

Primary Social Security Strategy Benefits

Cash Entitlements. Cash entitlements under maternity programs overwhelmingly take the form of earnings-related benefits (131 countries), although flat-rate benefits are paid (Iceland, New Zealand and Switzerland) as are lump-sum benefits (Taiwan).

The duration of paid maternity leave taken before and after confinement extends from 30 working days (Cape Verde, Rwanda and Tunisia) to 450 working days in Sweden. The most frequently specified leave period is between 12 and 15 weeks (69 countries), although longer leave periods are provided (49 countries, mainly post-socialist (20 countries) and West European (15 countries)), as are, less commonly, shorter leave periods (17 countries, mostly in Africa (9 countries) and the Middle East (3 countries)). Maternity leave extensions are commonly granted on medical grounds (40 countries, most conspicuously in Africa and post-socialist Central Asia) but also if there are multiple births (19 countries) or if employment is in a hazardous or arduous occupation (Vietnam). Extending pre-natal leave by the provision of sick leave occurs in Sweden when pregnant female employees in physically demanding work are unable to be given less demanding work by their employers. The extending of post-natal leave by the provision of an additional period of child-raising leave occurs in 17 countries. This leave can be taken by either partner in Finland and Italy, and can be taken at any time during the child's first four years of life in Iraq. Only in Sri Lanka is the maternity leave period halved for third and subsequent confinements.

Some countries permit shorter periods of paid leave after an adoption (8 countries), a miscarriage (3 countries) or an abortion (China).

Unpaid leave is an option in Armenia, where it can be taken on a full- or part-time basis and by either parent, grandparents or other relatives.

The distribution of maximum income-replacement rates is: under 50 percent (Botswana (25 percent) and South Africa (45 percent)); 50–75 percent (47 countries); and over 75 percent (82 countries, including full restitution in 61 countries).

Entitlement tapering because of the receipt of non-benefit income is distinctly uncommon, applying only under New Zealand's maternity assistance program and under Japan's maternity insurance program. In both cases the receipt of earned income or cash sickness benefits results in a reduction in entitlements or even their discontinuation.

In Sweden maternity benefits are taxable.

Specifying limits on earnings-related cash entitlements is far from common. Minimum cash entitlement rates are specified in only 10 countries, while nine countries specify a maximum rate. Moreover, while minimum earnings rates for the calculation of earnings-related cash entitlements are specified in only eight countries, maximum earnings rates are specified in 22 countries.

Additional benefits are commonly provided. Lump-sum entitlements are paid in some countries: birth grants (34 countries), maternity grants (24 countries), pre-natal grants (17 countries), funeral grants (St Kitts and Nevis and Grenada), adoption grants (Norway) and multiple-birth grants (Israel). Also, Albania pays compensation in the event of employment changes due to pregnancy. In-kind benefits are also provided in a few countries, such as free milk (Bolivia, El Salvador, France and Nicaragua) and layettes (Mexico).

In three countries, those who fail to satisfy the general qualifying criteria attached to social insurance programs receive a maternity lump-sum settlement payment (Norway and Barbados) or a flat-rate allowance for 12 months based on the minimum wage (Slovenia).

Supplementary Cash Benefits. These are paid with respect to dependents in only Greece, where the income-replacement rate is increased by 10 percent for each dependent.

Special Need Benefits. Additional cash entitlements are given to nursing mothers for varying periods of time (7 countries) and to working pregnant mothers or working fathers-to-be, subject to the satisfaction of an employment test, for six months (Iceland).

HEALTHCARE BENEFIT PROGRAMS

Introduction

As health status is a defining characteristic of employment injury, sickness, maternity and disability, and as healthcare is a prominent issue at either end of the dependency age spectrum — the very young and the very old — access to healthcare by social security recipients and their dependents and survivors' is clearly an integral part of their support provision. Indeed, the connection between ill-health and poverty is an intimate one.

The alleviation or prevention of poverty requires a social security system to provide a safety net that at least maintains adequate nutrition and good health. The restoration, improvement or, at the very least, maintenance of the health status of those protected by social security systems is thus an important subsidiary social security objective, one that is acknowledged in the ILO's conventions on minimum social security standards (ILO 1952a and 1969). To what extent and how this objective is achieved does, of course, vary considerably.

Primary and Supplementary Healthcare Strategies Adopted

A majority of countries do not have integrated health and social security systems. The most frequently adopted primary healthcare strategy is the publicly funded national health service, whereby health services (variously defined) are provided to the general community by health professionals who are under contract to the state or who are employed by either public or private hospitals that are under contract to the state. This strategy occurs in 86 countries. A further 11 countries — Albania, Australia, Bermuda, Canada, Kenya, Japan, Russia, Senegal, South Korea, Slovakia and Taiwan — have chosen the health insurance strategy, whereby the payment of designated health insurance contributions to a public, or state-mandated, agency by the individual and perhaps his or her employer, entitles the insured person to specific medical and hospital services or to healthcare cost reimbursements. Under these strategies access to health services is neither restricted to, nor determined by, social security program eligibility, and health services funding is not linked to social security program funding.

In a large minority of countries healthcare benefits are incorporated specifically into social security programs. The direct or indirect provision of healthcare benefits is part of one or more employment-based social security programs in 75 countries. To a very great extent, this has meant the provision of healthcare benefits under social insurance programs (66 countries), although employers are occasionally obligated to provide medical care as part of their statutory responsibility for sickness benefit provision (8 countries, 7 of which are in Africa, the other being China). Singapore permits its National Provident Fund members to make interim withdrawals from their accounts to cover medical and hospital costs. Filling the gaps in coverage under these employment-related programs occurs in all countries by means of one or more supplementary healthcare strategies.

The supplementary healthcare strategy most commonly adopted is the provision of health services to uncovered social security recipients and their dependents under a public health service (72 countries), although this may mean only access to limited maternity and child health services program (12 African countries). In some countries, health services supplementation is by means of mandatory employer-provided medical services (18 countries, 14 of which are in Africa, with the balance in Asia).

Healthcare benefits are provided under employment-injury programs independently of the primary healthcare strategy in 58 countries. This came about either because of the fragmentation of healthcare provision (17 countries) or because of the desire to avoid the transfer of employment injury-related healthcare costs either to publicly funded national health services (34 countries) or to national health insurance programs (7 countries).

Primary Healthcare Strategy Coverage

At least some social security recipients — most conspicuously, sickness, maternity and employment-injury recipients — are covered under primary health-care strategies in all countries.

In 97 countries there are universal healthcare benefit programs under which social security recipients and their dependents have access to health services, subject to the their availability, which is an important constraint in developing countries. These programs mainly take the form of national health services (86 countries), national health insurance programs (8 countries, with Kenya, Senegal and Slovakia restricting their health insurance program coverage to employees) and universal healthcare provision under sickness insurance programs (Finland, Israel and Norway). Universal public health services operate in all countries in Australasia, Central Asia and the Pacific Islands. They are, moreover, dominant in East Asia, East Africa, Eastern Europe and the Caribbean.

In the 75 countries with employment-based primary healthcare strategies coverage is extended to designated categories of social security recipients and their dependents and survivors. This practice is dominant in North, West and Central Africa, South-East Asia, and Central and South America. Coverage is extended to recipients of benefits under temporary and permanent employment-injury programs (64 countries), sickness programs (54 countries), maternity programs (48 countries), disability programs (31 countries), old-age programs (30 countries), survivors' programs (27 countries) and unemployment programs (Honduras and Mexico) (if aged between 60 and 64); to spouses of covered employees in the event of maternity (51 countries) or sickness (45 countries); to spouses of recipients under old-age programs (28 countries), survivors' programs (27 countries), disability programs (27 countries) and employment-injury programs (Algeria, provided the incapacity is at least 50 percent); to dependent children of covered employees in the event of sickness (46 countries); to dependents of recipients under old-age programs (27 countries), survivors' programs (25 countries) and disability programs (26 countries); and, rarely, to other dependents (Iran (dependent aged parents), Panama (dependent mother and disabled father aged 60 years or over), Paraguay (dependent parents aged 60 and over) and Tunisia (aged parents)).

Healthcare Strategy Eligibility

The eligibility criteria attached to primary healthcare strategies depend on the nature of those strategies. Countries with national health services all require beneficiaries to be residents and, generally, to satisfy a minimum residency period requirement, as well as, in a few instances, an income test (Burundi, Surinam, Trinidad and Tobago, and Zimbabwe). National health insurance programs contain residency requirements and, perhaps, a minimum contribution period requirement, which is usually no more stringent than those attached to contiguous sickness and/or maternity insurance programs, although Taiwan is an exception. Employment-related healthcare strategies usually have attached the same eligibility conditions as apply to contiguous social security programs, although more stringent conditions apply in Ecuador, Senegal and Vietnam.

In order to constrain access to healthcare services some countries either by requiring healthcare consumers to contribute towards their costs, by imposing limited fees for services rendered (27 countries, 18 of which are in Europe and Africa) or patient co-payments (21 countries, 10 of which are in Western Europe); or by simply limiting healthcare consumption, by placing limits on hospital stays (27 countries, largely in Africa, Asia and Latin America), by imposing statutory waiting periods (Colombia and Guinea), or by placing an expenditure ceiling on individuals' healthcare consumption (11 countries, mainly in Africa).

Primary Healthcare Strategy Benefits

Those eligible for healthcare services in any country have access to medical care and usually to hospital care, the two exceptions being Afghanistan and Azerbaijan, which provide only hospital care. The other forms of healthcare services most commonly provided are: pharmaceuticals (154 countries), prostheses (90 countries, most conspicuously in Europe, West and Central Africa, Central Asia, and Central and South America), transportation (71 countries, notably in Western Europe, Africa and Central Asia), dental care services (58 countries, largely in Western Europe, Central Asia and Central and South America) and rehabilitation services (52 countries, predominantly in Western Europe and Central Africa). A range of additional services are less commonly provided, namely: house calls (10 countries, half of which are in Europe), home nursing (Australia, Austria, Belgium, Denmark, El Salvador and the United Kingdom), optical services (Canada, Costa Rica, Ecuador and Ireland) and paramedical services (Canada, Denmark, Hong Kong and Taiwan).

The provision of healthcare services is on the basis of direct provision (123 countries), contracting out (35 countries) or cost reimbursement (30 countries). Direct provision is the modus operandi of national health services, although it also applies to social security programs in 35 countries, particularly in West Africa, and Central and South America, as well as to healthcare service provision in China by employers and in Slovakia by its health insurance organization. Contracting out is most popular amongst social insurance programs in Central and South America and Western Europe, although it is used by health insurance programs in Japan, Korea, Russia and Taiwan. Reimbursement is most common under employer-financed healthcare benefit programs, especially in Africa, as well as under most health insurance programs. It is also an approach adopted by 17 social insurance programs spread largely across Central Africa, Western

Europe and South East Asia.

Under health service contracting out arrangements, the service provider is typically a public provider (34 countries, with the Dominican Republic being the only country to contract out exclusively to the private sector), although most countries also contract out to private healthcare providers (28 countries), but only Egypt also contracts out to employers.

Under health cost reimbursement arrangements the refund is typically 100 percent, although in 10 countries the reimbursement rate falls to between 70 and 90 percent.

CONCLUSION

Short-term social security contingencies have been addressed by most countries by the adoption of the social insurance strategy. The initial programs on or before the turn of the century built on the burgeoning European tradition of voluntarism, manifested in the rapid expansion during the last half of the nineteenth century in the voluntary protection offered by mutual aid and co-operative societies. Over the subsequent century the global coverage of programs addressing these contingencies gradually broadened, although unemployment programs have failed to receive the same degree of global acceptance as sickness and maternity programs. Nevertheless, they can no longer be perceived to be limited to a group of industrialized countries, due largely to the adoption of labor legislation in many Third World countries requiring employers to provide paid sickness and maternity leave and to pay termination or redundancy indemnity.

It is, indeed, evident that the employers' role in the provision of sickness, maternity, unemployment entitlements and even healthcare services is a significant one, especially in Third World countries. Other than their role as an important financier of social insurance programs, employers are used in many countries either to provide basic coverage (or to fill the primary strategy coverage gaps) or to provide basic entitlements (or to augment primary strategy entitlements) through direct provision. This is particularly evident in Africa.

Major watersheds in the development of short-term contingency programs are rare. The 1930s and 1940s saw the emergence of the social assistance strategy in two countries — New Zealand and Australia — both of which had by then long tradition in the use of this approach to social security. Few countries followed, however, in their wake. In the 1950s, the social allowance strategy was adopted in two countries — Denmark and Iceland — both of which were committed to this approach to social security. Again, few countries followed suit. In the 1980s the marketization model was applied in the one country — Chile — adventurous enough, some might say desperate enough, to explore the other radical alternative. Again, however, this model was subsequently adopted by very few countries. Most countries were content to stay with their original strategies, preferring to tinker with program coverage, eligibility conditions and entitlement generosity to meet changing social security needs in changing socioeconomic and political environments.

Short-term social security programs, like their long-term counterparts, mostly cater to the needs of those in the workforce, to whom they promise at least a respite from poverty. To those not protected they are, again, an irrelevancy.

7

Family Support

INTRODUCTION

As a branch of social security, family support comprises entitlements paid for children — child benefits — and for members of designated family compositions — family benefits. It stands in stark contradistinction to other branches of social security because eligibility is not contingent upon the interruption or cessation of earnings. It is, rather, a recognition of three considerations. First, that family size and family composition have a direct impact on family living standards, to the point ultimately that a poverty-line may be breached. Second, that the payment of a "social wage" — in the form of family support — reduces or constrains wage demand pressures on employers. Finally, that the cost of child raising tends to reduce or inhibit the birth rate.

Family support programs were first introduced in the 1920s, although some states of the United States began tinkering with means-tested mothers' pensions before the First World War, as did some Canadian provinces (Skidmore 1995, Skocpol 1992, Shewell 1998). Estonia was the first country to introduce a family support program (1922), in the hope of increasing its birth rate, by adopting the social insurance strategy to provide child benefits. New Zealand followed in 1926, choosing instead the social assistance strategy to provide child benefits to families in need, so reducing wage demand pressures (Uttley 1989). This desire to constrain wage demand pressure was also evident in Western Europe in the 1920s, but the initial preferred strategy was to encourage voluntarism. In Belgium and France regional or industry-based, employer-sponsored equalization funds were established in the 1920s to distribute the cost of wage supplementation —in the form of child allowances — across all participating employers (ILO 1984: 97). In the early 1930s, in the midst of a depression, Belgium (1930) and France (1932) both created statutory programs by making employer contributions towards the cost of child benefits mandatory under social insurance programs. Soon after, the United States, building on earlier state-initiated "Mothers' Aid" or "Endowment of Motherhood" legislation dating back to 1911, introduced its Aid to Dependent Children program that targeted indigent families (1935) (Macarov 1978: 59). Following in Belgium's and France's wake were Italy and Chile (for salaried employees only), then Hungary and Spain (1938).

It was, however, during the Second World War that family support programs received their first major impetus. Twenty more countries established such programs, of which one half adopted the social allowance strategy (Australia (1941), Canada, Ireland, Romania and the five countries that were then part of the Soviet Union (1944) and the United Kingdom (1945), while the other half followed the then European social insurance mainstream (the Netherlands (1939), Egypt and Brazil (large families only) (1941), Bulgaria, Morocco and Portugal (1942), Lebanon, Switzerland (cantonal laws) and Uruguay (1943) and Tunisia (1944)).

The post-Second World War period saw the global coverage of family support programs extended considerably, albeit with a restricted regional focus. They were established as social allowance programs in all continental Western European countries by the mid-1950s, with only Luxembourg (1947) and Greece (1958) adopting the social insurance strategy. They simultaneously traveled quickly to Africa, most conspicuously to West and Middle Africa, and to a large part of South America, where the social insurance strategy had a stranglehold. Japan (1971) was the only Asian country outside post-socialist Central Asia to establish a child benefit program, choosing the social insurance strategy, while Hong Kong (1971) and Sri Lanka (1990) have established the only family benefit programs, both adopting the social assistance strategy. Similarly, outside South America Costa Rica's (1974) and Nicaragua's (1982) social insurance programs stand alone in Latin America. In the Middle East, interest in following in Lebanon's footsteps was limited to only Iran (1953) and Israel (1959), with the former adopting the employer liability strategy, and the latter choosing the social allowance strategy. Interest in the Pacific Islands has been limited to Nauru (1956) and the Cook Islands (1978), both of which have adopted the social allowance strategy.

By 1995, 74 countries had established child benefit programs, of which 17 had also set up family benefit programs. Only seven countries had established family benefit programs in isolation (Costa Rica, Hong Kong, Lithuania, Mauritius, Moldova, Sri Lanka and the United States).

CHILD BENEFITS PROGRAMS

Primary and Supplementary Strategies Adopted

Of the 74 countries that have child benefits programs most have adopted the social insurance strategy (43 countries), whilst most of the rest have opted for social allowances (22 countries). The social assistance strategy has been adopted by five countries (Kyrgyzstan, New Zealand, Poland, Slovakia and Slovenia). And the employer liability strategy has been the choice of only four countries (Bolivia, Burundi, Iran and Paraguay).

A change of social security strategy has been most uncommon. The most radical strategy change has occurred in Canada and Iceland, both of which abandoned their child benefits programs in favor of fiscal welfare measures. New Zealand has also changed its approach twice, first by abolishing its income test just after the Second World War (Uttley 1989), only to then reinstitute it in the early 1990s.

The augmenting of primary social security strategies has occurred in only 11 countries. This has largely involved the adoption of social assistance (9 countries) either to cater to the needy who are ineligible for a primary strategy (Belgium, Gabon and Spain) or to provide supplementary benefits (Armenia, Australia, Belarus, Japan and the Ukraine). Coverage extension by means of social allowances has taken place in Argentina (to social security recipients) and Belarus (to the unemployed, to mean-tested beneficiaries and to children aged over 3); by means of social assistance in Japan (to low-income unemployed and to the self-employed); and by means of employer liability measures in Zaire (to employees in exempt territories).

Primary Social Security Strategy Coverage

The coverage of child benefit programs is usually mutli-targeted. The most frequently targeted children are those in families headed by a person in employment (73 countries), the only exception is Kyrgyzstan, which focuses its program on orphans, children in sole-parent families, and students who have disabled or unemployed parents. Sixteen countries go further by specifying that family heads must be currently working on a substantial basis (variously defined). Coverage extension to children in family units whose head is out of the workforce occurs in 61 countries. In only 25 countries is coverage extended to all children in any family unit, although this may be constrained by the specification of a minimum number of children, as in France (at least 2 children) or Cyprus (4 or more children). Only Malta restricts coverage to its resident citizens.

Employment Coverage. Covered employees generally include farm employees (37 countries) and domestic workers (excluded in only Nicaragua and Tunisia). Earnings are generally not considered a barrier. High-income employees (variously defined) are excluded in only four countries (Belarus, Brazil, Colombia and Japan), while low-income employees (variously defined) are excluded in only Algeria and Morocco. Covered employees, however, overwhelmingly exclude the self-employed (included in only Equatorial Guinea, Malta, Surinam and Switzerland (on a limited basis only)) and farmers (included in only Bulgaria and Switzerland (on a limited basis only)). Employment coverage is, however, incomplete in some countries, with coverage gaps existing on an industry basis (France and Bolivia, both of which have special systems for those excluded) and a geographical basis (Zaire, where the coverage gap is filled by a supplementary employer liability program).

Voluntary coverage under social insurance programs is extremely rare: in only Nicaragua (for the self-employed, uncovered employees, previously covered employees and farmers) and Portugal (designated uncovered employees).

Special systems for particular population categories are rather more common, especially for public employees (22 countries), although they do exist for farm employees (Algeria (on a limited basis only), Czech Republic, France and Italy); for the self-employed (Austria (in agriculture only), Gabon and Italy); for students (Bulgaria and Cameroon (for apprentices with families only); for designated occupational groups (Bolivia and France); for designated industry groups (Bolivia and Morocco).

Primary Social Security Strategy Eligibility

Categorical Criteria. The categorical criteria that define the eligible child benefit categories relate to both the family unit and the child.

What constitutes an eligible family is sometimes defined so as to include all families (25 countries), but usually a secondary criterion is applied to the family head, namely that he or she must also be: a social security beneficiary (50 countries); an employee (46 countries); a lone parent (18 countries); a deceased social security recipient's widow or widower (8 African countries); an unemployed person (Italy (in prescribed categories), Kyrgyzstan (only those with student children), Madagascar and Portugal); a student (Czech Republic (advanced-level only), Equatorial Guinea and Tunisia (aged under 18 or trainees of any age); or aged over 60 or 60 percent disabled (Colombia).

The categorical criteria attached to children relate to age, dependency, gender, relationship to the family head, and disability and employment status. In most countries child eligibility begins at birth, although Chile qualifies a fetus from the fifth month of pregnancy, while an older cut-in age on one is specified in Bolivia and Niger and two in Senegal (2). The age at which a child's eligibility ceases, unless he or she is either disabled or a student (including apprentice), varies markedly. The modal cutout age is between 15 and 17 (44 countries). A lower cutout age of between 11 and 14 has been set in 24 countries, of which 15 are in Africa. The youngest cutout ages are three (Belarus and Japan) and six (the Cook Islands). Only three countries have set a higher cutout age of between 17 and 19 (Austria, Bolivia and Chile). Continued eligibility is granted to unmarried children up to age 18 in Cyprus); to dependent and unmarried daughters who are unemployed and working at home in France and Tunisia (to age 20 years), Madagascar (to age 21) and Lebanon (to age 25); to a person who is replacing a lone parent in Belgium (up to age 25); and to a person seeking employment in Germany (to age 21) and Malta (over age 16). Students continue to qualify beyond the specified cut-off age in 57 countries, of which 38 set an age limit of between 17 and 20, with the remainder specifying an age limit of 21 or over (up to 27 in Germany). Similarly, disabled children continue to qualify in 48 countries. Twenty-two countries set no age limit in the event of mental retardation. A further 22 countries specify an age limit of between 17 and 21, with even higher cut-off ages applying in three countries (Sweden (23 for the mentally retarded attending special schools) and the Czech Republic and Slovakia (both 26).

In Mali a family must prove that an otherwise eligible child has received pediatric care during his or her preschool years.

The other eligible children categories in evidence are: great-grandchildren (Chile), grandchildren (Belgium and Chile), siblings (Belgium and Italy), nieces and nephews (Italy), orphaned children (Chile), abandoned children (Chile), stepchildren (Belgium) and other dependent minors (Belgium).

General Qualifying Eligibility Criteria. Most countries do not attach general qualifying criteria to their child benefits programs, and those that do generally set only modest requirements relating to minimum periods of employment, contribution or residency, or to the maximum number of children.

Minimum employment period requirements of up to a year are the most common, being specified by 17 countries, of which 15 are in Africa, with the others being Greece and Colombia, where the period of employment must be with the same employer.

Minimum contribution period requirements are rare, attached in only Yugoslavia (1 year) and Iran (720 working days).

Minimum residency period requirements apply only in the United Kingdom (26 weeks in last 52 weeks), Denmark and Slovakia (1 year, for aliens only) and Austria (5 years for alien, unless they have been employed for more than 3 months).

A maximum number of eligible children in any family is specified in 13 countries, typically between four and six (11 countries), although a larger maximum number is specified in Italy (7) and Guinea (10).

Means-Assessment Criteria. An income test applies in all five countries with social assistance programs, as well as under Yugoslavia's social insurance program (as a statutory maximum income cutout point) and, interestingly, under Australia's social allowance program (as a statutory income cutout point set at an affluence income threshold).

Primary Social Security Strategy Benefits

Cash Entitlements. Cash entitlements under child benefit programs mainly take the form of flat-rate benefits (63 countries), with benefits relating to minimum wages being paid in 10 mainly post-socialist countries, and with earnings-related benefits provided only in Tunisia.

Cash entitlements sometimes vary either with the number of children (27 countries, of which 18 are in Europe), either inversely (12 countries) or directly (15 countries), or with the age of the child (6 countries), again either inversely (Russia and Nicaragua) or directly (Austria, Czech Republic, Latvia and the Netherlands).

Entitlement tapering because of the receipt of other income applies under most social assistance programs (the exceptions being Poland and Slovakia) as well as under some social insurance programs (Greece, Italy, Nicaragua and Yugoslavia).

Specifying limits on cash entitlements is done only in Tunisia, which specifies a maximum earnings rate for benefit calculation purposes.

Child benefits are paid to each parent where both are insured under social insurance programs in Brazil.

Most periodic entitlements under child benefit programs are not regularly adjusted in line with inflation. Only 12 countries do so, largely on an ad hoc basis (7 countries). Annual adjustments are made in Australia, Denmark and Italy. Biannual adjustments are made in the Netherlands, while quarterly adjustments are made in Israel.

Additional children's benefits are commonly provided in many countries. The most frequently provided are general welfare services (13 African countries). In a few countries lump-sum grants are paid, namely: funeral grants (Bolivia, Cape Verde and Portugal), marriage grants (Argentina and Iran), death grants (Colombia) and start-in-life grants (Estonia). In-kind benefits are also provided in Colombia. Gratuities, as additional monthly payments, are provided in Argentina (13 per year) and Belgium (14 per year).

Special Need Benefits. Additional cash entitlements are given in many countries on the presumption of need. These are paid with respect to children in particular family circumstances, namely: low-income families (Australia, Germany and Japan); families headed by a lone parent (11 European countries), with a disabled member present (Estonia, Italy and Uruguay), headed by a social security recipient (Australia, Denmark and Belgium), with a large number of children (Argentina), with a guardian present (Estonia)), with a non-working parent present (Estonia) or with a widowed parent present (Colombia); and families with particular presumed needs because they living in remote or disadvantaged regions (Argentina, Norway and Switzerland), because of multiple births (Denmark and Ireland) or because they require a carer (Portugal).

Special Need benefits are also paid with respect to children with particular characteristics, namely: of school age (9 countries), with a disability requiring domiciliary care (Australia, Belarus, Ireland and the Ukraine), of a young age (Finland, France and Norway), a student (Malta and Switzerland (paid as a higher education allowances)), an orphan (Denmark), an unemployed youth (Malta), infected by HIV or AIDS (Belarus), suffering a sickness requiring constant care (Poland), and being the first school-age child (Belgium).

FAMILY BENEFITS PROGRAMS

Primary and Supplementary Strategies Adopted

The 24 countries that have family benefits programs can be found in all geographical regions, although they are most heavily concentrated in Western Europe, Eastern Europe Australasia and North America. The most frequently adopted strategy is social assistance (11 countries), followed by social insurance (8 countries), social allowances (Armenia, Chile, Denmark and Finland) and, finally, employer liability measures (Burundi).

No country is known to have changed its social security strategy for the provision of family benefits.

The augmenting of primary social security strategies has occurred in only Argentina, which has a supplementary social allowance program to support families headed by social security recipients.

Primary Social Security Strategy Coverage

As with child benefit programs, the coverage of family benefit programs is usually mutli-targeted. Most frequently targeted are those families headed by a person in employment (23 countries), although Argentina, Burundi and the Czech Republic further require that the employed family head must be currently working on a continuous or substantial basis (variously defined) and Greece exempts employees in receipt of equivalent allowances from their employers. Coverage extension to designated family units whose head is out of the workforce occurs in all countries.

Employment Coverage. Covered employees under employment-related programs generally include farm employees (excluded in only 2 countries). Earnings are not a barrier, as no country excludes either high- or low-income employees. Covered employees, however, generally exclude farmers (covered in only Bulgaria and then only collective farmers) and the self-employed (covered in only Malta). Aliens are excluded in Malta. Employment coverage is, however, incomplete in two countries, with coverage gaps existing on an industry basis (France) and a geographical basis (Sri Lanka).

Voluntary coverage is not available under any social insurance program.

Special systems for particular population categories are somewhat more common, notably for public employees (Burundi, Cape Verde and France (but only public utility employees)), farm employees (Czech Republic, and Finland), students (Bulgaria) and designated industry categories (France).

Primary Social Security Program Eligibility

Categorical Criteria. The categorical criteria that define the eligible population categories under family benefit programs relate to the composition of the family unit.

What constitutes an eligible family unit is defined by whether it contains on of the following: a lone parent (11 countries, of which 3 countries designate only a lone mother (Armenia, Bulgaria and Moldova); a social security recipient (10 countries); a non-working spouse (Argentina, Burundi, Chile, Lebanon, Malta and Tunisia); a member of an advanced age (variously defines); a disabled member (Chile, Costa Rica and Poland); a student (Argentina, Burundi (but only apprentices with a dependent wife), the Czech Republic and Tunisia); a widow with at least one child (Chile and Costa Rica); a dependent aged parent with limited income (Cape Verde); a dependent aged mother (Chile); a mother under the age of 18 (Moldova); a working mother (Moldova); and parents with children (Ireland and Lithuania), with three children under age 15 (Mauritius), or with at least one child under the age three, or if disabled aged under seven (the Czech Republic, provided he or she is cared for at home) and France.

General Qualifying Eligibility Criteria. The general qualifying criteria are not attached to family benefits programs in most countries. A minimum residency period is specified only in Denmark (1 year, aliens only) and Hong Kong (5 years). A maximum payment period after which eligibility ceases is specified in only Ireland (1 year, for family income supplements only) and Sri Lanka (2 years, for family allowances only). A minimum employment period requirement is specified only in Moldova (1 year, applied to only working mothers aged over 18).

Means-Assessment Criteria. An income test applies in all 11 countries with social assistance programs, as well as under Costa Rica's social insurance program (as a statutory maximum income cutout point). An assets test is also applies in Hong Kong.

Primary Social Security Strategy Benefits

Cash Entitlements. Cash entitlements under family benefit programs generally take the form of flat-rate benefits (22 countries), with minimum wage-related benefits being paid Lebanon and Moldova. Ireland provides a family income supplement equal to 60 percent of the gap between family income and an income threshold that depends on the number of children.

The periodic cash entitlements provided are diverse. They include: adult dependents supplements (11 countries), lone parent's benefits (8 countries), lone mother's benefits (3 countries), families-with-children supplements (6 countries) and working mothers' supplements (Moldova).

The entitlements provided sometimes vary either with the number of dependents, either directly as in Costa Rica (for adult dependents' supplements), France (for lone-parent benefits and families-with-children supplements) and Ireland (for families-with-children supplements) or inversely in Costa Rica and Tunisia (for adult dependents' payments); or with their age as in Moldova (for families-with-children supplements).

Entitlement tapering because of the receipt of income occurs under most social assistance programs, the exceptions being Ireland, Malta, Mauritius, Poland and Sri Lanka, while assets are also taken into consideration in Australia.

Most periodic family benefit entitlements are not regularly adjusted in line with inflation. Those that are adjusted are done so largely on an ad hoc basis (Chile, Hong Kong and Moldova), although Denmark does so on an annual basis and Australia does so on a biannual basis.

Additional benefits that are sometimes provided to families include general welfare services (Tunisia and the United States), lump-sum family grants (Malta) and funeral grants for deceased spouses (Cape Verde).

Special Need Benefits. Additional cash entitlements are given in many countries on the basis of presumed need. These include paid parental leave to care for a sick child (in 4 post-socialist countries as well as Portugal, São Tomé and Principe and Sweden); supplements for families living in remote or disadvantaged regions (Argentina and Australia (but for lone-parent families only), for families with a disabled child (as paid parental leave) (Estonia), for families with an income below a threshold income level (Moldova), for families receiving family income supplements who need child-care assistance (Australia) and for lone parent families who need assistance to cover the costs of schooling, housing, and child care (Hong Kong) or telephones (Australia).

CONCLUSION

Social security programs that provide support to families with one or more children or adult dependents or to families with particular compositions are common, but not widespread, globally. Child benefit programs are almost universally offered throughout Europe and Australasia and are quite conspicuous in Middle and West Africa and in South America. They have, however, barely achieved a toe-hold in Asia, the Pacific Islands and the Middle East. They are simply not available in North America, although Canada had such a program after the Second World War but abolished it in favor of fiscal welfare measures.

Family benefit programs are spread even more thinly across the globe, being concentrated mainly in Europe and Australasia. They are entirely absent in the Pacific Islands. These programs are usually mutli-targeted, focusing largely on families headed by a person in employment, acknowledging the reality that the provision of family benefits — a social wage — improves their standard of living without burdening employers with higher earnings. In this setting, the impact on family support programs of a diversity of cultural values and socioeconomic circumstances can be readily seen from the array of dependents who attract such support.

Family support programs also define the circumstances in which unacceptable social costs are incurred if one or both parents are required to work to support dependents; lone parenthood is the conspicuous example.

8

Administration and Finance

INTRODUCTION

There is considerable diversity in the ways social security is both administered and financed globally. The most common approach is for a centralized independent agency, under central government control, to collect employer and employee contributions and to disburse program benefits.

SOCIAL SECURITY ADMINISTRATION

In all countries social security administration is, primarily, a central government responsibility. Regional governments have a role to play in 15 countries, seven of which have federal political structures (Australia, Canada, Germany, India, Russia, Switzerland and the United States). Local government plays a role in 10 countries, five of which are in Western Europe (Denmark, Finland, Luxembourg, the Netherlands and Switzerland). However, the involvement of all three levels of government is rare, restricted to six countries (China, Denmark, Japan, Lithuania, North Korea and Switzerland). Two microstates (the Marshall Islands and Micronesia) have chosen to contract out their social security program administration to a public social security agency in another country (the United States), as has Palau, a United Nations Trust Territory administered by the United States. The Cook Islands has chosen to contract out its social security administration to an insurance company.

Governmental Modes of Social Security Administration: Institutional Arrangements

The most common public mode of social security program administration is the independent (parastatal or quasi-governmental) agency (109 countries), although public agencies under direct governmental control — typically a ministry or department of state — are used by 69 countries to administer at least one of their social security programs, while the use of specialized subagencies within a public agency is the preferred approach in 46 countries to the administration of at least one of their social security programs.

The nomenclature of the responsible agencies supervising one or more national social security programs — usually headed by a minister of state — is suggestive of the diverse national orientations of social security policy. Most frequently the supervisory agency is designated as Labor (or Employment or Manpower) (122 countries) reflecting the dominance of employment-related social security programs. The other frequently used designations are Social Welfare (or Social Services) (23 countries), Health (or Hygiene) (18 countries), Social Security (15 countries), Finance (15 countries), Social Affairs (or Social Protection) (13 countries) and Interior Affairs (or Home Affairs) (8 countries). Other less frequently designated responsible agencies are: Prime Minister's Office (or Cabinet Office (Bahamas, Barbados and St Lucia), Family (Luxembourg), Human Resource Development (Canada), Human Development (Bolivia), Housing and Economic Development (Bolivia), Consumer Affairs and Social Services (Trinidad and Tobago), Environment, Youth and Family (Austria), Economic Development (Burkina Faso) and the Comptroller-General (Peru).

Independent Social Security Agencies. The independent social security agencies that exist in 109 countries are all statutory creations of the central governments, although they operate in conjunction with regional independent agencies in France and Germany. Uniquely, in Pakistan the social security agencies responsible for sickness, maternity and employment-injury programs are regionally based and under regional government supervision. These independent agencies are typically designated as Institutes or Funds, although the use of public corporation does happen (as, for example, in Indonesia (Purwoko 1996: 59–60)). However, separate statutory trust funds, comprising all National Provident Funds, exist in only 20 countries.

Independent social security agencies operate under the general supervision of either ministries or departments (82 countries), most frequently designated Labor (or Employment or Manpower) (58 countries), Health (or Hygiene) (12 countries, seven of which are in Africa) or Social Welfare (or Social Affairs or Social Protection) (10 countries). Specific supervisory committees, commissions, boards or councils exist in 24 countries, of which 12 are in Central America and the Pacific Islands. These are usually national in their focus, although India has regional supervisory committees, and Libya permits local supervision by municipal committees. In most instances, all independent agencies operating in a country are under supervision by one body, although, different bodies sometimes supervise different independent agencies (Bolivia, Cape Verde, Colombia, Greece, Iceland, the Philippines and Slovenia). Multiple supervision of a single independent agency does happen, albeit rarely

(Libya and Burkina Faso).

Most independent social security agencies have a statutory governance or management board (or commission) that establishes organizational policies and approves appropriate procedures, practices and regulations within the context of the enabling statute; accepts overall responsibility for management and organizational conduct; and advises the responsible minister on social security policy. Membership is appointed by the responsible minister, although there may be a statutory requirement that it be bipartite (Austria, Denmark, France, Madagascar, Senegal and Slovenia), more commonly tripartite (46 countries (42 percent)) or even quadripartite (Burkina-Faso, El Salvador and Poland).

Public Social Security Agencies. In the 69 countries with public social security agencies, a variety of nomenclatures apply. Most frequently they are departments of Social Security (29 countries) or Social Welfare (or Social Services) (28 countries), although other designations are used: Social Affairs (or Social Protection) (10 countries, 7 of which are post-socialist), Labor (or, Employment) (9 countries, 4 of which are post-socialist), Health (Brazil and Chile, Health and Welfare (Japan), Human Resource Development (Canada), or Policy and Planning (Sri Lanka).

Specialized Public Social Security Subagencies. The assignment of social security program administration responsibilities to administrative subunits within a public agency — typically an administration, bureau, office or service — occurs in 46 countries, most prevalently in Europe, North America and the Caribbean. The most frequent subunit nomenclature is Social Security (32 countries). While most administrative subunits have broad-based functional responsibilities, it is quite common to have Employment Services (or Labor Bureaux or Labor Offices) involved in the administration of unemployment programs (29 countries). A specialized Child (or Family) Allowance Bureau (or Office) is used to administer family support programs in Belgium, Costa Rica and Luxembourg.

Governmental Modes of Social Security: Administrative Arrangements

Most public social security administrative units have a mode of administration that embraces both program management (benefit eligibility determination and payment) and, where applicable, financial management (contribution collection and, where applicable, portfolio management).

Administrative Complexity. Administrative complexity is viewed from the perspective of social security recipients and contributors. Most countries deliver their social security programs through a single public social security administrative unit (107 countries), a practice that is least prevalent in Europe and, to an even lesser extent, in Asia. A further 40 countries use two public administrative units, typically, one for employment-related injury programs, the other for the remaining social security programs. This administrative arrangement is most popular, but not dominant, in Europe, where the administrative arrangements in place have evolved from the networked voluntary sickness and pension funds that constituted the early administrative structures under the Bismarckian social insurance model. The use of three public administrative units occurs in a further 14 countries, five of which are in Eastern Europe. Eleven countries have an even greater degree of administrative fragmentation, involving four public administrative units (Canada, France, Japan, Slovenia and Yugoslavia), five administrative units (Austria and Denmark, or even six or more administrative units (Belgium, Chile and Luxembourg). The adoption of the multiple-unit public mode of social security administration reflects the perceived desirability of making specialist agencies responsible for delivering different social security programs (43 countries).

The delivery of social security programs by public administrative units in 20 countries also involves a range of other non-governmental agencies, including sickness funds (Austria, Germany, Luxembourg and Switzerland), health insurance societies (Australia, Bermuda and South Korea), unemployment funds (Denmark and Sweden), accident insurance funds (Germany and Switzerland), family allowance funds (Colombia and Switzerland), pension funds (Iceland) and mutual benefit organizations (Belgium).

Administrative Decentralization. This occurs in only 66 countries as either benefit administration decentralization (66 countries) and/or contribution collection decentralization (46 countries), with the highest incidence occurring in North America and Australasia, the post-socialist countries in Eastern Europe and Central Asia, and Western Europe. This decentralization of administration takes a variety of forms. Most commonly it involves a responsible public administrative unit with a regional office structure (34 countries), a district office structure (35 countries) and/or a local office structure (27 countries), as is typical in North America, Australasia and the post-socialist countries. In other instances, decentralization involves the contracting out of services to regional government agencies (14 countries); local government agencies (10 countries); other central government agencies with either a regional office structure (Ireland (regional health boards) or a local office structure (7 countries); local self-governing agencies (Belgium, Denmark, France, Germany and Switzerland); trade unions (China, Denmark, Iceland and Argentina); or regional self-governing agencies (Yugoslavia).

Separation of Functions. The practice of separating program and financial management occurs in only 26 countries, half of which are in Western Europe, which also has one of the highest incidences of this practice, exceeded only by North America. This complicates social security decision making as it makes inter-agency collaboration necessary, especially over benefit eligibility determination.

Benefit Administration. Responsibility for benefit administration rests with the social security program unit in all countries. The benefit application process, however, very occasionally involves local government agencies (Luxembourg (for the receipt of unemployment claims) and Lithuania (for the processing of old-age, disability, survivors' and family assistance claims)) or local agents (Australia (for the receipt of unemployment claims)). The benefit payment process more common involves other organizations. Employers sometimes pay particular benefits on behalf of the social security administrative unit (25 countries), as do regional government agencies (14 countries, half of which have federal political structures), local government agencies (China, Denmark, Japan, the Netherlands, North Korea and Switzerland), other central government agencies (Cuba, Czech Republic, Iceland, Norway and Slovakia), local self-governing agencies (Belgium, Denmark, France, Germany and Switzerland), trade unions (China, Denmark, Iceland and Argentina), public payment agencies (Belgium) and local or regional self-governing agencies (Yugoslavia).

Contribution Administration. Responsibility for contribution administration rests predominantly with the social security administrative unit, although it is separately administered in 26 countries, typically by the income tax collection agency. It is less common to have other organizations involved in the contribution collection process. Regional government agencies occasionally collect contributions on behalf of the responsible administrative unit (8 countries, half of which have a federal political structure), as do local government agencies (China, Finland and Switzerland), local self-governing agencies (Denmark, Germany and Switzerland), other central government agencies (the Netherlands and Sweden), joint collection agencies (France) or regional self-governing agencies (Yugoslavia).

Public-Private Modes of Social Security Administration

The delivery of benefits under employer liability and mandated occupational or private pension or savings programs is a joint responsibility of a variety of organizations — governmental agencies, private business, membership organizations and even judicial agencies — under regulatory regimes enforced by governmental agencies.

Employers, and the private sector more generally, play a pivotal role in social security administration under either the mandated occupational and personal pension and savings programs in 25 countries or employer liability programs in 115 countries, comprising 47 countries with primary workers' compensation programs and 72 countries with other primary or supplementary employer liability programs.

Workers' Compensation Programs. In only four of the 47 countries with workers' compensation programs are employers alone required to administer and to pay cash entitlements directly to work injury beneficiaries (Bangladesh, China, Hong Kong and Myanmar).

Insurance carriers contribute to the administration of work-injury benefit claims in 43 countries that require or permit employers to insure their employment injury risks with an insurance carrier. In most countries these insurance carriers must be private (29 countries), but some mandate only public carriers (7 countries) or both (7 countries). Argentina and Belgium permit insurance to be carried with employer mutual societies. Benefit administration by insurance carriers in some countries is in conjunction with the judicial agencies or compensation boards.

Judicial involvement in the administration of employment injury claims happens in only seven countries. This involves a court either determining benefit entitlement (Morocco, Nigeria, Solomon Islands (for survivors' benefits only), the United States (3 states only) and Fiji) or conciliating and arbitrating benefit-entitlement disputes (Bermuda), although dispute settlement can be the responsibility of a specialist labor tribunal (Belgium). Local courts in Bermuda and Fiji also dispense lump-sum disability and survivors' benefits.

Common-law actions for negligence by the employer are permitted in some Australian States.

The administration of employment-injury claims by a public compensation board (variously titled) occurs in only five countries: Australia, Canada, St Vincent and the Grenadines (for permanent disability and survivors' benefits only), the United States (about half of the states) and Western Samoa.

Responsibility for enforcing employer compliance with workers' compensation program obligations falls to a ministry (or department) of Labor (or Employment) in 54 countries with such programs, although alternative regulatory arrangements are not uncommon, indicative of the national orientations of their workers' compensation programs. Some countries use a social security administrative unit as the enforcement agency (Argentina, Dominica, Panama, Switzerland and Uruguay). Others have established a specialized regulatory board or commission (Belgium, Denmark and Pakistan) or use a ministry with the designation Social Affairs (Finland and Tunisia), Internal (or Home) Affairs (Bermuda and Nauru) and Finance (Portugal).

In Kenya, Trinidad and Tobago and Uganda regulatory enforcement agencies also pay employment-injury benefits when employers lodge funds with them, perhaps as a guarantee bond (Trinidad and Tobago).

Other Employer Liability Programs. Employers are required in many countries to pay social security benefits directly under primary and supplementary employer liability programs with respect to sickness (56 countries), maternity (38 countries), employment-related injuries (supplementary programs) (19 countries), unemployment (18 countries), permanent disability (Colombia and Pakistan), survivors' (Colombia), old age (Colombia and North Korea) and family benefits (Burundi). They are also obligated in 26 countries to provide healthcare services directly.

Responsibility for enforcing employer compliance with statutory requirements is given to a ministry (or department) of Labor (or Employment) in most countries with employer liability programs (58 countries), although 22 countries use their social security administrative unit as the enforcement agency for at least one such program.

Mandated Occupational or Personal Pension or Savings Programs. Of the 27 countries that have mandated occupational or personal pension or savings programs, most use commercial pension funds and insurance companies (22 countries), with the remainder mandating pension or savings funds established and administered by industry associations, employers or trade unions (workers' associations).

Most countries that have either privatised complementary benefit provision or permitted primary coverage contracting out, use commercial private pension funds and insurance companies to deliver social security outcomes (20 countries).

The mandated occupational pension programs in France and Greece are administered by funds jointly managed by employees and employers, while in Bolivia they are administered by workers' associations. This arrangement is a legacy of their earlier incarnation as industry-based, occupation-based or enterprise-based occupational pension plans established as an outcome of collective labor agreements.

Employers administer the mandated private savings programs established in Afghanistan (for work injury benefits) and in Guatemala (for unemployment benefits).

Responsibility for enforcing compliance with statutory requirements under mandated occupational or personal pension or savings programs rests with a variety of public agencies. The most commonly used enforcement agency is a social security agency (12 countries, most notably in those that permit contracting out). It should be noted, however, that in these countries a separate regulatory regime exists governing the operation of voluntary occupational or personal pension or savings plans. Regulatory enforcement is by ministries (or departments) of Labor (or Employment) (Afghanistan, Colombia, Guatemala, Japan and Venezuela) and Social Affairs (Finland and France), Health and Social Affairs (Côte d'Ivoire); or by a Superintendent (variously titled) of Pension Funds (Australia, Argentina, Chile and Peru), of National Health (Colombia, for private health providers), or of National Banking (Colombia, for commercial pension funds). Peru also has an investment classification agency that regulates pension fund portfolio management practices by issuing regulations, after an investment risk assessment, on acceptable capital market products.

SOCIAL SECURITY FINANCE

Social security systems in 165 countries are financed, at least in part, by employer and/or employee contributions, of which 110 countries provide government financial supplementation. The remaining seven countries operate non-contributory social security systems, five of which involve only employer-financed programs (Bangladesh, Botswana, Malawi, North Korea and Sierra Leone), with the balance involving both government- and employer-financed programs (Nauru and Hong Kong).

Old-Age, Disability and Survivors' Program Financing

Long-term contingency strategies, whether primary or supplementary, are overwhelmingly contributory (159 countries), but some are government-financed or -subsidized (43 countries) and only one is entirely employer-financed (North Korea, where, admittedly, the distinction between government and employer is rather blurred). The contributory programs are usually financed by a common set of contributions designated for old-age, disability and/or survivors' benefits (154 countries), although in five countries funds are drawn from sickness and/or maternity contribution revenue to finance disability benefits (Algeria, Belgium, France, Guinea and Thailand) and survivors' benefits (Algeria and France).

Designated old-age, invalidity and/or survivors' contribution revenue is used to finance other social security program benefits in a minority of countries: employment-related permanent disability benefits (44 countries), employment-related survivors' benefits (43 countries) and employment-related temporary disability benefits (37 countries), both most frequently in Central Asia, Eastern Europe and the Caribbean; maternity benefits (43 countries) and sickness benefits (40 countries), both most frequently in Central Asia, Eastern Europe and the Caribbean; unemployment (18 countries, half of which are in Europe); child benefits (121 countries mostly in Europe); and family benefits (Bulgaria, Czech Republic, Malta and Moldova).

Most long-term contingency contribution regimes require both employers and employees to contribute. Some countries, however, imposed only either employer contributions (Bulgaria, Cuba, Estonia, Lebanon, Pakistan, Poland and Romania) or employee contributions (Afghanistan, Chile, Peru and Surinam). Only three countries have opted for flat-rate contributions (Bermuda, Denmark (depending on employment status) and Macau) rather than earnings-related contributions. The standard contribution rates are usually based on actual earnings, rather than earnings categories (9 countries only), and are usually set at a uniform rate. Differential contribution rates are, however, occasionally set.

Contribution rate differentiation is common for particular contributor categories: the self-employed (47 countries); the voluntarily insured (14 countries); workers in arduous conditions (6 countries, where the rate usually exceeds the prevailing standard total contribution rate (Bulgaria, Burundi, Greece and Mauritius (sugar industry workers only)); farmers (Estonia, South Korea, Russia and Tunisia, where the rates are set above the standard employee rate); pensioners (Belgium (where disabled pensioners pay a rate below the standard employee contribution rate), Norway (where pensioners over age 69 pay a rate below the standard employee rate), Paraguay (disabled and old-aged pensioners pay a rate below the standard employee rate) and El Salvador (where sickness, maternity and work injury beneficiaries pay a rate between the standard employee and total contribution rate); those in designated industry or economic sectors (10 countries, 5 of which are in Europe); those in particular earnings categories (Egypt (where lower rates are paid by those in higher income categories) and Bahamas, Belize, Haiti, Ireland and Israel (where higher rates are paid by those in higher income categories)); those in designated geographic region (China, Italy, Norway and Yugoslavia); those employed by small firms (variously defined) (Finland and India); and those in designated age categories (Bermuda, Finland and Singapore (where older workers pay a lower contribution rate).

In a few cases only are employer contribution rates differentiated. Most notably a lower contribution rate applies where the employer's contribution is a substitute for contributions from low-earnings employees (Germany, Singapore and Zambia), where the employer is a publicly funded organization (Georgia and Moldova), or where a pensioner is employed (Belize). In Finland employer contributions vary according to employees' gender and age. In the Seychelles the employer contribution rates increase with the size of their wage bills. The tiny Marshall Islands has adopted the novel approach of setting a contribution rate for small business equal to 10 percent of twice the salary of the highest-paid employee.

Placing limits on contribution payments is common. This includes limiting contribution payments by the imposition of an earnings ceiling (67 countries, with the highest incidence in Latin America) and/or an earnings floor (21 countries, with the highest incidence in Central America). Entirely exempting low income earners, however, occurs in only the Netherlands, Norway and the United Kingdom.

The contribution rates payable vary markedly on a regional and national basis. The global average earnings-related total contribution rate is 15.4 percent of payroll, ranging from 30.2 percent in Eastern Europe to 6.0 percent in Central Africa. The highest total contribution rate can be found in Poland (45.0 percent). The global average employer contribution rate is 10.7 percent. The regions with an average employer contribution rate well above that global average are Eastern Europe (26.8 percent), Central Asia (24.0 percent), Western Europe (13.2 percent) and North Africa (12.6 percent), while the regions with an average employer contribution rate well below the global average are Central Africa (3.5 percent) and Central America (3.7 percent). The highest employer contribution rate can also be found in Poland (45.0 percent). The global average employee contribution is 4.7 percent. The regions with an average employee contribution rate well above that global average are South America (7.9 percent) and Western Europe (7.7 percent), while the region with an average employer contribution rate well below the global average is Central Asia (0.9 percent). The highest employee contribution rate can be found in Singapore (20.0 percent). The global average statutory contribution incidence is 31 percent for employees and 69 percent for employers, with the employees' share being lowest in Central Asia (3.4 percent) and highest in the Pacific Islands (48.8 percent).

Governmental involvement in funding occurs in 94 countries. This ranges from the provision of supplementary financial assistance to contributory programs (80 countries) to entire public financing of social allowance and social assistance programs (13 countries). Such government funding comes exclusively from central governments in most instances (88 countries), although joint funding does happen with regional government (Switzerland) or with local government (China, Finland and the Ukraine). The incidence of government funding is lowest in Africa and the Pacific Islands.

Government subsidies to contributory programs take many forms. Program deficit funding takes place in 35 countries, including Guyana, where, intriguingly, government loans are made for that purpose. The incidence of deficit funding is highest in post-socialist countries. A diverse array of subsidy approaches is used: subsidies based on a specified percentage of the payroll — under 1 percent (6 countries), 1-to-3 percent (6 countries) and over 3 percent (9 countries); periodically determined fixed subsidies (10 countries); annual subsidies (7 countries); administrative costs subsidies (6 countries); subsidies with respect to particular population categories — farmers (Finland), fishermen (South Korea), the self-employed (Finland), the unemployed and the non-employed (the Ukraine, for family benefits only), those living in underdeveloped districts (Yugoslavia) and the first five employees in small industrial and technical workshops (Iran); and subsidies from earmarked tax revenue (Panama (on alcohol)).

Sickness and Maternity Program Financing

Sickness and/or maternity strategies, whether primary or supplementary, are largely contributory (113 countries). Although entirely employer-financed benefits are common (64 countries), entirely government-financed ones are not (Australia (sickness assistance only), Hong Kong (supplementary sickness and maternity assistance only), Iceland (sickness program only), New Zealand, Trinidad and Tobago (supplementary sickness and maternity assistance only) and Nauru (sickness assistance only)). Eleven countries also require the payment of health insurance contributions, which are generally earnings-related — flat-rate contributions apply in only Kenya and Bermuda — and payable by both employers and employees — the exceptions being Canada and Russia (both requiring only employer contributions) and Australia and Kenya (both requiring only individual contributions). The contributory programs are financed by a common set of contributions designated for that purpose (60 countries); by old-age, invalidity and/or survivors' contribution revenue for maternity benefits (43 countries) and to sickness benefits (40 countries); child and/or family benefit contribution revenue for maternity benefits (9 countries, 8 of which are in Africa); and unemployment contribution revenue for both sickness and maternity benefits (Canada and South Africa).

The designated sickness and/or maternity contribution revenue collected is used to finance other social security program benefits in a minority of countries: employment-related temporary disability benefits (12 countries), employment-related survivors' benefits (6 countries) and employment-related permanent disability benefits (6 countries); and child and family benefits (Tunisia).

Most sickness and/or maternity contribution regimes require both employers and employees to contribute (46 countries). Some countries, however, only impose either employer contributions (13 countries, 10 of which are in Africa and Asia) or employee contributions (Chile).

The 60 countries that finance their sickness and/or maternity benefits from contribution revenue designated for that purpose have overwhelmingly adopted earnings-related contributions, for only Switzerland has adopted the flat-rate contribution approach. The contribution rates specified are usually based on actual earnings, although earnings categories are used in Japan (but only for employer contributions), Myanmar and the Philippines, they are set at a uniform rate. Differentiated contribution rates are quite rare: only China and Yugoslavia (by geographic region), Finland (by earnings) and Luxembourg (by whether a contributor is a wage or salary earner). Only two countries differentiate employer contribution rates alone (Germany (where a lower rate is specified when an employer's contributions substitute for contributions from low-earnings employees) and Egypt (where a lower rate is specified when employers provide cash and medical services to their employees)).

While contribution rate differentiation is uncommon, it does happen for particular contributor categories, namely, the self-employed (14 countries, 7 of which are in Latin America); and pensioners (11 countries, 7 of which are in Western Europe, including Belgium, which exempts those in receipt of a minimum pension, and France, which sets a rate below the employee contribution rate).

Placing limits on contribution payments is common. This includes limiting contribution payments by the imposition of an earnings ceiling (24 countries, half of which are in West and Central Africa) and/or an earnings floor (8 countries, 5 of which are in Central and South America). Entirely exempting low-income earners, however, does not occur.

The contribution rates that are set vary somewhat on a regional and national basis. The global average earnings-related total contribution rate is 7.9 percent of payroll, rising to 12.6 percent in Eastern Europe. The highest total contribution rate can be found in Hungary (23.5 percent). The global average employer contribution rate is 5.4 percent. The highest employer contribution rate is found in Poland (19.5 percent). The global average employee contribution is 2.5 percent. The highest employee contribution rate is found in Yugoslavia (15.2 percent at the maximum level, depending on profession and location). The global average statutory contribution incidence is 32 percent for employees and 68 percent for employers.

Governmental involvement in funding occurs in 44 countries. This ranges from the provision of supplementary financial assistance to contributory programs (36 countries) to the entire public financing of social allowance and social assistance programs (8 countries). Such government funding come exclusively from central governments in most instances (40 countries), although joint funding does happen with regional government (Switzerland and the United States) and/or local government (Armenia, Denmark and Switzerland). The incidence of government funding is lowest in Africa and the Pacific Islands.

The forms of government supplementary financial assistance to contributory programs are diverse. Program deficit funding is not common, whether for both sickness and maternity programs (only China, Czech Republic, Finland, Myanmar, Uruguay and Vietnam), for sickness programs alone (only Uruguay, and Vietnam), or for maternity programs alone (only Philippines). An array of subsidy approaches is used: periodically determined fixed subsidies for sickness benefits (eleven countries) and maternity benefits (10 countries); subsidies based on a specified percentage of the payroll — under 1 percent (5 countries), 1-to-3 percent (4 countries) and over 3 percent (Greece, 6.6 percent); administrative cost subsidies (Japan and Venezuela); subsidies based on earmarked tax revenue (France (taxes on alcohol and tobacco consumption and an insurance premium surcharge) and Belgium (an insurance premium surcharge)); subsidies to particular population categories — the unemployed (Germany (sickness program only) and Slovenia), low-income earners (Slovenia), those living in designated regions (Switzerland), those in authorized training (Germany) and females employed by exporters with a workforce that is 75 percent female (Jamaica); allocations to covering the whole cost incurred for particular population categories — the self-employed (Libya), and those not in employment (Russia) — and the whole cost of maternity benefits (Armenia).

Employment-Injury Program Financing

Employment-injury programs, whether primary or supplementary, are largely contributory (113 countries), although employer-financed benefits are common (67 countries), with entirely government-financed benefits are provided only in Denmark (temporary disability allowances only) and Hong Kong (temporary disability assistance only). The employer-financed benefits take two forms: those provided directly by the employer (self-insured) (24 countries) and those provided by an insurance carrier (43 countries) with which the employer must insure (30 countries) or may insure (13 countries).

A diversity of social security contributory funding sources is used to finance employment injury benefits: employment injury contribution revenue designated for that purpose (63 countries); old-age, invalidity and survivors' contribution revenue for employment-related permanent disability benefits (44 countries), for employment-related survivors' benefits (43 countries) and for employment-related temporary disability benefits (37 countries); and sickness and/or maternity contribution revenue for employment-related temporary disability benefits (12 countries), for employment-related survivors' benefits (6 countries) and for employment-related permanent disability benefits (6 countries).

The designated employment injury contribution revenue is not used in any country to finance other social security program benefits.

Of the 63 countries that finance their employment injury benefits from designated contribution revenue, most require only employers to contribute (59 countries) the exceptions being Guatemala, Italy and Nicaragua (with respect to war victims only), all of which require both employer and employee contributions, and Afghanistan, which insists on employee-only contributions. Earnings-related contributions are most favored, for only Italy has adopted a flat-rate contribution regime, and then only for employee contributions. The contribution rates specified are usually based on actual earnings, although earnings categories are used in Malaysia, Myanmar and the Philippines. Contribution rates are usually set at a uniform rate. Risk-related contribution rates are, however, not uncommon (27 countries). In Uruguay, distinctively, the occupational risk assessment for agricultural workers is made according to the proportion of land area under cultivation. The direct linking of employment injury contributions with occupational safety measures takes place in Greece, where the employers' contribution doubles if there is non-compliance with occupational safety laws.

Placing limits on contribution payments is common. This mainly means limiting contribution obligations by the imposition of an earnings ceiling (30 countries), with the highest incidence in the Caribbean, and West and Central Africa. Few countries specify an earnings floor (only Barbados, Congo and Mexico).

The contribution rates set vary only within quite a narrow range on a regional and national basis. The global average earnings-related total contribution rate is 2.2 percent, within a narrow regional range. The highest total contribution rate can be found in Somalia (6.0 percent), which is also the highest employer contribution rate, although contribution rates for high-risk occupations can be considerably higher (up to 16 percent in Italy). The global average employee contribution is a mere 0.1 percent. The global average statutory contribution incidence is 98 percent for employers and 2 percent for employees.

Government involvement in funding occurs in only 14 countries. This ranges from the provision of supplementary financial assistance to contributory programs (11 countries, half of which are in East Asia and the Middle East) to the entire public financing of supplementary temporary disability allowances (Denmark) and assistance (Hong Kong). Such government funding comes exclusively from central governments in most instances (13 countries), although funding does come exclusively from local government in China.

Supplementary financial assistance by government to contributory programs takes a variety of forms. Program deficit funding is rare; happening in only China and Jordan. An array of subsidy approaches is used: annual subsidies (Japan and Saudi Arabia); administrative cost subsidies (Luxembourg and South Korea); subsidies based on a specified percentage of the payroll (Guatemala (1.5 percent) and Israel (0.05 percent)); inflationary adjustment subsidies (Luxembourg); subsidies to target population categories: motor vehicle accident victims (Western Samoa, for healthcare costs only), general accident victims (New Zealand, for healthcare costs only), students, children in kindergartens and farm employees (Germany) and the self-employed (Libya).

Unemployment Program Financing

Unemployment programs, whether primary or supplementary, are largely contributory (61 countries), although entirely government-financed programs are not uncommon (23 countries) nor are entirely employer-financed benefits (18 countries). The social security contributory funding sources used to finance unemployment benefits are unemployment contribution revenue designated for that purpose (43 countries) and old-age, disability and survivors' contribution revenue (18 countries).

The designated unemployment contribution revenue is typically not used to finance other social security benefits, the exception being South Africa where it is used to finance sickness and maternity benefits.

The 43 countries that finance their unemployment benefits from contribution revenue designated for that purpose mostly require either both employer and employee contributions (25 countries) or employer contributions (16 countries), for only Colombia and Guatemala require employee contributions only. Earnings-related contributions are most common, with flat-rate contributions payable in only Denmark, Guatemala and Sweden (for employee contributions only) and Finland (for both employer and employee contributions). The contribution rates specified are typically based on actual earnings, with earnings categories used in only Spain. Contribution rates are usually set at a uniform rate, although differential rates are sometimes set on a regional basis (China and the United States), on an industry basis (the Netherlands) or on an earnings basis (France).

Placing limits on contribution payments is not common. Some countries limit contribution obligations by the imposition of an earnings ceiling (11 countries, mainly in Europe and North America) and/or an earnings floor (Barbados, Canada and Italy).

The contribution rates that are set vary very little on a regional and national basis. The global average earnings-related total contribution rate is 2.7 percent, within a narrow regional range. The highest total contribution rate can be found in Spain (7.8 percent), while the highest employer contribution rate set is in Bulgaria (7.0 percent). The global average employee contribution is a mere 0.8

percent. The global average statutory contribution incidence is 34 percent for employees and 66 percent for employers.

Governmental involvement in funding occurs in 47 countries. This ranges from the provision of supplementary financial assistance to contributory programs (24 countries, half of which are in post-socialist countries and seven are in Western Europe) to the entire public financing of unemployment assistance and unemployment allowances (23 countries). Such government funding comes almost entirely from central governments (45 countries), although joint national-local government funding does happen (7 post-socialist countries) as does joint regional-local government funding (Belarus) and local government funding (China).

Supplementary financial assistance by government to contributory programs takes a variety of forms. Program deficit funding is quite common (20 countries, including 13 post-socialist countries and 4 Western European countries). A variety of subsidy approaches are: annual subsidies (Argentina (only on a temporary basis), Luxembourg and Spain); administrative cost subsidies (Italy and Japan); subsidies for target unemployed population categories — farm employees (Italy), youth (Italy), government workers (Bulgaria) and vocational and higher education graduates (Bulgaria); wage subsidies for construction workers (Italy); subsidies based on a percentage of benefit costs (Japan, 25 percent), of employer contribution revenue collected (Iceland (0.05 percent), of payroll (Israel, 0.11 percent, but only 0.07 percent if earnings below half the average earnings); and subsidies from earmarked taxes (Denmark).

Child and Family Program Financing

Family and/or child programs, whether primary or supplementary, are predominantly government-financed (49 countries), although contributory programs are common (45 countries), with entirely employer-financed programs existing only in five countries (Bolivia, Burundi, Iran, Paraguay and Zaire). The social security contributory funding sources used to finance family and/or child benefits are: family and/or child benefit contribution revenue designated for that purpose (32 countries); old-age, invalidity and/or survivors' contribution revenue for child benefits (12 countries) and family benefits (4 countries); and sickness and/or maternity contribution revenue for both family and child benefits (Tunisia).

The designated family and/or child contribution revenue collected is used to finance maternity benefits in nine countries.

The 32 countries that finance their family and/or child benefits from designated contribution revenue have overwhelmingly imposed a contribution liability only on employers, the exceptions being France and Greece, both of which also impose joint employee contributions. All have adopted earnings-related contributions with a uniform rate applied to actual earnings.

The articulation of uniform, but different, contribution rates for target population categories is very uncommon. Only three countries do so, and then only for the self-employed (France sets a contribution rate higher than the total contribution rate, Israel sets a rate equal to that paid by employers, and Luxembourg sets a rate equal to that paid by government, the only other contributor).

Placing limits on contribution payments is typical. This includes limiting contribution payment by the imposition of an earnings ceiling (16 countries, 11 of which are in West and Central Africa) and/or an earnings floor (Congo and Italy). Entirely exempting low income earners, however, does not occur.

The contribution rates set vary somewhat on a regional and national basis. The global average earnings-related total contribution rate is 6.5 percent, rising to 8.5 percent in West Africa. The highest total contribution rate can be found in the Central African Republic (12.0 percent). The global average employer contribution is 5.4 percent. The highest employer contribution rate can also be found in the Central African Republic (12.0 percent). The global average employee contribution is 2.5 percent. The highest employee contribution rate can be found in Yugoslavia (11.4 percent). The global average statutory contribution incidence is 32 percent for employees and 68 percent for employers.

Government involvement in funding occurs in 65 countries. This ranges from the public provision of supplementary financial assistance to contributory programs (11 countries) to the entire public financing of social allowance and social assistance programs (39 countries). Such government funding comes almost exclusively from central governments in most instances (40 countries), although joint funding from regional governments does occur (Austria, Japan and Switzerland), as does joint funding from local government (Austria, Belarus, Japan and Russia).

Diverse forms of government supplementary financial assistance to contributory programs are in evidence. The deficit funding occurs in a few countries, but only for child benefit programs (Belgium, Burkina Faso and Mali). The subsidy approaches used include: subsidies from earmarked tax revenue (Chad, Costa Rica (sales tax) and Senegal (turnover tax)); subsidies based on a percentage of benefit costs (Japan, 30 percent); subsidies to particular population categories — small farmers and farm employees (Switzerland) and pensioners and means-tested beneficiaries (Argentina); allocations covering the whole cost incurred for the self-employed and the unemployed (Japan); annual subsidies (Italy); subsidies based on a percentage of total contribution revenue collected (Israel, 130 percent), of employer contribution revenue collected (Luxembourg, 1.7 percent), or of payroll (Israel, 1.67 percent); and an administrative cost subsidy (Luxembourg).

CONCLUSION

Social security programs are typically a central government responsibility financed by employer and employee contributions with government subsidies. Regional and local governments in a few countries do have a social security role to play, both administratively, and, to a lesser extent, financially. The involvement of all three levels of government is, however, rare.

Social security systems are typically administered by an independent social security agency, responsible, through a governing board, to a state ministry or department. Administrative functions are generally centralized.

Employer involvement in administration is most prevalent with employer liability programs, invariably under a regulatory regime administered by a state labor or manpower ministry or department.

Private sector involvement in social security administration is dominated by insurance carriers and pension funds with mandated responsibilities.

9

Comparative Social Security: The Challenge of Comparative Evaluation

INTRODUCTION

Comparative social security, as a field of study, is primarily concerned with describing and analyzing social security programs, to enhance understanding of the development and nature of social security systems. The field of comparative social security has blossomed over the last four decades. The pioneering works of Nelson (1953), Mendelsohn (1954), Clark (1960), Gordon (1963), Wilensky and Lebeau (1965), Rodgers with Greve and Morgan (1968), Gerig (1966), Kessler (1966) and Jenkins (1969) focused on cross-national comparisons that described and compared values, institutions, policies and programs in a selection of countries that share a set of reasonably homogeneous characteristics. Subsequent comparative research has tended to follow in this tradition (see, for example, Lally 1970, Kaim-Caudle 1973, Heclo 1974, Chow 1975, 1981 and 1985, Lawson and Reed 1975, Thursz and Vigilante 1975 and 1976, Stein 1976, Lemam 1977, Rodgers et al. 1977, Maddison 1980, Heckscher 1984, Jones 1985, Midgley 1986, Ackerman 1987, Dixon and Scheurell 1987, Bolderson 1988, Gordon 1988, Guest 1988, Crijns 1989, Bolderson and Mabbett 1991, Mitchell 1991, Ginsburg 1992, Pieters and Vansteenkiste 1995, Ramesh 1995b, Mok 1996, Toft 1996). Since the pioneering works, comparative studies have taken on a much wider variety of perspectives and focuses — although the epistemological and methodological challenges of the comparative evaluation of social security systems have been neglected — which has resulted in the emergence of a sizable descriptive and analytical body of literature.

An early focus of comparative research was on specific social security branches, notably: *unemployment* (ILO 1955, Blaustein and Craig 1977, Sinfield 1983, ISSA 1985, Rikkert 1986, Lawson 1987, Euzeby 1988, Reubens 1989, Kershen and Kessler 1990, Clasen 1992); *old-age and retirement* (Clark 1960, Shanes et al. 1968, Fisher 1970, Schulz et al. 1974, Wilson 1974,

Thompson 1979, Kaim-Caudle 1981, ISSA 1982a, Dapre et al. 1984; Tracy and Ward 1986, ILO 1989a, Tracy 1990 and 1991, Schulz 1992, Bellamy 1993, Orloff 1993, Pratt 1993, Williamson and Pampel 1993, Mackenzie 1995, Giarchi 1996, Shaver 1998); *employment injury* (Gordon 1963, Moulton and Voirin 1979, Palmer 1979, Greiner 1986, Ortolani 1986, Waterman and Brancoli 1986, Rys 1988); *family support* (OECD 1977b, Kamerman and Kahn 1978, 1982 and 1994, Bradshaw and Piachaud 1980, Kahn and Kamerman 1983, Borowczyk 1986, Oxley 1987, Watts 1987, Dapre 1989, Bradshaw et al. 1993, Knyester et al. 1994, McLaughlan and Glendinning 1994); *disability* (Palmer 1979; Wedekind 1985, Aguilar 1986, Burkhauser 1986, Bloch 1994, Lonsdale and Seddon 1994, Zeitzer 1994); *maternity* (ILO 1985b); *survivors* (Crutz 1991); and *sickness* (Kangas 1991).

The first regional comparative studies emerged in the mid-1960s, and all the global regions have now been charted: *Africa* (Gerig 1966, Kessler 1966, Moulton 1975, ILO 1977, Ejuba 1982, Dixon 1987c, Gruat 1990); *Latin America* (ILO 1972a and 1993; Mesa-Lago 1978, 1983, 1985a, 1985b, 1986, 1988, 1991a, 1991b, 1992a, 1992b and 1994, Paillas 1979, Tamburi 1985, Dixon and Scheurell 1990, McGreevey 1988 and 1990, World Bank 1995c); *Asia* (Wadhawan 1972, Chow 1975, Thompson 1978; Dixon and Kim 1985, Jones, 1990, Dixon and Chow 1992, Tyabji 1993, Inductivo 1997, ISSA 1996c, Kwon 1997, Jacobs 1998);*the Pacific Islands* (Wadhawan 1972, ILO 1985a, Dixon and Chow 1992, ISSA 1996c); *Europe* (Zelenka 1974, Lawson and Reed 1975, EISS 1981, Ashford 1986a, European Commission 1991, 1993 and 1996, Deleeck et al. 1992, Greve 1992, Mortensen 1992, Olsson et al. 1993, Reynaud 1995, George and Taylor-Gooby 1996);*the Caribbean* (Jenkins 1981, Mesa-Lago 1988, Mesa-Lago and Roca 1990); *the Middle East* (Dixon 1987b and 1987d); and *Eastern Europe* (Deakin 1992, Dixon and Macarov 1992, Rys 1994, Voirin 1993; Maydell and Hohnerlein 1994, Standing 1996).

Comparative studies that explore the relationship between national social security systems and a variety of socioeconomic phenomena also first emerged in the mid-1960s and have focused on: *the causation of a social security system development* (Cutright 1965, Fisher 1968, Singer 1968, Taira and Kilby 1969, Perrin 1969a, Gilbert 1981, Clark and Filinson 1991, Habibi 1994, Tang 1996b); *economic development* (Hassen 1965, Arroba 1966 and 1972, Kassalow 1968, Rimlinger 1968, Wolfe 1968, Gobin 1977, Cockburn 1980); *income distribution* (Paukert 1968a and 1968b, OECD 1977a, EISS 1979, George and Lawson 1980); *political regimes* (Hewitt 1977, Castles 1981 and 1982, Alber 1983); *poverty* (George and Lawson 1980, Saunders 1990; Deleeck et al. 1992, Siegenthaler 1996, Dixon and Macarov 1998, Shaver 1998); *demography* (Schulz 1981); *employment and labor markets* (Bakemans 1983, Tracy 1983, Euzeby 1988 and 1995, Aaron and Farwell 1984, Blackwell 1990 and 1994, Saunders 1990, Barr 1994a); *savings* (Koskela and Viren 1983); *early, partial and late retirement* (ISSA 1985, Berthet 1986, Bergman et al. 1987, Laczko 1988,

Walters 1988, Schmahl 1989, Tracy and Adams 1989, Simanis 1994, Royers and Russell 1995); *absenteeism* (Prins and De Graaf 1986); *welfare regimes* (Esping-Andersen 1990); *investment* (Yee 1994); *structural adjustment* (Grimaud 1995).

Comparative studies of the more technical dimensions of national social security systems began to emerge in the mid-1960s: *reform and transformation* (Benenson 1964, Parrott 1968, Clarke 1977, ISSA 1975 and 1977, EISS 1981, Thompson 1980b, Maydell and Hohnerlein 1994); *benefits* (Horlick 1970, Aldridge 1982, Tracy and Ward 1986, European Commission 1993 and 1996, Bolderson and Mabbett 1995, Whiteford 1995); *benefit adjustments* (Horlick and Lewis 1970, Horlick and Tracy 1974, ILO 1980); *contribution ceilings* (Horlick and Lucas 1971, Euzeby and Euzeby 1982); *administration* (Gerdes 1973, Ijeh 1980, Indri 1986, Nicolle 1986, Bloch 1994); *mandatory complementary pensions* (ISSA 1973a, 1993b and 1994, EISS 1975); *harmonization* (ILO 1977, Drover 1988, Banting 1992, Voirin 1992, Pieters and Vansteenkiste 1995, Liverpool 1995); *health services* (Roemer 1973, ISSA 1982b, Kvalheim 1980, Zschock 1982, Glaser 1987, Majnani d'Intignano 1991, Borzutzky 1993); *health insurance* (Fulcher 1974, Glaser 1988, Vogel 1990, Abel-Smith 1992); *welfare services* (ISSA 1974, Perez 1974); *finances* (Ijeh 1977, Arroba 1979, McArdle 1979, Rosa 1982a, Montas 1983, ILO 1984a, Moulton 1984, Gustafsson and Klevmarken 1988, Gutierrez 1989 and 1990, Camacho 1992, Mesa-Lago 1992b, Noord and Herd 1993, Ribe 1994, Reynaud 1995, ISSA 1996c); *maintenance* (ISSA 1978, Griffith et al. 1987, Scheiwe 1994); *retirement age* (Tracy 1979, Rix and Fisher 1982); *means tests* (Tracy 1983, Millar 1988, Oorschot and Schell 1989, Castles 1996, Evans 1996, Shaver 1998); *legal rights* (ILO 1983, Perrin 1985, Igle 1990); *benefit take-up rate* (Oorschot 1991); and *privatization* (Gluski 1994, ILO 1994).

Yet another focus that first developed from the late 1960s was the comparative analysis of social security target categories across countries: *immigrants* (Ribas 1968, ILO 1977, Dixon and Magill 1997); *farm employees* (Savy 1972, Thompson 1980a); *women* (ISSA 1973b, Adams and Winston 1980, Bonnar 1985, ISSA 1986b, Tracy and Ward 1986, Folbre 1993, Kingson and O'Grady-LaShane 1993, Sainsbury 1993 and 1996, Hauser et al. 1994, Hutton and Whiteford 1994, Meyers et al. 1994, Hill and Tigges 1995); *lone parents* (Cass and O'Loughlan 1984, Kisch 1987, Kamerman and Kahn 1989a, Millar and Whiteford 1993, Whiteford and Bradshaw 1994); *alien public employee* (Kritzer 1984); *atypical workers* (Kravaritou-Manitakis 1988, Beiback 1993a and 1993b, Blackwell 1994); *indigenous people* (Dixon and Scheurell 1994a); and *war veterans* (Dixon and Scheurell 1994b).

The comparative studies of countries that have adopted the same social security strategies are not common and began in the late 1960s: *National Provident Fund* (Wadhawan 1969, Gerdes 1970–71, Fletcher 1976, Dixon 1982, 1985b, 1987a, 1989a, 1989b, 1993, 1996b and 1996c, ISSA 1986a); *social assistance*

(Liebfried 1978 and 1979, Midgley 1984b and 1984c, Tang 1996a); *social insurance* (Kohler and Zacher 1982, Tracy and Papel 1991, Clasen 1997); and *social allowances* (Gal 1998).

Comparative studies in a Third World setting have begun to emerge since the pioneering research in the early 1980s by MacPherson (1982) and Midgley (1984a, 1984b, 1984c, 1993 and 1995) (see, for example, MacPherson and Midgley 1987, Benda-Beckmann et al. 1988, Tracy 1988, 1990 and 1991, Ahmed et al. 1991, Aikinson and Hill 1991, Gillion 1994, Benda-Beckmann and Benda-Beckmann 1995, Midgley 1995, Schmidt 1995, Tang 1996b).

Cross-national social security studies involving different cultures are also not too common (see, for example, Rimlinger 1971, Woodsworth 1977, Lapiidus and Swanson 1988, Kato 1991, Imbrogno 1991, Gould 1993, Seeleib-Kaiser 1995).

Studies taking a global perspective remain very thin on the ground (Dixon 1986, 1989c, 1996d and 1998a, ISSA 1989, 1992, 1993a, 1993c and 1996a). This is despite the efforts made, over a long time, by the US Social Security Administration and the International Labor Organization to collect and publish descriptive information on national social security systems (US SSA 1937–1998, ILO 1936, 1942, 1952b, 1953a, 1953b and 1954–92).

THE NEGLECT OF EVALUATIVE COMPARATIVE SOCIAL SECURITY

Despite the very evident growth in descriptive and analytical comparative social security research over the last 40 years, only Kaim-Caudle (1973) has taken up the epistemological and methodological challenges of the comparative evaluation of social security systems, as distinct from individual programs (see, for example, ISSA 1976, Bradshaw et al. 1993). Perhaps Rodgers, in the best neopositivist tradition, summed up, 30 years ago, the reason for this general reluctance when she concluded (Rodgers et al. 1968: 337):

if it is so difficult to evaluate the social policies and achievements of a particular country, what of comparative evaluations? Clearly any kind of League Table — "a table that ranks states or countries from highest to lowest on a given measure" (Rose 1993: 24) — except in relation to some very clear cut and quantifiable facts (e.g. the proportion of old people in each country living below a certain income level) is to be avoided, although one is always tempted to draw comparisons in these terms.

Indeed, those grounded in the epistemological tenets of neopositivism — with its *penchant* for empirical verification and reductionism (Alexander 1982, Halfpenny 1982) — can deal with the challenges of comparative evaluation only by restricting comparisons to those countries for which there are strictly comparable objective" social security system performance data — of the kind that would satisfy Rodgers' standard of "very clear cut and quantifiable facts" — which fits into a universally applicable conceptual framework ensuring "value-free" evaluation. This perspective embodies the dubious, if not specious or even fallacious, neopositivist myths of the fact-value dichotomy (Rein 1976, Amy 1984), of the "objectification of reality" (Berger and Luckman 1967) and of the need for "certainty" — a search that Gergen (1982: 209) describes as "a child's romance."

The intricate complexities of the mosaic that is the global social security reality — in terms of multiple and conflicting goals and objectives, and of diverse programmatic, administrative and financial arrangements — require the adoption of an evaluation perspective that transcends the constraints of neopositivism, even at the risk of its being cast out of the realm of objective knowledge by neopositivists (Popper 1972).

APPROACHES TO EVALUATING SOCIAL SECURITY SYSTEMS

There is a variety of evaluation methodologies applicable to the assessment of national social security systems (Dixon 1998b). They could be appraised by their *inputs* (by using as measures, say, public social security receipts or expenditure as a percentage of Gross National Product (GNP), public social security receipts or expenditure per capita, indices of average annual benefit expenditure per capita over time, or indices of the real average annual benefit expenditure per capita over time); by their *efficiency* (by using as a measure, say, the administrative cost per unit of social security benefit dispersed); by their *performance* (by using, say, program coverage measures (such as the percentage of population or workforce covered or the percentage program coverage of target population categories), benefit adequacy measures (such as cash entitlements as a percentage of a poverty-income threshold, of minimum earnings, of average earnings, or of GNP per capita), beneficiary needs-satisfaction or benefit-adequacy perception measures (such as measures of household financial security, of subjective deprivation and of subjective poverty), and macroeconomic measures (such as unemployment, inflation and economic growth); or by their *design features* (by rating the adequacy of their design features). Any of these methodologies will comparatively evaluate national social security systems.

Comparative Input Evaluation

The International Labor Organization (ILO) has long been reporting on the public cost of selected social security programs, as has the Organization for Economic Cooperation and Development (OECD) (ILO 1952b, 1953a and 1954–1992, OECD 1976, 1985, 1989 and 1994c). From these databases can be compiled comparative social security expenditure (or cost) or revenue indicators, usually social security expenditure as a percentage of Gross Domestic Product (GDP), trend GDP, Gross National Product (GNP) or aggregate earnings (Aaron 1967, Mendelsohn 1979; Castles 1982, Alber 1983, Wilensky et al. 1985, Simanis 1989, Esping-Andersen 1990, Andersen 1992, Jacobs 1998). From this type of data Kaim-Caudle (1973: 51–52) has concluded:

The interpretation of statistics relating to [public social security] cost, even if they are based on uniform definitions, standardized accounting and free from distortion by differences in the purchasing power of money, is still exceedingly difficult. . . .

The supposition that low cost necessarily implies low standards is certainly unjustified. . . .

In the same way, high levels of expenditure, whether per head of population or relative to G.N.P., are not necessarily an indication of high standards of service.

Kaim-Caudle (1973: 50) has argued, quite persuasively, that comparing levels of public expenditure on social security has "dangers, difficulties and limitations" (see also IMF 1986, OECD 1996). He considered that systemic cross-national comparisons on the basis of public social security expenditure as a percentage of GNP were of "restricted value" although perhaps useful and suggestive "if they are regarded with some skepticism" (p. 300). They should not, however, in his view, "be viewed as league tables and even less as revelations of truth" (p. 300).

Undoubtedly, public social security expenditure data permit a statistical portrayal of social security system input levels and trends over time, although a careful appraisal of the comparability of these levels and trends is obligatory and extensive qualifications must be attached to their interpretation. Thus, they say something about the relative state of the emperor's clothes, albeit without any sensitivity to the social values underpinning national social security systems. Indeed, the extent to which such a statistical portrayal reveals reality depends crucially on two factors. The first factor is the extent to which social security systems include benefits provided directly by employers or individuals, the cost of which is outside the public domain (Mendelsohn 1979: 223). The second factor is whether the required data is available in a consistent and reliable form (see, for example, OECD 1995, MacKellar and McGreevey 1997, Tang 1996b). On both counts this input evaluation methodology is found wanting.

The comparative input evaluation approach is reductionist in perspective and falls well short of meeting the comparative-evaluative challenge issued by Rys (1966: 268) of defining the "classification scales by which to judge the respective merits and shortcomings of individual members of the [social security] universe observed."

This means, of course, that input evaluation does not permit social security systems to be comparatively assessed on a global basis or ordinally ranked even on the basis of their full cost.

Comparative Efficiency and Performance Evaluation

Social security studies routinely consider *program efficiency* and *program performance*, typically using quantitative, inferential or judgmental analysis, drawing upon whatever national data are available, perhaps utilizing simulation methodologies (see, for example, de Lathouwer 1996, also Cutt et al. 1977, Dixon and Cutt 1975 and 1976, Dixon et al. 1984). An excellent example is Esping-Andersen's (1990) innovative OECD study, which, in passing, ranked the performances of long-term pensions, sickness and unemployment benefits, as a whole, in his 18-country cohort using critical indicators such as the degree of universality of coverage, the extent of differential benefits for different social groups, the extent to which programs exempted beneficiaries from entering the labor market, and the public-private pension balance.

The very evident reluctance to engage in a comparative evaluation of the efficiency or performance of social security systems *in toto* is not surprising, largely because there is no straight forward, accurate and comprehensive way of so doing (Dogan and Pelassy 1984, Merritt and Rokkan 1966). What might seem to be clear-cut systemic efficiency or performance indicators at the abstract level become methodological quagmires when it comes to their quantification in a comparative setting, especially on a global basis.

Social security administrative cost measures are problematic because of double counting and the existence of gaps. These occur when social security service delivery is an adjunct to the delivery of other services, when multiple public agencies are involved in social security administration, when inter-agency or inter-governmental administrative subsidies are provided, or when the non-government sector (including employers) provides significant administrative inputs (ILO 1988b: 6).

Social security program coverage measures are problematic because of the difficulties in determining, at any given moment, the number of people who are actually, rather than potentially, eligible for program benefits under general qualifying criteria specified, such as minimum residency, employment or contribution qualifying periods (ILO 1972b: 385, Macarov 1981: 24).

Social security program benefit adequacy measures are dubious because they ignore differential social security needs and the distribution of benefit payment above or below the chosen standard or benchmark (such as a poverty-income threshold, an average wage level, GDP per capita) (Aldrich 1982, Bolderson 1988, Haanes-Olsen and Horlick 1974, Horlick 1970, Tracy 1991, Jacobs 1998).

Needs satisfaction or benefit-adequacy perception measures may be biased by the form of question posed and the measurement scales used (Koniaris 1979, Shepherd and Mullins 1989).

The socioeconomic performance of social security systems can be judged by their impact on a set of internationally comparable indicators of, for example, material and social deprivation, household financial insecurity, family economic status, the incidence of poverty, and income distribution, not to mention unem-

ployment, inflation and economic growth (Atkinson 1990, Berghman and Muffels 1988, Deleeck et al. 1986, 1988 and 1992, Fields 1994, Foster 1984,
McGranahan 1977, Moroney 1979, Morris 1979, O'Higgins et al. 1994, Rainwater et al. 1986, Sawyer 1976, Scott 1981, Stephenson 1989, Townsend
1993). To undertake, for example, cross-national income distribution comparisons is a daunting task that requires, among other things, three consistent definitions: "income" (be it gross, disposable, net cash, permanent or current, perhaps
adjusted for any in-kind income received from kin groups, local communities,
employers or the state), "income unit" (be it the household, family or individual)
and "equivalence scales" (for weighting income units of different sizes and compositions) (see Atkinson 1983, Berge 1989, Buchmann et al. 1988, Danziger and
Taussig 1979, Gottschalk and Smeeding 1997, Plotnik 1984, Townsend 1987).
The ultimate methodological challenge is, of course, to be able to isolate the
impact of a social security system on those indicators.

In addition to this quite formidable list of evaluation challenges, two further
problems exist. The first is methodological: how to reconcile various complex
assessment indicators into a single indicator that will permit the assessment and
ordinal ranking of social security systems? The second is informational: how to
overcome the unavailability of reliable and compatible data, especially on a
global basis? (Estes 1984, McGranahan et al. 1985). On the latter issue, the
World Bank's global data has the following caveat attached (1995b: 385, similarly 1995a: 229):

statistical systems in many developing economies are still weak; statistical methods, coverage, practice, and definitions differ widely among countries; and cross-
country and cross-time comparisons involve complex technical problems that cannot be unequivocally resolved.

This means, of course, that efficiency and performance evaluation methodologies do not permit social security systems to be comparatively assessed on a
global basis or ordinally ranked even on the basis of their efficiency or their performance.

Comparative System Design Feature Evaluation

In a global comparative setting, the design features of national social security
systems are commonly described (see, especially, US SSA 1937–98), but rarely
evaluated. Kaim-Caudle (1973) is the very obvious exception. He evaluated 10
national social security systems by crudely rating the adequacy of their design
features. He was thus willing, clearly with some reluctance, to draw general
comparative-evaluative conclusions (pp. 301–2):

in spite of all the problems which arise in making detailed comparisons . . . based on personal judgment and not on slide-rule calculations, as a number of particulars have to be taken into account which, like apples and pears, cannot be added up.

On the basis of his personal judgment Kaim-Caudle established a league table: Netherlands first (5 points), Germany second (4 points), Denmark third (3 points), Austria and the United Kingdom equal fourth, (1 point), New Zealand sixth (no points), Ireland and Canada equal seventh (–2 points), Australia ninth (–4 points) and the United States tenth and last (–6 points). He concluded, however, that "these scores are no more than reasonable approximations" (p. 306). He also dismissed, almost out of hand, the idea that a more sophisticated design feature scoring system could be developed to quantify design feature merits and shortcomings (p.302):

Any attempt to produce indices by attaching weights to the different particulars would have to be so arbitrary that the results would be much less meaningful than those based on judgment.

A systematic qualitative assessment of a very comprehensive set of social security design features permits a more complex, and, indeed more rigorous, comparative evaluation of national social security systems than is possible using Kaim-Caudle's (1973: 301–2) path breaking, but relatively crude, aggregated "personal judgment" methodology.

This means, of course, that social security systems can be comparatively assessed on a global basis, in terms of their merits and shortcomings, and thus ordinally ranked on the basis of their design features.

A METHODOLOGY FOR COMPARATIVELY EVALUATING AND ORDINALLY RANKING SOCIAL SECURITY SYSTEMS

A social security system design feature evaluation methodology enables an assessment to be made of a country's statutory social security intention. There is, of course, a potential, sometimes an actual, implementation gap between what a social security system promises to deliver — in terms of statutory program coverage, benefit eligibility and benefit generosity — and what it ultimately delivers. This gap can, of course, become very significant in countries where public administration and/or public finances have largely or totally collapsed, or have become severely restricted, because of war, natural disasters or severe economic dislocation.

Methodology Conceptualization

Designing a methodology that evaluates systemic design features requires the conceptualization of scoring system that quantifies design feature merits and shortcomings. This approach meets Berk and Rossi's (1990: 31) requirement that an evaluation methodology should ensure that the empirical technique employed (the evaluation of systemic design feature merits and shortcomings) relates directly to the evaluation question posed (which countries have the best designed social security systems?). It involves, first, the comprehensive articulation of design features, categorized by whether they relate to constituent program coverage, program benefit-eligibility requirements, program benefits, and methods of financing or administrative arrangements. Then there must be an assignment of a score to each design feature, one that reflects its relative importance.

The attachment of a subjective score to the existence (or non-existence) of a specific design feature is the quantitative expression of a qualitative judgment about whether the inclusion of that design feature makes a social security system "more acceptable" (or its absence makes it "less acceptable"). Central to any such qualitative judgments must be a set of value premises about whether an "acceptable" social security system should seek to:

- cover all social security contingencies, which penalizes countries that have made the policy choice, whether for ideological, political or economic reasons, of either:
  - using other public policy strategies (such as tax expenditure strategies) to achieve social security goals; or
  - not establishing social security programs for particular contingencies;
- have embodied in its constituent programs:
  - universality of coverage, which penalizes countries that have made the policy choice of restricting coverage by excluding specific population categories, whether for ideological, political or economic reasons;
  - minimal restrictions with respect to their categorizing and general qualifying eligibility requirements, and the specification of needs-assessment criteria, which penalizes countries if they have made the policy choice of restricting eligibility on any basis other than need, whether for ideological, political or economic reasons;
  - provision of periodic cash entitlements that enable recipients to maintain their accustomed lifestyle, relative to the prevailing community living standards, which penalizes countries that have made the policy choice, whether for ideological, political or economic reasons, of:
    - providing benefits on any basis other than past earnings; and/or
    - not regularly adjusting such cash entitlements so as to ensure that they remain commensurate with prevailing community living standards;
  - provision of healthcare benefits that include appropriate medical, hospital and paramedical care, of a standard comparable to that available to the community as a whole, to those covered by social security programs (including dependents) and to social security recipients who are in need of such services for as long as such services are medically required, which penalizes countries that have made the policy choice, whether for ideological, political or economic reasons, of restricting the availability, and/or the range of healthcare benefits provided under the auspices of their social security systems; and

- provision of measures to encourage and/or enable the social security recipients who are able to work to enter the workforce, which penalizes countries that have made the policy choice of not introducing a set of welfare-to-work measures in an effort to reduce dependency;
- minimize its costs, and share them amongst employers, employees and government in such a way as to ensure that cost burden to individuals (as taxpayers and contributors) is progressive rather than regressive, which penalize countries that have made the policy choice, whether for ideological, political or economic reasons, of:
  - not adopting tripartite financing for all social security programs; and/or
  - limiting the degree of vertical income redistribution sought; and
- have a mode of administration that is as simple and as decentralized as possible, especially from the perspective of the end user, which penalizes countries that have made the policy choice, whether for ideological, political or economic reasons, of constructing a complex and/or centralized social security system.

The ILO's conventions on minimum social security standards (ILO 1952a, 1952c, 1964, 1966. 1967, 1968, 1969, 1988a and 1989a) constitute a long-standing and internationally accepted set of conservative, minimum-standard benchmarks that identify the design features that should be embodied in a "minimally acceptable" social security system (ILO 1989b). (For a comprehensive account of the early development of these social security standards see Tamburi 1981). Otting (1993: 169) considers that these conventions provide "an internationally accepted definition of the very idea of social security."

Methodology Operationalization

National Social Security Program Design Assessment. To operationalize this social security system design feature evaluation methodology involved the articulation of a comprehensive set of design features. The comparative-evaluative assessment methodology developed here focuses on 860 social security system design features (see Table 9.1).

The designated primary social security strategy has been assessed on three dimensions: coverage requirements, benefit-eligibility requirements and the benefits provided. Each of these dimensions was initially assigned a base-level score of 100. Deductions were then made if particular meritorious design features (design merits) were missing or if design features with particular shortcomings (design demerits) were included. Bonuses were added if design merits were included or if design demerits were missing. The deductions and bonuses assigned to the inclusion and exclusion of particular design features were generally relatively small (5, 10 or 15 points), so that the inclusion and exclusion of one design feature did not dominate the evaluation, except in those instances of significant design feature merit (up to 30 points) or shortcoming (up to 80 points).

Coverage requirements have been assessed by reference to the ILO's conventions on minimum social security standards. These establish three alternate min-

Table 9.1
Social Security System Design Feature Evaluative Dimensions

	PRIMARY COVER- AGE	STRATEGY: ELIGIB- ILITY	BENE- FITS	SUPPLE- MENTARY STRATEGIES	TOTAL
OLD-AGE PROGRAMS	21	18	32	3	74
DISABILITY PROGRAMS	22	17	36	3	78
SURVIVORS' PROGRAMS	23	39	33	3	98
SICKNESS PROGRAMS	27	10	19	3	59
MATERNITY PROGRAMS	25	13	35	3	76
EMPLOYMENT- RELATED TEMPORARY INJURY PROGRAMS	20	8	15	3	46
EMPLOYMENT- RELATED PERMANENT INJURY PROGRAMS	21	10	32	3	66
EMPLOYMENT- RELATED SURVIVORS'					

PROGRAMS	20	29	40	3	92
UNEMPLOYMENT PROGRAMS	12	15	34	3	64
FAMILY BENEFITS PROGRAMS	24	10	19	3	56
CHILD BENEFITS PROGRAMS	24	18	39	3	84
HEALTHCARE BENEFIT PROGRAMS	13	2	14	4	84
FINANCIAL ARRANGEMENTS					27
ADMINISTRATIVE ARRANGEMENTS					7
TOTAL	**252**	**189**	**348**	**37**	**860**

imum coverage standards: not less than 20 percent of all residents; all residents with means below a particular limit; or not less than 50 percent of all employees in industrial work places employing 20 persons or more. Thus, program coverage has been assessed on the basis of the degree of population coverage sought. Deductions were made for the exclusion from coverage of: people outside formal employment; the self-employed; employees in designated regions, occupations, industries, small business (on a sliding scale) or earning below a minimum income; people in particular program-relevant categories (such as nonmanual workers excluded from employment-injury programs coverage, or small families excluded for child benefit program coverage). Bonuses were added if voluntar coverage, or a special system, are available to excluded population categories or if coverage is extended to particular population categories facing distinctive social security risks (such as the inclusion of those incapacitated for work due to a childhood disability under disability program coverage).

Benefit-eligibility requirements have been assessed according to the degree of exclusion sought, as evidenced by the degree to which the categorizing and general qualifying eligibility requirements restricted eligibility, and by the degree to which any means assessment requirement focused eligibility on those most in need. Deductions were made for the exclusion of particular applicants from the receipt of benefits, such as those who fail to satisfy restrictive categorical requirements (such as retirement ages set above the life expectancy, less than total and permanent disability, advanced minimum ages for widows' pensions (on a sliding scale), advanced minimum ages and/or restricted maximum ages of dependents for child and family benefits (on a sliding scale); those in program-relevant population categories (such as pensioners made ineligible for healthcare benefits, survivors' without children made ineligible for survivors' benefits, female orphans made ineligible for survivors' benefits, female employees who have an employed husband made ineligible for sickness benefits, first-job seekers or women seeking to re-enter the workforce made ineligible for unemployment benefits, victims of particular types of employment accidents or illnesses made ineligible for employment-injury benefits); and those who fail to satisfy restrictive general qualifying eligibility requirements (such as long minimum qualifying periods for residency, contribution payments, covered employment, sickness, unemployment or marriage). Bonuses were added if liberal categorical requirements were specified (such as early retirement; low minimum degrees of disability (on a sliding scale)); if in particular program-relevant population categories were included (such as women having an abortion, lone mother and male partners made eligible for maternity benefits, those with a partial but permanent disability made eligible for general and employment-related disability benefits (on a sliding scale), widowers made eligible for survivors' benefits, road accident victims made eligible for employment injury benefits, or dependents of working age who are studying or disabled made eligible for family support benefits); or if liberal general qualifying eligibility requirements applied (such as no minimum qualifying periods specified in particular circumstances (as in the event of general accidents); or if income or asset tests are applied to concentrate benefits on those in most need.

Benefit provision has also been assessed by reference to with the ILO's conventions on minimum social security standards. These endorse only the use of periodic payments expressed either as a percentage of a beneficiary's previous earnings over a specified period of time, or as an income-tested, flat rate amount "sufficient to maintain the family of the beneficiary in health and decency" (ILO 1952a: article 65). Thus, program benefit provision has been assessed on the basis of both the degree of periodicity of payment and the degree of benefit generosity (relative, of course, to prevailing community living standards). Deductions were made when benefits are paid as a lump sum, a flat rate, as a proportion of average or minimum national earnings, or on the basis of past contributions; when benefits vary with income, assets, the period of past covered employment, or age; when a maximum payment period is specified (on a sliding scale); when no or only ad hoc automatic benefit adjustments are made; when maximum income-replacement rates are less than 50 percent (on a sliding scale) or when additional income tests apply to supplementary or special need benefits. Bonuses were added when maximum income-replacement rates are more than 70 percent (on a sliding scale); when supplementary and special need benefits are provided, especially those that enhance beneficiaries' ability to enter the workforce; when lump sum benefits are convertible to periodic payments and annuities; when minimum and maximum benefit rates are specified; when minimum and maximum earnings for benefit purposes are specified; and when automatic benefit adjustments are made on less than an annual basis.

Any supplementary social security strategies have been assessed according to whether they extend primary coverage, particularly to those most in need, and whether they supplement primary benefits, with bonus points being assigned accordingly.

A national social security program design assessment score has been calculated as follows, assuming equal weight is given to each social security program:

$$P = 0.3 \, ((100 - Cd + Cb) + (100 - Ed + Eb) + (100 - Bd + Bb) + Sb)$$

where, Cd is the sum of all primary strategy coverage design shortcoming deductions, Cb is the sum of all primary strategy coverage design merit bonuses, Ed is the sum of all primary strategy benefit-eligibility design shortcoming deductions, Eb is the sum of all primary strategy benefit-eligibility merit bonuses, Bd is the sum of all primary strategy benefit design shortcoming deductions, Bb is the aggregate primary strategy benefit merit bonuses, and Sb is the merit bonus assigned to any supplementary strategies.

National Social Security Healthcare Benefit Program Design Assessment. The overall assessment of a social security system's primary healthcare provision, in line with the ILO's conventions on minimum social security standards, depended on the degree to which adequate medical, paramedical and hospital services were intended to be provided to social security recipients and their dependents and to covered employees and their dependents.

Primary healthcare benefit program coverage has been assessed on the basis of the degree of population coverage intended. Deductions were thus made if restrictive coverage requirements are included that exclude social security recipients, their dependents or the dependents of covered workers, or if coverage is restricted because of limited service provision.

Primary healthcare benefit program eligibility requirements have been assessed according to the degree of exclusion sought. Deductions were thus made if the eligibility requirements are more rigorous than those applying to cash sickness and maternity benefits and if access is restricted exclusively to those with low incomes.

Primary healthcare benefit program benefits have been assessed according to the degree to which limits were placed on service provision and on the range of paramedical services provided. Deductions were thus made if healthcare provision is limited (by the specification of maximum hospital stay periods, statutory waiting periods, maximum health expenditure limits, cost reimbursements limits of less than 90 percent (on a sliding scale), copayment requirements, limited fees-for-service payments) or if the range of health services offered excludes certain services (prostheses, pharmaceuticals, transport and rehabilitation) or are very limited (maternity healthcare only). Bonuses were added if additional paramedical services are provided, specifically dental and optical care.

Any supplementary healthcare strategies have been assessed on the basis of the degree to which they extended primary healthcare coverage, with bonus points being assigned accordingly.

A national social security healthcare benefit program design assessment score (H) has been calculated in exactly the same way as a national social security program design assessment score (P). Hence:

$$H = 0.3 \,((100 - HCd + HCb) + (100 - HEd + HEb) + \\ (100 - HBd + HBb) + HS)$$

where, HCd is the sum of all primary healthcare benefit program coverage design shortcoming deductions, HCb is the sum of all primary healthcare coverage design merit bonuses, HEd is the sum of all primary healthcare benefit-eligibility design shortcoming deductions, HEb is the sum of all primary healthcare benefit design merit bonuses, HBd is the sum of all primary healthcare benefit design shortcoming deductions, HBb is the sum of all primary healthcare benefit design merit bonuses, and HS is the design merit bonus assigned to any supplementary healthcare strategies.

National Social Security Financing Assessment. The ILO's conventions on minimum social security standards require that the costs of social security protection be met by means of contributions or taxes "in a manner which avoids hardship to persons of small means" (1952a: article 67). Thus the social security financial arrangements have been assessed on the basis of the share of statutory cost burden carried by employers, employees and government and on the degree of regressivity of this cost burden to individuals (as taxpayers or contributors). Deductions were thus made if employer contributions are 15 percent or more (on a sliding scale); if employee contributions are 7.5 percent or more (on a sliding scale); if contributions are paid at a flat rate (on a sliding scale); if health insurance contributions are paid (on a sliding scale); if either employers or employees pay either the whole cost of a social security program or make no contributions whatever; if lower contribution rates apply to higher income earnings; if either maximum contribution rates or maximum earnings ceilings for contribution purposes are specified; or if government deficit finances programs. Bonuses were given if total contributions are less than 15 percent, provided no more than three programs are entirely paid either by employers or individuals (on a sliding scale); if employer contributions substitute for employee contributions at low earnings levels; if those receiving low earnings pay either a lower or no contribution; or if a minimum earnings level for contribution purposes is specified.

A national social security financing assessment score (F) has been calculated as follows:

$$F = (100 - Fd + Fb)$$

where, Fd is the sum of all social security financing design shortcoming deductions, and Fb is the sum of all social security financing design merit bonuses.

Social Security Administration Assessment. The social security administrative arrangements have been assessed according to the degree of administrative complexity and on the degree of administrative decentralization. Deductions were thus made if a social security system's administration is particularly complex (such as where there are multiple lines of accountability; where multiple agencies deliver social security services (on a sliding scale); or where either inter-agency or inter-governmental collaboration is required). A bonus was added if benefit administration is decentralized.

A national social security administration assessment score (A) has been calculated:

$$A = (100 - Ad + Ab)$$

where, Ad is the sum of all social security administration design shortcoming deductions, and Ab is the sum of all social security administration design merit bonuses.

National Social Security System Design Assessment. A national social security system design assessment score — the basis for an ordinal ranking of social security systems — has been calculated as follows:

$$R = a\,((Psum + H)/11) + b(F) + c(A).$$

where, Psum is the sum of all the national social security program design assessment scores, F is the national social security financing assessment score, H is the national social security health services design assessment score, A is the national social security administration assessment score, and a, b and c are coefficients of relative importance that sum to unity, assigned the values of 0.8, 0.15 and 0.05, respectively.

CONCLUSION

Comparative social security, as a field of study, has blossomed over the last four decades. The point has now been reached where social security policies and practices in all regions of the world, and in most countries, have, to varying degrees, been described and analyzed. Comparative social security research extends from technical studies, to thematic and issue studies, to regional studies, even to global studies. The result has been an enhanced understanding of the development, nature and consequences of social security programs and systems. Despite this remarkable growth in descriptive and analytical comparative social security research, only Kaim-Caudle (1973) has taken up the epistemological and methodological challenges of the comparative evaluation of social security systems.

This reluctance to engage in comparative-evaluative research is not too surprising, given the neopositivist tradition within the social sciences. The inclination amongst social scientists is to disparage, if not to condemn, any evaluative methodology that does not restrict itself to comparisons of those countries for which there is strictly comparable "objective" and "factual" social security system input or performance data that fit into a universally applicable conceptual framework to ensure "value-free" evaluation. This perspective is difficult to sustain.

A variety of evaluation methodologies can be applied to national social security systems: input evaluation, efficiency evaluation, performance evaluation, or design-feature evaluation. All of these approaches enable national social security systems to be evaluated. Each has its strengths and weaknesses, but, in the end, the availability of compatible and reliable data most constrains the evaluator. Design-feature evaluation is the only feasible approach in a global setting.

The design-feature evaluation methodology adopted here involved the systematic attachment of a subjective score to the existence (or non-existence) of each of 860 design features in 172 social security system. Central to any such qualitative judgments is a set of value premises about whether the inclusion of particular design feature makes a social security system "more acceptable" or its absence makes it "less acceptable." The ILO's conventions on minimum social security standards provided the necessary benchmarks. The output is a global ranking to national social security systems — a league table — which, as Rose (1995: 113, see also 1993:73–75) quite correctly points out, "ignore[s] whether a country is not only making progress in relation to its own past, but also catching up in relation to other nations." It does, however, provide the necessary base for a subsequent dynamic cross-national evaluative study.

10

A Global Ranking of
National Social Security
Systems and Programs

INTRODUCTION

The basis for the ordinal ranking of social security programs and systems (given in Appendix 10.1 (country rank order), 10.2 (country alphabetical order) and 10.3 (regional country rankings)) is the inclusion or exclusion of 860 particular program design features that make them "more" or "less" acceptable, according to a set of benchmarks embodying the ILO's conventions on minimum social security standards (ILO 1952a, 1952c, 1964, 1966. 1967, 1968, 1969, 1988a and 1989a) (see Appendix 10.4). These league tables have been compiled on the basis of statutory intent. Some countries — particularly those in post-socialist East Europe and Central Asia — that have been identified as having well-designed programs may indeed have social security systems that are severely restricted, even inoperative, because of war, natural disasters or severe economic dislocation.

GLOBAL SOCIAL SECURITY PROGRAM RANKINGS

Old-Age Programs

Most of the best-designed old-age programs can be found in Western Europe. The very best are in Scandinavia — conspicuously Finland, Sweden (2nd) and Denmark (3rd) — followed by Portugal, France, and Australia and Italy (equal 4th), Canada (8th) and Austria, Iceland and Turkmenistan (equal 9th). In Africa and the Middle East unquestionably the best-designed programs are in Mauritius and Turkey, respectively. In Latin America, the Pacific Islands and Eastern Europe this honor is held, respectively, by Nicaragua just ahead of Brazil, by the Cook Islands and Nauru (in that order) and by Belarus and the Ukraine (equal ranking).

Disability Programs

Western Europe's dominance of the disability program league table is somewhat weakened by the best-designed disability programs found in the Antipodes. The best-designed program is clearly Australia's, followed by Portugal (2nd), Austria (3rd), Finland (4th), Norway (5th), Brazil, Nicaragua and Sweden (equal 6th), Denmark (9th) and Japan, Spain and Turkey (equal 10th). In Africa the best-designed programs can be found in the cluster of Libya (1st), the Congo (2nd) and Niger and Togo (equal 3rd). In Eastern Europe they are found in the Czech Republic and Russia (equal 1st), closely followed by Moldova. In the Pacific Islands, the Cook Islands has the best-designed program. In North America, Canada clearly leads the United States.

Survivors' Programs

The higher echelons of the best-designed survivors' program rankings are not dominated by Western Europe. The best-designed program honor is shared by Iceland and Kazakhstan, closely followed by Georgia (3rd), Spain (4th), Denmark and Japan (equal 5th), Uzbekistan (7th), Australia and Sweden (equal 8th) and Greece and Norway (equal 10th). In Africa, Egypt clearly leads the best-designed program list, as do Uruguay in Latin America and the Cook Islands in the Pacific Islands. The rank order in Eastern Europe is Russia (1st), closely followed by Moldova and Estonia (equal and close 2nd) and in the Middle East it is Kuwait (1st) and Israel (a close 2nd). In North America, Canada is very marginally ahead of the United States.

Sickness Programs

Western Europe is dominant in the higher echelons of the sickness program league table, but the design strengths in three Eastern European countries are evident. The best-designed program is found in Scandinavia — Sweden — followed closely by France (2nd) and then Australia, Austria, Germany and Slovenia (equal 3rd), Russia (7th), Norway and Peru (equal 8th) and Yugoslavia (10th). Algeria clearly leads the African rankings, as do Peru in Latin America, Iraq in the Middle East, and Nauru in the Pacific Islands. Turkmenistan has the best-designed program in Asia, by a very small margin over Georgia and Uzbekistan (equal 2nd). In North America, Canada is well ahead of the United States.

Maternity Programs

Although Western Europe occupies a significant position in the maternity program league table, it is not dominant, however, because of the presence of Eastern European, Asian and African countries. The best-designed program is found in France, followed by Armenia (2nd), Denmark and Hungary (equal 3rd), Iceland (5th), Poland (6th), Bulgaria and Slovakia (equal 7th) and Côte d'Ivoire,

Luxembourg Sweden and Russia (equal 9th). Uruguay and Israel conspicuously have the best-designed programs in Latin America and the Middle East, respectively. Canada has a considerably better designed program than the United States.

Employment-Injury Programs

Five of the 10 best-designed employment-injury programs are West European. The very best are notably in Luxembourg (1st), followed by Russia (2nd), Austria and France (equal 3rd), New Zealand (5th), Sweden (6th), Brazil and Germany (equal 7th), Hungary and Belgium (9th). The clearly best-designed programs in the other regions are in Gabon (Africa), Malaysia (Asia), Israel (Middle East) and Papua New Guinea (Pacific Islands). These rankings differ, however, when constituent employment-injury programs are considered individually.

Employment-Related Temporary Disability Programs. New Zealand and Sweden equally share the honor of having the best-designed programs, closely followed by Belgium and Malaysia (equal 3rd), Germany (5th), Brazil, Cuba, Lithuania and Slovakia (equal 6th) and Estonia, France, Hungary, Luxembourg, Russia, Trinidad and Tobago, and Yugoslavia (equal 10th). In Africa the best-designed programs can be found in Algeria (1st), very closely followed by Côte d'Ivoire (2nd), Congo (3rd) and Gabon (4th). In the remaining regions, the best-designed programs are in Canada (North America), Israel (Middle East) and Papua New Guinea (Pacific Islands).

Employment-Related Permanent Disability Programs. Luxembourg emerges as having the best-designed program, closely followed by the Netherlands and New Zealand (equal 2nd), France and Italy (equal 4th), Austria, Sweden and Switzerland (equal 6th) and Brazil, Malaysia, Russia and Spain (equal 9th). The clearly best-designed programs in the remaining regions are in Canada (North America), Tunisia (Africa), Israel (Middle East), and Kiribati and Papua New Guinea (equal ranking) (Pacific Islands).

Employment-Related Survivors' Programs. Austria and Luxembourg have the equal best-designed programs, followed by Belarus (3rd), Russia (4th), Georgia (5th), Germany, Mexico and Moldova (equal 6th), France (9th) and Kazakhstan, Kyrgyzstan, Turkmenistan, Ukraine and Uzbekistan (equal 10th). The manifestly best-designed programs in the remaining regions are in Canada (North America), New Zealand (Australasia), Rwanda, just ahead of Egypt (2nd), (Africa), Israel (Middle East) and Papua New Guinea (Pacific Islands).

Unemployment Programs

West European countries are not prominent in the unemployment program league table's higher echelons, although Finland shares equal top ranking with Australia. They are followed by the Ukraine (3rd), Romania (4th), Austria and New Zealand (equal 5th), Turkmenistan, Uzbekistan and Russia (equal 7th), Germany and Sweden (equal 10th). Of the relatively few countries that provide this program in Africa, Mauritius has the best-designed one, which is also true of Uruguay in Latin America and Israel in the Middle East. In North America, the United States is unmistakably ahead of Canada.

Family Support Programs

Western European countries are only modestly represented amongst the providers of the best-designed family support programs. Australia has the best-designed family support program in the world, just ahead of Chile (2nd), both of which are much better designed than those of Armenia and France (equal 3rd), Denmark (5th), Ireland and Finland (equal 6th), Argentina (8th) and Bulgaria and Tunisia (equal 9th). Of the relatively few countries that provide such programs in the Middle East, Lebanon, incontestably, has the best designed one, which is also true of Nauru in the Pacific Islands.

Healthcare Benefit Programs

Western Europe dominates the healthcare benefit program rankings. Top billing goes to Austria, Denmark, Germany and Spain (equal ranking), followed by Australia, Finland, the Netherlands and New Zealand (equal 5th), Belgium, Greece, Ireland, Israel and Japan (equal 9th). In Latin America, Uruguay has the best-designed program, while in Africa this honor is shared equally by South Africa and Mauritius, and is held in the Pacific Islands by Fiji .

GLOBAL SOCIAL SECURITY SYSTEMS FINANCE AND ADMINISTRATION RANKINGS

Ranking of Social Security Financial Arrangements

Because the ranking of social security financial arrangements is crucially dependent on the magnitude of the social security cost burden, the countries that ranked highest are those with the least developed, and thus lowest cost, social security systems — Somalia and Azerbaijan. However, at the regional level, where relative costs are generally more comparable, the degree of regressivity of the social security cost burden on individuals (as taxpayers or contributors) comes more into play.

Western Europe. The West European social security financing rankings reveal a set of very wide extremes. Cyprus heads the rankings because of its relatively underdeveloped social security system (ranked equal 78th in the global social security financing rankings with Bolivia, Côte d'Ivoire, Dominican Republic and Pakistan). Then follows Ireland (2nd) (equal 92nd), Iceland (3rd) (equal 97th), the United Kingdom (4th) (equal 107th), Portugal and Switzerland (equal 5th) (equal 128th), Luxembourg (7th) (equal 139th), Spain (8th) (142nd), Italy (9th) (equal 143rd) and Denmark and Sweden (equal 10th) (equal 146th). At the bottom of the table are Austria (20th and last) (171st and second last ranking in the world), Finland (19th) (169th) and Malta (18th) (168th).

North America. Canada (equal 95th in the global social security financing ranking with Costa Rica) heads the United States (equal 111th) and both are in accord with the upper levels of the Western Europe rankings.

Australasia. Australia (equal 121st in the global social security rankings with Armenia and Burkina Faso) is marginally ahead of New Zealand (equal 128th).

Eastern Europe. The Eastern European social security financing rankings have extremes similar to those of Western Europe. Moldova is clearly at the top of the table (equal 97th in the global rankings with Cameroon, the Central African Republic, Iceland and Togo) and Bulgaria is at the bottom (and is also at the bottom of the global rankings). The rankings, overall, reflect the extent to which post-socialist countries have transformed their social security financing methods from those that prevailed under socialism. Thus Moldova, Albania (2nd) (equal 113th) and the Ukraine (3rd) (120th) have embodied better designed financing arrangements than Bulgaria, Romania (15th) (167th) and Hungary (14th) (equal 162nd).

Latin America. The Latin American social security financing rankings have wide extremes and the rank ordering generally reflects the relative cost of social security systems, although the degree of regressivity of the chosen method of financing becomes a factor of importance at the lower levels. At the top are the Caribbean countries with relatively underdeveloped social security systems — Jamaica (1st) (equal 8th on the global rankings with Indonesia), Bahamas and the British Virgin Islands (equal 2nd) (equal 10th), and Haiti (4th) (17th). The lower orders are filled by Brazil (36th and last) (170th on the global rankings), Argentina (35th) (equal 164th), Peru (34th) (159th) and Chile (33rd) (158th), all of which are in the bottom cohort of 14 counties in the global rankings.

Asia. As with the Latin American social security financing rankings, the Asian rankings have wide extremes and generally reflect the relative cost of social security systems, although the degree of regressivity of the chosen method of financing becomes a factor of more importance at the lower levels. Countries with the least-developed social security systems are dominant at the top of the Asia rankings, and some are at the top of the global rankings — Azerbaijan (1st) (2nd in the global rankings), Macau (2nd) (7th), Indonesia (3rd) (8th), and Thailand (equal 4th) (equal 13th) — but so is the more affluent South Korea (equal 4th) (equal 13th). At the bottom of the Asian rankings are four post-socialist countries — Kyrgyzstan (26th and last) (equal 162nd), Turkmenistan and Georgia (equal 26th) (equal 137th) and China and Singapore (equal 23rd) (equal 134th).

Africa. The African social security financing rankings, in line with those for Latin America and Asia, also have wide extremes and generally reflect the relative cost of social security systems, although the degree of regressivity in the chosen method of financing becomes a factor at the lower levels. The countries with least-developed social security systems are dominant at the top of the Africa rankings, and some are at the top of the global rankings — Somalia (1st) (also 1st in the global rankings), Malawi (2nd) (3rd) and Liberia and Sierra Leone (equal 3rd) (equal 5th). At the other extreme can be found Egypt (45th) (166th), Guinea (44th) (equal 132nd with Lithuania) and Mauritius (42nd) (equal 124th).

The Middle East. The extremes of the Middle East social security rankings are not wide by the standards set by the other regions, but the rank ordering does primarily reflect differential social security costs. The top group reflects the degree of under-development of the social security systems in Oman (1st) (equal 18th), Bahrain (2nd) (equal 36th) and Kuwait (3rd) (equal 97th). At the foot of the table are the more established systems in Turkey (12th and last) (equal 146th), Lebanon (11th) (equal 134th) and Iran (10th) (equal 65th).

The Pacific Islands. The extremes of the Pacific Islands social security financing rankings are narrower than those in evidence in the Middle East, and the rank ordering strongly reflects the region's relatively underdeveloped social security systems. At the top is Vanuatu (1st) (equal 3rd) and at the bottom are Nauru (12th) (equal 74th) and Fiji (11th) (equal 62nd). Except for Nauru and Fiji, the remaining Pacific Island countries are in the group of 50 counties in the top one-third of the global rankings.

Ranking of Social Security Administrative Arrangements

Because assessment of social security administrative arrangements is limited to two dimensions — the degree of administrative complexity and the degree of administrative decentralization — the global rankings reveal a set of very narrow extremes. The honor of having the best-designed set of social security administrative arrangements is shared by 31 countries, while second place is shared by seven countries and third place by 103 countries. North America stands out as the region with the poorest administration design standards — with both the United States (159th in the global rankings) and Canada (163rd) towards the bottom of the global rankings — a product of the administrative fragmentation caused by the constitutional division of responsibilities within a federal political structure. Western Europe stands out as the region having widest extremes with respect to administration design standards, a product of its historical legacy of administrative fragmentation, especially in (in ascending order) Luxembourg and Belgium (equal 170th and second last), France, Denmark, Austria and Finland, all of which are in the group of countries constituting the bottom 10 percent of the global rankings. The only other regions with any significant ranking spread are Eastern Europe and Latin America, where Russia (equal 159th) and Venezuela (equal 163rd) are clearly at the bottom of the regional rank order. The poorest administrative design standards in Africa can be found in Egypt, which is also the poorest in the world (172nd), closely followed by Burkina Faso (equal 163rd), while in Asia it is clearly Sri Lanka (equal 163rd).

REGIONAL SOCIAL SECURITY SYSTEMS RANKINGS

Australasia

The social security systems in Australia and New Zealand are amongst the best-designed in the world, as one or other of these countries appears in the upper levels of most of the social security program league tables, the obvious exception being maternity programs. Of the two countries, Australia has, most definitely, the best-designed system, despite its relatively weak set of employment-injury programs, which is New Zealand's conspicuous design strength.

Europe

European social security systems are also amongst the best designed in the world. The Scandinavian countries dominate the upper bracket of the European rankings — with Sweden (1st), Denmark (3rd) and Finland (5th), interspersed by France (2nd) and Russia (4th). The lower stratum of the regional league table are dominated by Eastern European countries, along with Malta (34th).

Western Europe. Sweden has the best-designed social security system in Western Europe, although there is little to differentiate it from that of France (2nd) and Denmark (3rd). While all three systems comprise programs that are of a relatively high design standard, the relative weakness of the French system is its unemployment program, while in Denmark it is its set of employment-injury programs. Following some way behind are Finland (4th), Austria (5th) and Spain (6th). Bringing up the rear is Malta (20th and last) and Cyprus (19th), which are, however, only marginally behind the United Kingdom (18th).

Eastern Europe. Russia clearly has the best-designed social security system in Eastern Europe, although it has long been beset with the serious financial problems that have become commonplace in all post-socialist countries and have ensured their inability to meet their statutory social security obligations. Belarus (2nd) and the Ukraine (3rd) are in a cluster, with Belarus' relative weakness being its unemployment program, while Ukraine's is its disability and survivors' programs. Both, however, are well separated from Poland (4th) and the others. At the bottom of the rank order are Lithuania (16th) and Moldova (15th).

North America

North American social security systems design standards lag well behind those in Europe and, indeed, even behind the best-designed systems in Latin America, Africa, Asia and the Middle East. Canada has a manifestly better-designed system than does the United States, the former's lack of family support programs notwithstanding. The only social security program in either country that is in the top 10 in its league table category is Canada's old-age program (ranked 8th).

Latin America

The Latin American rankings reveal a very wide distribution, with the best-designed social security systems to be found in South America. At the other extreme, the Caribbean has the poorest design standards.

South America. Bolivia tops the regional league table, followed by Uruguay (2nd) and Brazil (3rd), all which are on a par with countries in the lower Western Europe rankings (notably, Greece and the Netherlands (equal 16th), and the United Kingdom (18th)). Bolivia's relative design strength is in its financing arrangements. Uruguay tops the Latin American program-design league table for survivors', maternity, unemployment and healthcare benefit programs. Brazil's disability and employment-injury programs stand out (both being equal 6th and equal 7th best-designed programs, respectively, in their categories in the world). Chile (5th in the South American league table) has world-class designed family support programs (ranked 2nd in the world). Above Surinam, at the foot of the South American league table, are Peru (11th), which, intriguingly, has a sickness program that stands out (equal 8th in the world), Guyana (10th) and Venezuela (9th).

Central America. This region is only marginally behind South America in its social security system design standards. Nicaragua (1st) and Mexico (2nd) stand out, relative to the rest of the region and, indeed, to Latin America as a whole. Nicaragua's design strength is its disability program (equal 6th in the world) and its old-age program (the best-designed in Latin America). Mexico's design strength is its employment-related survivors' program (equal 6th in the world). Belize is unmistakably at the bottom of the Central American rank order.

The Caribbean. This is the weakest region in Latin America, by a considerable margin. Only the Bahamas, which has the best-designed social security system in this region, and Trinidad and Tobago (2nd) are in the Latin American top 10, albeit as ninth and tenth respectively. At the other extreme, six countries fall bellow the minimum design standards set for South America (by Peru) and for Central America (by Belize). Indeed, Montserrat (16th and last) competes with Surinam as having one of the poorest designed social security systems in the world.

Africa

The distribution amongst African social security system design ranking is wide, but not as wide as in Latin America, with which the best are comparable, while the poorest are somewhat superior. The best-designed African system can be found in North Africa; while at the other end of the spectrum comes the Southern Africa region.

North Africa. This region's social security systems are unequivocally the best designed in Africa, and better than in any of the regions in Latin America. Their design standards are largely comparable to those in Malta and Cyprus. Tunisia unquestionably has the best-designed system, which is in the same class as

Greece, the Netherlands and the United Kingdom in Western Europe and with Bolivia and Uruguay in Latin America. Tunisia's design strength is its family support programs (equal 9th in the world). Of the remaining five countries in the region, three are in the African top 10: Algeria (3rd, with Africa's best-designed sickness program), Libya (4th, with Africa's best-designed disability program) and Egypt (equal 9th, with Africa's best-designed survivors' program). At the bottom of the regional league table is Sudan, which is still only just in the bottom half of the African league table (24th).

Middle Africa. This region's social security systems design standards match those of the middle league countries in Central America (namely Panama (4th), Honduras (5th) and El Salvador (6th)). The best two — Congo and Zaire (in that order) — are ranked eighth and equal ninth in Africa. Congo's relative design strengths are its disability and maternity programs. The region's poorest designed system — the Central African Republic — is still in the middle of the African league table (23rd).

West Africa. Design standards of social security systems in this region correspond to those achieved in the Caribbean, although its poorest design system — Sierra Leone (19th and last) — is clearly better than Surinam's. Cape Verde, undoubtedly the region's best-designed system, compares favorably with Malta and is the only country from this region in the African top 10 (5th). Its relative design strengths are its sickness and family support programs. Next come Togo (2nd) and Gabon (3rd, with Africa's best designed set of employment-injury programs). Côte d'Ivoire (10th) stands out only because of its maternity program (equal 9th in the world). The poorest designed system in the region is in Sierra Leone, which is also the poorest designed in Africa

East Africa. Social security design standards in the Mauritius system stand out in this region, making it the second ranking country in Africa. Its design strength rests with its old-age and unemployment programs, which are the best designed in Africa. Following Mauritius are Burundi (2nd) and Rwanda (3rd). The region's poorest designed system — Malawi — is rather better than Sierra Leone's (West Africa).

Southern Africa. The best-designed system in this region is South Africa, which is in the African top 10 (6th). Its design strength is its healthcare benefit program. The poorest designed system — Swaziland — is rather better than Malawi's (East Africa).

Asia

The overall design standards of social security systems in Asia are somewhat lower than those in Latin America and Africa, although Asia's best are better than Latin America's or Africa's best. The top of the Asian league table is dominated by post-socialist countries in Central Asia (4 of the top five rankings), all of which face long-standing financial problems. Outside Central Asia, the best-designed social security systems can be found in East Asia. The weakest sub-region in Asia is South Asia.

Central Asia. Social security system design standards in this region are comparable to those in Central and South America, although all countries are confronting difficulties in achieving their statutory social security intentions. Armenia has the best-designed system, with world-class maternity and family support programs (ranked, respectively, the 2nd and equal 3rd in the world). It is followed by Kyrgyzstan (2nd) and Turkmenistan (3rd), which has Asia's best-designed old-age and sickness programs. All but the poorest designed system — Azerbaijan) — are comparable to all but the very best-designed systems in post-socialist Eastern Europe

East Asia. Japan sits most comfortably at the top of the East Asian league table. Its social security design standards exceed that of any Latin American or African country, not to mention both Canada and the United States, and are on a par in Western Europe with Norway (11th) and Switzerland (12th). Its design strengths rest with its survivors' program (equal 5th in the world), its disability program (equal 10th in the world) and its healthcare benefit program (equal 9th in the world). Some considerable distance behind Japan come Hong Kong (2nd) and China (3rd) clustered together and ranked in the Asian top 10 (7th and 8th respectively). Macau's new and under-developed system is at the bottom of the East Asian table, with a design standard, however, that is rather better than the lower orders of the African and Latin American league tables.

South-East Asia. This region's standards of social security system design are clearly below those achieved in any region in Latin America or Africa. The Philippines has the best-designed social security system (ranked 9th in Asia), followed by Singapore (2nd) and Malaysia (3rd). Malaysia stands out because of its employment-related temporary and permanent disability programs (ranked, respectively, as equal 3rd and equal 9th in the world). Indonesia is at the bottom of the region's league table (6th), corresponding to The Gambia in West Africa and Swaziland in South Africa.

South Asia. This is the weakest region in Asia. Its best-designed social security system is in Pakistan, which is just behind the Philippines on the Asian league table (in 10th place). In a cluster well behind Pakistan are India (2nd) and Sri Lanka (3rd). Myanmar sits indisputably at the bottom of the South Asia league table, with a social security system that is, however, better designed than that of Azerbaijan (Central Asia) or Macau (East Asia).

The Middle East

The design standards of social security systems in the Middle East are comparable, overall, to those in Asia, with the Middle East's best — Israel — of a standard comparable to Asia's best — Armenia and Japan. Indeed, Israel's social security design standards exceeds those of any North American, Latin American or African country, and bear comparison with those of Norway and Switzerland in Western Europe. Israel's design strengths are its maternity, employment injury, unemployment and family support programs, which are the best designed in the region. Following behind Israel are Iran (2nd) and Turkey (3rd), which stands out because of its disability program (equal 10th in the world) and its old-age program (the region's best designed one). The region's poorest designed system is wealthy Kuwait's, which, nevertheless, has the distinction of having the region's best-designed survivors' program. Kuwait's design standards are just a little lower than those of Malawi (East Africa) and Macau (East Asia) and thus considerably above the worst in Latin America, Africa and Asia.

The Pacific Islands

This is undoubtedly the least-developed region in the world in terms of social security design standards. Its constituent systems are comparable in their design standards to those in the bottom half of the Asian league table, the lowest one-third in the African league table, and the lowest-quarter of the Latin American league table. Its best — the Solomon Islands and Kiribati (in that order) — are comparable to Uganda and Zimbabwe in Africa, to Malaysia in Asia, and to Bahrain in the Middle East, but well below Peru in Latin America. The region's poorest designed system is the Cook Islands', which has a somewhat better design standard than that of Macau (East Asia).

GLOBAL SOCIAL SECURITY SYSTEMS RANKINGS

The First-Tier Systems

Australia has the best-designed social security system in the world. In second place comes Sweden, followed by France (3rd), Denmark (4th) and New Zealand (5th), all of which have design scores that are within 5 percent of the best-designed system. That Australia and New Zealand are included in this group may surprise those who equate the social assistance strategy with a residualist safety net, either by design or benign neglect, for those who miss entirely or fall through the dominant poverty prevention net. However, as Esping-Andersen (1996c: 263) has recently concluded in the Australian context, "selectivity can be both efficient and legitimate" because the net is broad and the means testing innocuous. Australia's premier position in the global social security design league table is attributable to the fact that its disability, unemployment and family support programs are the best- (or equal best-) designed in the world, and that its sickness, old-age, healthcare and survivors' programs are all amongst the best designed in the world. This has been the result of three developments in its approach to social assistance. The first has been the growing use of categorical targeting to provide wider support for those within particular target population categories, which is most notable in its disability program. The second development has been the increasing use of a means-testing mechanism at the program level both to concentrate benefit expenditure on those in most need (especially its old-age program (Saunders 1991, Shaver 1998)) and to exclude from benefit eligibility those above a specified affluence threshold (especially child benefit programs). The third development has been the provision of supplementary and special benefits to provide additional support to those in particular social security categories considered to be in greatest need. The outcome of these developments is that Australia's social assistance system, arguably, provides a social security safety-net that provides modest benefit to many, with additional support provided to those deemed to be in most need, and that is financed, without imposing significant contribution burdens on employees or employers, from taxation revenue.

In rather stark contrast to Australia, Sweden has designed what Ginsberg (1992: 32) has described as "the largest, most expensive and possibly the most egalitarian state welfare system in the West," based on the principles of coverage universality and benefit adequacy, which makes financing its Achilles' heel (see also Haanes-Olsen 1994a and 1994b). Sweden's sickness and employment-related temporary disability programs are the best designed in the world. Its other social security programs, except for family support and healthcare benefit programs, are all in the top levels of the relevant program league table.

France, in third place, has adopted the more traditional social insurance approach. Its maternity program is undoubtedly the best in the world, and its sickness, family support, employment injury and old-age programs rank highly, but not so its disability, survivors', unemployment and healthcare benefit programs. Its financing of social security is its primary design blemish.

Both Denmark (4th) and New Zealand (5th) have their social security design high spots, but design inadequacies are evident elsewhere. Denmark has the equal best-designed healthcare benefit program, and highly ranked programs for maternity, old-age and survivors, but the social security costs involved have produced a flawed approach to their financing. New Zealand has highly ranked programs for health care, employment injury and unemployment, but its approach to financing is far less flawed than that of Denmark.

A further 14 countries have designed social security systems that have a design score between 5 and 10 percent below that of the best-designed system. This means that the first-tier category comprises, essentially, the top 10 percent of all social security systems, and includes nine West European countries (Finland (7th), Austria (8th), Spain (9th), Germany (10th), Belgium (equal 12th), Luxembourg (14th), Portugal (15th), Norway (17th) and Switzerland (18th)); three East European countries (Russia (6th), Belarus (11th) and the Ukraine (equal 12th)); as well as Israel (16th) and Armenia (19th). The inclusion of Russia's social security system as one of the 10 best designed in the world, and of three post-socialist countries the first-tier systems, is a reflection of all four countries' socialist origins. All of them, however, are beset with transitional financial crises that seriously inhibit their ability to deliver their statutory social security obligations.

The Second-Tier Systems

Thirty-eight countries have social security systems with a design score that is between 10 and 20 percent below that of the best-designed system, essentially comprising some 20 percent of all social security systems. This group contains most of the remaining Western European countries (namely, Iceland (21st), Ireland and Italy (equal 23rd), Greece and the Netherlands (equal 33rd), the United Kingdom (equal 37th), Cyprus (40th) and Malta (58th)), most of the remaining East European countries, and the better designed systems in Latin America (9 countries, notably Bolivia (27th), Uruguay (equal 33rd) and Brazil (equal 37th)), Asia (5 countries, most notably Japan (20th)), Africa (4 countries, notably Tunisia (30th)), North America (Canada (46th)) and the Middle East (Iran (55th)).

Of all the second-tier systems, five countries stand out as disappointments. The Netherlands, with its world-class employment-related permanent disability program, Brazil, with its world-class disability and employment-injury, and Argentina all have expenditure programs of design standards comparable to those of mid-level Western European countries — benchmarked by Iceland, Ireland, Greece and Italy — but all three had their rankings seriously diminished by the very significant design flaws in their chosen financing arrangements (on the global social security financing league table, Brazil ranked a dismal 170th, and Argentina and the Netherlands ranked only marginally better at equal 164th). The United Kingdom's disappointingly low ranking occurred because it had no social security expenditure program high spots — even on a Western European regional basis — which meant its relative design strength is its financing arrangements (ranked 107th globally and 4th in Western Europe). Canada's even lower ranking (46th), despite its world-class old-age program, was largely because it had abandoned its family support program in favor of a tax expenditure program.

Amongst the second-tier countries can be found, however, two with surprisingly high rankings: Tunisia (30th), designated by the World Bank as a lower-middle-income country) and Nicaragua (42nd), designated as a low-income country (World Bank 1995a). Both countries have expenditure programs that achieve an overall design standard at or just below that achieved by Malta, designated an upper-middle-income country, which is located at the lower levels of the Western European rankings. Both Tunisia and Nicaragua, however, have program design high spots considerably above those achieved by Malta, and both have considerably better designed financing arrangements.

The Third-Tier Systems

Forty-nine countries have designed social security systems that have a design score between 20 and 30 percent below the best-designed system, and comprise just under 30 percent of all social security systems. These include the United States (62nd); the poorest designed systems in Western Europe (Malta) (58th) and Eastern Europe (Moldova (73rd) and Lithuania (86th); all but the poorest designed systems in Central America (4 countries), South America (5 countries) and North Africa (3 countries); and the relatively better designed systems in the rest of Africa (18 countries), the Caribbean (7 countries), Asia (5 countries) and the Middle East (3 countries).

In this third tier, two countries stand out as conspicuously dissimilar to the rest because of their relatively high standards of living: the United States (62nd), which has achieved design standards comparable to those in Ecuador, and Hong Kong (75th). Both countries have chosen to design expenditure programs of a standard well below that of any other developed countries — indeed at a level comparable only to the best in Central America — which enabled them to have as their relative design strength their systems' financing arrangements, which are comparable to those in all but the very upper bracket of countries in the Western European rankings — just below those in the United Kingdom.

The Fourth-Tier Systems

The 66 countries in this category have a design ranking score that is more than 30 percent below that of the best-designed system, and comprise just under 40 percent of all social security systems. This group includes all Pacific Island countries, just over half of Asia and Middle East; almost half of Africa, and about one-third of Latin America. Not surprisingly, 31 of these countries are designated as low-income countries, almost half of which are in Africa; 24 are designated as lower-middle-income countries; and nine are designated upper-middle-income countries.

The particularly incongruous countries within this fourth tier — because of their relatively high levels of income — are Kuwait, ranked 163rd, because it has a very restricted system; and Singapore, ranked 117th because of its chosen financial arrangements, which sought to achieve objectives other than those related to social security.

CONCLUSION

While Western Europe dominates the first-tier social security system rankings, with 12 of the top 19 countries (or, put another way, 60 percent of European countries were in the first-tier category), Australia has the best-designed social security system in the world. It is, however, significantly better designed than Sweden's second-placed system. With expenditure program design, however, there is little to choose between Australia and the next ranked Western European countries — Sweden, France and Denmark. This rank ordering may come as a surprise to those who equate the social assistance strategy with a residualist safety net. In essence, however, Australia has, by Western European standards, a relatively low social security cost burden, financed without significantly burdening employers or employees, because its social assistance system provides modest benefit to many, a product of the gradual liberalization of its means-tests, with additional support being available to those deemed to be in most need. This approach stands in stark contrast to the Scandinavian approach premised on the relatively more expensive principles of universal coverage and benefit adequacy.

The global rankings threw up some other surprises. First, there are the surprisingly poor performers. The most notable of these is the United States, which is the only developed Western country with a third-tier social security system. This reflects a past disinclination to construct a Western European-style social security system, preferring, on the whole, to leave employers and individuals to take responsibility for meeting social security needs. Hong Kong and Singapore also fall into this category. Hong Kong has a third-tier system because it clings to the residualist social assistance model. Singapore has a fourth-tier system because it has designed a set of financial arrangements that seek to achieve social and economic goals that are far removed from the social security arena. The Netherlands might have been expected to be in the ranks of the first tier, but its chosen financing arrangements have very significant design flaws that outweighed the meritorious design feature embedded in its expenditure programs. Malta's standing as a third-tier rather than a second-tier system is also very much a product of its chosen financing arrangements. Of those at the very bottom of the global ranking, only wealthy Kuwait stands out as anomalous because it has an under-developed social security system of relatively recent origin.

Then, of course, there were the surprisingly good performers. While the inclusion of four post-socialist countries in the first tier is not surprising given their socialist origins, (and it must be remembered that these countries may be unable to deliver their statutory social security obligations), the gaining of a place by Israel may surprise some. Israel's financing design strength enabled it to gain a higher ranking over the two upper second-tier West European countries — Iceland and Ireland — both of which had comparable expenditure program design standards.

The inclusion of Tunisia and Nicaragua in the second tier occurred because both have expenditure programs design standard high spots of global standing and a set of financing arrangements that leave little to be desired.

On a regional basis, a few meritorious program design performances can be identified: Mauritius in Africa, Japan in Asia, Bolivia in Latin America, all of which are second-tier systems, and the Solomon Islands and Kiribati stand out in the Pacific Islands.

At the program level the first-tier countries dominate. Australia has the best-designed disability, unemployment (shared with Finland) and family support programs. Sweden has the best-designed sickness program and shares best-design standing with New Zealand for employment-related temporary disability programs. Austria and Luxembourg have equal best-design standing for their employment-related survivors' programs. Luxembourg has the honors for the best-designed employment-related permanent disability program. France has the best-designed maternity program. Finland also has top billing for its old-age program. Iceland (a second-tier system) and Kazakhstan (a fourth-tier system) have equal best-designed survivors' programs.

Other meritorious program design performances include Brazil and Nicaragua for their disability programs; Japan, for its survivors' program; Peru, for its sickness program; Iceland and Côte d'Ivoire (both fourth-tier systems), for their maternity programs; Malaysia (also a fourth-tier system), for its employment-related temporary disability program; the Netherlands, for its employment-related permanent injury program; Mexico, for its employment-related survivors' program; and Chile and Tunisia, for their family support programs.

APPENDIX 10.1:   **GLOBAL SOCIAL SECURITY**
                         RANKINGS: RANK ORDER, 1995

COUNTRY	RANKING	SOCIAL SECURITY DESIGN SCORE
AUSTRALIA	1	1038
SWEDEN	2	1012
FRANCE	3	1009
DENMARK	4	1005
NEW ZEALAND	5	998
RUSSIA	6	985
FINLAND	7	971
AUSTRIA	8	969
SPAIN	9	965
GERMANY	10	958
BELARUS	11	956
BELGIUM	12	955
UKRAINE	12	955
LUXEMBOURG	14	949
PORTUGAL	15	948
ISRAEL	16	943
NORWAY	17	942

SWITZERLAND	18	941
ARMENIA	19	940
JAPAN	20	934
ICELAND	21	932
POLAND	22	921
IRELAND	23	919
ITALY	23	919
ESTONIA	25	911
SLOVAKIA	26	908
BOLIVIA	27	906
ALBANIA	28	902
KYRGYZSTAN	28	902
TUNISIA	30	898
CZECH REP.	31	897
TURKMENISTAN	32	896
GREECE	33	895
NETHERLANDS	33	895
URUGUAY	33	895
UZBEKISTAN	33	895
BRAZIL	37	888
UNITED KINGDOM	37	888

BULGARIA	39	886
CYPRUS	40	883
HUNGARY	41	879
NICARAGUA	42	878
GEORGIA	43	877
ARGENTINA	44	871
LATVIA	44	871
CANADA	46	869
MAURITIUS	47	865
MEXICO	48	864
CHILE	49	862
YUGOSLAVIA	50	859
ALGERIA	51	854
SLOVENIA	52	849
ROMANIA	53	844
LIBYA	54	843
IRAN	55	842
COSTA RICA	56	836
BAHAMAS	57	834
MALTA	58	830
CAPE VERDE	59	829

TRINIDAD AND TOBAGO	59	829
TURKEY	59	829
ECUADOR	62	827
UNITED STATES	62	827
SOUTH AFRICA	64	821
BARBADOS	65	816
COLOMBIA	66	811
BURUNDI	67	810
PARAGUAY	68	809
CONGO	69	804
PANAMA	69	804
EGYPT	71	800
ZAIRE	71	800
MOLDOVA	73	799
RWANDA	74	797
HONG KONG	75	795
TOGO	76	789
VENEZUELA	76	789
BRITISH VIRGIN ISLANDS	78	786
GABON	79	783

CHINA	80	782
CUBA	81	781
MOROCCO	82	780
NIGER	82	780
MALI	84	778
BENIN	85	774
LITHUANIA	86	772
CHAD	87	769
HONDURAS	87	769
PHILIPPINES	89	767
PAKISTAN	90	764
CAMEROON	91	763
DOMINICA	92	761
TAIWAN	93	756
ZAMBIA	94	754
CENTRAL AFRICAN REP.	95	751
EL SALVADOR	96	748
GUINEA	97	748
LEBANON	98	746
ST KITTS AND NEVIS	99	745

EQUATORIAL GUINEA	100	743
SUDAN	101	740
GUATEMALA	102	738
IRAQ	103	737
MADAGASCAR	104	734
GUYANA	105	733
ST VINCENT AND THE GRENADINES	106	729
CÔTE D'IVOIRE	107	720
INDIA	108	716
SRI LANKA	109	715
JAMAICA	110	710
DOMINICAN REP.	111	709
MAURITANIA	112	705
BURKINA FASO	113	701
KENYA	114	698
KAZAKHSTAN	115	689
PERU	116	684
SINGAPORE	117	683
NIGERIA	118	680
JORDAN	119	679

SAUDI ARABIA	120	674
SOLOMON ISLANDS	121	667
UGANDA	121	667
BAHRAIN	123	666
MALAYSIA	124	664
ZIMBABWE	125	662
KIRIBATI	126	661
SENEGAL	127	659
SEYCHELLES	128	653
WESTERN SAMOA	129	648
KOREA, SOUTH	130	647
VIETNAM	131	639
BELIZE	132	638
OMAN	133	634
ST LUCIA	133	634
SYRIA	135	631
FIJI	136	625
ETHIOPIA	137	624
BERMUDA	138	616
SÃO TOMÉ AND PRINCIPE	139	610

TANZANIA	139	610
THAILAND	141	605
BOTSWANA	142	604
LIBERIA	143	599
PAPUA NEW GUINEA	144	594
AFGHANISTAN	145	593
GHANA	145	593
GAMBIA, THE	147	590
SWAZILAND	147	590
HAITI	149	587
KOREA, NORTH	150	585
INDONESIA	151	584
BANGLADESH	152	566
NEPAL	153	556
YEMEN	153	556
NAURU	155	554
SOMALIA	156	542
GRENADA	157	538
MYANMAR	158	532
ANTIGUA-BARBUDA	159	498
COOK ISLANDS	160	486

MACAU	161	464
MALAWI	162	462
KUWAIT	163	451
SIERRA LEONE	164	429
PALAU	165	412
MICRONESIA	166	411
MARSHALL ISLANDS	167	409
VANUATU	168	402
MONTSERRAT	169	390
TUVALU	170	375
SURINAM	171	320
AZERBAIJAN	172	318

APPENDIX 10.2:   GLOBAL SOCIAL SECURITY
                   RANKINGS: ALPHABETICAL   ORDER,
                   1995

COUNTRY	RANKING	SOCIAL SECURITY DESIGN SCORE
AFGHANISTAN	145	593
ALBANIA	28	902
ALGERIA	51	854
ANTIGUA-BARBUDA	159	498
ARGENTINA	44	871
ARMENIA	19	940
AUSTRALIA	1	1038
AUSTRIA	8	969
AZERBAIJAN	172	318
BAHAMAS	57	834
BAHRAIN	123	666
BANGLADESH	152	566
BARBADOS	65	816
BELARUS	11	956
BELGIUM	12	955
BELIZE	132	638
BENIN	85	774

BERMUDA	138	616
BOLIVIA	27	906
BOTSWANA	142	604
BRAZIL	37	888
BRITISH VIRGIN ISLANDS	78	786
BULGARIA	39	886
BURKINA FASO	113	701
BURUNDI	67	810
CAMEROON	91	763
CANADA	46	869
CAPE VERDE	59	829
CENTRAL AFRICAN REP.	95	751
CHAD	87	769
CHILE	49	862
CHINA	80	782
COLOMBIA	66	811
CONGO	69	804
COOK ISLANDS	160	486
COSTA RICA	56	836
CÔTE D'IVOIRE	107	720

CUBA	81	781
CYPRUS	40	883
CZECH REP	31	897
DENMARK	4	1005
DOMINICA	92	761
DOMINICAN REP.	111	709
ECUADOR	62	827
EGYPT	71	800
EL SALVADOR	96	748
EQUATORIAL GUINEA	100	743
ESTONIA	25	911
ETHIOPIA	137	624
FIJI	136	625
FINLAND	7	971
FRANCE	3	1009
GABON	79	783
GAMBIA, THE	147	590
GEORGIA	43	877
GERMANY	10	958
GHANA	145	593
GREECE	33	895

GRENADA	157	538
GUATEMALA	102	738
GUINEA	97	748
GUYANA	105	733
HAITI	149	587
HONDURAS	87	769
HONG KONG	75	795
HUNGARY	41	879
ICELAND	21	932
INDIA	108	716
INDONESIA	151	584
IRAN	55	842
IRAQ	103	737
IRELAND	23	919
ISRAEL	16	943
ITALY	23	919
JAMAICA	110	710
JAPAN	20	934
JORDAN	119	679
KAZAKHSTAN	115	689
KENYA	114	698

KIRIBATI	126	661
KOREA, NORTH	150	585
KOREA, SOUTH	130	647
KUWAIT	163	451
KYRGYZSTAN	28	902
LATVIA	44	871
LEBANON	98	746
LIBERIA	143	599
LIBYA	54	843
LITHUANIA	86	772
LUXEMBOURG	14	949
MACAU	161	464
MADAGASCAR	104	734
MALAWI	162	462
MALAYSIA	124	664
MALI	84	778
MALTA	58	830
MARSHALL ISLANDS	167	409
MAURITANIA	112	705
MAURITIUS	47	865
MEXICO	48	864

MICRONESIA	166	411
MOLDOVA	73	799
MONTSERRAT	169	390
MOROCCO	82	780
MYANMAR	158	532
NAURU	155	554
NEPAL	153	556
NETHERLANDS	33	895
NEW ZEALAND	5	998
NICARAGUA	42	878
NIGER	82	780
NIGERIA	118	680
NORWAY	17	942
OMAN	133	634
PAKISTAN	90	764
PALAU	165	412
PANAMA	69	804
PAPUA NEW GUINEA	144	594
PARAGUAY	68	809
PERU	116	684
PHILIPPINES	89	767

POLAND	22	921
PORTUGAL	15	948
ROMANIA	53	844
RUSSIA	6	985
RWANDA	74	797
SÃO TOMÉ & PRINCIPE	139	610
SAUDI ARABIA	120	674
SENEGAL	127	659
SEYCHELLES	128	653
SIERRA LEONE	164	429
SINGAPORE	117	683
SLOVAKIA	26	908
SLOVENIA	52	849
SOLOMON ISLANDS	121	667
SOMALIA	156	542
SOUTH AFRICA	64	821
SPAIN	9	965
SRI LANKA	109	715
ST KITTS & NEVIS	99	745
ST LUCIA	133	634

ST VINCENT & THE	106	729
GRENADINES		
SUDAN	101	740
SURINAM	171	320
SWAZILAND	147	590
SWEDEN	2	1012
SWITZERLAND	18	941
SYRIA	135	631
TAIWAN	93	756
TANZANIA	139	610
THAILAND	141	605
TOGO	76	789
TRINIDAD & TOBAGO	59	829
TUNISIA	30	898
TURKEY	59	829
TURKMENISTAN	32	896
TUVALU	170	375
UGANDA	121	667
UKRAINE	12	955
UNITED KINGDOM	37	888
URUGUAY	33	895

UNITED STATES	62	827
UZBEKISTAN	33	895
VANUATU	168	402
VENEZUELA	76	789
VIETNAM	131	639
WESTERN SAMOA	129	648
YEMEN	153	556
YUGOSLAVIA	50	859
ZAIRE	71	800
ZAMBIA	94	754
ZIMBABWE	125	662

APPENDIX 10.3: REGIONAL SOCIAL SECURITY RANKINGS:
RANK ORDER, 1995

REGION/ COUNTRY	RANKING	SOCIAL SECURITY DESIGN SCORE	REGIONAL DESIGN SCORE
AFRICA			
TUNISIA	1	898	
MAURITIUS	2	865	
ALGERIA	3	854	
LIBYA	4	843	
CAPE VERDE	5	829	
SOUTH AFRICA	6	821	
BURUNDI	7	810	
CONGO	8	804	
EGYPT	9	800	
ZAIRE	9	800	
RWANDA	11	797	
TOGO	12	789	
GABON	13	783	
MOROCCO	14	780	
NIGER	14	780	
MALI	16	778	

BENIN	17	774
CHAD	18	769
CAMEROON	19	763
ZAMBIA	20	754
CENTRAL AFRICAN REP.	21	751
GUINEA	22	748
EQUATORIAL GUINEA	23	743
SUDAN	24	740
MADAGASCAR	25	734
CÔTE D'IVOIRE	26	720
MAURITANIA	27	705
BURKINA FASO	28	701
KENYA	29	698
NIGERIA	30	680
UGANDA	31	667
ZIMBABWE	32	662
SENEGAL	33	659
SEYCHELLES	34	653
ETHIOPIA	35	624
SÃO TOMÉ & PRINCIPE	36	610
TANZANIA	36	610

BOTSWANA	38	604
LIBERIA	39	599
GHANA	40	593
GAMBIA, THE	41	590
SWAZILAND	41	590
SOMALIA	43	542
MALAWI	44	462
SIERRA LEONE	45	429

716

ASIA

ARMENIA	1	940
JAPAN	2	934
KYRGYZSTAN	3	902
TURKMENISTAN	4	896
UZBEKISTAN	5	895
GEORGIA	6	877
HONG KONG	7	795
CHINA	8	782
PHILIPPINES	9	767
PAKISTAN	10	764
TAIWAN	11	756

INDIA	12	716
SRI LANKA	13	715
KAZAKHSTAN	14	689
SINGAPORE	15	683
MALAYSIA	16	664
KOREA, SOUTH	17	647
VIETNAM	18	639
THAILAND	19	605
AFGHANISTAN	20	593
KOREA, NORTH	21	585
INDONESIA	22	584
BANGLADESH	23	566
NEPAL	24	556
MYANMAR	25	532
MACAU	26	464
AZERBAIJAN	27	318

699

AUSTRALASIA

AUSTRALIA	1	1038
NEW ZEALAND	2	998

1018

EUROPE

SWEDEN	1	1012
FRANCE	2	1009
DENMARK	3	1005
RUSSIA	4	985
FINLAND	5	971
AUSTRIA	6	969
SPAIN	7	965
GERMANY	8	958
BELARUS	9	956
BELGIUM	10	955
UKRAINE	10	955
LUXEMBOURG	12	949
PORTUGAL	13	948
NORWAY	14	942
SWITZERLAND	15	941
ICELAND	16	932
POLAND	17	921
IRELAND	18	919
ITALY	18	919
ESTONIA	20	911

SLOVAKIA	21	908
ALBANIA	22	902
CZECH REP.	23	897
GREECE	24	895
NETHERLANDS	24	895
UNITED KINGDOM	26	888
BULGARIA	27	886
CYPRUS	28	883
HUNGARY	29	879
LATVIA	30	871
YUGOSLAVIA	31	859
SLOVENIA	32	849
ROMANIA	33	844
MALTA	34	830
MOLDOVA	35	799
LITHUANIA	36	772

916

NORTH AMERICA

CANADA	1	869
UNITED STATES	2	827

848

LATIN AMERICA

BOLIVIA	1	906
URUGUAY	2	895
BRAZIL	3	888
NICARAGUA	4	878
ARGENTINA	5	871
MEXICO	6	864
CHILE	7	862
COSTA RICA	8	836
BAHAMAS	9	834
TRINIDAD & TOBAGO	10	829
ECUADOR	11	827
BARBADOS	12	816
COLOMBIA	13	811
PARAGUAY	14	809
PANAMA	15	804
VENEZUELA	16	789

BRITISH VIRGIN ISLANDS	17	786
CUBA	18	781
HONDURAS	19	769
DOMINICA	20	761
EL SALVADOR	21	748
ST KITTS & NEVIS	22	745
GUATEMALA	23	738
GUYANA	24	733
ST VINCENT & THE GRENADINES	25	729
JAMAICA	26	710
DOMINICAN REP.	27	709
PERU	28	684
BELIZE	29	638
ST LUCIA	30	634
BERMUDA	31	616
HAITI	32	587
GRENADA	33	538
ANTIGUA-BARBUDA	34	498
MONTSERRAT	35	390

SURINAM	36	320

740

MIDDLE EAST

ISRAEL	1	943
IRAN	2	842
TURKEY	3	829
LEBANON	4	746
IRAQ	5	737
JORDAN	6	679
SAUDI ARABIA	7	674
BAHRAIN	8	666
OMAN	9	634
SYRIA	10	631
YEMEN	11	556
KUWAIT	12	451

699

PACIFIC ISLANDS

SOLOMON ISLANDS	1	667
KIRIBATI	2	661
WESTERN SAMOA	3	648
FIJI	4	625

PAPUA NEW GUINEA	5	594
NAURU	6	554
COOK ISLANDS	7	486
PALAU	8	412
MICRONESIA	9	411
MARSHALL ISLANDS	10	409
VANUATU	11	402
TUVALU	12	375

520

APPENDIX 10.4: SOCIAL SECURITY DESIGN SCORES, 1995

REGION/COUNTRY	SOCIAL SECURITY SYSTEM CONSTITUENT SCORE:														
	1	2	3	4	5	6	7	8	9	10	11	12	13	14	15
NORTH AFRICA															
ALGERIA	107	92	92	100	90	113	120	98		56	82	100	76	86	854
EGYPT	107	97	98	93	75	105	113	122	73		85	85	36	88	800
LIBYA	103	107	67	85	90	97	113	87	73		79	95	94	82	843
MOROCCO	87	83	75	90	90	102	112	110		48	62	100	71	78	780
SUDAN	80	60	62	88	83	105	102	108			77	100	89	70	740
TUNISIA	95	101	68	83	72	100	122	118	58	92	84	102	83	90	898
WEST AFRICA															
BENIN	80	100	62	70	90	102	115	108		56	54	100	77	76	774
BURKINA FASO	82	102	60		92	103	110	107		57	63	90	62	70	701

CAMEROON	77	88	67	70	88	107	118	108	56	52	100	73	76	763
CAPE VERDE	88	90	58	95	80	102	112	110	84	73	100	87	81	829
CÔTE D'IVOIRE	70	58	62		103	112	115	113	57	68	100	79	69	720
EQUATORIAL GUINEA	72	72	68	83	85	107	97	90	56	55	100	82	71	743
GABON	77	78	67	78	83	112	115	120	71	81	100	61	80	783
GAMBIA, THE	58	52	80			102	107	87		65	100	93	50	590
GHANA	82	80	83			97	88	88		43	100	90	51	593
GUINEA	70	87	70	83	92	103	113	113	51	61	100	56	77	748
LIBERIA	53	73	57			100	103	107		29	100	113	47	599
MALI	75	88	67	77	87	108	118	108	55	63	100	75	77	778
MAURITANIA	75	103	57		83	103	110	110	56	57	100	71	69	705
NIGER	77	105	73	77	92	102	115	103	54	63	100	70	78	780
NIGERIA	67	60	60	77	80	93	88	77		72	100	94	61	680
SÃO TOMÉ & PRINCIPE	77	77	68	78	80	103				72	100	104	50	610
SENEGAL	68	57	58		88	102	115	103	52	51	100	69	63	659

SIERRA LEONE	82	105	67	77	90	90	92	77		58	30	100	113	26	429
TOGO	80	73	57	77	82	102	108	107			72	100	73	79	789
MIDDLE AFRICA															
CEN. AFR. REP.	63	88	55	77	82	103	117	113		56	55	100	73	74	751
CHAD	77	106	67	77	80	102	115	108		55	55	100	92	73	769
CONGO	83	92	67	77	92	112	118	103		56	73	100	77	80	804
ZAIRE				70	80	102	108	107		64	62	100	95	76	800
EAST AFRICA															
BURUNDI	83	97	62	73	78	103	113	115		83	67	100	83	79	810
ETHIOPIA	50	48	47	77	58	77	83	85			53	100	102	53	624
KENYA	70	58	77	77	80	103	92	107			45	100	89	64	698
MADAGASCAR	77	63	52	80	92	105	120	100		58	59	100	66	73	734
MALAWI						100	88	97	80		47	100	114	30	462
MAURITIUS	122	101	95	77	87	108	112	98		30	87	100	61	91	865
RWANDA	65	97	90	77	80	108	112	123			76	100	97	75	797

253

	1	2	3	4	5	6	7	8	9	10	11	12	13	14	15
SEYCHELLES	87	82	43	97	93	102	93				83	100	72	62	653
SOMALIA	58	53	72		77	105	105	110			40	100	116	40	542
TANZANIA	48	50	68	57	83	93	95	98	75		67	100	77	56	610
UGANDA	68	67	88		90	100	100	95			58	100	91	60	667
ZAMBIA						100	110	112	73		65	105	93	70	754
SOUTHERN AFRICA															
BOTSWANA	100	91		77	73	95	90	100	62		62	100	99	51	604
SOUTH AFRICA	72	60	85	78	78	108	107	97	67		87	105	77	82	821
SWAZILAND	62	55	72		82	102	97	100			43	100	96	49	590
ZIMBABWE			60			103	112	102			58	100	101	58	662
CENTRAL ASIA															
ARMENIA	97	88	97	95	110	108	108	103	105	103	78	105	62	99	940
AZERBAIJAN									112		17	105	115	12	318
GEORGIA	97	103	122	97	93	108	103	130	92		77	105	54	93	877

	1	2	3	4	5	6	7	8	9	10	11	12	13	14	15
KAZAKHSTAN	102	102	123			108	103	125	98	75	70	105	69	67	689
KYRGYZSTAN	105	103	110	93	93	108	103	125	115		75	105	38	99	902
TURKMENISTAN	123	103	105	98	93	108	103	125	115		75	102	54	95	896
UZBEKISTAN	100	102	115	97	98	108	103	125	115		73	105	59	94	895
EAST ASIA															
CHINA	102	65	88	88	90	108	113	87	72		77	105	55	81	782
HONG KONG	117	90		88	87	107	98	98	85	29	95	95	65	81	795
JAPAN	107	117	117	88	97	106	105	103	95	58	98	100	61	99	934
KOREA, NORTH	53			80	80	102	108	83			62	97	82	52	585
KOREA, SOUTH	80	82	85			87	100	87			82	100	107	55	647
MACAU	67	62					73		65		73	100	111	31	464
TAIWAN	88	75	92	82	70	93	88	98			85	100	97	70	756
SOUTH ASIA															
AFGHANISTAN	65	93		77	90	80	85	83			37	100	66	55	593
BANGLADESH				57	75	82	93	70	63		58	100	103	45	566

INDIA	62	50	73	67	82	88	95	100	73		68	105	75	69	716
MYANMAR	43			70	67	90	97	87			54	100	97	42	532
NEPAL		52	70			87	80	80	63		62	100	77	49	556
PAKISTAN	80	70	65	90	78	97	112	107	60		58	105	79	74	764
SRI LANKA	65	53	72		78	100	97	103	87	26	83	90	76	69	715
SOUTH-EAST ASIA															
INDONESIA	60	47	67			95	100	85			55	100	110	46	584
MALAYSIA	67	92	100			122	125	105			75	100	77	62	664
PHILIPPINES	82	102	92	80	93	100	107	90			77	100	80	75	767
SINGAPORE	83	70	75	72	80	97	98	97			85	100	55	69	683
THAILAND		57		80	68	87	88	95			67	100	107	49	605
VIETNAM	92	57	70	65	75	90	83	75			65	100	67	61	639
AUSTRALASIA															
AUSTRALIA	127	133	113	108	90	100	123	100	125	109	100	105	62	112	1038

	106	115	103	90	88	123	130	117	117	89	100	102	60	107	998
NEW ZEALAND	106	115	103	90	88	123	130	117	117	89	100	102	60	107	998
WESTERN EUROPE															
AUSTRIA	123	125	108	108	102	110	127	135	117	65	102	90	24	111	969
BELGIUM	117	108	88	100	92	122	115	122	112	83	98	87	47	105	955
CYPRUS	88	90	77	90	90	107	112	96	87	55	92	100	79	89	883
DENMARK	130	118	117	100	108	113	118	115	97	102	102	90	48	111	1005
FINLAND	146	123	105	87	102	102	110	110	125	96	100	92	33	110	971
FRANCE	128	115	105	110	118	117	128	127	88	103	97	90	43	112	1009
GERMANY	103	97	98	108	101	120	113	128	113	69	102	102	46	105	958
GREECE	115	110	112	97	86	95	112	108	87	55	98	95	44	98	895
ICELAND	123	113	123	85	107	107	107	107	93		95	105	73	96	932
IRELAND	108	80	93	85	83	98	110	93	98	96	98	95	75	95	919
ITALY	127	103	90	77	95	98	137	115	87	76	97	105	49	100	925
LUXEMBOURG	92	92	90	100	103	117	132	135	103	79	97	87	51	104	949

257

MALTA	83	83	80	83	97	102	105	102	85	91	93	100	34	91	830
NETHERLANDS	93	103	97	92	88	105	130	103	102	69	100	105	37	98	895
NORWAY	117	122	112	105	102	113	113	108	93	67	97	95	40	104	942
PORTUGAL	129	128	103	90	98	103	88	118	102	64	90	95	60	101	948
SPAIN	105	117	118	97	95	102	125	120	108	67	102	100	50	105	965
SWEDEN	132	120	113	112	103	123	127	117	113	63	97	105	48	111	1012
SWITZERLAND	110	115	110	100	83	115	127	113	78	63	90	95	60	100	941
UNITED KINGDOM	107	90	88	85	85	110	98	102	90	65	93	95	69	92	888
EASTERN EUROPE															
ALBANIA	113	108	88	92	88	103	113	115	87	56	75	95	66	94	902
BELARUS	122	105	105	100	100	108	117	133	95	73	87	105	48	104	956
BULGARIA	95	110	100	97	105	88	103	115	112	92	82	105	23	100	886
CZECH REP	108	113	87	95	90	110	120	115	68	78	82	95	49	97	897
ESTONIA	85	93	107	102	100	117	112	122	87	74	82	102	51	98	911
HUNGARY	95	100	82	95	108	117	123	120	75	65	82	102	38	96	879

258

LATVIA	105	105	78	97	93	113	110	102	93	63	78	95	46	94	871
LITHUANIA	78	77	53	98	100	118	90	87	70	30	75	102	56	80	772
MOLDOVA	112	112	107			108	120	128	88	32	68	105	73	80	799
POLAND	98	95	78	100	106	115	118	112	108	91	82	95	47	100	921
ROMANIA	90	95	80	97	95	110	102	90	118	67	78	97	35	93	844
RUSSIA	117	113	108	107	103	117	125	132	115	71	90	92	45	109	985
SLOVAKIA	112	110	72	102	105	118	118	108	63	69	78	100	61	96	908
SLOVENIA	98	80	92	108	98	108	102	107	70	71	77	100	42	92	849
UKRAINE	122	88	98	90	102	108	102	125	122	75	80	105	63	101	955
YUGOSLAVIA	105	88	92	103	96	117	102	117	73	65	67	100	43	93	859
NORTH AMERICA															
CANADA	125	93	108	72	80	108	103	122	77		92	90	74	89	869
UNITED STATES	115	88	107	65	63	97	98	95	84	29	95	92	67	85	827

CENTRAL AMERICA

BELIZE	82	70	75	80	82	95	102			14	82	100	69	61	638
COSTA RICA	112	93	100	88	83	108	118	123			87	100	74	84	836
EL SALVADOR	88	88	63	83	83	102	118	93			60	100	87	71	748
GUATEMALA	97	107	82	80	87	100	87		63		69	100	85	70	738
HONDURAS	83	77	57	82	78	80	98	83	68		84	100	96	72	769
MEXICO	92	88	90	102	87	112	115	128	68		75	105	77	87	864
NICARAGUA	119	120	85	82	85	105	105	112		58	73	100	95	86	878
PANAMA	98	97	63	72	80	108	107	118			83	100	102	75	804

CARIBBEAN

ANTIGUA-BARBUDA	80	63	55	78	75						75	100	92	39	498
BAHAMAS	102	92	92	95	87	100	112	103			75	100	108	78	834
BARBADOS	87	77	73	78	87	101	110	102	67		82	100	92	78	816
BERMUDA	82	60	58			98	103	97			82	100	96	53	616

BRITISH VIRGIN ISLANDS	78	67	82	80	85	105	113	105	75	100	108	72	786
CUBA	92	85	83	97	92	118	113	110	83	95	66	79	781
DOMINICA	92	77	72	73	77	98	107	102	73	100	101	70	761
DOMINICAN REP.	99	102	78	78	78	83	75	82	65	105	79	67	709
GRENADA	82	70	72	83	80				68	100	105	41	538
HAITI	58	52	60			99	100	90	61	100	106	47	587
JAMAICA	73	70	70		82	105	113	94	70	105	110	62	710
MONTSERRAT	70	57	75						58	100	101	24	390
ST KITTS AND NEVIS	87	77	72	73	78	97	110	97	78	100	91	70	745
ST LUCIA	75	57	65	73	77	97	98		77	100	90	56	634
ST VINCENT AND THE GRENADINES	82	70	62	73	77	100	82	98	78	100	103	66	729

TRINIDAD AND TOBAGO	97	88	80	92	93	117	108	118	85	95	73	100	99	79	829
SOUTH AMERICA															
ARGENTINA	85	113	88	90	85	105	102	107	85	95	95	105	37	95	871
BOLIVIA	108	85	95	88	90	112	112	110	73	63	80	97	79	92	906
BRAZIL	117	120	97	102	87	118	125	118	77	61	81	97	25	100	888
CHILE	77	100	82	97	85	110	112	100	73	108	93	92	42	94	862
COLOMBIA	108	110	98	65	73	102	98	107	67	34	76	105	51	85	811
ECUADOR	100	73	92	73	87	97	112	122	62		74	100	87	81	827
GUYANA	75	80	73	70	78	87	103	112			82	100	87	69	733
PARAGUAY	100	82	88	80	78	98	102	102		56	70	100	91	78	809
PERU	70	75	82	105	92	103	103	95			62	100	41	72	684
SURINAM	65									56	43	100	101	15	320
URUGUAY	107	95	110	90	102	100	102	110	88	60	97	100	49	96	895
VENEZUELA	100	93	88	77	75	93	95	100	70		95	90	66	81	789

MIDDLE EAST

BAHRAIN	92	85	70			95	108	105		60	90	100	98	59	666
IRAN	90	97	77	85	77	102	112	97	77		80	105	65	87	842
IRAQ	87	85	70	92	82	100	107	95			48	100	88	69	737
ISRAEL	105	100	95	82	92	108	120	115	82	64	98	100	81	96	943
JORDAN	93	62	48		70	98	98	95	72		83	100	71	65	679
KUWAIT	93	85	96								77	100	97	32	451
LEBANON	72	67	83	82	82	102	92	98		87	77	105	55	76	746
OMAN	85	72	63			98	93	102			73	100	105	53	634
SAUDI ARABIA	80	95	57	70		93	112	96			88	105	80	63	674
SYRIA	93	67	68		83	105	107	98			75	105	88	56	631
TURKEY	118	117	87	87		100	110	112	65		90	105	48	88	829
YEMEN	45	55	55			102	92	80			73	100	94	46	556

PACIFIC ISLANDS

COOK ISLANDS	92	78	108						49	70	100	98	36	486
FIJI	77	70	87		97	97	98			80	105	88	55	625
KIRIBATI	68	50	70	68	103	100	97			77	100	100	58	661
MARSHALL ISLANDS	85	75	77							53	100	99	26	409
MICRONESIA,	82	70	72	83					63	53	100	107	25	411
NAURU	92	65	70		77					77	100	81	48	554
PALAU	78	72	73							53	100	107	25	412
PAPUA NEW GUINEA	58	40	58		112	100	103			62	100	104	48	594
SOLOMON ISLANDS	77	53	73		110	92	92	72		73	100	101	58	667
TUVALU	55	45	63							62	100	108	20	375
VANUATU	63	53	73							60	100	114	23	402
WESTERN SAMOA	82	70	80		108	95	98			77	100	103	55	648

11

Social Security Towards 2000 and Beyond

INTRODUCTION

Social security is, globally, in a state of flux. Governments are seeking to extricate themselves from the horns of many social security dilemmas, which are quite markedly different in developed, developing and post-socialist countries.

DEVELOPED COUNTRIES

Governments in most developed countries are now faced with the consequences of the past success of their social security systems, typically achieved over the 30 years following the end of the Second World War (Logue 1979). They have achieved universality of employment coverage or, in some instances, even population coverage. They now contain more liberal eligibility criteria. They also provide entitlements that, arguably, ensure an acceptable level of income replacement if the middle classes confront a social security contingency (Goodin and LeGrand 1987). These achievements were made possible by the adoption of financing methods involving inter-generational transfers that captured the benefits of post-Second World War productivity and population growth (Aaron 1966). Yet it is in these financing methods that the contemporary seeds of disenchantment can be found (Sabelhaus 1994).

Universal coverage, liberal eligibility criteria and benefit generosity are all very well, provided the social security categories protected do not increase too dramatically. When they do, they bring to the forefront questions of social security's financial viability (see, for example, Kingson 1994, Noord and Herd 1993). The first signs of trouble could be detected in the late 1970s (Alber 1988b, Boskin 1978, Cohen and Goldfinger 1979, Flora 1986, OECD 1981, Rosa 1982a).

The unpredicted, but certainly not unforeseeable, burgeoning of social security expenditure, which has been the major cause of public expenditures growth over the last 30 or so years, is a consequence of the juxtaposition of three factors (Cantillon 1990, Carter and Shipman 1996, Dornbusch 1997, Gustafsson and Klevmarken 1988, Hagemann and Nicoletti 1989, ILO 1989b, MacKeller and Bird 1997, Rosa 1982a and 1982b, Simanis 1989, Tanzi and Schuknecht 1996, Taverne 1995). The first is population aging — associated with the post-war baby-boom, increasing life expectancy, declining fertility rates and declining workforce participation rates amongst the older age groups — long seen as remote prospects. The second is a slowing down of economic growth — long the victim of unrealistic expectations. The third is the emergence of intractable unemployment — long dismissed as the fault of the unemployed. Addressing this escalating social security cost burden, in the face of a diminishing workforce, constitutes the supreme challenge still to be addressed by governments in all developed countries.

Yet the experts publicly disagree on both the immediacy and seriousness of this challenge. Saner heads, like Abel-Smith (1993: 260), reflecting on the imponderables and unknowables of actuarial, economic and demographic projections, mindful, no doubt, that even slight under- or over-estimations can play havoc with social security revenue and expenditures projections, points out that such projections "amount to no more than possible future scenarios. They are no more robust than the assumptions underlying them." He concludes (p. 265) that social scientists are not able to "predict the future with all its complex and economic and political dimensions" (see also Barker 1996, Bernstein 1997, George 1996, Roush 1996). In the US context, Myers (1996: 23) considers that the "use of 'crisis' is unduly alarmist (even wrong) because the decisive moment . . . is likely to be more than twenty to thirty years hence" (see also Myers 1993 and 1994, Barker 1996; Jallende 1992). Jones (1996: 27) makes an even stronger statement: "Pensions are not facing a crisis [in the United States]. The program as currently structured and financed can pay full benefits today, tomorrow and for another thirty years or more." The European Commission (1996: 24) has concluded: "Sustainability of public pay-as-you-go schemes could be ensured through a range of piecemeal reforms, mainly through reductions in benefits" (see also Abrahamson 1988).

This does not, however, deter the prophets of doom, with their rhetoric of crisis and their "doom-laden tracts" (Littlewood, 1998: 1), from prognosticating that without radical reform social security's future is bleak, which they state with a certainty that belies the complexities of the constellation of political, economic, demographic and social dimensions that impact on social security policy. Peters (1995: 272) captures the spirit of these prophecies with his comments on United States situation: "The massive debts, the unprecedented unfunded [social security] liabilities, and the unsustainable taxes that future generations will have to pay is nothing less than fiscal child abuse." Kotlickoff (1996b:22) maintains that unless social security reforms are made "it will mean our kids paying almost 20% of their earnings for pensions," which would "further transfer from young savers to old spenders in our society and reduce our perilously low rate of savings" (see also Aaron and Burtless 1989, Aaron et al. 1989, Genovese 1990, Gramlich 1996, Marrota 1997, Schobel 1992). In the Austrian setting, Prinz (1995: 17) puts this potential inter-generational conflict argument another way: "inequities between the baby-boom and after baby-boom cohorts could indeed threaten the implicit [social security] generational contract."

Social security's pending financial "crisis" — the precommitment of future generations to unsustainable forced transfers — has given credence to the neoliberal's new orthodoxy of "anti-statism" (Freeden 1978; also see, for example, Alesalo 1993 and 1997, Kangas and Palme 1993) and the call, with almost missionary zeal, for radical systemic surgery. However politically unpalatable such surgery may be, it is, so the neoliberals assert, inevitable and must come sooner rather than later, as the unfunded social security liabilities can only get worse because the alternatives of higher taxes or higher public debts are considered to be tantamount to spending tomorrow's wealth today. Social security is thus perceived as being failure-prone (MacKeller and McGreevey 1997). Allegations about its dire consequences abound. It has undermined public confidence in government; as Jallande (1992: 41) remarks: "Individuals feel increasingly powerless *vis-à-vis* bureaucratic regulations that are impersonal, remote and ill-adapted to specific situations."

Social security is said to have sapped the social moral fiber, by discouraging work and savings, by promoting family breakdowns and by encouraging the formation of de facto and lone-parent family units. It does not offer, moreover, a fair return on tax and contribution outlays. It has also become unaffordable, so it is vehemently said at times, because of its gross inefficiencies and waste, to the point where it now constrains economic growth (see, for example, Offe 1996, OECD 1997, Williams 1995). These perceptions have given rise to the forces driving social security reform.

Not in dispute is the nature and seriousness of the social security challenges to be faced — essentially how best to adapt to recent economic and social change — but rather the urgency of those challenges, and the appropriateness of the presumed panacea (ISSA 1992b). To the neoliberal critic nothing less than the restoration of free market forces can solve the problems of the dysfunctional Welfare State. At the same time, of course, this solution creates lucrative business opportunities by, for example, expanding the market for existing occupational and personal pension and savings plans. The rhetoric of the marketplace has become a mantra that will bend any socioeconomic reality to the will of the invisible hand. The proffered panacea involves the adoption of two policy tactics: incentive-driven social security measures, aimed at promoting work and savings, and ipso facto economic growth, in expectation that reduction in both poverty and inequality will follow; and targeting measures, aimed at simultaneously alleviating poverty and reducing social security expenditure.

Influential international social security policy actors (Midgley 1997) — particularly international agencies (Deacon et al. 1997) — have sought legitimacy for their market forces approach not by explicitly drawing upon a particular ideology, but rather by referring to the "supremacy" that economic metaphors currently exercise over the public policy domain, leaving implicit, or even denying, their underlying ideological premises. So much so that the social security policy debate has been intellectually and epistemologically hijacked by a very virulent strain of neoliberalism, with its economic preoccupations and its politics of self-interest. Karl Gustaf Scherman, President of the International Social Security Association, has taken due note of this (ISSA 1996b: 9): "It seems that the economy and economic theory have recently been allowed to dominate the debate and decisions on how to reform social security."

The ascendancy of economic dogma has come about because of the wide appeal of neoliberalism, with its simplicities, its absolutism and its ideological additives — egoistic utilitarianism, the seductive allure of rationality and the unquestioning certainties of neopositivism. Typical is the World Bank's (1994) "three pillar" strategy: *for the workers*, a combination of competitive, mandatory and tax-induced voluntary defined-contribution plans; and *for the deserving poor*, minimally government-funded, means-tested modest flat-rate pensions (see also Gilbert 1992, Haar 1989, Horsman and Marshall 1994, James 1996, James 1994, Keane 1988, Kotlikoff 1996b, Maydell 1994, Offe 1996). The adoption of this approach, of course, requires a technical realignment of social security funding responsibilities between the state, the employer, the family and the individual. Neoliberalism's disdain for the idea of a rational values discourse means that the social security debate agenda is set by "scientific" economic forecasts; an exercise, it could be argued, in economic sophistry.

It is not surprising that neoliberalism has acquired almost hegemonic proportions, because it goes largely unchallenged on technical grounds, notwithstanding serious reservations about the superiority of the marketplace, and because it arrogantly disdains rational values discourse. This has led to what Alesalo (1997: 76) describes as "the homogenization of socioeconomic values" and, ultimately, to the emergence of a dominant discourse coalition, one that shares the neoliberal "social construct" (Hajer 1993: 43) and determines the contextual constraints on what constitutes the "positivistically-approved mode of discourse" (Fay 1975). Even the forums in which neoliberal social security grand designs are being deconstructed into concrete policy arguments by these coalitions are ones where the ideological premises of neoliberalism are unquestioningly accepted, such as the corporate boardrooms, industry conferences, treasury departmental meeting, and gatherings of sympathetic political parties. This is certainly the experience in Chile (Holzmann 1996), Hong Kong (Dixon 1995a), Singapore (Ramesh 1992) and the United States (Cloward and Piven 1992).

There is certainly a convenient conjunction in neoliberal ideology between economic imperatives — fair returns and economic efficiency — and moral imperatives — individual and family responsibility, personal choice and dignity based contractual relationships — as posited by the New Right, a political movement that "combines eighteenth century liberalism and populist conservatism (Kouzmin et al. 1996: 234) and, increasingly, the New Left, the crypto-neoliberal reformers operating within a Social Democratic tradition. This casts a gloomy gray shadow over the social justice visions and humane good intentions of the founders of the Welfare State, conceived to soften the "sharper edges of capitalism" and to be the "crowning achievement of post war prosperity" (D. Cox 1998: 1), and to initiate a golden age (Pinker 1995, see also Eichengreen 1996). The Welfare State, nevertheless, still has its advocates (Bryson 1992, Jenkins 1993, Mishra 1984, Stephens 1995, Wilson and Wilson 1995). The neoliberals — never the utopians — assert that the Welfare State must be surrendered to the dark tide of its ineluctable destiny, because of its unaffordable predisposition towards coverage universality and benefit generosity, both of which have been stretched too far. As Robert Cox (1998: 2) has remarked: "If the welfare state has become a butterfly, many are still calling it a caterpillar." At stake are not just social security's current and future economic and financial viability, for any realignment that diminishes the role of the state must also reduce its distributive and redistributive role (Alesalo 1993, Bowles and Gintis 1995, Bryson 1992).

The opponents of neoliberalism endeavor to shift the social security debate away from a technical economic efficiency focus towards abstract discussions of the normative dimensions of social security reform — the ethical precepts surrounding what is a fair and equitable distribution of entitlements and financial burdens — and the broader issues of social justice — conceptualized, perhaps, as social rights, universality and solidarity across generations and across income groups (R. H. Cox 1998). Such a normative policy debate would be reminiscent of that which took place in the optimistic economic milieu of the halcyon days of the 1950s and 1960s, when the democratic socialists and social democrats were assiduously constructing their welfare states (Ashford 1993, Muller 1994). This comparison, however, highlights the legacy following in the wake of the Welfare State constructionists' perceived economic illiteracy or even, as some would say, economic irresponsibility, which casts a shadow of incredulousness over those who seek to follow in their wake. The pendulum has shifted; some would say from social progress to social dumping (Abrahamson 1991), or from modernity to post-modernity (Bauman 1997, Leonard 1997). Pessimism, uncertainty generated by realism leading to existential individualism, has long replaced optimism, certainty generated by hope leading to a good and fair society, as a defining feature of the economic milieu.

From this neoliberal milieu has came the new orthodoxy in economic policy-making, with its supply-side preoccupations, which has three fundamental postulates. First, that budgets should be balanced rather than used as a Keynesian tool for managing demand. Second, that unemployment should be regarded as a labor market problem, best solved by deregulation. Finally, that inflation should be controlled by means of monetary policy, tactically using interest rates, preferably designed and implemented by an independent central bank. This milieu and its policy prescriptions have challenged past perceptions of "governmentality," those competing cultures and mentalities of government that Foucault has argued are engendered by modern societies (Gordon et al. 1988). As a result, the notion of "un-governability" has gained a certain credibility because it cleverly links the libertarian's wish to reduce the size of government and the conservative's worry about disorder (Rowlands 1990: 267). Governments are now under pressure from the neoliberals to re-engineer themselves.

A significant part of any government neoliberal re-engineering must involve aligning and realigning the modalities of state social security intervention in accordance with a set of economically efficient, and thus the "correct," reforms (see, for example, Schieber and Shoven 1996, OECD 1988, World Bank 1994). These prescriptions — such as privatization, marketization, re-casting the state-individual-family responsibility boundaries, welfare-to-work programs and work-for-welfare programs — are posited as inevitabilities rather than possibilities and supposedly constitute an irresistible force that dictates the only possible reform path, one that, arguably, as Wright (1994: 128–9) observes, in a more general context,

is based on a simplistic view of bureaucracy, a naive view of the market, an idealized view of the private sector, an insensitivity to the hidden costs of reform, an over-optimism about outcomes, and, perhaps more fundamentally, a misleading view of the state.

These omnipotent reform prescriptions — designed in the abstract — appear in a spectrum reflecting various degrees of radicalness: away from pay-as-you-go financing of defined-benefit entitlements modestly towards the partially funded, or more radically, the fully funded financing of tightly targeted, publicly provided, defined-benefit entitlements; towards, even more radically, the fully funded financing of mandated defined-contribution or defined-benefit entitlements; or towards, *in extremis*, the abdication by the state from any social security responsibility, by means of individualization and familialization.

Indeed, governments are now confronting vexing reform incongruities — because even abstract policy prescriptions cannot be implemented in the abstract — as they seek to reduce social tensions, especially those associated with anomie and despair, without destroying their economies (Kirsch 1988) or losing electoral support. Maintaining strong economic and political support may well prove to be mutually incompatible with achieving such social security policy goals (Esping-Andersen 1996a), notwithstanding the World Bank's (1994) "three pillars" strategy. Indeed, that the 1997 New Zealand referendum's very decisively rejection of the idea of compulsory private pensions must be worrying to any government that is keen to explore the privatization options.

Governments are also now struggling to find ways to redesign their tax-financed or -subsidized social security systems. They are seeking to reduce budget deficits, or even to balance their budgets, to achieve macro-economic objectives, most notably to enhance their countries' international competitiveness in the regional and global marketplaces. They want to do this without leaving gaping holes in their social security safety-nets, ever mindful of ensuring equity for future generations, and always cognizant of the prevailing welfare politics concomitant with generational tensions. In redesigning a social security system the crucial question is how to harmonize it with policy initiatives in any or all of the following domains: employment policies (to create jobs and provide retraining opportunities), wages policies (to deal with working poor), taxation policies (to encourage work and appropriate forms of saving), savings policies (to encourage appropriate forms of saving), microeconomic policies (to deal with structural unemployment), and macroeconomic policies (to encourage economic growth and to minimize cyclical unemployment and inflation). Governments are searching for a middle way that does not alienate totally either the politically influential welfare lobbies (especially those focused on senior-citizens or welfare professionals) or the electorally significant post-war baby boomers throughout the developed world (Abrahamson 1994, Baldwin 1990a and 1990b, Battle 1996, Borowski 1991, Burkhauser et al. 1994, Campbell 1994b, Castles and Pierson 1996, Castles 1996, Clasen and Gould 1995, Cutler 1997, Day 1993, George and Wilding 1994, Huber and Stephens 1993, Haanes-Olsen 1994a, Heclo 1975, Kingson 1991, Mebane 1994, Pratt 1993, Prinz 1995, Quadagno 1989, Richman 1995, Rochefort 1990, Taylor-Gooby 1996).

Governments are also agonizing over how best to reconstruct their social security systems by reducing coverage, tightening eligibility criteria, reducing benefit generosity, raising the revenue base, and/or reassigning financial burdens. The tactics from which they can choose to address these issues are many and varied:

- *restricting coverage* can be achieved by narrowing presumed need categories by redefining the population categories that are covered by social security programs so as to exclude particular population categories or to make their coverage voluntary, such as by exempting from coverage particular individuals (such as aliens or those with adequate private provision) or employees in particular forms of employment (such as temporary, casual, unpaid or family labor), or by imposing coverage earnings floors and ceilings.
- *restricting eligibility* by redefining the categorical criteria that determine the population categories that fall within a social security category (by, for example, adjusting age, gender, marital status, degree of disability, health status, number and type of dependents, and employment status requirements). Alternatively, the general qualifying conditions can be tightened (such as by imposing or extending minimum residency, contribution, employment or waiting period requirements; by imposing or increasing minimum or maximum age requirements; by eliminat-

ing incentives to claim entitlements (such as by eliminating rewards for early retirement); or by rewarding the deferment of entitlement claims (such as by rewarding deferred retirement));

- *improving income or means target efficiency* by imposing or adjusting income or
asset cutout points, by imposing or adjusting income and/or asset disregard limits and their attendant claw-back rates, or by imposing or adjusting the personal
income tax liability on pensions and benefits, so as to focus expenditure on
those below either a poverty or an affluence income threshold;

- *reducing benefit generosity* by reducing income-replacement rates, by abolishing
supplementary and special benefits, by reducing maximum benefit payment periods, by adopting a two-tier or three-tier benefit structure, by replacing earnings-
related with flat-rate or contribution-based benefits, by lowering maximum or
minimum benefit rates, by abolishing any form of periodic adjustment, by changing the basis upon which benefits are periodically adjusted, by reducing the periodicity of benefit adjustments or by lowering the earnings benchmark upon
which benefits are based;

- *raising the revenue base* by raising general taxation revenue (by, for example,
raising income, profit or commodity tax revenues), by raising one or more of the
contribution rates, by broadening the contribution base (by, for example, extending coverage) or by increasing the rate of return on social security reserves (by,
for example, redefining any investment portfolio constraints, or perhaps by privatizing investment portfolio management responsibilities); or

- *redistributing the cost burdens* by adjusting government subsidies, by adjusting
employer and/or employee statutory contribution incidents, by entirely recasting
social security funding arrangements, perhaps by shifting all or part of cost burden to the individual, perhaps by mandating personal pension or savings plans or
by renouncing a statutory responsibility, thereby creating a vacuum to be filled
on a discretionary basis by individuals (such as by withdrawing unemployment
benefits from particular population categories) or by families (perhaps by making family support for particular population categories either mandatory
(perhaps, for the aged and children) or necessary because of the withdrawal of
benefits (perhaps, for adolescent first job seekers or adolescent unmarried mothers)).

Social security privatization is now on the political agenda globally. While
it may not be seen as a magical elixir, it is certainly seen as a means of clearly
identifying who is paying for what. Privatization at least offers hope — some
might say naive hope — that perceived social security problems will not get any
worse (Kotlickoff 1996a). Precisely how vague privatization aspirations could or
should be translated into new social security programs remains a political challenge still to be met in the light of the plethora of interest and pressure groups
to be placated (Campbell 1992 and 1994a, Duskin 1991, Gilbert and Park 1996,
Kopits 1993, Ramesh 1992, Taverne 1995). With time, Kingson and Williamson (1996: 28) may well be proved right when they assert, in the United States'
setting, that the

real social security crisis is the possibility that the advocates of means-testing and marketization may succeed. Should this occur, political support for the pension system will be eroded, the moral base of the communitarian institutions will be diminished, and America's families — especially the low income ones — will be placed at greater economic risk.

It may also be true of Gilbert and Park (1996: 19), who go somewhat further and suggest that the shifting public-private mix in the United States will mean that the public social security programs will:

* "provide declining support for those most in need";
* "heighten the need for greater regulation of private schemes"; and
* create "a two-tiered system of pensions": "whittled-down" public pensions for the low income earners, private pensions for the middle- and upper-income groups.

Current social security recipients, and those likely to join their ranks in the foreseeable future, feel threatened by the privatization rhetoric, to the point of being willing to protests politically even at the mere suggestion that existing social security program benefits or eligibility should, in any way, be curtailed. They have come to expect, and depend on, a certain level of public social security provision. The middle-aged baby boomers, as taxpayers and social security contributors, are beginning to feel threatened by the real possibility that although they will be living longer, healthier lives their future income security needs may not being entirely met by public programs with the generous funding that they, themselves, financed for an earlier generation. They face the daunting dual task of paying for today's pensioners and saving for their own old age, and hence the prospect of impoverishment, particularly if they fall victim to unemployment. Thus they, themselves, threaten to demand restraint on transfers to those who are feather-bedded by the Welfare State which they are financing (Baldwin 1990a and 1990b, Borowski 1991, Becker 1994, Cutler 1997, Ponza et al. 1988, Richman 1995, Sherman 1992, Silverstein and Parrott 1997).

Adding to governments' woes are the politically influential mercantilist business lobbies, which continually plead for reductions in their statutory social security contribution obligations, as well as other tax burdens, even though they may well have shifted those burdens forward on to their consumers or backward on to their employees. Although it must be acknowledged that any social security reform has implications for international competitiveness that need to be understood, achieving international competitiveness is not contingent upon social security reform (Thompson 1998).

Exacerbating this dilemma is the all-too-evident inability of social security systems to address adequately a range of contemporaneous and contingency issues. Foremost amongst them would be the consequences of economic recession, economic structural adjustment in the context of economic globalization and changing social values, most notably: persistent poverty (Berghman and

Muffels 1988, Deleeck et al. 1992, Dixon and Macarov 1998, George and Lawson 1980, Rieger and Liebfried 1998, Townsend 1993); increasing, and increasingly more protracted, unemployment (Esping-Andersen 1996b); the growth in atypical work practices (Beiback 1993a and 1993b, Cousins 1992, Furugori 1993, Kravaritou-Manitakis 1988); the treatment of women (Hill and Tigges 1995, Kingson and O'Grady-LaShane 1993, Meyer et al. 1994, Olsen 1994) and ethnic minorities (Dixon and Scheurell 1994a); and the consequences of transnational population movements (Dixon and Magill 1997, Maydell 1994, Pieters and Vansteenkiste 1995) caused by multilateral economic cooperation (as in the European Union) or by economic or political refugees. These issues bring into question the appropriateness of hermetic social security systems compartmentalized within national jurisdictions and thus the need for a globalization of social security.

The social security problems facing developed countries are as diverse as approaches to their solution are complex (Espina 1996). Recent social security policy reviews and reforms are in process, or have recently taken place, in a variety of developed countries, such as *Australia* (Rosenman and Warburton 1996), *Belgium* (OECD 1994b); *Canada* (Battle 1996); *Denmark* (Hasling 1996); *France* (OECD 1994a, Campbell 1994b); *Germany* (*Economist* 19 February 1994: 59–60); *Italy* (Marchettini 1995, Salafia 1995); *Japan* (Clark 1996, Kato 1991, Murakmi 1995 and 1997); *the Netherlands* (Bierlaagh and Sporken 1994, Oorschot 1998); *Portugal* (Terribile 1996); *Spain* (Puidak 1994); *Sweden* (Haanes-Olsen 1994a and 1994b, Stephens 1996, Sweden 1995); and *the United Kingdom* (Kritzer 1994, UK 1998) and more countries are likely to follow suit (Maydell 1994). Social security is, undoubtedly, in transition throughout the developed world, where the search for greater public social security cost-effectiveness will continue well into the twenty-first century (OECD 1997). The resuscitation of the legitimacy of public social security's poverty alleviation role may be one of its by-products, particularly if the World Bank's advocacy of its "three pillars" strategy falls upon sympathetic government ears.

DEVELOPING COUNTRIES

Governments in most developing countries, in stark contrast to their counterparts in developed countries, are now faced with the consequences of the failure of their social security systems (Gillion 1994, Iyer 1993, Schmidt 1995). They have failed to achieve anything like universality of employment coverage, because of the difficulties of penetrating the rural sector in the face of irregular employment patterns, temporary or seasonal rural-urban migration, illiteracy, poor communications systems or geographic isolation (see, for example, Amin 1980, Mallet 1980, Savy 1972). Instead, they prefer to focus on the politically more important urban middle class interest groups (see, for example, Chang 1985, Deyo 1992, Ku 1995, Malloy 1979, Mesa-Lago 1978, Ramesh 1995a,

Rimlinger 1971). They have failed to provide pensions and benefits that keep even these privileged groups out of poverty, especially when faced with the rampant inflation that is a symptom of economic crisis and dislocation. They have also failed to address the growing and serious income inequalities that exist within developing countries (Asian Development Bank 1990, 1993 and 1994, Brand 1994, Oxfam 1995, Rodgers and Hoeven 1995, Townsend 1993).

Social security systems in developing countries do not reach the poor, particularly not the rural poor, and especially not women. The pre-eminent employment-based strategies — social insurance, employer liability and National Provident Funds — all cater to the urban industrial workforce, ignoring rural peasants, those in the urban informal sectors, and those outside the workforce (Amin 1980, Mallet 1980). Social assistance has the potential to address contemporary poverty, but only if it achieves a high degree of poverty target efficiency, if the entitlements granted are adequate to lift recipients out of poverty, and if fiscal capacity and budgetary priorities permit the required program expenditure (Midgley 1993). Meeting the challenge of these three preconditions is beyond capabilities of those relatively few developing countries that have adopted the social assistance strategy. Indeed, social assistance has not been widely used to ameliorate poverty by providing those most in need, irrespective of their current or past employment or contribution status, with either income supplementation (as, for example, in Mauritius, where means-tested child benefits are paid to families with at least three children) or income support (as, for example, in India, where very modest means-tested old-age pensions are provided to the elderly poor without access to family support, provided they are of good moral character and not engaged in begging —the shadow of the Poor Law tradition certainly still lingers beyond de-colonization (Midgley 1984a, 1984b and 1984c, Isuani 1985)! Indeed, it can be argued that at the margin social security may well exacerbate poverty by the behavioral responses it induces, most notably the incentive to have more children when the number of children is a categorical criterion or when more children attract more entitlements, although there is a conspicuous lack of empirical evidence in support of this hypothesis.

The juxtaposition of the relatively widespread provision of lump-sum benefits, inadequacy of flat-rate benefits, the low levels of income replacement achieved, and the general absence of benefit indexation, limits the extent to which social security systems in developing countries can keep their beneficiaries out of poverty. Unless lump-sum benefits are sufficient to provide a future source of income, and are used to that effect, they will not prevent poverty (see, for example, Musiga 1976). Unless the periodic payments are adequate to meet basic human needs and indexed, inflation exacerbates their inadequacy.

Redistributive social security strategies are not considered by governments to be an appropriate way of alleviating poverty. As Morató (1990: 1) notes, poverty is usually conceptualized as "merely a by-product of development," a consequence of inequality. There is a reluctance in all but a few developing countries to use social security programs to provide either income replacement for the urban unemployed or income supplementation for low-income urban families, which limits their effectiveness as a mechanism for preventing, let alone ameliorating, urban poverty and inequality. This reluctance exists even when poverty and inequality are caused by governments' implementing, perhaps at the behest of international financial institutions, interventionist or laissez-faire economic restructuring policies encouraged and rationalized by those who advocate a commitment to "trickle-down" development strategies, which are based on the premise that with growth comes reduced poverty and greater equality, but have, in effect, "float up" consequences (Morató 1990: 1). Such reluctance is then, of course, rationalized by reference to the perceived moral hazard risks and the political, social and economic consequences that might flow from any resultant inherently conflict-laden vertical income redistribution (Dixon 1994 and 1996a, Leal de Araujo 1972, Midgley 1984a, 1984b, 1984c, 1988 and 1993, Tracy 1991).

Even more worrying is the fact that few developing countries are willing, or able, even to harmonize social security strategies with broader socioeconomic development strategies targeting the amelioration of poverty (Arroba 1966 and 1972, Cockburn 1980, Fisher 1968, Midgley 1997, Moles 1971, Rys 1974), notably the "social fund" measures originally experimented with in Bolivia in the late 1980s and subsequently implemented elsewhere (Vivian 1995). Because of the absence of such coordinated policy making, social security has become irrelevant to any national antipoverty strategy and anachronistic in the economic development context, perhaps even impeding, rather than aiding, a developing country's capacity to respond to the problems of economic development, structural adjustment and, ultimately, poverty and inequality.

In those developing countries that have tripartite funding of social insurance systems, government subsidies are generally financed by regressive tax regimes (see, for example, Mesa-Lago 1978). This results in the transfer of resources from the poorest if they are excluded from coverage but pay taxes, to those not-so-poor in the formal wage sector who are covered (Arroba 1966, Midgley 1984a). Where the social security financing role of government is quite restricted, this regressive income redistribution process is probably quite limited, although any social security reforms involving greater government funding could initiate such a regressive redistributive process (see Dixon 1989a, Fisher 1968, Malloy 1979, Mathew 1979a and 1979b; Paukert 1968a and 1968b). Indeed, employer contributions can have quite a significant regressive impact on income distribution, if those contributions can be readily shifted forwards to consumers (as higher commodity prices over time) or, perhaps, backwards to workers (as lower real earnings over time) because of commodity and labor market imperfections.

In some developing countries, social security institutions — especially National Provident Funds — have become significant financial institutions. Fully funded social security systems have the capacity to generate savings, depending on the contribution rates, contribution ceilings, the benefit rates, the social security (and other) contingencies covered and the level of any government subsidies provided. The growth in revenue (contributions plus investment and other income) usually exceeds the growth in expenditure (benefits plus administrative expenses), thus ensuring an accumulation of reserves (Arroba 1966, Cockburn 1980, Dixon 1989a, Iyer 1971, Reviglio 1967, Fisher 1968). This is inevitable for a variety of reasons. First, because the focus is largely on long-term social security contingencies, contributions are collected for a considerable period before benefits are payable. Second, the typical age structure in developing countries is skewed toward the younger age groups, which means that the proportion of beneficiaries to contributors is relatively low. Third, industrialization and urbanization draw more people into covered employment, thus ensuring continued growth in the number of contributors. Finally, inflation increases revenue, because contributions are tied to money earnings, while having no significant impact on expenditure. Whether such responsibility for the investment of these reserves should be in public or private hands is a moot point.

Those with Benthamite distaste for the public sector and a penchant for economic efficiency argue, persuasively, that the private sector should manage the investment of reserves generated by partially or fully funded social security systems because it is more likely to achieve higher real rates of return on those reserves (World Bank 1994). Singapore, for example, is experimenting with the contracting-out of investment services for a proportion of its substantial National Provident Fund reserves (Dixon 1996a). Private sector involvement in investment management offers the promise of greater domestic capital market depth and liquidity (Crespo 1994, Singh 1996), provided any contractual constraints or regulatory regimes imposed on the private sector are liberal in the range of permitted financial instruments and conservative in permitting international investments (Holzmann 1996, Montas 1983).

Those with a collectivist's distrust the private sector and a penchant for social justice argue, just as persuasively, that the marketplace does not always get it right — pointing the finger at the poor financial management performance of Chilean privatized pension funds, which produced their first-ever negative rate of return in 1995 (Love 1996: 24). They also acknowledge that while the private sector may be efficient at should set the priorities for the investment of public social security reserves on the basis of the prevailing political attitudes towards the appropriate socioeconomic roles of social security institutions. These investment priorities can be articulated as asset portfolio management constraints in the enabling legislation, or as part of the institutional or regulatory arrangements surrounding the investment decision-making process (Kertonegoro 1986).

For funded social security the primary asset portfolio management objective depends on whether defined-benefit or defined-contribution programs are being financed. For defined-benefit programs the primary concern is to maintain their actuarial viability, set in the context of the agreed levels of government subsidy. For defined-contribution programs, whether publicly or privately administered, the primary concern is to enable them to earn an adequate positive real rate of interest on funds invested. A secondary asset portfolio management policy goal for publicly administered programs — National Provident Funds — is to provide a relatively cheap source of development finance for use by government. These twin objectives are not necessarily inherently incompatible for either defined-benefit programs (because they may receive government subsidies to support their defined-benefit programs) or defined-contribution programs (because, by definition, they offer no guaranteed benefits). Thus, during periods of relatively modest inflation, when the real rate of interest is at least positive, the achievement of both objectives is relatively easy. When, however, inflation causes the real rate of interest to become negative, then the simultaneous achievement of both objectives becomes substantially more difficult. The available evidence suggests that under these circumstances the social security objective of publicly administered social security programs becomes a little blurred (Dixon 1993, Thompson 1978).

Prudent asset portfolio management policies that may be appropriate when there is currency stability are challenged in times of currency depreciation. For publicly administered, funded social security programs, a prudent policy of purchasing low-yield, high-security, government and government-guaranteed bonds and loans remains the dominant feature of their asset portfolio management policies. This traditional conservatism is, however, placed under threat as such risk-averse social security institutions increasingly seek ways of protecting their members and beneficiaries from the full impact of inflation, perhaps by entering the capital market and thus confronting the challenges of managing rather than avoiding risk. For privately administered, funded social security programs, the dominant feature of their portfolio management policies is the balancing of risk-differentiated financial instruments to maximize returns, while prudently managing risk considering the prevailing regulatory regime. Inflation, and with it the prospect of negative real rates of return, threaten prudent risk management as higher expected returns are more willingly traded off against higher risks. Unquestionably, financial assets do not provide a hedge against inflation, unless they are indexed in line with the inflation, which commonly they are not. However, protecting accumulated reserves from currency depreciation must remain the major financial challenge facing funded social security systems in the future (Lee 1980).

In meeting the challenge of currency depreciation, funded social security systems — especially those that are publicly administered — are confronted with a variety of externally and self-imposed constraints that limit their maneuverability. First, they are usually required to hold a significant proportion of their portfolios in government, semi-government or government-guaranteed securities or loans, whether by law or ministerial decree, or as prudence may dictate. This is an appropriate policy, however, only if the rate of return on such investments is competitive with other investment opportunities carrying a comparable degree of risk. Second, some social security institutions are having difficulties finding sufficient investment opportunities in which to invest their reserves at an acceptable rate of return (Yee 1994), because they are not permitted or prepared to invest in real property, to provide venture (equity or loan) capital to the private sector, or to take advantage of investment opportunities outside the country in which they operate. Each of these strategies offers the promise of market rates of return, although the risks are rather higher than those attached to government and semi-government securities and loans.

Several authorities (Arroba 1966, Fisher 1968, Cockburn 1980, Midgley 1997) have argued over many years, the accumulated reserves of funded social security systems can and should be harnessed, at least in part, to promote social and economic development. Governments can, if they so choose, use these reserves to the advantage of the poor, by improving their quality of life (for example, improving healthcare or housing) or improving their economic well-being (creating employment opportunities or supporting small-scale enterprises). It is but a question of political priorities and political will.

Social security systems can be designed so that they are compatible with domestic economic and social realities in the developing country context, but the idea that they must reflect European systems must first be challenged (Atkinson and Hills 1991). They can be designed to ameliorate poverty directly (through progressive vertical income redistribution) or indirectly (by contributing to the financing of social and economic developmental strategies that address the pressing problems of poverty and deprivation). But it takes political will for this to happen. It also requires imaginative and innovative social security policy-making (Guhan 1994, Hardiman and Midgley 1988, Iyer 1993, Midgley 1993).

Many governments are, however, seeking to enhance the performance of their social security systems, as a means of addressing pressing social and personal tragedies associated with socioeconomic change and modernization, in order to ensure social stability in the face of prevailing social inequalities (Grimaud 1995, Kirsch 1988). They are doing this by adding new social security branches, by broadening program coverage (especially to rural workers, independent farmers and other self-employed) and by increasing benefit generosity. They are endeavoring to do this, however, without draining their meager public coffers, which are already over-burdened with public expenditure demands. Adding further to governments' woes are the all-too-common investment and contribution revenue shortfalls being experienced in funded systems, caused by negative real investment yields, and the consequences of rapacious governments unwilling to pay competitive interest rates on borrowed funds, corrupt and inefficient administrators, dishonest employers, and employees eager to avoid their contribution liabilities (Murray and Bueikman 1992). Employees see their contributions as an inter-temporal transfer of consumption that they can ill-afford, given their current living standards and the meager pensions and benefits promised, which will, in all likelihood, be quickly eaten away by inflation. MacKeller and McGreevey, document this for Latin America and elsewhere, drawing upon World Bank reports (McGreevey 1990, MacKellar and McGreevey 1997).

The budgetary and macroeconomic realities in most developing countries leave governments with little room to maneuver when contemplating social security reforms. They cannot consider such reforms merely from a financial and economic perspective, for who wins and who loses from any social security reform raises extremely sensitive political issues. Given the inevitable prospects of an aging population, albeit one associated with a bulging workforce — because of the juxtaposition of declining fertility rates and high workforce participation rates in the older age groups — then, as MacKellar and Bird (1997: 3) suggest "policy makers will look for ways to complement, if not replace, transfer-based social security arrangements with savings-based ones." Thus, the international financial institutions' general advocacy of privatization — invariably, the competitive, mandatory defined-contribution strategy — may well fall upon eager ears. It offers the promise of a multilevel, pluralistic social security structure, and the hope of replicating the Chilean "economic miracle" of the 1980s (Bosworth et al. 1994, Castaneda 1992, Gillion and Bonilla 1992 Gluski 1994, Holzmann 1996, ILO 1994, Kritzer 1996b, Mackenzie 1995, Ryser 1992, Vittas and Iglesias 1992, World Bank 1994), but hopefully not the sobering negative rate of return achieved by Chile's private pension funds — 2.5 percent in 1995 (Love 1996: 24). Malaysia and Singapore would appear keen to take up the privatization clarion call, as they are in the process of redefining state-private boundaries around their social security systems (Hoon 1995, Ramesh 1992).

Privatization offers the promise of enhanced economic performance. It may increase domestic savings, provided the mandatory savings gains are not offset by voluntary savings losses. It may produce greater domestic capital market efficiency, depth and liquidity, provided there is effective competition between pension funds and provided regulatory regimes are liberal in the range of permitted financial instruments and conservative in permitting international investments. It may lessen labor-market distortions, provided employers are discouraged from hiring unregistered employees. The dream is that privatization will allow governments to impose little or no social security contribution burdens on employers and taxpayers and will prevent governments from penalizing future generations (Holzmann 1996, Montas 1983, Tanner 1996). For the employee, however, while it may offer the prospect of a more secure benefit, it certainly promises a benefit of uncertain magnitude, which is an inherent feature of the mandatory defined-contribution social security strategy. Any replacement of social insurance by this strategy represents the abandonment of risk pooling, a fundamental tenet of social insurance for over 100 years.

The social security problems facing developing countries are as daunting as approaches to their solution are tenuous. Social security is in transition in pockets of the developing world, most notably in Latin America (Huber 1996), where the Chilean model of privatization vies for support with the Argentinean public/private mixed model (Campbell 1992, Mesa and Bertranou 1997). The search for enhanced social security performance has begun and will continue beyond the year 2000. One of the consequences of this search may well be the gradual demise of the risk pooling principle.

POST-SOCIALIST COUNTRIES

Governments in post-socialist countries are, in stark contrast to their counterparts in either developed or other developing countries, now faced with the consequences of the past use of their social security systems to achieve ideological goals (Dixon 1981b, Dixon and Kim 1992, George and Manning 1980). Under communist rule, social security systems provided generous cradle-to-grave protection to loyal state workers, so as to consolidate socialism by obviating at least the excesses of the alienation generated by the governing regime and the inevitable loss of freedom. This was paid for by state employers ever eager to provide much-needed work incentives and to minimize work indiscipline, particularly as they operated in an economic environment where production costs were more illusory than real, and where economic efficiency was always subservient to communist ideology.

The communist world, however, began crumbling in the early 1990s with the sudden collapse and disintegration of the Soviet Union. This forced upon its former republics, as well as the dependent socialist countries of Eastern Europe, the daunting task of simultaneous political and economic transformation, with the inevitably concomitant, social transmutation (Atkinson and Micklewright 1992, Brzezinski 1993, Huntington 1993, Miller 1992, Przeworski 1991). The political transformation challenge involves solving the paradox of grafting stable democracies (DiPalma 1990) on to societies that lack the preconditions for democracy, namely, a functioning market economy, a strong civil society, a large middle class, competent elites and corporative institutional arrangements. The economic transformation challenge involves the introduction of labor, capital and currency markets; the liberalization of foreign trade and foreign capital investment controls; the corporatization, commercialization and privatization of state enterprises; and the encouragement of private enterprise. The social transformation challenge involves removing Sztompka's (1996: 38) syndrome of distrust (see also Rose 1994), including distrust of public institutions (Sztompka 1996: 52), as the lost socialist life-world has yet to be replaced by another (Gregova 1996).

The process of transforming socialist planned economies in Eastern Europe, Central Asia and elsewhere into market economies has, however, been both more difficult and more protracted than expected (Adams and Brock 1993, Asian Development Bank 1995, Barr 1994a, Batt 1991). The rapid dismantling of central planning systems has almost invariably produced structural dislocation, the symptoms of which are macroeconomic imbalances — inflation, the sudden loss of employment and a resultant dramatic decline in living standards (Barr 1994a, Coria 1994a and 1994b, George and Rimachevskaya 1993, Sredkova 1996). Interestingly, however, this did not occur so dramatically in China, where concern for social and political stability has meant that market reform and the dismantling of the "iron rice bowl" have been phased in more gradually without any concomitant shift towards democratization (Dixon and Newman 1998, Leung 1994). As a result, the social fabric in most post-socialist countries, so badly rent by these dislocations, requires re-weaving by thoughtful social and political innovation. But persistent budget deficits, often because of shortfalls in tax revenue and a desire by governments to shield state-owned enterprises from the shock of market adjustments, have constrained or even reduced the degree to which governments can protect those who have been made most vulnerable by this transition process, especially the aged, disabled people and the unemployed (see for example, Chan and Chow 1992, Chow 1988a, 1988b, and 1995, George and Rimachevskaya 1992, Maydell 1994, Sredkova 1996), to the point at which some governments have had to delay payment of pensions and benefits. This has happened at a time when the traditional social security institutions — state-owned enterprises — have, themselves, been forced to begin shedding their social security cost responsibilities and thus burdens (see, for example, Commander and Jackman 1993, Chow 1995, Estrin et al. 1994, Stoesz and Lusk 1995). A crucial part of this socioeconomic transition is the challenge of dismantling the inherited social security systems, which were once the envy of many, but which the governments concerned can now no longer afford, while preserving a safety net for the vulnerable that does not have gaping holes (Barr 1994b, Deacon and Szalai 1990, George 1991, Maret and Schwartz 1994, Myles and Brym 1992, Myles 1996, Paul 1991, Rajnes and Turner 1996, Rossler 1996, Rhys 1994, Voirin 1993, Zukowski 1994).

There has begun a process of reconceptualizing social security, the key to which is "pluralism"; the shift from state and state-enterprise dependency towards marketization, the inevitable result of which has been a shrinking of the public sector's involvement in, and commitment to, social security. Hungary is, indeed, speeding towards the creation of a mandated personal pension system, which will make it the first post-socialist country to reform its pension system. Elsewhere, however, social security reform has been constrained because democratization has produced new political parties, some of which have roots going back to the old discredited regimes, which have been focusing their core policies on the maintenance of the old socialist welfare legacy, in an effort to position themselves as the sole protector of the working class (see, for example, Ruzica 1995).

The initial social security policy priority of most emerging post-socialist countries has been to extricate their governments from a social security funding quagmire by imposing contributions on the employers that reflect their past social security outlays, associated with minuscule contribution impositions on employees, mere token gestures in most cases. This has only exacerbated the foremost of many yet unaddressed social security problems; that is, how best to reduce the social security cost burden on former state-owned enterprises, so that they can become financially viable economic units able to compete in an open economy seeking integration into the competitive global economy. This means that social security financing responsibilities must be recast, with the prospect looming of employees becoming the major loser. It also means that the achieved levels of benefit generosity will have to be critically questioned. Unfortunately, these challenging policy issues must be confronted at a time when economic dislocation, caused by market reform, has dramatically reduced both job security and attained living standards, and when democracy in these post-socialist countries is only in its fragile infancy, both of which, consequently, make any decisions that create social security losers even more unpalatable.

The social security problems facing post-socialist countries are as bewildering as approaches to their solution are indubitable. Social security is definitely in significant transition in the post-socialist world, where the search for affordable social security systems will accelerate towards the year 2000, as the cost of the status quo becomes increasingly more apparent. One consequence of this transition is, of course, the death of a short-lived social security tradition, although it will haunt these countries well into the twenty-first century.

CONCLUSION

Social security was born in Europe almost 500 years ago. For 350 years it changed very little, as its fundamental Poor Law values were never questioned. The excesses of the European Industrial Revolution, however, sowed the seeds of change in the middle of the nineteenth century. Slowly these seeds began to germinate, before blossoming in the closing decades of that century. A veritable revolution in the way European societies viewed social security then took place.

Social security's global spread over the last 100 years has involved the transplanting of essentially nineteenth-century European values and twentieth-century administrative and financial practices. The result has been global predominance of the social insurance strategy, as most countries sought to construct income-replacement safety nets that promised to keep their burgeoning middle classes out of poverty. Social security, administered as it invariably must be, has favored the literate, the assertive and the informed, and thus has been irrelevant in terms of the human needs of most people, including, unfortunately, the most vulnerable — those most in need — in most countries for most of the twentieth century.

Social security has always had its specters present. Like all ghosts, unless they are exorcised they will continue to haunt. In most countries the twin social security ghosts are irrelevancy and inadequacy, but their exorcism raises the specter of an unaffordable burgeoning of social security costs, a ghost that already haunts developed and post-socialist countries. The major global challenge is how best to enhance the cost-effectiveness of social security systems so that they are better able to meet the current and future social security needs of their host communities. This requires governments to address the thorny political issue of unrealistic or conflicting community expectations, to confront the Poor Law ghost of deterrence, and to reconsider the social security obligations of employers, employees and taxpayers, with the specter of privatization looming menacingly on the horizon. This challenge has certainly set the global social security agenda until well beyond the year 2000.

References

Aaron, B. and Farwell, D. F. eds. 1984. *International Society for Labor and Social Security: Reports and Proceedings from the 10th International Congress. Washington, DC: September 7–10, 1984.* Washington, DC: Bureau of National Affairs.

Aaron, H. 1966. "The Social Insurance Paradox." *Canadian Journal of Economics* 3 2 (2): 371–79.

Aaron, H. 1967. "Social Security: International Comparisons." In Eckstein, O. ed., *Studies in the Economics of Income Maintenance.* Washington, DC: Brookings Institute.

Aaron, H. J. and Burtless, G. T. 1989. "Fiscal Policy and the Dynamic Inconsistency of Social Security Forecasts." *American Economic Review* 79, May: 91–96.

Aaron, H. J., Bosworth, B. P. and Burtless, G. T. 1989. *Can America Afford to Grow Old? Paying for Social Security.* Washington, DC: Brookings Institution.

Abel-Smith, B. 1992a. "The Beveridge Report: Its Origins and Outcomes." *International Social Security Review* 45 (1–2): 5–17.

Abel-Smith, B. 1992b. "Health Insurance in Developing Countries: Lessons from Experience." *Health Policy and Planning* 7 (3): 215–26.

Abel-Smith, B. 1993. "Age, Work, and Social Security: The Policy Context." In Atkinson, A. B. and Rein, M. eds., *Age, Work, and Social Security.* London: St Martin's Press.

Abrahamson, P. ed. 1988. *Welfare State in Crisis: The Crumbling of the Scandinavian Model?* Kobenhaven: Foraget Sociologi.

Abrahamson, P. 1991. "Welfare and Poverty in the Europe of the 1990s: Social Progress or Social Dumping." *International Journal of Health Services* 21 (2): 237–64.

Abrahamson, P. 1994. "The Scandinavian Welfare Model in a Time of Change." In Cave, W. ed., *The Welfare State in Transition: Problems and Prospects of the Welfare Model.* Copenhagen: Danish Cultural Institute.

Ackerman, W. 1987. "State, Security and Insurance: An Analysis of Social Security

Policy in Some Western Societies." *The Geneva Papers on Risk and Insurance* 10: 3–41.

Adams, C. T. and Winston, K. T. 1980. *Mothers at Work: Public Policies in the United States. Sweden and China*. New York: Longmans.

Adams, W. and Brock, J. W. 1993. *Adam Smith Goes to Moscow: A Dialogue on Radical Reform*. Princeton, NJ: Princeton University Press.

Aguilar, R. C. Raporteur 1986. *Developments and Trends in Social Security Benefits, in the Light of Increasing Importance of Rehabilitation Measures: Report of the Permanent Committee on Insurance against Employment Accidents and Occupational Diseases to the International Social Security Association XXII General Assembly* (Report XXIII, Montreal, 2–12 September). Geneva: International Social Security Association.

Ahmed, E., Dreze, J., Hills, J. and Sen, A. eds. 1991. *Social Security in Developing Countries*. Oxford: Clarendon Press.

Aire, J. U. 1974. "Problems of Social Security in Nigeria." *Quarterly Journal of Administration*. 8 (4): 409–25.

Alber, J. 1983. "Some Causes of Social Security Expenditure Development in Western Europe 1949–1979." In Loney, M., Boswell, D. and Clarke, J. eds., *Social Policy and Social Welfare*. Milton Keynes: Open University.

Alber, J. 1988a. "Continuities and Change in the Idea of the Welfare State." *Politics & Society* 16 (4): 451–68.

Alber, J. 1988b. "Is There a Crisis of the Welfare State? Cross-National Evidence from Europe, North America, and Japan." *European Sociological Review* 3 (4): 181–207.

Alcock, P. 1996. "The Advantages and Disadvantages of the Contribution Base in Targeting Benefits: A Social Analysis of the Insurance Scheme in the United Kingdom." *International Social Security Review* 49 (1): 31–49.

Aldridge, J. 1982. "Earnings Replacement Rate of Old-age Benefits in 12 Countries, 1969–1980." *Social Security Bulletin*. 45 (11): 3–11.

Alesalo, M. 1993. "The Rise of Neo-Liberalism in Finland: From Politics of Equal Opportunity to the Search for Scientific Excellence." *Science Studies* 6 (2): 35–47.

Alesalo, M. 1997. "Variations in State Responsiveness: The Science System and Competing Theories of the State." *International Sociology* 12 (1): 73–92.

Alexander, J. C. 1982. *Positivism, Presupposition, and Current Controversies*. London: Routledge and Kegan Paul.

Allardt, E. 1987. "The Civic Conception of the Welfare State." In Rose, R. and Shiratorie, R. eds., *The Welfare State — East and West*. Oxford: Oxford University Press.

Ameresekere, R. V. W. E. 1994. "Social Security System in Sri Lanka." In *Asia Regional Conference on Social Security (September 14–16, 1993), Conference Proceedings*. Hong Kong: Hong Kong Council of Social Services.

Amin, N. M. 1980. "Social Security Protection for the Rural Population: Approaches in Malaysia." *International Social Security Review* 33 (2): 165–75.

Amy, D. J. 1984. "Why Policy Analysis and Ethics are Incompatible." *Journal of Policy Analysis and Management*. 3 (4): 573–91.

Andersen, B. R. 1992. "The Lessons from the Welfare State." In Greve, B. ed., *Social*

Policy in Europe: Latest Evolution and Perspectives for the Future. Copenhagen: Danish National Institute for Social Research.

Andersen, B. R. 1993. "The Nordic Welfare State under Pressure: The Danish Experience." *Journal of Aging and Social Policy* 21 (2): 109–20.

Anderson, S. 1987. "The Elitist Origins of the Japanese Welfare State Before 1945: Bureaucrats, Military Officers, Social Interests and Politicians." *Transactions of the Asiatic Society of Japan* (4th series) 2: 259–77.

Anderson, S. 1993. *Welfare Policy and Politics in Japan: Beyond the Developmental State.* New York: Paragon House.

Armstrong, B. N. 1932. *Insuring the Essentials.* New York: Macmillan.

Arroba, G. 1966. "Social Security and the National Economy." *International Review of Actuarial and Statistical Problems of Social Security* 13 (3): 129–81.

Arroba, G. 1972. "Social Security Planning and National Planning in the Developing Countries." *International Social Security Review* 25 (2): 215–42.

Arroba, G. 1979. "The Financing of Social Security in Latin America." In *Methods of Financing Social Security.* Geneva: International Social Security Association.

Arrow, K. J. 1963. *Social Choice and Individual Values* (2nd ed.). New York: Wiley.

Arrow, K. J. 1976. "Values and Collective Decision-making." In Laslett, P. and Runciman, W. G. eds., *Philosophy, Politics and Society.* Oxford: Basil Blackwell.

Artus, P. 1994. "The Financing of Retirement Schemes, Savings and Growth." *International Social Security Review* 47 (2): 3–16.

Asamoah, Y. and Nortey, D. N. A. 1987. "Ghana." In Dixon, J. ed., *Social Welfare in Africa.* London: Croom Helm.

Asher, M. G. 1991. *Social Adequacy and Equity of Social Security Arrangements in Singapore.* Singapore: Times Academic Press for the Centre of Advanced Studies, National University of Singapore.

Asher, M. G. 1998. "The Future of Retirement Protection in Southeast Asia." *International Social Security Review* 51 (1): 3–30

Ashford, D. E. ed. 1986a. *Nationalizing Social Security in Europe and America.* Greenwich: JAI Press.

Ashford, D. E. ed. 1986b. *The Emergence of the Welfare State.* Oxford: Blackwells Publishers.

Ashford, D. E. ed. 1987. *The Boundaries of the Welfare State.* Oxford: Blackwells Publishers.

Ashford, D. E. 1993. "The Historical and Political Foundations of the Welfare State: A Lost Opportunity for the Left." *Journal of Policy History* 5 (3): 311–34.

Asian Development Bank 1990. *Poverty Alleviation: Insights and Strategies.* Manila: Asian Development Bank.

Asian Development Bank 1993. *Rural Poverty in Developing Asia,* Vol. 1: *Bangladesh, India and Sri Lanka.* Manila: Asian Development Bank.

Asian Development Bank 1994. *Escaping the Poverty Trap: Lessons from Asia.* Manila: Asian Development Bank.

Asian Development Bank 1995. *From Centrally Planned to Market Economies: The Asian Approach.* Manila: Asian Development Bank.

Atkinson, A. B. and Mogensen, G. V. eds. 1993. *Welfare and Work Incentives: A North European Perspective.* Oxford: Clarendon Press.

Atkinson, A. B. and Rein, M 1993. *Age, Work and Social Security.* Oxford:

Clarendon.

Atkinson, A. B. 1983. *The Economics of Inequality* (2nd ed.). Oxford: Clarendon.

Atkinson, A. B. 1987. "Income Maintenance and Social Insurance." In Auerbach, A. J. and Feldstein, M. eds., *Handbook of Public Economics* (Vol II). New York: North Holland.

Atkinson, A. B. 1990. *Comparing Poverty Rates Internationally: Lessons from Recent Studies in OECD Countries.* London: London School of Economics.

Atkinson, A. B. and Hills, G. 1991. "Social Security in Developed Countries: Are There Lessons for Developing Countries." In Ahmed, E., Dreze, J., Hills, J. and Sen, A. eds., 1991. *Social Security in Developing Countries.* Oxford: Clarendon Press.

Atkinson, A. B. and Micklewright, J. 1992. *Economic Transformation in Eastern Europe and the Distribution of Income.* Cambridge: Cambridge University Press.

Australia 1974. *Report of the National Committee of Inquiry into Compensation and Rehabilitation in Australia* [Woodhouse Report]. Canberra: Australian Government Publishing Service.

Backman, G. and Sharma, S. 1998. "Changing Social Welfare Systems in the Nordic Nations: Some Observations and Analysis." *Journal of International and Comparative Social Welfare* 14: 34–45.

Baernreither, J. M. 1883. *English Associations of Workingmen.* London: Swan Sonnnenschein.

Bakayoko, A. and Ehouman, S. 1987. "Ivory Coast." In Dixon, J. ed., *Social Welfare in Africa.* London: Routledge.

Baldwin, P. 1990a. "Class Interests and the Post-War Welfare State in Europe: A Historical Perspective." *International Social Security Review* 43 (3): 255–69.

Baldwin, P. 1990b.*The Politics of Social Solidarity.* Cambridge: Cambridge University Press.

Baldwin, P, 1992. "Beveridge in the Longue Duree." *International Social Security Review* 45 (1–2): 53–72.

Banting, K. G. 1992. "Economic Integration and Social Policy: Canada and the United States." In Hunsley, T. ed., *Social Policy in the Global Economy.* Kingston: Queen's University Press.

Barker, D, 1996. "The Assumptions are too Pessimistic." *Challenge* 39 (6): 31–32.

Barr, N. 1989. "Social Insurance as an Efficiency Device." *Journal of Public Policy* 9 (1): 59–82.

Barr, N. 1992. "Economic Theory and the Welfare State: A Survey and Interpretation." *Journal of Economic Literature* 30 (3): 741–803.

Barr, N. ed. 1994a. *Labor Markets and Social Policy in Central and Eastern Europe.* New York: Oxford University Press.

Barr, N. 1994b. "Income Transfers: Social Insurance." In Barr, N. ed., *Labor Markets and Social Policy in Central and Eastern Europe.* New York: Oxford University Press.

Barry, N. 1998. *Welfare.* Milton Keynes: Open University.

Batt, J. 1991. *East and Central Europe: From Reform to Transformation.* London: Pinter

Battle, K. 1996. "Why Solange Denis Smiled: Public Pension Reform in the 1990s." *Canadian Review of Social Policy* 38, Fall: 125–38.

Bauman, Z. 1997. *Postmodernity and Its Discontents*. Oxford: Polity.

Becker, G. 1994. "Cut the Graybeards a Smaller Slice of the Pie." *Business Week* 28 March: 20.

Beckerman, W. 1979. "The Impact of Income Maintenance Payments on Poverty in Britain, 1975." *Economic Journal* 89 (2): 261–79.

Beiback, K.-J. 1993a. "The Protection of Atypical Workers in the Australian, British and German Social Security Systems." *International Social Security Review* 66 (2): 21–42.

Beiback, K.-J. 1993b. "Protection of Atypical Work and Family Benefits: Comparison of the Australian, German and British Social Security Systems." *Policy Studies Review* 12 (1/2): 182–96.

Bekemans, L. 1983. *Social Security and Employment*. Assen: Vangorcum.

Bellamy, D. F. and Irving, A. 1989. "Canada." In Dixon, J. and Scheurell, R. P. eds. *Social Welfare in Developed Market Countries*. London: Routledge.

Bellamy, D. F. 1993. "Continuities in Providing for Old Age: Cross-national and Cross-cultural Comparisons." *Policy Studies Review* 12 (1/2): 159–81.

Benda-Beckmann, F. von and Benda-Beckmann, K. von 1995. "Rural Populations, Social Security, and Legal Pluralism in the Central Moluccas of Eastern Indonesia." In Dixon, J. and Scheurell, R. P. eds., *International Perspectives on Social Security*. Westport, CT: Greenwood.

Benda-Beckmann, F. von, Benda-Beckmann, K. von, Brun, O. B. and Hirz, F. eds. 1988. *Between Kinship and the State: Social Security and the Law in Developing Countries*. Dordretcht: Foris Publications.

Benenson, M. 1964. *Actuarial Problems in the Transition from Provident Funds to Pension Insurance*. Geneva: International Social Security Association.

Bentham, J. [1789] 1970. *An Introduction to the Principles of Morals and Legislation*. London: Athlone.

Berge, E. 1989. "On the Study of Households: Some Methodological Considerations on the Use of Household Data." *International Sociology* 4 (2): 113–30

Berger, P. and Luckman, T. 1967. *The Social Construction of Reality*. New York: Ancore Books.

Berghman, J. and Muffels, R. 1988. *Social Indicators of Poverty: The Netherlands*. Le Tilberg, the Netherlands: Institute for Social Scientific Research, IVZ.

Bergman, S., Nagele, G. and Tokarski, W. 1987. *Early Retirement: Approaches and Variations: An International Perspective*. Jerusalem: JDC–Brookdale Institute of Gerontology and Adult Human Development Monograph Series, in conjunction with the Soziale Gerontologie, Fachbereich Sozialwesen, Gesamthochschule Univsersat Kassel, Germany.

Berk, R. A. and Rossi, P. H. 1990. *Thinking About Program Evaluation*. Beverly Hills, CA: Sage.

Berkowitz, M. 1981. "Social Policy and the Disabled: The Main Issues." In *Social Security and Disability: Issues in Policy Research* (Studies and Research 17). Geneva: International Social Security Association.

Bernheim, B. D. and Leven, L. 1989. "Social Security and Personal Savings: An Analysis of Expectations." *American Economic Review* 79, May: 97–102.

Bernstein, A. 1997. "Commentary: Social Security: Is the Sky Really Falling?" *Business Week* February 10: 92.

Bernstein, M. H. 1955. *Regulating Business by Independent Commission*. Princeton, NJ: University of Princeton Press.

Berthet, C. Raporteur 1986. *Relations Between Unemployment and Old-Age Insurances: Report of the Permanent Committee on Unemployment Insurance and Employment Maintenance to the International Social Security Association XXII General Assembly* (Report XVIII, Montreal, 2–12 September). Geneva: International Social Security Association.

Beveridge, W. H. 1944. *Full Employment in a Free Society*. London: Allen and Unwin.

Beveridge, W. H. 1945. *The Price of Peace*. New York: Norton.

Bierlaagh, H. and Sporken, E. 1994. "A Healthier Climate for Investment." *International Tax Review* 5 (7): 21–22.

Blackwell, J. 1990. *The Labor Market Impact of Social Policy*. Paris: Organization for Economic Co-operation and Development

Blackwell, J. 1994. "Changing Work Patterns and Their Implication for Social Protection." In Baldwin, S. and Falkingham, J. eds., *Social Security and Social Change*. Brighton, England: Wheatsheaf.

Blaustein, S. J. and Craig, I. 1977. *An International Review of Unemployment Insurance Schemes*. Kalamazoo: W. E. Upjohn Institute for Employment Research.

Bloch, F. S. 1994. "Assessing Disability: A Six-Nation Study of Disability Pension Claim Processing and Appeals." *International Social Security Review* 47 (1): 15–36.

Boaz, R. F. 1989. "Social Security Rules and the Early Acceptance of Social Security Benefits." *Social Science Quarterly* 70 (1): 72–87.

Bolderson, H. 1988. "Comparing Social Policies: Some Problems of Method and the Case of Social Security Benefits in Australia, Britain and the USA." *Journal of Social Policy* 17 (3): 267–88.

Bolderson, H. and Mabbett, D. 1991. *Social Policy and Social Security: A Comparative Study of Australia, Britain and the USA*. Brookfield, VT: Avebury.

Bolderson, H. and Mabbett, D. 1995. "Mongrels and Thoroughbreds: A Cross-National Look at Social Security Systems." *European Journal of Political Research* 28: 119–39.

Bolderson, H. and Mabbett, D. 1996. "Cost Containment in Complex Social Security Systems: The Limitations of Targeting." *International Social Security Review* 49 (1): 3–18.

Bolitho, W. 1986. "The Letter Killeth, the Spirit Gives the Life." *Australian Journal of Public Administration* 45 (4): 334–8.

Bonnar, D. 1985. "Women, Poverty and Policy: A World Wide Challenge." *Journal of International and Comparative Social Welfare* 1 (2): 7–19.

Booth, W. C. 1892. *Life and Labor of the People of London*. London: Macmillan.

Borowczyk, E. 1986. "State Policy in Favor of the Family in East European Countries." *International Social Security Review* 39 (2): 190–203.

Borowski, A. 1991. "The Economics and Politics of Retirement Incomes Policy in Australia." *International Social Security Review* 44 (1–2): 27–40.

Borzutzky, S. 1983. "Chilean Politics and Social Security Policies." Ph.D. thesis, University of Pittsburgh, Pittsburgh.

Borzutzky, S. 1990. "Chile." In Dixon, J. and Scheurell, R. P. eds., *Social Welfare in*

Latin America. London: Routledge.

Borzutzky, S. 1993. "Social Security and Health Policies in Latin America: The Changing Roles of the State and the Private Sector." *Latin American Research Review* 28 (2): 246–56.

Boskin, M. J. 1977. "Social Security and Retirement Decisions." *Economic Inquiry* 15, January: 1–25.

Boskin, M. J. 1978. *The Crisis in Social Security*. San Francisco: Institute for Contemporary Studies.

Bosworth, B., Dornbusch, R. and Laban, R. 1994. *The Chilean Economy: Policy Lessons and Challenges*. Washington, DC: Brookings Institution.

Bowles, S. and Gintis, H. 1995. "Productivity-enhancing Egalitarian Policies." *International Labor Review* 134 (4–5): 559–86.

Boye, S. 1977. "The Cost of Social Security, 1960–71: Some National Economic Aspects." *International Labor Review* 115 (3): 305–25.

Bradley, H. L. 1994. New Pension Improvements and Supplements in Singapore." *Social Security Bulletin* 57 (2): 85–86.

Bradshaw, J., Ditch, J. Holmes, H. and Whiteford, P. 1993. "A Comparative Study of Child Support in Fifteen Countries." *Journal of European Social Policy* 3 (4): 255–77.

Bradshaw, J. and Piachaud, D. 1980. *Child Support in the European Community*. London: Bradford Square Press.

Brand, H. 1994. "The World Bank, The Monetary Fund and Poverty." *International Journal of Health Services* 24 (3): 567–78.

Brennan, [H.] G. and Friedman, D. 1981. "A Libertarian Perspective on Welfare." In Brown, P. G., Johnson, C. and Vernier, P. eds., *Income Support: Conceptual and Policy Issues*. Totowa, NJ: Rowman and Littlefield.

Bridges, S. (1978). "Why the Social Insurance Budget is too Large in a Democracy: A Comment." *Economic Inquiry* 16, January: 133–42.

Briggs, A. 1965. "The Welfare State in Historical Perspective." In Zald, M. N. ed., *Social Welfare Institutions: A Sociological Reader*. New York: Wiley.

Bromely, D. W. 1990. "The Ideology of Efficiency: Searching for a Theory of Policy Analysis." *Journal of Environmental Economics and Management*. 19 (1): 86–107.

Brookes, N. 1979. "The Tax Expenditure Concept." *Canadian Taxation* 1 (1): 25–40.

Brooks, E. E. and Nyirenda, V. G. 1987. "Zambia." In Dixon, J. ed., *Social Welfare in Africa*. London: Croom Helm.

Browning, E. K. 1975. "Why the Social Insurance Budget is too Large in a Democracy." *Economic Inquiry* 13, September: 373–87.

Bruce, M. 1966. *The Coming of the Welfare State*. New York: Schocken Books.

Bryson, J. and Ring, P. S. 1990. "A Transaction-Based Approach to Policy Intervention." *Policy Sciences* 23 (3): 205–29.

Bryson, L. 1892. *Welfare and the State. Who Benefits?* London: Macmillan.

Brzezinski, Z. 1993. "The Great Transformation." *The National Interest* 33: 3–13.

Buchanan, J. M. 1959. "Positive Economics, Welfare Economics, and Political Economy." *Journal of Law and Economics* 2 (2): 125–42.

Buchmann, B., Rainwater, L., Schmausss, G. and Smeeding, T. 1988. "Equivalence Scales, Well Being, Inequality and Poverty: Sensitivity Estimates Across Ten

Countries Using the Luxembourg Income Study (LIS) Database." *Review of Income and Wealth* 34 (2): 113–42.

Burchardt, T. and Hills, J. 1997. *Private Welfare Insurance and Social Security.* York: York Publishing Services in association with the Roundtree Trust.

Burden, T. 1998. *Social Policy and Welfare: A Clear Guide.* London: Pluto Press.

Burkhauser, R. V. 1986. "Disability Policy in the United States, Sweden and the Netherlands." In Berkowitz, M. and Hill, M. A. eds., *Disability and the Labor Market: Economic Problems, Policies and Programs.* Ithaca, NY: ILR Press, New York State School of Industrial Relations, Cornell University.

Burkhauser, R. V., Duncan, G. J. and Hauser, R. 1994. "Sharing Prosperity Across the Age Distribution: A Comparison of the United States and Germany." *The Gerontologist* 34, April: 150–60.

Butare, T. 1994. "International Comparisons of Social Security and Retirement Funds from a National Savings Perspective." *International Social Security Review* 47 (2): 17–36.

Butler, S. 1991. "Privatization and Public Purposes." In Gormley, W. T. ed., *Privatization and its Alternatives.* Madison, WI: University of Wisconsin Press.

Cain, G. and Watts, H. 1973. *Income Maintenance and Labor Supply.* New York: Academic Press.

Callen, T. and Nolan, B. 1998. "Ireland." In Dixon, J. and Macarov, D. eds., *Poverty: A Persistent Global Reality.* London: Routledge.

Camacho, L. A. 1992. "Financing Social Security in Latin America: New Perspectives in the Light of Current Economic Development." *International Social Security Review* 45 (3): 19–38.

Cameron, C. 1972. *Income Support Schemes: Bibliography and Annotations to Academic Literature, including References to Newspaper Citations.* Madison, WI: Institute for Research on Poverty, University of Wisconsin–Maddison.

Campbell, G. R. 1992. "Argentine Privatization and Other Reforms." *Social Security Bulletin* 55 (3): 80.

Campbell, G. R. 1994a. "Bolivia Plans to Privatize Pension Program." *Social Security Bulletin,* 57 (2): 81.

Campbell, G. R. 1994b. "Financial Stress Leads France to Weigh Third Tier." *Social Security Bulletin* 57 (1): 111–12.

Cantillon, B. 1990. "Socio-demographic Changes and Social Security." *International Social Security Review* 43 (4): 399–425.

Carney, T. 1994. *Social Security in Australia.* Melbourne: Oxford University Press.

Carter, M. N. and Shipman, W. G. 1996. "The Coming Global Pension Crisis." *Foreign Affairs* 75 (6): S1–S16.

Cass, B. and O'Loughlan, M. A. 1984. *Social Policies for Single Parent Families in Australia: An Analysis and Comparison with Sweden* (Report 40). Sydney: Social Welfare Research Centre, University of New South Wales.

Castaneda, T. 1992. *Combating Poverty: Innovative Social Reform in Chile During the 1980s.* San Francisco: ICS Press.

Castellino, O. 1982. "Italy." In Rosa, J.-J. ed., *The World Crisis in Social Security.* San Francisco: Institute for Contemporary Studies.

Castillo, R. B. 1993. "'Analysis of a National Private Pension Scheme: The Case of Chile': Comments." *International Labor Review* 132 (3): 407–16.

Castles, F. 1981. "How Does Politics Matter? Structure and Agency in the Determination of Public Policy Outcomes." *European Journal of Political Research* 9 (2): 119–32.

Castles, F. 1982. "The Impact of Parties on Public Expenditure." In Castles, F. ed., *The Impact of Parties*. London: Sage.

Castles, F. 1985. *The Working Class and Welfare*. Wellington: Allen and Unwin/ Port Nicholson.

Castles, F. 1996. "Needs-Based Strategies for Social Protection in Australia and New Zealand." In Esping-Andersen, G. ed., *Welfare States in Transition: National Adaptions in Global Economies*. London: Sage.

Castle, F. and Pierson, C. 1996. "A New Convergence? Recent Policy Developments in the United Kingdom, Australia and New Zealand." *Policy and Politics* 24 (3): 233–46.

Ceniceros, R. 1997. "Mexico's Pension Scramble." *Business Insurance* 31 (9) March 3: 3 and 31.

Central Provident Fund Study Group 1986. "Special Issue — Report of the Central Provident Fund Study Group." *Singapore Economic Review* 31 (1): 1–108.

Cerney, P. 1990. *The Changing Architecture of Politics: Structure, Agency and the Future of the State*. London: Sage.

Chan, C. and Chow, N. W. S. 1992. *More Welfare After Economic Reform: Welfare Development in the People's Republic of China*. Hong Kong: University of Hong Kong, Department of Social Work and Social Administration.

Chan, R. K. H. 1996. *Welfare in Newly-Industrialised Society: The Construction of a Welfare State in Hong Kong*. Aldershot, Hants.: Avery.

Chan, Y. C. 1994. "The Role of the Central Provident Fund in Singapore." In *Asia Regional Conference on Social Security (September 14–16, 1993), Conference Proceedings*. Hong Kong: Hong Kong Council of Social Services.

Chang, I.-H. 1985. "Korea, South." In Dixon, J. and Kim, H. S. eds., *Social Welfare in Asia*. London: Croom Helm.

Chen, X.-B. 1994. "Social Security System Reform in Hainan Province, PRC." In *Asia Regional Conference on Social Security (September 14–16, 1998), Conference Proceedings*. Hong Kong: Hong Kong Council of Social Services.

Chester, T. E. 1977. "Social Security, Work and Poverty." *National Westminster Bank Quarterly* November: 38–46.

Chow, N. W. S. 1975. "A Comparative Study of Social Security Systems in East and South East Asian Countries." Ph.D. thesis, University of Hong Kong, Hong Kong.

Chow, N. W. S. 1981. "Social Security Provision in Singapore and Hong Kong." *Journal of Social Policy* 10 (3): 353–66.

Chow, N. W. S. 1985a. "Social Security Provisions in Singapore, Hong Kong, Taiwan and South Korea." *Journal of International and Comparative Social Welfare* 2 (1 and 2): 1–10.

Chow, N. W. S. 1985b. "Hong Kong" In Dixon J. and Kim, H. S. eds., *Social Welfare in Asia*. London: Croom Helm.

Chow, N. W. S. 1988a. *The Administration and Financing of Social Security in China*. Hong Kong: Centre of Asian Studies, University of Hong Kong.

Chow, N. W. S. 1988b. "Scope for Reform in the Social Security System of the People's Republic of China." *Asia News Sheet* (International Social Security

Association) 18 (3): 22–8.

Chow, N. W. S. 1988c. "Western and Chinese Ideas of Social Welfare." *International Social Work* 30 (1): 31–41.

Chow, N. W. S. 1995. "Social Security Reforms in China." In Dixon, J. and Scheurell, R. P. eds., *International Perspectives on Social Security*. Westport, CT: Greenwood.

Chowdhry, D. P. 1985. "India." In Dixon, J. and Kim, H. S. eds., *Social Welfare in Asia*. London: Croom Helm.

Ciggno, A. and Rosati, F. C. 1996. "Jointly Determined Savings and Fertility Behavior: The Theory, and Estimates for Germany, Italy, the UK and USA." *European Economic Review* 40 (8): 1561–89.

Clark, R. L. 1996. "Japanese Pension Plans in Transition." *Benefits Quarterly* 12 (1): 59–74.

Clark, R. M. 1960. *Economic Security for the Aged in the United States and Canada*. Ottawa: Queen's Printer.

Clarke, C. E. 1977. "Actuarial Aspects of Converting Provident Funds into Social Security Schemes." In *First Meeting of the Committee* [on Provident Funds] *and Round Table Meeting on Provident Funds*. Geneva: International Social Security Association.

Clark, R. and Filinson, R. 1991. "Multinational Corporate Penetration, Industrialism, Region and Social Security Expenditures." *International Journal of Aging and Human Development* 32 (2): 143–59.

Clasen, J. 1992. "Unemployment Insurance in Two Countries: A Comparative Analysis of great Britain and West Germany in the 1980s" *Journal of European Social Policy* 2 (4): 279–300.

Clasen, J. 1997. *Social Insurance in Europe*. Bristol: Policy Press.

Clasen, J. and Gould, A. 1995. "Stability and Change in Welfare States: Germany and Sweden in the 1990s." *Polity and Politics*. 23 (3): 189–202.

Cloward, R, A. and Piven, F. F. 1992. "Welfare State Politics in the United States." In Ferge, Z. and Kolberg, J. E. eds., *Social Policy in a Changing Europe*. Frankfurt am Main, Germany: Campus Verlag/Boulder, CO: Westview.

Coal Mines Provident Fund, India 1986. "Development of Research for the Purpose of Improving Provident Fund Benefits and Services." In *Eighth Meeting of the Committee* [on Provident Funds]. Geneva: ISSA.

Coarse, R. 1937. "The Nature of Firms." *Economica* (new series) 4 (3): 386–405.

Coates, A. W. 1964. "Value Judgments in Economics." *Yorkshire Bulletin of Economic and Social Research* 16 (1): 127–43.

Cockburn, C. 1980. "The Role of Social Security in Development." *International Social Security Review* 33 (3/4): 337–58.

Cohen, S. S. and Goldfinger, C. 1979. "From Permacrisis to Real Crisis in French Social Security." In Lindburg, L. ed., *Stress and Contradiction in Modern Capitalism*. Lexington, MA: Lexington Books.

Collins, M. 1990. "A Guaranteed Minimum Income in France." *Social Policy and Administration* 24 (2): 120–24.

Commander, S. and Jackman, R. 1993. *Providing Social Benefits in Russia: Redefining the Roles of Firms and Government* (Policy Research Working Paper 1184). Washington, DC: World Bank.

Corden, A. 1983. *Taking Up a Means Tested Benefit, The Process of Claiming Family Income Supplements*. London: Her Majesty's Stationary Office

Coria, G. A. 1994a. "Poverty, Food Consumption, and Nutrition During the Transition of the Market Economy in Eastern Europe." *American Economic Association Papers and Proceedings* May: 297–303.

Coria, G. A. 1994b. *Crisis in Mortality, Health and Nutrition, Central and Eastern Europe in Transition: Public Policy and Social Conditions* (Regional Monitoring Report 2). Florence: United Nations International Children's Emergency Fund.

Cousins, M. 1992. "Social Security and Atypical Workers in Ireland." *International Labor Review* 131 (6): 647–60.

Cox, D. 1998. "Australia." In Dixon, J. and Macarov, D. eds., *Poverty: A Persistent Global Reality*. London: Routledge.

Cox, R. H. 1998. "The Consequences of Welfare Reform: How Conceptions of Social Rights are Changing." *Journal of Social Policy* 27 (1): 1–16.

Creedy, J. and Disney, R. 1988. "The New Pension Scheme in Britain." *Fiscal Studies* 9 (2): 57–71.

Creedy, J. 1994. "Two-tier State Pensions: Labor Supply and Income Distribution." *Manchester School of Economic and Social Studies* 62 (2): 167–83.

Crescentini, L. 1993. "Italy: Voluntary Compensatory Pension Scheme — the 1993 Law." *International Social Security Review* 46 (4): 72–74.

Crespo, M. (994. "Shot in the Arm." *Financial World* 163 (7) March 29: 102–5.

Crijns, L. H. J. 1989. *Social Security in the United States and Canada (Lessons to be Drawn in the Context of European Integration*. Amsterdam: European Institute of Public Administration.

Cross, S. T. 1994. "Mexican Private Pension Trends: From Termination Indemnity Substitute to True Retirement Plan." *IBIS Review* 8 (12): 2–9 and 20.

Crutz, H. 1991. "Survivors' Pensions and Death Benefits: Current Issues and Future Perspectives." *International Social Security Review* 44 (1–2): 95–110.

Culverhouse, A. F. 1990. "U.K. Places Greater Reliance on Private Sector for Pensions." *Journal of Compensation and Benefits* 5 (6): 379–82.

Cutler, N. E. 1997. Baby Boomers, Financial Literacy, and the Privatization of Social Security." *Journal of the American Society of Clu and Chfc* 51 (2): 26–30.

Cutright, P. 1965. "Political Structures, Economic Development and National Social Security Programs." *American Journal of Sociology* 70: 537–50.

Cutt, J., Dixon, J. and Nagorcka, B. N. 1977. *Income Support Policy Evaluation in Australia: A Dynamic Approach* (Administrative Studies Program, Research Monograph 2). Canberra: Australian National University Press.

Czechoslovakia 1992. Federal Ministry of Labor and Social Affairs. "Czechoslovakia." In Dixon, J. and Macarov, D. eds., *Social Welfare in Socialist Countries*. London: Routledge.

Danisoglu, E. 1987. "Turkey." In Dixon, J. ed., *Social Welfare in the Middle East*. London: Routledge.

Danziger, S. and Taussig, M. 1979. "The Income Unit and the Anatomy of Income Distribution." *Review of Income and Wealth* 25 (4): 365–75.

Dapre, B. 1989. *Assistance to Families with Children Through Cash Transfers or Tax Credits: A Comparative Study*. Canberra: Australian Department of Social Security.

Dapre, B. et al. 1984. *Retirement Income Provisions Overseas*. Canberra: Australian

Department of Social Security.

Dasgupta, R. 1993. "Social Security and Mutual Assistance in India: A Preliminary Account." *International Social Security Review* 46 (3): 53–68.

Davis, P. 1996. *Pension Funds: Retirement Income Security and Capital Markets —* *An International Perspective.* Oxford: Oxford University Press.

Davidson, A. 1989. *Two Models of Welfare: The Origins and Developemnt of the Welfare State in Sweden and New Zealand: 1888–1988.* Uppsala: Acta Universitatis Upsaliensis.

Day, C. L. 1993. "Public Opinion Towards Costs and Benefits of Social Security and Medicare." *Research on Aging* 15, September: 279–98.

Day, P. 1989. *A New History of Social Welfare.* Englewood Cliffs, NJ: Prentice Hall.

Daykin, C. D. 1995. "Financial Management and Control of Supplementary Pension Schemes." *International Social Security Review* 48 (3–4): 75–89.

Deacon, A. 1982. "An End to the Means Test? Social Security and the Atlee Government." *Journal of Social Policy* 11 (2): 289–306.

Deakin, B. ed. 1992. *Social Policy, Social Justice and Citizenship in Eastern Europe.* Brookfield, VT: Avebury.

Deacon, B., with Hulse, M. and Stubbs, P. 1997. *International Organizations and the Future of Welfare.* London: Sage.

Deacon, B. and Szalai, J. 1990. *What Future for Socialist Welfare?* Aldershot, Hants.: Avebury.

Deleeck, H., de Lathouwer, L. and van den Bosch, K., 1986. *Indicators of Social Security 1976–1985.* Antwerpen: University of Antwerp, Centre for Social Policy.

Deleeck, H., de Lathouwer, L. and van den Bosch, K. 1988. *Indicators of Social Security: A Comparative Analysis of Five Countries.* Antwerp: University of Antwerp, Centre for Social Policy.

Deleeck, H. van den Bosch, K. and de Lathouwer, L. eds. 1992. *Poverty and the Adequacy of Social Security in the EC.* Aldershot, Hants.: Avebury.

Deyo, F. C. 1992. "The Political Economy of Social Policy Formulation: East Asia's Newly Industrializing Countries." In Appelbaum, R. P. and Henderson, J. eds., *States and Development In the Asia Pacific Rim.* Newbury Park, CA: Sage.

Diamond, P. A. 1977. "A Framework for Social Security Analysis." *Journal of Public Economics* 8 (3): 275–98.

Diamond, P. and Valdes-Prieto, S. 1994. "Social Security Reform." In Bosworth, B. P., Dornbusch, R. and Laban, R. eds, *The Chilean Economy: Policy, Lessons and Challenges.* Washington, DC: The Bookings Institute.

DiPalma, G. 1990. *To Craft Democracies.* Berkeley, CA: University of California Press.

Disney, R. and Whitehouse, E. 1992. "Personal Pensions and the Review of Contracting Out Terms." *Fiscal Studies* 13 (1): 38–53

Dixon, J. 1977. *Australia's Policy Towards the Aged: 1890–1972* (Canberra Series in Administrative Studies 3). Canberra: Canberra College of Advanced Education.

Dixon, J. 1978/79. "The Evolution of Australia's Social Security System 1890–1972: The Social Insurance Debate." *Social Security Quarterly* 5 (2): 1–10.

Dixon, J. 1981a. "Australia's Policy Towards the Aged: 1890–1978." In Howe, A. ed., *Towards an Older Australia.* Brisbane: Queensland University Press.

Dixon, J. 1981b. *The Chinese Welfare System: 1949–1979.* New York: Praeger.

Dixon, J. 1981c. "The Workers' Social Assistance System in China: 1949–1979." *International Social Work* 21 (1): 1–13.

Dixon, J. 1982. "Provident Funds in the Third World: A Cross National Review." *Public Administration and Development* 2, 325–44.

Dixon, J. 1983."Australia's Income Security Systems: Its Origins, Its Features and Its Dilemma." *International Social Security Review* 36 (1): 19–44.

Dixon, J. 1984. "The People's Republic of China: Politics and Social Welfare." In Wade, L. L. and Groth, A. J. eds., *Comparative Resource Allocation*. Beverly Hills, CA: Public Policy Organization–Sage Yearbook.

Dixon, J. 1985a. "People's Republic of China." In Dixon, J. and Kim, H. S. eds., *Social Welfare in Asia*. London: Croom Helm.

Dixon, J. 1985b. "Provident Funds: Their Nature and Performance." In *Social Security in the South Pacific*. Bangkok: International Labor Organization.

Dixon, J. 1986. *Social Security Traditions and Their Global Applications*. Canberra: International Fellowship for Social and Economic Development.

Dixon, J. 1987a. "Provident Funds: An Assessment of Their Social Security, Social and Economic Performance and Prospects." In Schulz, J. and Davis-Friedmann, D. eds., *Aging China: Family, Economics, and Government Policies in Transition*. Washington, DC: The Gerontological Society of America.

Dixon, J. 1987b. "Social Security in the Middle East." In Dixon, J. ed., *Social Welfare in the Middle East*. London: Croom Helm.

Dixon, J. ed. 1987c. *Social Welfare in Africa*. London: Routledge.

Dixon, J. ed. 1987d. *Social Welfare in the Middle East*. London: Routledge.

Dixon, J. 1988. "The Changing Nature of Public Administration in Australia." *Public Personnel Management* 17 (2): 231–6.

Dixon, J. 1989a. "A Comparative Perspective on Provident Funds: Their Present and Future Explored." *Journal of International and Comparative Social Welfare* 5 (2): 1–28.

Dixon, J. 1989b. *National Provident Funds: The Enfant Terrible of Social Security*. Canberra: International Fellowship for Social and Economic Development.

Dixon, J. 1989c. "Social Security Traditions and Their Global Context." In Mohan, B. ed., *Dimensions of International and Comparative Social Welfare*. Canberra: International Fellowship for Social and Economic Development.

Dixon, J. 1992a. "The Management of Social Services Round Table: General Rapporteur's Report." In *The Management of Social Services, Proceedings, Copenhagen, 1991*. Brussels: International Institute of Administrative Sciences.

Dixon, J. 1992b. "China." In Dixon, J. and Macarov, D. eds., *Social Welfare in Socialist Countries*. London: Routledge.

Dixon, J. 1993. "National Provident Funds: The Challenge of Harmonizing Social Security, Social and Economic Objectives." *Policy Studies Review* 12 (1–2): 197–213.

Dixon, J. 1994. "Social Security in the Nineties — Challenges and Prospects: Reflections on the Connection between Social Security and Poverty." In *Asia Regional Conference on Social Security (September 14–16, 1993) Conference Proceedings*. Hong Kong: Hong Kong Council of Social Services.

Dixon, J. 1995a. *Mandatory Occupational Retirement Savings: Towards a Program Design Agenda for Hong Kong* (Working Paper 17 (2/95)). Hong Kong: Centre for

Public Policy Studies., Lingnan College.

Dixon, J. 1995b. "Social Security and the Ghosts that Haunt it." In Dixon, J. and Scheurell R. P. eds., *International Perspectives on Social Security*. Westport, CT: Greenwood.

Dixon, J. 1996a. "Social Security and Poverty Alleviation: Debunking a Myth." In Mok, H. ed., *Eradicating Poverty and Employment.*. Hong Kong: Hong Kong Social Security Society and Department of Applied Social Studies, Hong Kong Polytechnic University.

Dixon, J. 1996b. "Mandatory Occupational Retirement Savings as a Social Security Strategy in Asia: Something Old, Something Borrowed, Something New." *Canadian Review of Social Policy* 38, Autumn: 72–87.

Dixon, J. 1996c. "National Provident Funds: A Sustainable but Inadequate Approach to Aged Income Security in Asia." In Calleja, J. ed., *The Report of United Nations Expert Group Meeting on Sustainable Development of Social and Economic Systems: Meeting the Challenges of Ageing Population in Developing Countries*. Malta: International Institute on Ageing.

Dixon, J. 1996d. "Social Security in Transition: An Explorations of Emerging Global Trends." *Proceedings of the 27th International Council on Social Welfare International Conference* (Vol. 1). Hong Kong: International Council on Social Welfare.

Dixon, J. 1998a. "An Exploration of Emerging Global Trends in Social Security." In MacPherson, S. and Won H.-W. eds., *Social Development:. World in Transition*. Aldershot, Hants.: Ashgate.

Dixon, J., 1998b. "Comparative Social Security: The Challenge of Evaluation." *Comparative Public Policy Analysis* 1 (1): 66–94.

Dixon, J. and Chow, N. W. S. 1992. "Social Security in the Asia-Pacific Region." *Journal of International and Comparative Social Welfare* 8 (1 and 2): 1–23.

Dixon, J. and Cutt, J. 1975. "Income Supporting Options for Australia: An Approach to Assessment." In Scott, R. and Richardson, J. eds., *Labor's First Thousand Days*. Canberra: Australian Institute of Political Science.

Dixon, J. and Cutt, J. 1976. "An Approach to the Assessment of Income-Support Options." *Social Security Quarterly* 3 (4): 15–21.

Dixon, J. and Kim, H. S. eds., 1985. *Social Welfare in the Asia*. London: Croom Helm.

Dixon, J. and Kim, H. S. 1992. "Social Welfare under Socialism." In Dixon, J. and Macarov, D. eds., *Social Welfare in Socialist Countries*. London: Routledge.

Dixon, J. and Kouzmin, A. 1994. "Management Innovations for Improving Governance: Changes and Trends in Australian Public Administration and Finance." *Asian Review of Public Administration* 6 (1and2): 33–91.

Dixon, J., Kouzmin, A. and Korac-Kakabadse, N. 1998. "Managerialism — Something Old, Something Borrowed, and Little New: Prescription Versus Effective Organizational Change in Public Agencies." *International Journal of Public Sector Management* 11 (1): 54–76.

Dixon, J., Kouzmin, A., and Wilson, J. 1995. "Commercialising 'Washminster' in Australia: What Lessons?" *Public Money and Management* 15 (1): 1–8.

Dixon, J. and Macarov, D. eds. 1992. *Social Welfare in Socialist Countries*. London: Routledge.

Dixon, J. and Macarov. D. eds. 1998. *Poverty: A Persistent Global Reality.* London: Routledge.

Dixon, J. and Magill, R. guest eds. 1997. *Journal of International and Comparative Social Welfare.* Symposium: "Crossing the Border: Migration and Social Security Policy." 12: 1–112.

Dixon, J., Nagorcka, B. N. and Cutt, J. 1984. "Evaluating Poverty Programs: The Usefulness of Dynamic Continuous Simulation Modeling." In Goldstein, R. and Sachs, S. M. eds., *Applied Poverty Research.* Totowa, NJ: Littlefield Adams.

Dixon, J. and Newman, D. 1998. *Entering the Chinese Market: The Risks and Discounted Rewards.* Westport, CT: Quorum Books.

Dixon, J. and Scheurell, R. P. 1987. "Social Security in Australia and the United States: A Comparison of Value Premises and Practices." *Journal of International and Comparative Social Welfare* 3 (1 and 2): 1–18.

Dixon, J. and Scheurell, R. P. eds. 1989. *Social Welfare in Developed Market Countries.* London: Routledge.

Dixon, J. and Scheurell, R. P. eds. 1990. *Social Welfare in Latin America.* London: Routledge.

Dixon, J. and Scheurell, R. P. eds. 1994a. *Social Welfare with Indigenous Populations.* London: Routledge.

Dixon, J. and Scheurell, R. P. guest eds. 1994b. *Journal of International and Comparative Social Welfare* Symposium: "Social Welfare of Veterans of Military Service." 10: 1–86.

Dixon, J. and Scheurell, R. P. eds. 1995. *Social Security Programs: A Cross Cultural Comparative Perspective.* Westport, CT: Greenwood in association with the Policy Studies Organization.

Dogan, M. and Pelassy, D. 1984. *How to Compare Nations.* Chathan, NJ: Chathan House.

Dolgoff, R. and Feldstein, D. 1984. *Understanding Social Welfare* (2nd ed.). New York: Longman.

Donahue, R. 1989. *The Privatization Decision: Public Ends, Private Means.* New York: Basic Books.

Dornbusch, R. 1997. "Japan's Pension Crisis: Growth the Only Way Out." *Business Week* 35 (11)January 27: 18

Dreyfus, M. 1993. "The Labor Movement and Mutual Benefit Societies: Towards an International Approach." *International Social Security Review* 46 (3): 19–28.

Drover, G. 1988. "Social Policy Harmonization: Canadian Debate, the European and Tasman Experience." In Drover, G. ed., *Free Trade and Social Policy.* Ottawa: Canadian Council on Social Development.

Dumont, J.-P. 1993. "Mutualism in the World: Ignorance, Inequalities and Market Pressures." *International Social Security Review* 46 (3): 99–112.

Duskin, E. 1991. "Changing the Mix of Public and Private Pensions: The Issues." In *Private Pensions and Public Policy* (OECD Social Policy Studies 9). Paris: Organization of Economic Co-operation and Development.

Dworkin, G. 1971. "Paternalism." In Wasserstrom, S. ed., *Morality and Law.* Belmont, CA: Wadsworth.

Dworkin, G. 1981. "Paternalism and Welfare Policy." In Brown, P. G., Johnson, C. and Vernier, P. eds., *Income Support: Conceptual and Policy Issues.* Totowa, NJ:

Rowman and Littlefield.

Eekelaar, M. J. and Pearl, D. eds. 1989. *An Aging World: Dilemmas and Challenges for Law and Social Policy.* Oxford: Clarendon Press.

Eichengreen, B. 1996. "Institutions and Economic Growth After World War II." In Crafts, N. and Toniolo, G. eds., *Economic Growth Since 1945.* Cambridge: Cambridge University Press.

EISS (European Institute of Social Security) 1975. "Complementary Systems of Social Security." In *1973 Yearbook of the European Institute of Social Security.* Brussels: Aurelia.

EISS 1979. "Social Security and the Redistribution of Income." In *1974–1977 Yearbook of the European Institute of Social Security.* Deventer, the Netherlands: Kluwer.

EISS 1981. "Social Security Reforms in Europe." In *1978–1980 Yearbook of the European Institute of Social Security.* Deventer, the Netherlands: Kluwer.

Ejuba, E. J. 1982. "Social Security Developments in French-Speaking Countries South of the Sahara: Trends since 1970." In *Report on the ILO/Norway African Regional Training Course for Social Security Managers and Administrative Officials, Nairobi, 24 November to 12 December 1980.* Geneva: International Labor Organization.

Elliott, J. E. 1987. "Moral and Ethical Considerations in Karl Marx's Robust Vision of the Future Society." *International Journal of Social Economics* 14 (10): 3–26.

Engler, A. 1995. *Apostles of Greed: Capitalism and the Myth of the Market.* London: Pluto Press.

Espina, A. 1996. "Reform of Pension Schemes in the OECD Countries." *International Labor Review* 135 (2): 181–206.

Esping-Andersen, G. 1990. *The Three Worlds of Welfare Capitalism.* Oxford: Polity.

Esping-Andersen, G. 1996a. "After the Global Age? Welfare State Dilemmas in a Global Economy." In Esping-Andersen, G. ed., *Welfare States in Transition: National Adaptions in Global Economies.* London: Sage.

Esping-Andersen, G. 1996b. "Welfare States Without Work: The Impasse of Labor Shedding and Familialism in Continental Europe." In Esping-Andersen, G. ed., *Welfare States in Transition: National Adaptions in Global Economies.* London: Sage.

Esping-Andersen, G. 1996c. "Positive-Sum Solutions in a World of Trade-Offs?" in Esping-Andersen, G. ed., *Welfare States in Transition: National Adaptions in Global Economies.* London: Sage.

Esping-Andersen, G. and Korpi, W. 1987. "From Poor Relief Towards Institutional Welfare States: The Development of Scandinavian Social Policy." In Erikson, R., Hansen, E. J., Riognden, S. and Uusitalo, H. eds., *The Scandinavian Model: Welfare States and Welfare Research.* New York: M. E. Sharp.

Estes, R. 1984. *The Social Progress of Nations.* New York: Praeger.

Estes, R. 1988. *Trends in World Social Development: The Social Progress of Nations, 1970–87.* New York: Praeger.

Estrin, A. 1992. "Peru's Privatization Option for Pension and Health Systems." *Social Security Bulletin* 55 (3): 79–80.

Estrin, A. 1996. "Malawi Moves to establish a Social Security System." *Social Security Bulletin* 59 (2): 73.

Estrin, S., Shaffer, M. and Singh, I. 1994. "The Provision of Social Benefits in State-owned, Privatized and Private Firms in Poland." Paper presented at the Workshop on Enterprise Adjustment in Eastern Europe, World Bank, Policy Research Department, Washington, DC, September 22–23 (distributed by the World Bank).

Etzioni, A. 1988. *The Moral Dimension: Towards a New Economics*. New York: The Free Press.

European Commission, 1991. *Supplementary Social Security Schemes: The Role of Occupational Pension Schemes in the Social Protection of Workers and Their Implications for Freedom of Movement* (SEC (91) 1332 final, Brussels, 22 July).Brussels: European Commission.

European Commission 1993. *Social Protection in Europe*. Luxembourg: Office for Official Publications of the European Commission.

European Commission, 1994. *Growth, Competitiveness, Employment: The Challenges and Way Forward into the 21st Century* (White Paper. Brussels: ECSC-EC-EAEC). Brussels: European Commission.

European Commission 1996. *Social Protection in Europe*. Luxembourg: Office for Official Publications of the European Commission.

Eusepi, G. 1987. "The Third Revolution in Economic Thinking: Social Economy in a New Perspective." *International Journal of Social Economics* 14 (7–8): 160–69.

Euzeby, A. 1988. "Unemployment Compensation and Employment in Industrialized Market Economies." *International Social Security Review* 41 (1): 15–24.

Euzeby, A. 1995. "Reduce or Rationalize Social Security Contributions to Reduce Unemployment." *International Labor Review* 134 (2): 227–42.

Euzeby, A. and Euzeby, C. 1982. "The Significance of Ceilings on Social Security Contributions in Europe." *Benefits International* 11(6): 11–16.

Evans, M. 1996. *Means-testing the Unemployed in Britain, France and Germany*. London: London School of Economic and Sunntory and Toyota International Centres for Economic and Related Disciplines.

Fay, B. 1975. *Social Theory and Political Practice*. London: Allen and Unwin.

Feldstein, M. 1974. "Social Security, Induced Retirement and Aggregate Capital Accumulation." *Journal of Political Economy* 82 (4): 905–26.

Feldstein, M. 1996. "Social Security and Savings: New Time Series Evidence." *National Tax Journal* 49 (2): 151–64.

Ferge, Z. 1996. "The Changed Welfare Paradigm: The Individualisation of the Social." *Social Policy and Administration* 31 (1): 20–44.

Ferrera, M. 1989. "Italy." In Dixon, J. and Scheurell R. P. eds., *Social Welfare in Developed Market Countries*. London: Routledge.

Fields, G. 1994. "Poverty Changes in Developing Countries." In Hoeven, R, van der and Anker, R. eds., *Poverty Monitoring: An International Concern*. New York: St. Martin's Press.

Fisher, P. 1968. "Social Security and Development Planning: Some Issues." In Kasalow, E. M. ed., *The Role of Social Security in Economic Development*. Washington, DC: Department of Health, Education and Welfare.

Fisher, P. 1970. "Minimum Old-Age Pensions." *International Labor Review* 102 (2): 298–318.

Fitzgerald, T. 1990. "Economics: Broad and Narrow." *Australian Society* 9 (12): 21–4.

Fletcher, L. P. 1976. "The Provident Fund Approach to Social Security in the Eastern

Caribbean." *Journal of Social Policy* 5 (1): 1–17.

Flora, P. ed. 1986. *Growth to Limits: The Western Welfare States Since World War II*. New York: Walter de Gruyter.

Flora, P. and Alber, J 1981a. "Modernisation, Democratisation, and the Development of Welfare States in Western Europe." In Flora, P. and Heidenheimer, A. J. eds., *The Development of the Welfare States in Europe and America*. New Brunswick and London: Transaction Books.

Flora, P. and Alber, J 1981b. "The Historical Core and Changing Boundaries of the Welfare State." In Flora, P. and Heidenheimer, A. J. eds., *The Development of the Welfare States in Europe and America*. New Brunswick and London: Transaction Books.

Flora, P. and Heidenheimer, A. J. eds. 1981. *The Development of the Welfare States in Europe and America*. New Brunswick and London: Transaction Books.

Folbre, N. 1993. *Women and Social Security in Latin America, the Caribbean and Sub-Sahara Africa* (Interdepartmental Projects and Activities Working Paper). Geneva: International Labor Organization.

Forsund, H. M. 1989. "Norway." In Dixon, J. and Scheurell R. P. eds., *Social Welfare in Developed Market Countries*. London: Routledge.

Foster, J. 1984. "On Economic Poverty: A Survey of Aggregate Measures." *Advances in Econometrics* 3 (2): 215–51.

Fraser, D. 1973. *The Evolution of the British Welfare State*. London: Macmillan.

Freeden, M. 1978. *The New Liberalism: An Ideology of Social Reform*. Oxford: Clarendon Press.

Freud, S. 1951. *Civilization and its Discontents*. London: Hogarth Press.

Frey, R. G. ed. 1984. *Utility and Rights*. Minneapolis: University of Minnesota Press.

Friedman, M. 1953. *Essays in Positive Economics*. Chicago: University of Chicago Press.

Friedman, M. 1970. *Capitalism and Freedom*. Chicago: Chicago University Press.

Friedman, R., Gilbert, N. and Shere, M. eds. 1987. *Modern Welfare States: A Comparative View of Trends and Prospects*. New York: New York University Press.

Fry, J. 1969. *Medicine in Three Societies: Comparison of Medical Care in the USSR, USA and UK*. London: MTP Press.

Fuery, M. et al. 1988. *Occupational Superannuation Arrangements in Overseas Countries* (Social Security Review Background/Discussion Paper 25). Canberra: Australian Department of Social Security.

Fulcher, D. H. 1974. *Medical Care Systems: Public and Private Health Coverage in Selected Industrialized Countries*. Geneva: ILO.

Furugori, T. 1993. "The Impact of a Flexible Labour Market on the Social Security System." *Review of Social Policy* (Social Development Research Centre, Tokyo) 2: 11–25.

Gal, J. 1998. "Categorical Benefits in Welfare States: Findings from Great Britain and Israel." *International Social Security Review* 51 (1): 71–102.

Gardner, R. K. and Judd, H. O. 1954. *The Development of Social Administration*. London: Oxford University Press.

Genovese, F. C. 1990. The Deficit and Social Security." *American Journal of Economics and Sociology* 49, April: 151–52.

George, V. 1968. *Social Security: Beveridge and After*. London: Routledge.

George, V. 1973. *Social Security and Society*. London: Routledge and Kegan Paul.

George, V. 1991. "Social Security in the USSR." *International Social Security Review* 44 (4): 47–64.

George, V. 1996."The Demand for Welfare." In George, V. and Taylor-Gooby, P. eds., *European Welfare Policy: Squaring the Welfare Circle*. Basingstock, Hampshire: Macmillan.

George, V. and Lawson, R. 1980. *Poverty and Inequality in Common Market Countries*. London: Routledge and Kegan Paul.

George, V. and Manning, N. 1980. *Socialism, Social Welfare and the Soviet Union*. London: Routledge and Kegan Paul.

George, V. and Rimachevskaya, N. 1993. "Poverty in Russia." *International Social Security Review* 46 (1): 67–78.

George, V. and Taylor-Gooby, P. eds. 1996. *European Welfare Policy: Squaring the Welfare Circle*. Basingstock, Hampshire: Macmillan.

George, V. and Wilding, P. 1994. *Welfare and Ideology*. Brighton: Harvester Wheatsheaf.

Georgiou, P. 1973. "The Goal Paradigm and Notes Towards a Counter Paradigm." *Administrative Science Quarterly* 18 (3): 291–310.

Gerdes, K. E. and Pehrson, K. L. 1998. "Philippines." In Dixon, J. and Macarov, D. eds., *Poverty: A Persistent Global Reality*. London: Routledge.

Gerdes, V. 1970–71. "African Provident Funds." *Industrial and Labor Relations Review* 24, 572–87.

Gerdes, V. 1973. "African Social Security Administration." *International Review of Administrative Sciences* 39 (2): 167–79.

Gergen, K. 1982. *Towards Transformation in Social Knowledge*. New York: Springer-Verlag.

Gerig, D. S. 1966. "Social Security in New African Countries." *Social Security Bulletin* 29 (1): 3–11.

Gethaiga, W. W. and Williams, L. P. 1987. "Kenya." In Dixon, J. ed., *Social Welfare in Africa*. London: Routledge.

Giarchi, G. 1996. *Care for the Elderly in Europe*. Aldershot: Gower.

Gilbert, N. 1981. "Social Security in Developing Countries." In Wallace, H. M. and Ebrahim, G. eds., *Maternal and Child Health Around the World*. London: Macmillan.

Gilbert, N. 1992. "From Entitlement to Incentives: The Changing Philosophy of Social Protection." *International Social Security Review* 45 (3): 5–18.

Gilbert, N. and Park, N.-H. 1996. "Privatization, Provision, Targeting: Trends and Policy Implications for Social Security in the United States." *International Social Security Review* 49 (1): 19–30.

Gillion, C. 1994. "Social Security and Protection in the Developing World." *Monthly Labor Review* 117, September: 24–31.

Gillion, C. and Bonilla, A. 1992. "Analysis of a National Private Pension Scheme: The Case of Chile." *International Labor Review* 131 (2): 171–95.

Gilman, S. C., Stupak, R Jr, and Collier, T. J. Jr 1993. "Machiavelli Reinvented: Integrity, Power, and Democratic Responsibility." *Public Manager* 22 (3): 24–6.

Ginneken, W. van, Join-Lambert, L. and Lecaillon, J. 1979. "Persistent Poverty in the Industrialized Market Economies." *International Labor Review* 118 (6): 699–711.

Ginsburg, N. 1992. *Divisions of Welfare: A Critical Introduction to Comparative Social Policy*. London: Sage.

Glaser. W. A. 1987. *Paying for Hospitals: Foreign Lessons for the United States*. San Fransisco: Jossey-Bass.

Glaser, W. A. 1988. *Financial Decisions in European Health Insurance: Foreign Lessons for the United States*. San Fransisco: Jossey-Bass.

Gluski. A. R. 1994. "Recent Reforms of National Pension Plans and the Future Development of Latin American Capital Markets." *Colombia Journal of World Business*. 29 (2): 54–65.

Gobin. M. 1977. "The Role of Social Security in the Development of the Caribbean Territories." *International Social Security Review*. 30 (1): 7–20.

Godfrey. V. N. 1974a. "Broader Role for National Provident Funds — Zambian Experience." *International Labor Review*. 109 (2): 137–52.

Godfrey. V. N. 1974b. "The Ability of National Provident Funds to Meet Social Needs: The Zambian Experience." *African Social Security Series* (International Social Security Association): 13–14.

Goldman. J. and Hollman. A. N. 1936. *Democracy in Denmark*. Washington, DC: National Home Library Foundation.

Goodin, R. E. 1982. "Freedom and the Welfare State: Theoretical Foundations." *Journal of Social Policy* 11 (2): 149–76.

Goodin, R. E. 1990. "Stabilizing Expectations: The Role of Earnings-Related Benefits in Social Welfare Policy." *Ethics* 100, April: 530–53.

Goodin, R. E. and LeGrand, J. 1987. *Not Only the Poor: The Middle Classes and the Welfare State*. London: Macmillan Press.

Goodin, R. E. and Schmidtz, D. 1998. *Social Welfare and Individual Responsibility*. Cambridge: Cambridge University Press.

Goodman, R. and Peng, I. 1996. "The East Asian Welfare States: Peripatetic Learning, Adaptive Change, and Nation-building." In Esping-Andersen, G. ed., *Welfare States in Transition: National Adaptions in Global Economies*. London: Sage.

Goodwin, L. 1972. *Do the Poor Want to Work? A Social-Psychological Study of Work Orientation*. Washington, DC: Brookings Institution.

Gordon, C., Burchell, G. and Miller, P. eds. 1988. *The Foucault Effect: The Culture and Mentality of Government*. Brighton: Harvester Wheatsheaf.

Gordon, M. S. 1963. "Industrial Injuries in Europe and the British Commonwealth before World War II." In Cheit, E. F. and Gordon, M. S. eds., *Occupational Disability and Public Policy*. New York: Wiley.

Gordon, M. S. 1988. *Social Security Policies in Industrial Societies: A Comparative Analysis*. Cambridge: Cambridge University Press.

Gormley, W. T. Jr 1994. "Privatization Revisited." *Policy Studies Review* 13 (3/4): 215–34.

Gottschalk, P. and Smeeding, T. M. 1997. Empirical Evidence on Income Inequality in Industrialised Countries. Unpublished paper (mimeo).

Gough, I. 1979. *The Political Economy of the Welfare State*. Basingstoke: Macmillan.

Gough, I., Eardley, T., Bradshaw, J., Ditch, J. and Whiteford, P. 1996. *Social*

Assistance in OECD Countries (DSS Research Report 46). London: Department of Social Security with the Organization for Economic Co-operation and Development.

Gould, A. 1993. *Capitalist Welfare Systems: A Comparison of Japan, Britain and Sweden*, New York: Longman.

Gouldner, A. W. 1955. "Metaphysical Pathos and the Theory of Bureaucracy." *American Political Science Review* 49 (2): 496–507.

Gouldner, A. W. 1970. *The Coming Crises of Western Sociology*. London: Heinemann.

Graham, J. 1984. *Take-up of Family Income Supplement. Knowledge, Attitudes and Experience, Claimants and Non-claimants*. Stormont: Department of Finance and Personnel, Public Policy Research Unit, Social Research Division.

Gramlich, E. M. 1996. "Different Approaches to Dealing with Social Security." *American Economic Review* 86 (2): 358–62.

Gregova, M. 1996. "Restructuring of the 'Life-world of Socialism'." *International Sociology* 11 (1): 63–78.

Greiner, D. Raporteur 1986. *Present State and Evolution of Occupational Diseases in the Light of the Recognition of New Types of Diseases: Report of the Permanent Committee on Insurance Against Employment Accidents and Occupational Diseases to the International Social Security Association XXII General Assembly* (Report XV, Montreal, 2–12 September). Geneva: International Social Security Association.

Gretschmann, K. 1991. "Analyzing the Public Sector: The Received View of Economics and its Shortcomings." In Kaufmann, F. X. ed., *The Public Sector: Challenge for Coordination and Learning*. Berlin: Walter de Gruyter

Greve, B. ed. 1992. *Social Policy in Europe: Latest Evolution and Perspectives for the Future*. Copenhagen: Danish National Institute for Social Research.

Griffiths, B., Cooper, S. and McVicar, N. 1987. *Overseas Countries Maintenance Provisions*. Canberra: Australian Department of Social Security.

Griffiths, D. 1974. *The Waiting Poor: An Argument for Abolition of the Waiting Period on Unemployment and Sickness Benefits*. Victoria, Australia: Brotherhood of St. Lawrence.

Grimal, H. 1978. *Decolonization: The British, French, Dutch and Belgian Empires 1919–1963* (Tr. Vos, S. de). London: Routledge and Kegan Paul.

Grimaud, M. 1995. *The Impact of Structural Adjustment Programmes on Social Security in African Countries*. Geneva: International Social Security Association.

Gruat, J.-V. 1990."Social Security Schemes in Africa: Current Trends and Problems." *International Labor Review* 129 (4): 405–21.

Guest, D. 1985. *The Emergence of Social Security in Canada*. Vancouver: University of British Colombia Press.

Guest, D. 1988. "Canadian and American Income Security Responses to Five Major Risks: A Comparison." In Drover, G. ed., *Free Trade and Social Policy*. Ottawa: Canadian Council on Social Development.

Guhan, S. 1994. "Social Security Options for Developing Countries." *International Labor Review* 133 (1): 35–53.

Guitton, H. 1987. "The Rational and the Non-Rational in Economics." *International Journal of Social Economics* 14 (3/4/5): 33–36.

Gustafsson, B. A. and Klevmarken, N. A. 1988. *The Political Economy of Social Security*. Amsterdam: Elsevier.

Gutierrez, A. 1989. "Pensions Schemes in Latin America, Some Financial Problems." *International Social Security Review* 42 (1): 16–42.

Gutierrez, A. 1990. "The Financing of Social Security and the Macro-economy: The Case of Latin America." *International Social Security Review* 43 (3): 287–302.

Haanes-Olsen, L. 1994a. "Sweden: A Welfare State in Need." *Social Security Bulletin* 57 (1): 109.

Haanes-Olsen, L. 1994b. "Far-reaching Social Security Pension Reform Proposed in Sweden." *Social Security Bulletin* 57 (2): 82–83.

Haanes-Olsen, L. and Horlick, M. 1974. "The Earnings Replacement Rates of Old-age Pensions for Workers Retiring at the End of 1972." *Social Security Bulletin* 37 (1): 9–18.

Haar, J. 1989. "International Developments in Pension Funds: Policy Choices Facing OECD Countries." *Employee Benefits Journal* 14 (4): 12–15.

Habibi, N. 1994. "Budgetary Policy and Political Liberty: A Cross-sectional Analysis." *World Development* 22 (4): 579–86.

Hagemann, R. P. and Nicoletti, G. 1989. "Population Ageing: Economic Effects and Some Implications for Financing Public Pensions." *OECD Economic Studies* 12, Spring: 59–110.

Hajer, M. A. 1993. "Discourse Coalitions and the Institutionalisation of Practice." In Fischer, F. and Forester, J. eds., *The Argumentative Turn of Policy Analysis and Planning*. London: UCL Press.

Halfpenny, P. 1982. *Positivism and Sociology*. London: Allen and Unwin.

Hallen, G. C. 1967. *Social Security in India*. Meerut: Rastogi.

Hardiman, M. and Midgley, J. 1988. *The Social Dimensions of Development: Social Policy and Planning in the Third World*. Aldershot: Gower.

Harding, L. F. 1994. "'Parental Responsibility' — A Dominant Theme in British Child and Family Policy for the 1990s." *International Journal of Sociology and Social Policy* 14 (1 and 2): 84–108.

Harris, C. P. 1977. "Income Security Programmes and the Philosophy of Social Security Policy." *International Social Work* 20 (1): 30–42.

Harris, R. and Selden, A. 1979. *Over-ruled on Welfare: The Increasing Desire for Choice in Education and Medicine and its Frustration by 'Representative Government* (Hobart Papers 13). London: Institute of Economic Affairs.

Hasling, L. 1997. "Labor-Market Pensions in Denmark." *Benefits and Compensation International* 25 (8): 21–24.

Hassen, N. 1965. *Social Security in the Framework of Economic Development*. Aligarh: Aligarh Muslem University Press.

Hassen, N. 1972. *The Social Security System in India*. Aligarh: Aligarh Muslim University Press.

Hauser, R., Rolf, G. and Tibitanzl, F. 1994. "Old Age Security for Women in Twelve EC Countries." *Journal of European Social Policy* 4 (1): 1–16.

Hayek, F. A. 1960. *The Constitution of Liberty*. London: Routledge and Kegan Paul.

Heckscher, G. 1984) *The Welfare State and Beyond: Success and Problems in Scandinavia*. Minneapolis: University of Minnesota.

Heclo, H. 1974. *Modern Social Policies in Britain and Sweden: From Relief to Income*

Maintenance. New haven: Yale University Press.

Hecloi, H. 1975. "Frontiers of Social Policy in Europe and America." *Policy Sciences* 6 (4): 403–12.

Hegyesi, G., Gondos, A. and Orsos, E. 1992. "Hungary." In Dixon, J. and Macarov, D. eds., *Social Welfare in Socialist Countries.* London: Routledge.

Hennock, E. P. 1987. *British Social Reform and German Precedents; The Case of Social Insurance, 1880–1914.* Oxford: Oxford University Press.

Hewitt, C. 1977. "The Effect of Political Democracy and Social Democracy on Equality in Industrial Societies, A Cross-National Comparison." *American Sociological Review* 42 (3): 450–64.

Higuchi, T. 1970. "The Special Treatment of Employment Injury in Social Security." *International Labor Review* 102 (2): 109–26.

Higuchi, T. 1985. "Employment Injury Protection." In *Social Security in the South Pacific.* Bangkok: International Labor Organization.

Hill, D. C. D. and Tigges, L. M. 1995. "Gendering Welfare State Theory: A Cross-national Study of Women's Public Pension Quality." *Gender and Society* 9, February: 99–119.

Hills, J., Ditch, J. and Glennerster, H. eds., 1994. *Beveridge and Social Security.* Oxford: Oxford University Press.

Hirtz, F. 1988. "Coping with Adversity in the Philippine Lowlands." In Benda-Beckmann, F. von, Benda-Beckmann, K. von, Brun, O. B. and Hirz, F. eds., *Between Kinship and the State: Social Security and Law in Developing Countries.* Dordrecht: Foris.

Hirtz, F. 1990. "Managing Insecurity — State Social Policy and Family Networks in the Rural Philippines. Past and Present." Ph.D. thesis, University of Bielefeld, Bielefeld, Germany.

Hirtz, F. 1995. "An Examination of the Roles of the State, Networks, and the Family in Philippine Social Security." In Dixon, J. and Scheurell, R. P. eds., *International Perspectives on Social Security.* Westport, CT: Greenwood.

Hofmeister, H. 1982. "Austria." In Kohler, P. A. and Zacher, H. F. eds., *The Evolution of Social Insurance, 1881–1981: Studies of Germany, France, Great Britain, Austria and Switzerland.* London: Frances Pinter.

Holzmann, R. 1996. *Pension Reform, Financial Market Development, and Economic Growth: Preliminary Evidence from Chile* (IMF Working Paer WP/96/94 (August)). Washington, DC: International Monetary Fund.

Hoon, L. S. 1995. "The EPF Rises to the Challenge." *AsiaMoney* 6 (1): 9–11.

Horlick, M. 1970. "The Earnings Replacement Rates of Old-age Benefits: An International Comparison." *Social Security Bulletin* 33 (3): 3–16.

Horlick, M. 1987." The Relationship Between Public and Private Pension Schemes: An Introductory Overview." *Social Security Bulletin* 50 (7): 3–6.

Horlick, M. and Lewis, D. E. 1970. "Adjustment of Old-age Pensions in Foreign Programs." *Social Security Bulletin* 33 (5): 12–15.

Horlick, M. and Lucas, R. 1971. "The Role of Contribution Ceilings in Social Security Programs: Comparison of Five Countries." *Social Security Bulletin* 34 (2): 19–31.

Horlick, M. and Tracy, M. 1974. "Adjustment of Old Age Pensions in Foreign Programs." *Social Security Bulletin* 37 (7): 33–36.

Horseman, M. and Marshall, A. 1994. *After the Nation-State: Citizens, Tribalism and the New World Disorder*. London: HarperCollins.

Howlett, M. and Ramesh M. 1993. "Patterns of Policy Choice: Policy Styles, Policy Learning and the Privatization Experience." *Policy Studies Review* 12 (1/2): 3–24.

Huber, E. 1996. "Social Policy in Latin America: Neoliberal versus Social Democratic Models." In Esping-Andersen, G. ed., *Welfare States in Transition: National Adaptions in Global Economies*. London: Sage.

Huber E. and Stephens, J. D. 1993. "Political Parties and Public Pensions: A Quantitative Analysis." *Acta Sociologica* 36 (4): 309–25.

Hui, S. Y. and Fung, W. 1994. "The Development of Social Security System for Macau: with Reference to the People's Republic of China." In *Asia Regional Conference on Social Security (September 14–16, 1993) Conference Proceedings*. Hong Kong: Hong Kong Council of Social Services.

Hutchins, K. 1993. "Mutual Benefit Societies in Hungary: 1830–1941." *International Social Security Review* 46 (3): 79–98.

Hutton, S. and Whiteford, P. 1994. "Gender and Retirement Incomes: A Comparative Analysis." In Baldwin, S. and Falkingham, J. eds., *Social Security and Social Change*. Brighton, Surrey: Wheatsheaf.

Ichien, M. 1995. "Japanese Social Security: Its Past, Present and Future." In Dixon, J. and Scheurell, R. P. eds., *International Perspectives on Social Security*. Westport, CT: Greenwood.

Igle, G. 1990. *Flexibility and Protection of Rights in the Field of Social Security*. Munich: MaxPlanckInstitute.

Igle, G. 1994. "The Contingencies Covered by Social Security Systems." In Maydell, B. von and Hohnerlein, E. M. eds., *The Transformation of Social Security Systems in Central and Eastern Europe*. Louvain: Peeters.

Ijeh, M. C. 1977. "Alternative Approaches to the Problem of Arrears in Employer Contributions." *African Social Security Documentation* 2: 8–13.

Ijeh, M. C. 1980. "Decentralisation of Provident Fund Administration." In *Fourth Meeting of the Committee* [on Provident Funds]. Geneva: International Social Security Association.

ILO (International Labor Office) 1936. *Studies and Reports* (Series M 16). Geneva: ILO.

ILO 1942. *Approaches in Social Security: An International Survey* (Series M 18, Montreal, McGill University). Geneva: ILO.

ILO 1944. *Social Security: Principles and Problems Arising out of the War, Part 1: Principles* (Reports IV (1) and IV (2) to the 26th Session of the International labor Conference). Geneva: ILO.

ILO 1952a. *Social Security (Minimum Standards) Convention, 1952* (No. 102). Geneva: ILO.

ILO 1952b. "The Cost of Social Security." *International Labor Review* 65 (6) June: 726–91.

ILO 1952c. *Maternity Protection Convention (Revised. 1952,* (No. 103). Geneva: ILO.

ILO 1953a. "The Cost of Social Security." *International Labor Review* 67 (6): 292–303.

ILO 1953b. "*Approaches to Social Security — An International Survey.*" *Studies and Reports Series* (Social Insurance) 18). Geneva: ILO.

ILO 1954–1992. *The Cost of Social Security* (various editions). Geneva: ILO.

ILO 1955. *Unemployment Insurance Schemes* (Studies and Reports, New Series 42). Geneva: ILO.

ILO 1964. *Employment Injury Benefits Convention, 1964* (No. 121). Geneva: ILO.

ILO 1966. *Revision of Conventions Nos. 35, 36, 37, 38 39 and 40 Concerning Old-Age, Invalidity and Survivors' Pensions* (Report V, Part 1, International Labor Conference, 50th Session). Geneva: ILO.

ILO 1967. *Invalidity, Old-Age and Survivors' Benefits Convention, 1967* (No. 128). Geneva: ILO.

ILO 1968. *Revision of Conventions Nos. 24 and 25 Concerning Sickness Insurance* (Report VI, Part 1, International Labor Conference, 52nd Session). Geneva: ILO.

ILO 1969. "*Medical Care and Sickness Benefits Convention, 1969* (No. 130)." Geneva: ILO.

ILO 1970. *Introduction to Social Security.* Geneva: ILO.

ILO 1972a. "Social Security in Latin America: Evolution and Prospects." *International Social Security Review* 25 (3): 305–56.

ILO 1972b. *The Cost of Social Security.* Geneva: ILO.

ILO 1977. *Improvements and Harmonisation of Social Security Systems in Africa.* Geneva, ILO.

ILO 1980. *Pensions and Inflation: An International Discussion* (2nd Impression). Geneva, ILO.

ILO, Department of Social Security 1981. "Assessment of Disability." In *Social Security and Disability: Issues in Policy Research* (Studies and Research 17). Geneva: ISSA.

ILO 1983. *Maintenance of Rights in Social Security* (Report V, International Labor Conference, 69th Session). Geneva: ILO.

ILO 1984a. *Financing Social Security: The Options an International Analysis.* Geneva, ILO.

ILO 1984b. *Introduction to Social Security.* Geneva, ILO.

ILO 1985a. *Social Security in the South Pacific.* Bangkok: ILO.

ILO 1985b. *Maternity Benefits in the Eighties: A Global Survey (1964–84).* Geneva: ILO.

ILO 1988a. *Employment Promotion and Protection against Unemployment Convention, 1988* (No. 168). Geneva: ILO.

ILO 1988b. *The Cost of Social Security.* Geneva: ILO.

ILO 1989a. *Social Security Protection in Old-Age.* Geneva: ILO.

ILO 1989b. *From Pyramid to Pillar.* Geneva: ILO.

ILO 1992. *Social and Labor Bulletin* 4. Geneva: ILO.

ILO 1993. *Report of the Tripartite Regional Meeting of Experts on Social Security in the Americas* (GB 258/ESP/7/7). Geneva: ILO.

ILO 1994. "Privatization of Pensions in Latin America." *International Labor Review* 133 (1): 134–41.

Imbrogno, S. 1991. "State and Welfare: Comparative Social Policy in the USA and the USSR." *Journal of International and Comparative Social Welfare* 7 (1 and 2): 15–30.

IMF (International Monetary Fund) 1986. *A Manual on Government Finance Statistics.* Washington, DC: IMF

Indri, M. Raporteur 1986. *Administrative Decentralisation of National Social Security Schemes: Report of the Permanent Committee on Organization and Methods to the International Social Security Association XXII General Assembly* (Report XIX, Montreal, 2–12 September). Geneva: International Social Security Association.

Ingleson, J. 1993. "Mutual Benefit Societies in Indonesia." *International Social Security Review* 46 (3): 69–78.

Inductivo, H. 1997. "Social Security in the Asia and Pacific Region: The Present Situation." In *Current Social Security Issues in Asia and the Pacific* (Social Security Documentation Asia and Pacific Series, 21). Manila: International Social Security Association.

Ippolito, R. A. 1986. *Pensions, Economics and Public Policy.* Homewood, Il: Dow Jones.

ISSA (International Social Security Association) 1973a. *Complementary Pension Institutes or Complimentary Pension Schemes.* Geneva: ISSA.

ISSA 1973b. *Women and Social Security.* Geneva: ISSA.

ISSA 1974. *The Role of Social Services in Social Security.* Geneva: ISSA.

ISSA 1975. "Transformation of Provident Funds into Pension Schemes." *International Social Security Review* 28 (3): 276–89.

ISSA 1976. *Methods of Evaluating the Effectiveness of Social Security Programmmes* (Studies and Research 8). Geneva: ISSA

ISSA 1977. "Transformation of Provident Funds into Pension Schemes." In *First Meeting of the Committee* [on Provident Funds] *and Round Table Meeting on Provident Funds.* Geneva: ISSA.

ISSA 1978. *Social Security Provision in Case of Divorce.* Geneva: ISSA.

ISSA 1979. *Methods of Financing Social Security.* Geneva: ISSA.

ISSA 1982a. *Social Security and the Elderly* (Background Document for the World Assembly on Aging, Vienna, 26 July–6 August, 1982). Geneva: ISSA.

ISSA 1982b. *Medical Care Under Social Security in Developing Countries.* Geneva: ISSA.

ISSA 1985. *Social Security, Unemployment and Premature Retirement* (Studies and Research 22). Geneva: ISSA.

ISSA 1986a. *Eighth Meeting of the Committee* [on Provident Funds]. Geneva: ISSA.

ISSA 1986b. *Pension Schemes for Women and the Importance of New Structures of Remunerated Employment as they Affect Pension Schemes for Women* (Report 2, ISSA 22nd General Assembly, Geneva, 1986). Geneva: ISSA.

ISSA 1989. "Development and Trends in Social Security: 1987–89." *International Social Security Review* 42 (3): 247–349

ISSA 1992a. "Development and Trends in Social Security: 1990–92." *International Social Security Review* 45 (4): 5–64.

ISSA 1992b. *Social Security Tomorrow: Permanence and Change* (Studies and Research 36). Geneva: ISSA.

ISSA 1993a. *Trends in Social Security* 3, March. Geneva: ILO.

ISSA 1993b. "Complementary Retirement Pensions in Europe." *International Social Security Review* 46 (4): 67–71.

ISSA 1993c. *Trends in Social Security* 4, August. Geneva: ILO.

ISSA 1994. *Complementary Pensions: European Perspectives* (Social Security Documentation, European Series 21). Geneva: ISSA.

ISSA 1996a. "Developments and Trends in Social Security, 1993–1995: Report of the Secretary General." *International Social Security Review* 49 (2): 5–83.

ISSA 1996b. *Asia and Pacific News Sheet* 24 (4), December.

ISSA 1996c. *Financing Retirement Benefits: The Asia and Pacific Experience* (Social Security Documentation, Asia and Pacific Series 20). Geneva: ISSA

Isuani, E. A. 1985. "Social Security and Public Assistance" in Mesa-Lago, C. ed., *The Crisis of Social Security and Health Care*. Pittsburgh: Center for Latin American Studies, University of Pittsburgh.

Iyer, S. M. 1971. "The Role of National Provident Funds and Pension Schemes in Capital Formation." In *Fifth International Conference of Social Security Actuaries and Statisticians*. Geneva: ISSA.

Iyer. S. M. 1993."Pension Reform in Developing Countries." *International Labor Review* 132 (2): 187–207.

Jacobs, D. 1998. *Social Welfare Systems in East Asia: A Comparative Analysis Including Private Welfare* (Case/10). London: Centre for Analysis of Social Exclusion, London School of Economics.

Janssen, M. C. and Muller, H. 1982. "Switzerland." In Rosa, J.-J. ed., *The World Crisis in Social Security*. San Fransisco: Institute for Contemporary Studies.

Jallande, J.-P. 1992. "Is the Crisis Behind Us? Issues Facing Social Security Systems in Western Europe." In Ferge, Z. and Kolberg, J. E. eds., *Social Policy in a Changing Europe*. Frankfurt am Main, Germany: Campus Verlag/Boulder, CO: Westview.

James, E. 1996. "Providing Better Protection and Promoting Growth: A Defense of *Averting the Old Age Crisis.*" *International Social Security Review* 49 (3): 3–16

James, M. 1994. "How to Reform Australia's Social Security System." *IPA Review* 46 (4): 32–35.

Jayasuriya, L., Fernando, G. and Allbrook, M. 1985. "Sri Lanka." In Dixon, J. and Kim, H. S. eds., *Social Welfare in Asia*. London: Croom Helm.

Jenkins, M. 1981. "Social Security Trends in the English Speaking Caribbean." *International Labor Review* 120 (6): 631–43.

Jenkins, M. 1993. "Extending Social Security Protection to the Entire Population: Problems and Issues." *International Social Security Review* 46 (2): 3–21.

Jenkins, S. ed. 1969. *Social Security in International Perspective: Essays in Honor of Eveline M. Burns*. New York: Colombia University Press.

Jersey, Employment and Social Security Review Committee 1995. *A Review of the Social Security and Health Insurance Schemes in Jersey: Continuity and Change*. Jersey, Department of Employment and Social Security.

Jones, C. 1985. *Patterns of Social Policy: An Introduction to Comparative Analysis*. London: Tavistock.

Jones, C. 1990. "Hong Kong, Singapore, South Korea and Taiwan: the Oikonomic Welfare State." *Government and Opporsition*, 25: 446–62.

Jones, H. M. 1974. *Revolution and Romanticism*. Cambridge, MA: Harvard University Press.

Jones, T. W. 1996. A Strategy to Maintain Social Security Benefits." *Challenge* 39 (6): 25–27.

Joynathsing, M. 1987. "Mauritius." In Dixon, J. ed., *Social Welfare in Africa*. London: Routledge.

Kahn, A. J. and Kamerman, S. B. 1983. *Income Transfers for Families with Children: An Eight Country Study*. Philadelphia: Temple University Press.

Kahn, R. L. 1974. "Organizational Development: Some Problems and Prospects." *Journal of Applied Behavioural Science* 10 (4): 485–502.

Kaim-Caudle, P. R. 1973. *Comparative Social Policy and Social Security*. London: Martin Robertson.

Kaim-Caudle, P. R. 1981. *Cross-National Comparisons of Social Service Pensions for the Elderly* (Discussion Paper Series). Sydney: University of New South Wales, Social Welfare Research Centre.

Kaim-Caudle, P. R. 1993. "The Unintended Effects of Social Policy Measures." *Policy Studies Review* 12 (1 and 2): 102–13.

Kalirajan, K. and Wiboonchutikula, P. 1986. "The Social Security System in Singapore." *ASEAN Economic Bulletin* 3: 129–44.

Kamerman, S. and Khan, A. J. 1978. *Family Policy: Government and Families in Fourteen Countries*. New York: Colombia University Press.

Kamerman, S. and Khan, A. J. 1982. "Income Transfers, Work, and the Economic Well-being of Families with Children: A Comparative Study." *International Social Security Review* 35 (3): 345–82.

Kamerman, S. and Khan, A. J. 1989a. "Single Parent Female Headed Families in Western Europe: Social Change and Response." *International Social Security Review* 42 (1): 3–34.

Kamerman, S. and Khan, A. J. 1989b. *Privatization and the Welfare State*. Princeton: Princeton University Press.

Kamerman, S. and Khan, A. J. 1994. "Family Policy and the Under-35s: Money, Services and Time in a Policy Package." *International Social Security Review* 47 (3–4): 31–44.

Kanbur, R. and Besley, T. 1990. *The Principles of Targeting* (Working Paper 85). Washington, DC: World Bank.

Kangas, O. 1991. *The Politics of Social Rights: Studies on Dimensions of Sickness Insurance in OECD Countries*. Stockholm: Swedish Institute for Social Research.

Kangas, O. and Palme, J. 1993. "Statism Eroded? Labor-Market Benefits and Challenges to the Scandinavian Welfare States." In Hansen, E. J., Eerikson, R., Ringen, S. and Uuisitalo, H. eds., *Welfare Trends in Scandinavian Countries*. Armonk, NY: M. E. Sharpe.

Kaseke, E. 1995. "Social Security and Redistribution: The Case of Zimbabwe." In Dixon, J. and Scheurell, R. P. eds., *International Perspectives on Social Security*. Westport, CT: Greenwood.

Kaseke, E. 1998. "Zimbabwe." In Dixon, J. and Macarov, D. eds., *Poverty: A Persistent Global Reality*. London: Routledge.

Kashef, A. S. M. 1987. "Egypt." In Dixon, J. ed., *Social Welfare in the Middle East*. London: Routledge.

Kassalow, E. M. ed. 1968. *The Role of Social Security in Economic Development*. Washington, DC: Department of Health, Education and Welfare.

Kato, J. 1991. "Public Pension Reform in the United States and Japan: A Study of Comparative Public Policy." *Comparative Political Studies* 24, April: 100–26.

Keane, J. 1988. "Introduction." In Keane, J. ed., *Civil Society and the State*. Guilford, Surrey: Verso.

Keeley, M., Robins, P., Speigelman, R. and West, R. 1978. "The Labor Supply Effects and Cost of Alternative NIT Programs." *Journal of Human Resources* 13 (2): 3–36.

Keithley, J. 1989. "United Kingdom." In Dixon, J and Scheurell R. P. eds., *Social Welfare in Developed Market Countries*. London: Routledge.

Kershen, N. and Kessler, F. 1990. "Unemployment Benefits in France and the Federal Republic of Germany: Social Protection or Employment Market Regulation." *International Social Security Review* 43 (3): 270–86.

Kertonegoro, S. 1986. "Investment Strategies for the Protection of the Value of Provident Fund Balances." In *Eighth Meeting of the Committee* [on Provident Funds]. Geneva: ISSA.

Kessler, J. A. 1966. *A Glimpse into Social Security in Africa*. Washington. DC: Department of Health. Education and Welfare. Social Security Administration.

Kewley, T. H. 1972. *Social Security in Australia, 1900–1972*. Sydney: Sydney University Press.

Keyes. G. 1990. "Guatemala." In Dixon, J. and Scheurell R. P. eds., *Social Welfare in Latin America*. London: Routledge.

Keynes, J. M. 1936. *The General Theory of Employment, Interest and Money*. London: Macmillan.

Kim, H. S. 1992. "North Korea." In Dixon, J. and Macarov, D. eds., *Social Welfare in Socialist Countries*. London: Routledge.

Kingson, E. R. 1991. "The Graying of the Baby Boom in the United States: Framing the Policy Debate." *International Social Security Review* 44 (1–2): 5–26.

Kingson, E. R. 1994. "Testing the Boundaries of Universality: What's Mean? What's Not?" *The Gerontologist* 34 December: 736–42.

Kingson, E. R. and O'Grady-LaShane, R. 1993. "The Effects of Caregiving on Women's Social Security Benefits." *The Gerontologist* 33, April: 230–39.

Kingson, E. R. and Williamson, J. 1996. "Undermining Social Security's Basic Objective." *Challenge* 39 (6): 28–30.

Kirsch, G. 1988. "Social Security: Reducing Social Tensions without Destroying the Economy." In *Policy Issues in Social Security*. Seoul: Korean Development Institute.

Kisch, J. 1987. *Overseas Countries' Assistance to Sole Parents*. Canberra: Australian Department of Social Security.

Klienig, J. 1984. *Paternalism*. Totowa, NJ: Rowman and Littlefield.

Knibbs, G. H. 1910. *Social Insurance Report*. Melbourne: Commonwealth Government Printer.

Knightley, P. 1994. "Mercer Greece and Turkey Seminar: London." *Benefits and Compensation International* 23 (7): 21–4.

Knyester, A., Strohmeirer, K. P. and Schulze, H.-J. 1994. "Social Policy and Forms of Family Life in Europe." *International Social Security Review* 47 (3–4): 11–30.

Kohler, P. A. and Zacher, H. F. eds. 1982. *The Evolution of Social Insurance, 1881–1981: Studies of Germany, France, Great Britain, Austria and Switzerland*. London: Frances Pinter.

Kolakowski, L. 1972. *Positivist Philosophy: From Hume to the Vienna Circle* (Tr.

Guterman, N.). London: Pelican.

Kolb, R. 1989. "One Hundred Years of German Pension Insurance Legislation." *International Social Security Review* 42 (2): 195–202.

Koniaris, T. B. 1979. *The Usefulness of Social Welfare Indicators for the Measurement of the Quality of Social Insurance Schemes.* Thessaloniki: Aristotle University of Thessaloniki, Faculty of Law and Economics.

Kopits, G. 1993. "Reforming Social Security Systems." *Finance and Development* 30, June: 21–23.

Koskela, E. and Viren, M. 1983, "Social Security and Household Savings in an International Cross Section." *American Economic Review* 73 (2): 212–17.

Kotlikoff, L. J. 1987. "Social Security and Savings." In *The New Palgrave: A Dictionary of Economics.* New York: Macmillan.

Kotlikoff, L. J. 1989. "On the Contribution of Economics to the Evaluation and Formation of Social Security Policy." *American Economic Review* 79 (2): 184–90.

Kotlikoff, L. J. 1996a. "Privatizing Social Security at Home and Abroad." *American Economic Review* 86 (2): 184–90.

Kotlikoff, L. [J.] 1996b. "Rescuing Social Security." *Challenge* 39 (6): 21–22.

Kouzmin, A. and Dixon, J. 1993. "The Dimensions of Quality in Public Management: Australian Perspectives and Experiences." In Hill, H. and Klages, H. eds., *Qualitats und Erfolgsorientierte Vervaltung: Aktualle Tendenzen und Entwurfe* [Quality and Success-Oriented Administrative Management: Current Trends and Models]. Berlin: Dunker and Humbolt.

Kouzmin, A. and Korac-Kakabadse, N. 1997. "From Phobias and Ideological Prescription Towards Multiple Models in Transformation Management for Socialist Economies in Transition." *Administration and Society* 29 (2): 139–88.

Kouzmin, A., Korac-Kakabadse, N. and Jarman, A. M. C. 1996. "Economic Rationalism, Risk and Institutional Vulnerability." *Risk Decision and Policy* 1 (2): 229–56.

Kouzmin, A., Leivesley, R, and Korac-Kakabadse, N. 1997. "From Managerialism and Economic Rationalism: Towards 'Reinventing' Economic Ideology and Administrative Diversity." *Administrative Theory and Praxis* 19 (1):19–46.

Kravaritou-Manitakis, Y. 1988. *New Forms of Work: Labor Law and Social Security Aspects in the European Community.* Luxembourg: European Foundation for the Improvement of Living and Working Conditions.

Kritzer, B. E. 1984. *Social Security Provisions for Public Employees in Several Countries.* Washington, DC: US Social Security Administration, Office of International Policy.

Kritzer, B. E. 1994. "New Social Security Measures in the United Kingdom." *Social Security Bulletin* 57 (1): 112.

Kritzer, B. E. 1995. "Peru Modifies Pension System." *Social Security Bulletin* 58 (4): 140.

Kritzer, B. E. 1996a. "Uruguay Sets Up Dual System of Public and Private Pensions." *Social Security Bulletin* 59 (1): 97–98.

Kritzer, B. E. 1996b. "Privatizing Social Security: The Chilean Experience." *Social Security Bulletin* 59 (3): 45–55.

Krueger, A. B. and Pischke, J.-S. 1992. "The Effect of Social Security on Labor

Supply: A Cohort Analysis of Notch Generation." *Journal of Labor Economics* 10, October: 412–37.

Ku, Y.-W. 1995. The Development of State Welfare in the Asian NICs with Special Reference to Taiwan." *Social Policy and Administration* 29 (4): 345–64.

Ku, Y.-W. 1998. "Can We Afford It? The Development of National Health Insurance in Taiwan." In Goodman, R., White, G. and Kwon, H.-J. eds., *In Search of an East Asian Welfare State*. London: Routledge.

Kvalheim, A. 1980. *The Cost of Healthcare in Member States of the Council of Europe and in Finland*. Strasbourg: Council of Europe.

Kwon, H.-J. 1997. "Beyond European Welfare Regimes: Comparative Perspectives on East Asian Welfare Systems." *Journal of Social Policy* 26 (4):467–84.

Laczko, F. 1988. "Partial Retirement: An Alternative to Early Retirement? A Comparison of Phased Retirement Schemes in the United Kingdom, France and Scandinavia." *International Social Security Review* 41 (2): 149–69.

Lall, V. D. 1986. *Appraisal of Provident Fund and Allied Schemes: Opinion Survey Aiming Subscribers*. New Delhi: National Institute of Public Finance and Policy.

Lally, D. 1970. *National Social Security Systems*. Washington, DC: US Department of Health, Education and Welfare.

Lamount, C. 1965. *The Philosophy of Humanism*. New York: Fredreich Ungar.

Lampman, R. 1978. *Labor Supply and Social Welfare Benefits in the United States* (Special Report 22). Madison: Institute for Research on Poverty, University of Wisconsin-Maddison.

Lapiidus, G. and Swanson, G. 1988. *State and Welfare USA/USSR*. Berkeley, CA: Institute of International Studies, University of California. Berkeley.

Lathouwer, L. de 1996. "Microsimulatiuon in Comparative Social Policy: A Case Study of Unemployment Schemes for Belgium and the Netherlands." In Harding, A. ed., *Microsimulation and Public Policy*. New York: North-Holland.

Lawson, R. 1987. "Income Support During Unemployment: Comparisons in Western Europe 1945–1985." In *Balanced Development of Long-term Benefits: Proceedings of the European Institute of Social Security* (EISS Yearbook, 1985). Antwerp: Kluwer Law and Taxation Publishers.

Lawson, R. and Reed, B. 1975. *Social Security in the European Community*. London: Chateau House.

Lay-Sion, J. 1977. "Feasibility of a National Pension Scheme for Seychelles." In *First Meeting of the Committee* [on Provident Funds] *and Round Table Meeting on Provident Funds*. Geneva: ISSA.

Leal de Araujo 1972. "Social Security as an Instrument of Income Distribution in the Developing Countries." *International Social Security Review* 25 (2): 243–54.

Lee, A. S. Y. C. 1994. "Social Security in Hong Kong." In *Asia Regional Conference on Social Security (September 14–16, 1993) Conference Proceedings*. Hong Kong: Hong Kong Council of Social Services.

Lee, S. M. 1980. "Survey on Capital Investment Practices of Provident Funds, Including Investment in Housing." In *Fourth Meeting of the Committee* [on Provident Funds]. Geneva: ISSA.

LeGrand, J. 1990. "Equity versus Efficiency: The Elusive Trade-off." *Ethics* 100 (4): 554–68.

LeGrand, J. 1996. "Knights, Knaves or Pawns: Human Behaviour and Social Policy."

Journal of Social Policy 26 (2): 149–69.

Leibfried, S. 1978. "Public Assistance in the United States and the Federal Republic of Germany: Does Social Democracy Make a Difference." *Comparative Politics* 20 (1): 59–75.

Leibfried, S. 1979. "Public Assistance in the Federal Republic of Germany." In Partington, M. and Jowell, J. eds., *Welfare Law and Policy*. London: Frances Pinter.

Leimer, D. R. and Richardson, D. H. 1992. "Social Security, Uncertainty Adjustments and the Consumption Decision." *Economica* 59 (3): 311–35.

Leite, C. B. 1990. "Brazil." In Dixon, J. and Scheurell R. P. eds., *Social Welfare in Latin America*. London: Routledge.

Leite, C. B. 1995. "Industrial Accidents: Why Should They Have Special Preferential Conditions." In Dixon, J. and Scheurell R. P. eds., *International Perspectives on Social Security*. Westport, CT: Greenwood.

Lemam, C. 1977. "Patterns of Policy Development: Social Security in the United States and Canada." *Public Policy* 25 (2): 261–91.

Leonard, P. 1997. *Postmodern Welfare: Reconstructing an Emancipatory Project*. Beverly Hills, CA: Sage.

Les, E. 1992. "Poland." In Dixon, J. and Macarov, D. eds., *Social Welfare in Socialist Countries*. London: Routledge.

Leung, J. C. B. 1994. "Dismantling the 'Iron Rice Bowel': Welfare Reform in the People's Republic of China." *Journal of Social Policy* 23 (3): 341–61.

Lin, C.-Y. 1994. "The Development of Health Insurance System in Taiwan, 1950–1990: A Historical and Political Approach." Unpublished paper, London School of Economics, London.

Linden, M. van der 1993. "Mutual Workers' Insurance: A Historical Outline." *International Social Security Review* 46 (3): 5–19.

Linden, M. van der 1996. *Social Security Mutualism: The Comparative History of Mutual Benefit Societies* (International and Comparative Social History, 2). Amsterdam and Bern: International Institute of Social History.

Lipton, M. and Ravaillion, M. 1993. *Poverty and Policy* (Working Paper 130). Washington, DC: World Bank.

Littlewood, M. 1998. *How To Create a Competitive Market in Pensions* (Choice in Welfare, 45). London: Institute of Economic Affairs Health and Welfare Unit.

Littman, M. S. 1989. "Poverty in the 1980s: Are the Poor Getting Poorer?" *Monthly Labor Review* 112, June: 13–18.

Liverpool, N. J. O. 1995. "Social Security in the Caribbean: Harmonizing Social Security Legislation in the English-speaking Caribbean." *International Social Security Review* 49 (1): 86–92.

Lockhart, C. 1991. "American Exceptionalism and Social Security: Complimentary Cultural and Structural Contributions to Social Program Development." *Review of Politics* 52 Summer: 510–29.

Logue, J. 1979. "The Welfare State: Victim of Its Success." *Daedalus* 108 (4): 69–87.

Lonsdale, S. and Seddon, J. 1994. "The Growth of Disability Benefits: An International Comparison." In Baldwin, S. and Falkingham, J. eds., *Social Security and Social Change*. Brighton, Surrey: Wheatsheaf.

Love, E. 1996. "Pension Funds: The Chilean Experience." *Asia and Pacific News Sheet*

(ISSA. 26 (4): 23–4.

Macarov, D. 1978. *The Design of Social Welfare*. New York: Holt, Rinehart and Winston.

Macarov, D. 1980. *Work and Welfare: The Unholy Alliance*. Beverly Hills, CA: Sage.

Macarov, D. 1981. "Welfare as Work's Handmaiden." *International Journal of Social Economics* 8 (5): 21–30.

Macarov, D. 1987. "Israel." In Dixon, J. ed., *Social Welfare in the Middle East*. London: Routledge.

Macarov, D. 1993. "Social Security as Poverty's Guardian." *Policy Studies Review* 12 (1 and 2): 92–101.

Macham, T. R. 1988. "Marxism: A Bourgeois Critique." *International Journal of Social Economics* 15 (11/12): 1–131.

MacKeller, [F.] L. and Bird, R. 1997. "Global Population Ageing, Social Security and Economic Growth: Some Results from a 2-Region Model." Paper presented at a Project LINK meeting, New York, March.

MacKeller, F. L. and McGreevey, W. 1997. "Social Security Reform in Developing and Formerly Socialist Economies" Unpublished paper, International Institute for Applied Systems Analysis, Luxembourg, Austria.

Mackenzie, G. A. 1995. "Reforming Latin America's Old Age Pension System." *Finance and Development* 32, March: 10–13.

MacPherson, S. 1982. *Social Policy in the Third World: The Social Dilemma of Underdevelopment*. Brighton: Wheatsheaf.

MacPherson, S. 1994. "Social Assistance in Hong Kong." In *Asia Regional Conference on Social Security (September 14–16, 1993) Conference Proceedings*. Hong Kong: Hong Kong Council of Social Services.

MacPherson, S. 1998. "Hong Kong." In Dixon J. and Macarov, D. eds., *Poverty: A Persistent Global Reality*. London: Routledge.

MacPherson, S. and Midgley, J. 1987. *Comparative Social Policy and the Third World*. Brighton, Surrey: Wheatsheaf

Maddison, B. A. 1980. *The Meaning of Social Policy: The Comparative Dimensions in Social Welfare*. London: Croom Helm.

Magill, R. S. 1989. "United States of America." In Dixon, J. and Scheurell R. P. eds., *Social Welfare in Developed Market Countries*. London: Routledge.

Mair, L. P. 1944. *Welfare in the British Colonies*. London: The Royal Institute of International Affairs.

Majnani d'Intignano, B. 1991. "Financing of Health Service Systems: Recent Developments and Reforms." *International Social Security Review* 44 (3): 5–22.

Majone, G. 1994. "The Rise of the Regulatory State in Europe." *West European Politics* 17 (3): 77–101.

Mallet, A. 1980. "Social Protection of the Rural Population." *International Social Security Review* 33 (3/4): 359–93.

Malloy, J. A. 1979. *The Politics of Social Security in Brazil*. Pittsburgh: University of Pittsburgh Press.

Mallya, W. J. and Mwankanye, H. A. 1987. "Tanzania." In Dixon, J. ed., 1990. *Social Welfare in Africa*. London: Routledge.

Marchettini, P. 1995. "Italy: Social Security Reinvents the Contribution Method." *Benefits and Compensation International* 25 (5): 2–11.

Maret, X. and Schwartz, G. 1994. "Poland: Social Protection and the Pension System During the Transition." *International Social Security Review* 47 (2): 51–70.

Marotta, G. 1997. "Social Security: Generational Equity." *Vital Speeches of the Day* 63 (12) April: 364–65.

Marsh, D. C. 1950. *National Insurance and Assistance in Great Britain.* London: Pitman.

Marshall, T. H. 1964. "Citizenship and Social Class." In Marshall, T. H. *Class, Citizenship and Social Development.* Garden City, NY: Doubelday.

Marshall, T. H. 1965. "The Right to Welfare." *Sociological Review* 13 (3): 261–72.

Marshall, T. H. 1975. *Social Policy.* London: Hutchinson.

Marshaw, J. 1979. "The Definition of Disability from the Perspective of Administration." In Berkowitz, E. D. ed., *Disability Policies and Government Programs.* New York: Praeger.

Marx, K. 1962 [1851]. "The Class Struggles in France 1848–1850." In *Karl Marx and Frederick Engels Selected Works* Vol. 1. London: Lawrence and Wishart.

Marx, K. 1970 [1875]. "Critique of the Gotha Programme." In *Karl Marx and Frederick Engels Selected Works.* Moscow: Progress Publishers.

Mashhour, N. 1998. "Tools and Means to Alleviate Poverty in Islam." *CROP* [Comparative Research Programme on Poverty] *Newsletter* 5 (2): 1–2.

Maslow, A. 1954. *Motivation and Personality.* New York: Harper and Row.

Mathew, T. I. 1979a. "Introduction on Concepts, Methods and Programmes of Social Security with Particular Reference to ILO's Role and Activities in Promotion of Social Security in Developing Countries in Asia." In *Social Security and National Developmentt.* Bangkok: International Labor Organization.

Mathew, T. I. 1979b. "Concepts, Methods and Programmes of Social Security with particular Reference to Role and Activities in Promotion of Social Security in Developing Countries in Asia." In *Report of a Regional Seminar, Role of trade Unions in Social Security in Asia and the Pacific.* Bangkok: International Labor Organization.

Maydell, B. von 1994. "Perspectives on the Future of Social Security." *International Labor Review* 133 (4): 501–10.

Maydell, B. von and Hohnerlein, E. M. eds. 1994. *The Transformation of Social Security Systems in Central and Eastern Europe.* Louvain: Peeters.

McArdle, F. B. 1979. "Sources of Revenue of Social Security Systems in Ten Industrial Countries." In *Social Security in a Changing World.* Washington, DC: Department of Health, Education and Welfare.

McCallum, J. 1989. "Australia." In Dixon, J. and Scheurell R. P. eds., *Social Welfare in Developed Market Countries.* London: Routledge.

McDonald, P. and Sorrano, G. 1994. "Legislation to Secure Financial Support of Aged Parents by Their Adult Children." *International Journal of Sociology and Social Policy* 14 (1 and 2): 109–23.

McGranahan, D. 1977. *International Comparability of Statistics on Income Distribution* (Report 79.6). Geneva: United nations Research Institute for Social Development.

McGranahan, D., Pizarro, E. and Richard, C. 1985. *Measurement and Analysis of Socioeconomic Development* (Report 85.5). Geneva: United Nations Research Institute for Social Development.

McGreevey, W. 1990. *Social Security in Latin America: Issues and Options for the World Bank* (Discussion Paper 110). Washington, DC: World Bank.

McGregor, D. 1960. *The Human Side of Enterprise.* New York: McGraw-Hill.

McKendrick, B. and Dudas, E. 1987. "South Africa." In Dixon, J. ed., *Social Welfare in Africa.* London: Routledge.

McLaughlin, E. and Glendinning, C. 1994. "Principles and Practice of Social Security Payments for Carers." *International Social Security Review* 47 (3–4): 137–56.

Mead, L. 1986. *Beyond Entitlement: Social Obligations of Citizenship.* New York: Basic Books

Mead, L. 1996. "Raising Work Levels Among the Poor." In Darby, M. R. ed., *Reducing Poverty in America: Views and Approaches.* Thousand Oaks, CA: Sage.

Mebane, W. R. Jr 1994. "Fiscal Constraints and Electoral Manipulation in American Social Welfare." *American Political Science Review* 88 (1) March: 77–94.

Melling, J. 1991. "Industrial Capitalism and the Welfare of the State: The Role of the Employer in the Comparative Development of Welfare States: A Review of Recent Research." *Sociology* 25, May: 219–39.

Mendelsohn, R. 1954. *Social Security in the British Commonwealth: Great Britain, Canada, Australia and New Zealand.* London: Athlone Press.

Mendelsohn, R. 1979. *The Condition of the People: Social Welfare in Australia 1900-1975.* Sydney: George Allen and Unwin

Merritt, R. and Rokkan, S. eds. 1966. *Comparing Nations: The Use of Quantitative Data in Cross-National Research.* New Haven: Yale University Press.

Mesa, A. A. de and Bertranou, F. 1997. "Learning From Social Security Reforms: Two Different Cases, Chile and Argentina." *World Development* 25 (3): 329–48.

Mesa-Lago, C. 1978. *Social Security in Latin America: Pressure Groups, Stratification and Inequality.* Pittsburgh: University of Pittsburgh Press.

Mesa-Lago, C. 1983. "Social Security and Extreme Poverty in Latin America." *Journal of Economic Development* 12 (1): 83–110.

Mesa-Lago, C. ed. 1985a. *The Crisis of Social Security and Health Care.* Pittsburgh: University of Pittsburgh Press.

Mesa-Lago, C. 1985b. "Alternative Strategies to the Social Security Crisis: Socialists, Market and Mixed Approaches." In Mesa-Lago, C. ed., *The Crisis of Social Security and Health Care.* Pittsburgh: University of Pittsburgh Press.

Mesa-Lago, C. 1986. "Comparative Study of the Development of Social Security in Latin America." *International Social Security Review* 39 (2): 127–51.

Mesa-Lago, C. 1988. "Social Insurance: The Experience of Three Countries in the English-speaking Caribbean." *International Labor Review* 127 (4): 479–96.

Mesa-Lago, C. 1991a. "Formal Social Security in Latin America and the Caribbean." In Ahmed, E. and Dreze, J. eds., *Social Security in Developing Countries.* Oxford: Clarendon Press.

Mesa-Lago, C. 1991b. *Social Security and Prospects for Equity in Latin America* (Discussion Paper 140). Washington, DC: World Bank.

Mesa-Lago, C. 1992a. *Social Security in Latin America: Issues and Options for the World Bank.* Pittsburgh: University of Pittsburgh Press.

Mesa-Lago, C. 1992b. *Ascent to Bankruptcy, Financing Social Security in Latin America.* Pittsburgh: University of Pittsburgh Press.

Mesa-Lago, C. 1994. *Changing Social Security in Latin America: Towards Alleviating the Social Cost of Economic Reform.* Boulder, CO: Lynne Rienner.

Mesa-Lago, C. and Roca, S. G. 1990. "Cuba." In Dixon, J. and Scheurell, R. P. eds., *Social Welfare in Socialist Countries.* London: Routledge.

Mesa-Lago, C. and Roca, S. G. 1992. "Cuba." In Dixon, J. and Macarov, D. eds., *Social Welfare in Socialist Countries.* London: Routledge.

Messere, K. and Owens, J. 1979. "The Treatment of Dependent Children Under Income Tax and Social Welfare Systems." *International Social Work* 22 (4): 29–36.

Metcalfe, L. and McQuillan, W. 1979. "Corporatism or Industrial Democracy." *Political Studies* 27 (2): 266–82.

Meyer, M. H., Street, D. and Quadagno, J. 1994. "The Impact of Family Status on Income Security and Healthcare in Old Age: A Comparison of Western Nations." *International Journal of Sociology and Social Policy* 14 (1–2): 53–83.

Midgley, J. 1984a. *Social Security, Inequality and the Third World.* New York: John Wiley and Sons.

Midgley, J. 1984b. "Social Assistance: An Alternative Form of Social Protection in Developing Countries." *International Social Security Review* 37 (3): 247–64.

Midgley, J. 1984c. "Poor Law Principles and Social Assistance in the Third World." *International Social Work* 27 (1): 19–29.

Midgley, J. 1986. "Industrialisaton and Welfare: The Case of the Four Little Tigers." *Social Policy and Administration* 20 (3): 225–38.

Midgley, J. 1988. "Inequality, the Third World and Development." *International Journal of Contemporary Sociology* 25 (3): 93–103.

Midgley, J. 1993. "Social Security and Third World Poverty." *Policy Studies Review* 12 (1–2): 133–43.

Midgley, J. 1995. "Social Security Policy in Developing Countries: Integrating State and Traditional Systems." *Focaal* 22/23: 219–30.

Midgley, J. 1997. *Social Welfare in Global Context.* Beverly Hills, CA: Sage.

Midgley, J. and Livermore, M. 1998. "United States of America." In Dixon, J. and Macarov, D. eds., *Poverty: A Persistent Global Reality.* London: Routledge.

Midgley, J. and Tracy, M. B. eds. 1996. *Challenges to Social Security: An International Exploration.* Westport, CT: Auburn House.

Midwinter, E. 1994. *The Development of Social Welfare in Britain.* Milton Keynes: Open University.

Mikul'shii, K. 1975. "Improvements of Distribution According to Labor in Comecon Countries." *Problems of Econiomics* 18 (7): 24–42.

Millar, J. 1988. "Barriers to Equal Treatment and Equal Outcome: Means-testing and Unemployment." *Equal Treatment in Social Security* (Studies and Research 27). Geneva: ISSA.

Millar, J. and Whiteford, P. 1993. "Child Support in Lone Families: Policies in Australia and the UK." *Policy and Politics* 21 (1): 50–72.

Miller, R. ed. 1992. *The Development of Civil Society in Communist Systems.* Sydney: Allen and Unwin.

Mills, J. S. [1859] 1977. *Collected Works.* Toronto: University of Toronto Press.

Mishra, R. 1984. *The Welfare State in Crisis.* New York: St. Martin's Press.

Mishra, R. 1987. *International Social Work.* Beverly Hills, CA: Sage.

Mitchell, D. 1991. *Income Transfers in Ten Welfare States.* Aldershot: Avebury.

Mohan, B. 1996. "New Global Welfare: Excursions on Post-Industrial Development." *Journal of International and Comparative Social Welfare* 12: 1–10.

Mok, H. 1996. "Public Pensions in South Korea and Taiwan: Coping with the Financial Burden." *Canadian Journal of Social Policy* 38 (3): 30–42

Moles, R. R. 1971. "Social Security and Economic Planning." In *The Planning of Social Security*. Geneva: International Social Security Association.

Montas, H. P. 1983. "Problems and Perspectives in the Financing of Social Security in Latin America." *International Social Security Review* 36 (1): 70–87.

Moon, M. 1977. "The Treatment of Assets in Cash benefit Programs for the Aged and Disabled." In *The Treatment of Assets and Income from Assets in the Income-Conditioned Government Benefit Programs*. Washington, DC: Government Printing Office for the Federal Council on Aging.

Moon, M. 1979. "Supplementary Security Income, Asset Tests and Equity." *Policy Analysis* 6 (1) Winter: 1–20.

Morató, E. A. Jr 1990. "Alternative Delivery Systems for Poverty Alleviation Programmes." *Borneo Review* 1 (1): 1–15.

Morgan, J. N. 1993. "Equity Considerations and Means-tested Benefits." *Journal of Policy Analysis and Management* 12 (3): 773–78.

Morgenstern, S, 1994. "Compulsory Complementary Pension Schemes: France." In *Complementary Pensions: European Perspectives* (Social Security Documentation, European Series 21). Geneva: International Social Security Association.

Moroney, J. R. ed. 1979. *Income Inequality: Trends and International Comparisons.* Lexington: Lexington Books.

Morris, M. D. 1979. *Measuring the Condition of the World's Poor.* New York: Pergamon.

Mortensen, J. M. ed. 1992. *The Future of Pensions in the European Community.* London: Brassey's

Moulton, P. 1975. *Social Security in Africa: Trends, Problems and Prospects.* Geneva: ILO.

Moulton, P. 1984. "Methods of Financing Social Security in Industrial Countries: An International Analysis." In *Financing Social Security: The Options an International Analysis.* Geneva, ILO.

Moulton, P. and Voirin, M. 1979) "Employment Injury Prevention and Compensation in Africa." *International Labor Review* 118 (4): 473–86.

Muller, W. 1993. "The German System of Social Security — Its Structure and Actual Problems." Unpublished paper, Fachhochschule fur Sozialwesen, Esslingen, Germany.

Muller, W. C. 1989. "Germany, West." In Dixon J. and Scheurell R. P. eds., *Social Welfare in Developed Market Countries.* London: Routledge.

Muller, W. C. 1994. "Political Traditions and the Role of the State." *West European Politics* 17 (3): 32–51.

Mulozi, S. L. 1980. "Recent Developments and Future Prospects of Social Security in Africa — with special reference to Zambia." *Social Security Documentation African Series* (International Social Security Association) 3: 53–61.

Munnell, A. H. 1974. "The Impact of Social Security on Personal Savings." *National Tax Journal* 27 (3): 553–67.

Murakami, K. 1995. "The 1994 Pension Reform in Japan and Future Issues." *Benefits and Compensation International* 24 (8): 2–8.

Murakami, K. 19975. "Pension Problems and Proposals for Future Reform in Japan." *Benefits and Compensation International* 26 (8): 14–21.

Murray, C. 1984. *Losing Ground: American Social Policy, 1950–1980.* New York: Basic Books.

Murray, C. 1991. *The Emerging British Underclass.* London: Institute of Economic Affairs.

Murray, M. N. and Bueikman, D. S. 1992. "Social Insurance in Developing Countries — Are there Net Benefits to Programme Participation." *Journal of Developing Areas* 26 (2): 193–212.

Musiga, L. O. 1976. *A Survey of the Effectiveness of Provident Fund Payments in Kenya* (Report 8). Geneva: ISSA, Studies and Research.

Myers, R. J. 1993. "Social Security Will Outlive Us All." *American Demographics* 15, June: 57.

Myers, R. J. 1994. "The Role of Social Security in the Smoke-and-Mirrors Budget Deficit." *Benefits Quarterly* 10 (1): 17–21.

Myers, R. J. 1996. "The Social Security Sky is not Falling in." *Challenge* 39 (6): 23–24.

Myles, J. 1996. "When Markets Fail: Social Welfare in Canada and the United States." In Esping-Andersen, G. ed., *Welfare States in Transition: National Adaptions in Global Economies.* London: Sage.

Myles, J. and Brym, R. J. 1992. "Markets and Welfare: What East and West Can Learn from Each Other." In Ferge, Z. and Kolberg, J. E. eds., *Social Policy in a Changing Europe.* Frankfurt am Main, Germany: Campus Verlag/Boulder, CO: Westview.

Nagel, S. et al. 1997. "The Emergency Nations in 1996." *Development Policy Studies* 3 (3): 12–20.

Nagi, S. Z. 1979. "The Concept and Measurement of Disability." In Berkowitz, E. D. ed., *Disability Policies and Government Programs.* New York: Praeger.

Nelson, C. R. 1953. *Freedom and Welfare: Social Patterns in the Northern Countries of Europe.* Denmark: Krohns Bogtry Krevi.

Neulinger, J. 1990. *The Road to Eden, After All: A Human Metamorphosis.* Culemborg, the Netherlands: Giordano Bruno.

New Zealand 1970. *The Growth and Development of Social Security in New Zealand.* Wellington: Social Security Department.

Nicolle, M. Raporteur 1986. *Supporting Materials and Social Security Forms: Report of the Permanent Committee on Organization and Methods to the International Social Security Association XX General Assembly* (Report XX, Montreal, 2–12 September). Geneva: International Social Security Association.

Noord, P. van den and Herd, R. 1993. *Pension Liabilities in the Seven Major Economies* (Working Paper 142). Paris: Organization for Economic Co-operation and Development.

O'Brien, J. C. 1981. "The Economist's Quandary: Ethical Values." *International Journal of Social Economics* 8 (3): 26–46.

O'Brien, M. and Penna, S. 1998. *Theorising Welfare: Enlightenment and Modern Society.* London: Sage.

OECD (Organization for Economic Co-operation and Development) 1976. *Public Expenditure on Income Maintenance Programmes* (Studies in Resource Allocation). Paris: OECD.

OECD 1977a. *The Tax/Benefit Position of Selected Income Groups in OECD Member Countries in 1971–76.* Paris: OECD.

OECD 1977b. *The Treatment of Family Units in OECD Member Countries Under Tax Transfer Systems.* Paris: OECD.

OECD 1981. *The Welfare State in Crisis.* Paris: OECD.

OECD 1985. *Social Expenditure 1960–1990.* Paris: OECD.

OECD 1988. *Reforming Public Pensions.* Paris: OECD.

OECD 1989. *Historical Statistics: 1960–1987.* Paris: OECD.

OECD 1991a. *Private Pensions and Public Policy* (OECD Social Policy Studies 9). Paris: OECD.

OECD 1991b. *National Accounts. Detailed Tables.* Paris: OECD.

OECD 1994a. "France." *OECD Economic Outlook* 55, June: 64–68.

OECD 1994b. "Belgium." *OECD Economic Outlook* 55, June: 86–88.

OECD 1994c. *Employment Outlook.* Paris: OECD.

OECD 1995. *Forecasting and Controlling Transfer Programme Costs — Definition and Methods.* Paris: OECD.

OECD 1996. *Social Expenditure Statistics of OECD Member Countries.* (Labour Market and Social Policy Occasional Papers, 17). Paris: OECD.

OECD 1997. *Managing the Cost of Transfer Programmes.* Paris: OECD.

Offe, K. 1996. *Modernity and the State: East, West.* Cambridge: Polity.

Ofori, Y. 1976. "Ten years of the Ghana Social Security System." *International Social Security Review* 29 (3): 250–7.

O'Higgins, M., Schmaus, G. and Stephenson, G. 1989. "Income Distribution and Redistribution: A Microdata Analysis of Seven Countries, *Review of Income and Wealth* 35 (2): 107–32.

Olson, L. K. 1994. "Women and Social Security: A Progressive Approach." *Journal of Aging and Social Policy* 6 (1–2): 77–93.

Olsson, S. E 1989. "Sweden." In Dixon, J. and Scheurell, R. P. eds., *Social Welfare in Developed Market Countries.* London: Routledge.

Olsson, S. [E.] 1990. *Social Policy and the Welfare State in Sweden.* Lund: Arvik.

Olsson, S. [E.], Hansen, H. and Eriksson, I. 1993. *Social Security in Sweden and Other European Countries — Three Essays.* Stockholm: Swedish Department of Finance.

Olsson, S. [E.], Hansen, H. and Eriksson, I. 1993. *Social Security in Sweden and Other European Countries — Three Essays.* Stockholm: Swedish Department of Finance.

Oorschot, W. van. 1991. "Non Take Up of Social Security Benefits in Europe." *Journal of European Social Policy* I (1): 15–30.

Oorschot, W. van. 1998. "From Solidarity to Selectivity: The Reconstruction of the Dutch Social Security System 1980–2000." In Brunsdon, E., Dean, H. and Woods, R. eds., *Social Poliocy Review 10*, London: Social Policy Association.

Oorschot, W. van and Schell, J. 1989. *Means-Testing in Europe, a Growing Concern.* Tilburg, the Netherlands: Reeks Sociale Zekerheidswetenschap Studies.

Orloff, A. S. 1993. *The Politics of Pensions: A Comparative Analysis of Britain, Canada and the United States, 1880–1940.* Madison, WI: The University of Wisconsin Press.

Ormerod, P. 1998. *Butterfly Economics*. New York: Faber.

Ortolani, G. Raporteur 1986. *Cash Benefits in Insurance Schemes Against Employment Accidents and Occupational Diseases: Report of the Permanent Committee on Insurance Against Employment Accidents and Occupational Diseases to the International Social Security Association XXII General Assembly* (Report XIV, Montreal, 2–12 September). Geneva: International Social Security Association.

Otting, A. 1993. "International Labor Standards: A Framework for Social Security." *International Labor Review* 132 (1). 169–83.

Oxfam 1995. *Oxfam Poverty Report*. Oxford: Oxfam.

Oxley, C. 1987. *The Structure of General Family Provision in Australia and Overseas: A Comparative Study* (Social Security Review Background/Discussion Paper 17). Canberra: Australian Department of Social Security.

Paillas, C. A. 1979. "Pensions in Latin America: The Present Situation." *International Social Security Review* 32 (3): 288–303.

Palmer, G. 1979. *Compensation for Incapacity. A Study of Law and Social Change in New Zealand and Australia*. Wellington: Oxford University Press.

Parijs, P. van ed., 1992. *Arguing for Basic Income: Ethical Foundations for Radical Reform*. London: Verso.

Parnes, H. S. ed. 1983. *Policy Issues on Work and Retirement*. Kalamazoo: W. E. Upjohn Institute for Employment Research.

Parrott, A. L. 1968. "Problems Arising From the Translation from Provident Funds to Pension Schemes." *International Social Security Review* 21 (4): 530–57.

Parrott, A. L. 1992. "Social Security: Does the Wartime Dream have to Become a Peacetime Nightmare." *International Labor Review* 131 (3): 367–86.

Paukert, F. 1968a. "Social Security and Income Redistribution: Comparative Experiences." In Kassalow, E. M. ed., *The Role of Social Security in Economic Development*. Washington, DC: Government Printing Office.

Paukert, F. 1968b. "Social Security and Income Distribution: A Comparative Study." *International Labor Review* 98 (5): 425–50.

Paul, G. 1991. *Poverty Alleviation and Social Safety Net Schemes for Economies in Transition* (Working Paper, WP/91/14). Washington, DC: International Monetary Fund.

Peachman, J. A., Aaron, H. and Taussig, M. K. 1968. *Social Security Perspectives for Reform*. Washington, DC: Brookings Institution.

Perez, R. A. 1974. "Social Services and Social Security in Latin America." In *The Role of Social Services in Social Security*. Geneva: ISSA.

Perez, R. A. 1990. "Colombia." In Dixon, J. and Scheurell R. P. eds., *Social Welfare in Latin America* . London: Routledge.

Perrin, G. 1969a. "Reflections on Fifty Years of Social Security." *International Labor Review* 99 (2): 249–69.

Perrin, G. 1969b. "The Future of Social Security." *International Social Security Review* 22 (1): 3–28.

Perrin, G. 1985. "The Recognition of the Right to Social Protection as a Human Right." *Labor and Society* 10 (2): 239–58.

Perrin, G. 1992. "The Beveridge Plan." *International Social Security Review* 45 (1–2): 39–53.

Peters, P. G. 1995. "Pensions and Reform." *Vital Speeches of the Day* 61 (9) February 15: 272–6.

Petersen, J. H. 1990. "The Danish 1891 Act on the Old Age Relief: A Response to Agrarian Demand and Pressure." *Journal of Social Policy* 19 (1): 69–91.

Pfeffer, I. 1956. *Insurance and Economic Theory*. Homewood, Il.: Richard D. Irwin.

Pfeffer, I and Klock, D. 1974. *Perspectives on Insurance*. Englewood Cliffs, NJ: Prentice Hall.

Pieters, D. and Vansteenkiste, S. 1995. "Social Security in the European Community: Co-ordination, Harmonization or Thirteen States." *International Journal of Public Administration* 18 (10): 1639–72.

Pilch, M. and Wood, V. 1960. *Pension Schemes*. London: Hutchinson.

Pinch, S. P. ed. 1996. *Worlds of Welfare*. London: Routledge.

Pinera, J. 1995–96. "Empowering Workers: The Privatization of Social Security in Chile." *Cato Journal* 15 (2–3): 155–66.

Pinker, R. 1979. *The Idea of Welfare*. London: Heinemann.

Pinker, R. 1983. "Traditions of Social Welfare." In Dixon, J. and Jayasuriya, D. L. eds., *Social Policy in the 1980's*. Canberra: Canberra College of Advanced Education in conjunction with the Australasian Social Policy and Administration Association.

Pinker, R. 1995. "Golden Ages and Welfare Alchemists." *Social Policy and Administration* 29 (2): 78–90.

Plotnik, R. 1984. *A Comparison of Measures of Horizontal Inequity Using Alternative Measures of Well-being* (Discussion Paper 752–784). Madison, WI: University of Wisconsin, Madison, Institute for Research on Poverty

Polanyi, K. 1957. *The Great Transformation: The Political and Economic Origins of Our Time*. Boston: Beacon Press.

Poloma, M. 1979. *Contemporary Sociological Theory*. New York: Macmillan.

Ponza, M., Duncan, G. J. and Corcoran, M. 1988. "The Guns of Autumn? Age Differences in Support for Income Transfers to the Young and Old." *Public Opinion Quarterly* 52 (4) (Winter): 441–66.

Popper, K. 1972. *Objective Knowledge*. Oxford: Oxford University Press.

Pratt, H. J. 1993. *Gray Agendas: Interest Groups and Public Pensions in Canada, Britain and the United States*. Ann Arbor: University of Michigan.

Price, M. 1994. "Australia's Pension Maze." *Pensions and Investments* 22 (8) April 18: 21.

Prins, R. and De Graaf, A. 1986. "Comparisons of Sickness Absence in Belgium, Germany, and Dutch Firms." *British Journal of Industrial Medicine* 43: 529–36.

Prinz, C. 1995. "Population Ageing and Intergenerational Equity in the Austrian Pension System: A Long-term Analysis of Cohorts Born in the Twentieth Century." Paper presented at The European Population Conference, 1995, Session IV(3), Vienna.

Przeworski, A. 1991. *Democracy and the Market: Political and Economic Reforms in Eastern Europe and Latin America*. Cambridge: Cambridge University Press.

Puidak, P. 1994. "Spain's Recent Developments." *Social Security Bulletin* 57 (4): 77–78.

Purdy, D. 1994. "Citizenship, Basic Income and the State." *New Left Review* 208: 30–48.

326

Purwoko, B. 1996. "Indonesian Social Security in Transition: An Empirical Analysis." *International Social Security Review* 49 (1): 51–71

Quadagno, J. 1989. "Generational Equality and the Politics of Welfare." *Politics & Society* 17, September: 353–76.

Queiro-Tajali, I. 1990. "Argentina." In Dixon, J. and Scheurell R. P. eds., *Social Welfare in Latin America*. London: Routledge.

Queisser, M. 1995. "Chile and Beyond: The Second Generation Pension Reforms in Latin America." *International Social Security Review* 48 (3 and 4): 23–40

Rainwater, L., Rein, M. and Schwartz, J. E. 1986. *Income Packaging in the Welfare state: A Comparative Study of Family Income*. Oxford: Clarendon Press.

Rajnes, D. M. and Turner, J. A. 1996. "Retirement Income System Reform in Central and Eastern Europe." *Benefits Quarterly* 12 (1): 49–58.

Ramasamy, B. and Hartono, O. P. 1992. "Post-retirement Income in Macau." In *Socio-economic Development and Quality of Life in Macau*. Macau: Centre of Macau Studies, University of Macau and Instituto Cultural de Macau.

Ramesh, M 1992. "Social Security in Singapore: Redrawing the Public-Private Boundary." *Asian Survey* 32, December: 1093–108.

Ramesh, M 1995a. "Politics of Illiberal Capitalism: The State, Industrialization, and Social Security in South Korea." In Dixon, J. and Scheurell, R. P. eds., *International Perspectives on Social Security*. Westport, CT: Greenwood.

Ramesh, M 1995b. "Social Security in South Korea and Singapore: Explaining the Differences." *Social Policy and Administration* 29 (3): 228–40.

Raviwongse, V. and Thodtankun, D. 1996. "Social Security in Thailand: Towards an Old Age Pension Scheme." *Canadian Review of Social Policy* 38, Autumn: 88–99.

Reichlin, P. and Siconolfi, P. 1996. "The Role of Social Security in an Economy with Asymmetrical Information and Financial Intermediaries." *Journal of Public Economics* 60 (2): 153–75.

Rein, M. 1976. *Social Science and Public Policy*. Baltimore: Penguin.

Reimers, C. and Honig, M. 1996. "Responses to Social Security by Men and Woman: Myopic and Far-Sighted Behaviour." *Journal of Human Resources* 31 (2): 359–82.

Reubens, B. G. 1989. "Unemployment Insurance in the United States and Europe, 1973–1983." *Monthly Labor Review* 112, April: 22–31.

Reviglio, F. 1967. "Social Security: A Means of Savings Mobilization for Economic Development." *International Monetary Fund Staff Papers* July: 324–68.

Reynaud, E. 1995. "Financing Retirement Pensions: Pay-as-you-go and Funded Systems in the European Union." *International Social Security Review* 48 (3 and 4): 41–57.

Reynaud, E. and Hege, A. 1996. "Italy: A Fundamental Transformation of the Pension System." *International Social Security Review* 49 (3): 65–74.

Reynaud, E. 1998. "Pensions in the European Union: Adapting to Economic and Social Change." *International Social Security Review* 51 (1): 31–46.

Ribas, J. J. 1968. "The Experience of the European Economic Community in Social Security for Migrant Workers 1959–1967." *International Social Security Review* 21 (3): 424–42.

Ribe, F. 1994. "Funded Social Security Systems: A Review of Issues in Four East Asian Countries." *Revista de Analisis Economico* 9 (1): 21–37.

Richman, L. S. 1995. "Why Baby-Boomers Won't be able to Retire." *Fortune* 132 (5)

September 4: 48.

Riebenack, M. 1905. *Railway Provident Institutions in English Speaking Countries.* Philadelphia: Pennsylvania Railway Co.

Rieger, E. anfd Liebfried, S. 1998. "Welfare State Limits to Globalization." *Politics & Society* 26 (3): 361–85.

Riker, W. H. 1982. *Liberalism Against Populism: A Confrontation Between the Theory of Democracy and the Theory of Social Choice.* San Francisco: W. H. Freeman.

Rikkert, H. K. Raporteur 1986. *Financing of Unemployment Protection Schemes: Report of the Permanent Committee on Unemployment Insurance and Employment Maintenance to the International Social Security Association XXII General Assembly* (Report XVII, Montreal, 2–12 September). Geneva: International Social Security Association.

Rimlinger, G. V. 1968. "Social Security and Industrialization" In Kasalow, E. M. ed., *The Role of Social Security in Economic Development.* Washington, DC: Department of Health, Education and Welfare.

Rimlinger, G. V. 1971. *Welfare Policy and Industrialization in Europe, America and Russia.* New York: Wiley.

Rix, S. E. and Fisher, P. 1982. *Retirement-Age Policy: An International Perspective.* New York: Pergamon.

Roberts, C. R. de 1993. "Complementary Retirement Pensions: Towards a Definition of Terms." *International Social Security Review* 46 (4): 51–66

Robinson, H. S. 1977. "Fiji National Provident Fund Augmented Annuity Scheme." In *First Meeting of the Committee* [on Provident Funds] *and Round Table Meeting on Provident Funds.* Geneva: ISSA.

Robinson. J. 1977. "What are the Questions?" *The Journal of Economic Literature* 15 (4): 125–54.

Rodgers, B. N. with Doran, A. and Jones, M. 1977. *The Study of Social Policy: A Comparative Approach.* London: George Allen and Unwin.

Rodgers, B. N. with Greve, J. and Morgan, J. S. 1968. *Comparative Social Administration.* London: George Allen and Unwin.

Rodgers, G. and Hoeven, R. van der 1995. *The Poverty Agenda: Trends and Policy Options.* Geneva: International Institute for Labor Studies.

Roduit, G. 1994. "Compulsory and Voluntary Complementary Pension Schemes: Switzerland." In *Complementary Pensions: European Perspectives* (Social Security Documentation, European Series 21). Geneva: International Social Security Association.

Roebroek, J. M. 1989. "Netherlands." In Dixon, J. and Scheurell R. P. eds., *Social Welfare in Developed Market Countries.* London: Routledge.

Roebroek, J. M. 1993. "Images of the Future: The Basic Income Challenge" *Policy Studies Review* 12 (1and 2): 114–32.

Roemer, M. 1973. "The Development of Health Services under Social Security in Latin America." *International Labor Review* 108 (1): 1–23.

Rosa, J.-J. ed. 1982a. *The World Crisis in Social Security.* San Fransisco: Institute for Contemporary Studies.

Rosa, J.-J. 1982b. "France." In Rosa, J.-J. ed., *The World Crisis in Social Security.* San Fransisco: Institute for Contemporary Studies.

Rose, R. 1994. "Postcommunism and the Problem of Trust." *Journal of Democracy* July: 18–30.

Rose, R. 1993. *Lesson-drawing in Public Policy*. Chatam, NJ: Chatam House.

Rose, R. 1995. "Making Progress and Catching up: Comparative Analysis for Social Policy-making." *International Social Science Journal* 47 (1): 113–25

Rosenman, L. and Warburton, J. 1996. "Restructuring Australian Retirement Incomes: Implications of Changing Work and Retirement Patterns." *International Social Security Review* 49 (4): 5–24.

Rossler, N. 1996. "Eastern Europe: How Supplementary Retirement Provision Fits into the New Philosophy." *Benefits and Compensation International* 25 (8): 15–19.

Rothschild, E. 1995a. "The Debate on Economic and Social Security in the Late Eighteenth Century: Lessons of a Road not to Take." Paper presented at the United Nations Research Institute for Social Development Conference on Rethinking Social Development. Copenhagen.

Rothschild, E. 1995b. "Social Security and Laissez Faire in Eighteenth Century Political Economy." *Population and Development Review* 21 (4): 711–45.

Roush, W. 1996. "Live Long and Prosper." *Science* 273, July 5.

Rowlands, D. 1990. "Privatization and Managerial Ideology." In Kouzmin, A, and Scott N. eds., *Dynamics in Australian Public Management: Selected Essays*. Melbourne: Macmillan.

Royers, J. and Russell, R. 1995. "Early Retirement Terms in Europe." *Benefits and Compensation International* 24 (7) March: 24–32.

Ruzica, M. 1992. "Yugoslavia." In Dixon, J. and Macarov, D. eds., *Social Welfare in Socialist Countries*. London: Routledge.

Ruzica, M. 1995. "Social Security in Yugoslavia: Change or Continuity in the 1990s." In Dixon, J. and Scheurell, R. P. eds., *International Perspectives on Social Security*. Westport, CT: Greenwood.

Rys, V. 1966. "Comparative Studies of Social Security: Problems and Perspectives."*Bulletin of the International Social Security Bulletin* 19 (3): 242–68.

Rys, V. 1974. "Problems of Social Security Planning in Industrialised and Developing Countries." *International Social Security Review* 27 (3): 314–68.

Rys, V. 1988. "Introductory Report on Social Protection Against Occupational Diseases." In *Report of the Regional Round Table Meeting on Social Protection Against Occupational Diseases, New Delhi, India (26–28 October 1987)*. Geneva: International Social Security Association.

Rys, V. 1994. "Social Security Reform in Central Europe: Issues and Strategies." *Journal of European Social Policy* 3 (3): 163–75.

Ryser, J. 1992. "And If Latin Markets Need Yet Another Spike . . ." *Global Finance* 6 (5): 57–59.

Sabelhaus, J. 1994. "Deficits and Other Intergenerational Transfers: Restoring the Missing Link." *Challenge* 37, January/February: 45–50.

Sainsbury, D. 1993. "Dual Welfare and Sex Segregation of Access to Social Benefits: Income Maintenance Policies in the UK, the US, the Netherlands, and Sweden." *Journal of Social Policy* 22 (1): 69–98.

Sainsbury, D. 1996. *Gender, Equality and Welfare States*. Cambridge: Cambridge

University Press.

Salafia, A. 1995. "Italy: The Draft Legislation for Reform of Italy's Statutory and Complementary Pension Schemes." *International Social Security Review* 48 (3–4): 143–50.

Sanda, A. O. 1987. "Nigeria." In Dixon, J. ed., *Social Welfare in Africa*. London: Croom Helm.

Santamaria, M. 1992. "Privatizing Social Security — The Case." *Colombia Journal of World Business* 27 (1): 38–56.

Sarma, A.M. 1979. "Analysis of the Employee Provident Funds, Family Pension and Deposit Linked Insurance Schemes." *Indian Journal of Social Work* 40 (1): 89–99.

Saunders, P. 1990. *An International Study of Poverty, Labor Market and Income Support Policies*. Sydney: University of New South Wales, Social Welfare Research Centre.

Saunders, P. 1991. "Selectivity and Targeting in Income Support: The Australian Experience." *Journal of Social Policy* 20 (3): 299–326.

Savy, R. 1972. *Social Security in Agriculture and Rural Areas*. Geneva: ILO.

Sawyer, M. 1976. *Income Distribution in OECD Countries*. Paris: OECD.

Scheiwe, K. 1994. "Who is Supported? Social Security for Families with Children Between Family Law and the Social Security Regulations in Belgium, Germany and the United Kingdom." *International Social Security Review* 47 (3–4): 45–68.

Schenk, Q. F. and Schenk, E. L. 1981. *Welfare, Society and the Helping Professions: An Introduction*. New York: Macmillan.

Schieber, S. J. and Shoven, J. B. 1996. "Social Security Reform: Around the World in 80 Ways." *American Economic Review* 86 (2): 373–77.

Schmahl, W. ed. 1989. *Redefining the Process of Retirement: An International Perspective*. Berlin: Springer-Verlag.

Schmidt, S. 1995. "Social Security in Developing Countries: Basic Tenets and Field of State Intervention." *International Social Work* 38 January: 7–26.

Schobel, B. D. 1992. "Sooner than you Think: The Coming Bankruptcy of Social Security." *Policy Review* 62, Fall: 41–2.

Schulz, J. H. 1981. *Social Welfare Programs in Asia and Their Population Implications*. New York: United Nations Fund for Population Activities.

Schulz, J. H. 1992. "Economic Support in Old Age: The Role of Social Insurance in Developing Countries." *International Social Security Review* 45 (4): 75–106.

Schulz, J. H., Carrin, G., Krupp, H., Pescke, M., Sclar, E. and Steenberge, J. V. 1974. *Providing Adequate Retirement Income Pension Reform in the United States and Abroad*. Hanover, NH: The University Press of New England.

Schwedtman, F. C. and Emery, J. A. 1911. *Accident Prevention and Relief*. New York: National Association of Manufacturers of the USA.

Schweinitz, K. de 1943. *England's Road to Social Security*. Philadelphia: University of Pennsylvania Press.

Scott, W. 1981. *Concepts and Measurement of Poverty* (Report, 81.1). Geneva: United nations Research Institute for Social Development.

Seeleib-Kaiser, M. 1995. "The Development of Social Assistance and Unemployment Insurance in Germany and Japan." *Social Policy and Administration* 29 (3): 269–93.

Seldon, A. 1957. *Pensions in a Free Society*. London: Institute of Economic Affairs.

Selden, A. 1998. "Pensions without the State." In Seldon, A. ed., *Re-Privatising Welfare: After the Lost Century*. London: Institute of Economic Affairs.

Self, P. 1993. *Government by the Market? The Politics of Public Choice*. London: Macmillan.

Shabangu, N. M. 1986. "Problems and Techniques in the Maintenance of Long Term Records by Provident Funds." In *Eighth Meeting of the Committee* [on Provident Funds]. Geneva: ISSA.

Shame, P. and Sat, K. W. 1978. "The Impact of Contractual Savings on Resource Mobilisation and Allocation: The Experience of Malaysia." *Malayan Economic Review* 23, April: 54–72.

Shaver, S. 1998. "Universality or Selectivity in Income Support to the Aged? A Comparative Assessment of the Issues." *Journal of Social Policy* 27 (2): 231–54.

Shepherd, H. S. and Mullins, L. C. 1989. "A Comparative Estimation of Perceived Income Adequacy Among Young and Old in Sweden and the United States." *Ageing and Society* 9 (3): 256–72.

Sherman, S. R. 1992. *Public Attitudes Towards Social Security 1966–1988*. Washington, DC: Social Security Administration, Office of Research and Statistics.

Shewell, H. 1998. "Canada." In Dixon J. and Macarov, D. eds., *Poverty: A Persistent Global Reality*. London: Routledge.

Shines. E. et al. 1968. *Old People in Three Industrial Societies*. London: Routledge and Kegan Paul.

Siegenthaler, J. K. 1996. "Poverty Among Single Elderly Women Under Different Systems of Old-Age Security: A Comparative Review." *Social Security Bulletin* 59 (3): 31–44.

Silburn, R 1998. "United Kingdom." In Dixon J. and Macarov, D. eds., *Poverty: A Persistent Global Reality*. London: Routledge.

Silverstein, M. and Parrott, T. M. 1997. "Attitudes Towards Public Support of the Elderly: Does Early Involvement With Grandparents Moderate Generational Tensions?" *Research on Aging* 19 (1): 108–26.

Simanis, J. G. 1989. "National Expenditures on Social Security and Health in Selected Countries." *Social Security Bulletin* 52 (12): 18–26.

Simanis, J. G. 1994. "Worldwide Trend Towards Raising the Retirement Age." *Social Security Bulletin* 57 (2): 83–4.

Simey, T. S. 1946. *Welfare and Planning in the West Indies*. Oxford: Clarendon.

Sinfield, A. 1983. "Unemployment." In Kohler, P. A. and Zacher, H. F. eds., *Beitrage zu Geschichte und Aktueller Situation der Sozialversicherung*. Berlin: Duncker and Humblot.

Singer, H. 1968. "Social Factors in Development: An Overview with Special Reference Emphasis on Social Security." In Kasalow, E. M. ed., *The Role of Social Security in Economic Development*. Washington, DC: Department of Health, Education and Welfare.

Singh, A. 1996. "Pension Reform, Stock Market, Capital Formation and Economic Growth: A Critical Commentary on the World Bank's Proposal." *International Social Security Review* 49 (3): 65–74.

Singhakowin, A. 1994. "The Development of Social Security in Thailand." In *Asia Regional Conference on Social Security (September 14–16, 1993) Conference*

Proceedings. Hong Kong: Hong Kong Council of Social Services.

Skidmore, M. J. 1995. "Social Security in the United States." In Dixon, J. and Scheurell, R. P. eds., *International Perspectives on Social Security.* Westport, CT: Greenwood.

Skocpol, T 1992. *Protecting Soldiers and Mothers: The Political Origins of Social Policy.* Cambridge MA: Harvard University Press.

Soeda, Y. 1990. "The Development of Social Assistance in Japan, 1966–83." In *Annals of the Institute of Social Science* (Tokyo: University of Tokyo) 23.

Song, S. and Chu, G. S.-F. 1997. "Social Security Reform in China: The Case of Old-Age Insurance." *Contemporary Economic Policy* 15 (2): 85–93.

Spielmeyer, G. 1965. "General Report." In *Ascertaining Entitlement to Compensation for Industrial Injury.* Brussels: International Institute of Administrative Sciences.

Spicker, P. 1998. "Le Trou de las Secu: social security in France." In Brunsdon, E., Dean, H. and Woods, R. eds., *Social Poliocy Review 10,* London: Social Policy Association.

Sredkova, K. 1996. "Unemployment Insurance in Bulgaria and Other East European Countries: The Transition to a Market Economy." *International Social Security Review* 49 (4): 38–52.

Stagner, R. 1978. "The Affluent Society Versus Early Retirement." *Ageing and Work* 1: 25–31.

Standing, G. 1996. "Social Protection in Central and Eastern Europe: A Tale of Slipping Anchors and Torn Safety Nets." In Esping-Andersen, G. ed., *Welfare States in Transition: National Adaptions in Global Economies.* London: Sage.

Stein, B. 1976. *Work and Welfare in Britain and the USA.* London: Macmillan.

Stephens, J. D. 1995. *The Scandinavian Welfare States* (Occasional Paper). Geneva: United Nations Research Institute for Social Development.

Stephens, J. D. 1996. "The Scandinavian Welfare States? Achievements, Crisis and Prospects." In Esping-Andersen, G. ed., *Welfare States in Transition: National Adaptions in Global Economies.* London: Sage.

Stitt, S. 1994. *Poverty and Poor Relief: Concepts and Reality.* Avebury: Aldershot.

Stock, J. H. and Wise, D. A. 1990. "Pensions, the Option Value of Work, and Retirement." *Econometrica* 58, September: 1,151–80.

Stoesz, D. and Lusk, M. W. 1995. "From Welfare State to Social Compact: Welfare Transformation in Poland." *Journal of Sociology and Social Welfare* 22 (4): 85–98.

Sugden, R. 1982. "Hard Luck Stories: The Problem of the Uninsured in a *laissez-faire* Society." *Journal of Social Policy* 11 (2): 201–16.

Surrey, S. S. 1985. *Tax Expenditure.* Cambridge, MA: Harvard University Press.

Sushama, P. C. 1985. "Malaysia." In Dixon, J. and Kim, H. S. eds., *Social Welfare in Asia.* London: Croom Helm.

Swaan, A. de 1988. *In Care of the State: Health, Education and Welfare in Europe and America in the Modern Era.* Cambridge: Polity Press.

Sweden 1995. *Fact Sheet on Sweden: Social Insurance in Sweden.* Stockholm: Swedish Institute.

Sztompka, P. 1996. "Trust and Emerging Democracy: Lessons from Poland." *International Sociology* 11 (1): 37–62.

Tabone, C. 1998. "Malta." In Dixon, J. and Macarov, D. eds., *Poverty: A Persistent Global Reality*. London: Routledge.

Taira, K. and Kilby, P. 1969. "Differences in Social Security Development in Selected Countries." *International Social Security Review* 22 (2): 210–45.

Takahashi, M. 1997. *The Emergence of a Welfare Society in Japan*. Aldershot, Hants.: Avebury.

Takahashi, T. and Someya,Y. 1985. "Japan." In Dixon, J. and Kim, H. S. eds., *Social Welfare in Asia*. London: Croom Helm.

Takayama, N. 1982. "Japan." In Rosa, J.-J. ed., *The World Crisis in Social Security*. San Fransisco: Institute for Contemporary Studies.

Tamburi, G. 1981. *The International Labor Organization and the Development of Social Insurance* (Social Security Department Working Paper). Geneva: ILO.

Tamburi, G. 1985. "Social Security in Latin America: Trends and Outlook." In Mesa-Lago, C. ed., *The Crisis of Social Security and Health Care*. Pittsburgh: University of Pittsburgh Press.

Tang, K.-L. 1996a. "Non-Contributory Pension System." In Midgley, J. and Sherraden, M. eds., *Alternatives to American Social Security*. Westport, CT: Greenwood.

Tang, K.-L. 1996b. "The Determinants of Social Security in Developing Countries: A Comparative Analysis." *International Social Work* 39 (4): 377–93.

Tanner, M. 1996. "It's Time to Privatize Social Security." *Challenge* 39 (6): 19–20.

Tanzi, V. and Schuknecht, L. 1996. "Reforming Government in Industrial Countries." *Finance and Development* 33, September: 2–5.

Tassel, D. D. van 1995. "The Long Shadow of the Almshouse: Searching for Security in Old Age." *TheGerontologist* 35 (1): 281–83.

Taverne, D. 1995. *The Pension Time Bomb in Europe*. London: Federal Trust.

Taylor-Gooby, P. 1996. "Eurosclerosis in European Welfare States: Regime Theory and Dynamic Change." *Policy and Politics* 24 (2): 109–24.

Terrell, K. 1993. "Public-Private Wage Differentials in Haiti: Do Public Servants Earn a Rent." *Journal of Development Economics* 12 (2): 293–314.

Terribile, F. 1996. "Portugal: Reforming the Social Security System." *OECD Observer* 201, August/September: 36–38

Thompson, K. 1978. "Trends and Problems of Social Security in Developing Countries in Asia." In *Social Security and National Development*. Bangkok: ILO, Regional Office for Asia.

Thompson, K. 1979. "Developments in Old Age Income Security in Asia and Oceania." *International Social Security Review* 32 (3): 304–16.

Thompson, K. 1980a. "Outline of Selected Rural Social Security Schemes in Developing Countries Outside Asia." In *Social Security Documentation: Asian Series*, 6. New Delhi: International Social Security Association, Regional Office for Asia and Oceania.

Thompson, K. 1980b. "Experiences Gained in the Conversion of Provident Funds into Pension Schemes." In *Fourth Meeting of the Committee* [on Provident Funds]. Geneva: ISSA.

Thompson, L. H. 1996. "Principles of Financing Social Security Pensions." *International Social Security Review* 49 (3): 45–64.

Thompson, L. 1998. *Older and Wiser: The Economics of Pensions*. Washington, DC:

Urban Institute Press.

Thurow, L. C. 1984. *Dangerous Currents: The State of Economics*. Oxford: Oxford University Press.

Thursz, D. and Vigilante, J. L. eds. 1975. *Meeting Human Needs: An Overview of Nine Countries*. Beverly Hills, CA: Sage.

Thursz, D. and Vigilante, J. L. eds. 1976. *Meeting Human Needs: Additional Perspectives from Thirteen Countries*. Beverly Hills, CA: Sage.

Tiano, R. and Alchini, L. 1994. "What's Happening in Colombia." *Benefits and Compensation International* 23 (9): 16.

Tierney, B. 1959. *Medieval Poor Laws*. Berkeley: University of California Press.

Titmuss, R. 1974. *Social Policy*. London: Allen and Unwin.

Titmuss, R. 1976. *Commitment to Welfare*. London: Allen and Unwin.

Toft, C. 1996. "Constitutional Choice, Multi-level Government and Social Security Systems in Great Britain, Germany and Denmark." *Policy and Politics* 24 (3): 247–62

Torgerson, D. 1986. "Between Knowledge and Politics: Three Faces of Policy Analysis." *Policy Sciences* 19 (1): 33–60.

Toso, S. G. 1993. "The Mutual Benefit Movement in Chile from its Origins to the Present Time." *International Social Security Review* 46 (3): 29–52.

Townsend, P. 1987. *Poverty and Labor in London*. London: Low Pay Unit and Poverty Research Trust.

Townsend, P. 1993. *The International Analysis of Poverty*. New York: Wheatsheaf.

Tracy, M. 1979. *Retirement Age Practices in Ten Industrial Societies* (Studies and Research, 14). Geneva: ISSA.

Tracy, M. B. 1983. "Older Men's Earnings Tests and Work Activity: A Six-National Study." *Research and Aging* 5, June: 155–72.

Tracy, M. B. 1988. "Integrating Cash Pension Benefits and Health Services for Agricultural Workers in Developing Countries." In Saunders, D. and Fischer, J. eds., *Visions for the Future: Social Work and the Pacific-Asian Perspective*. Manoa: University of Hawaii.

Tracy, M. B. 1990. "Towards a Comparative Approach to the Study of Old-Age Pension Programs in the Third World." In Kattakayam, J. H. ed., *Contemporary Social Issues: Essays in Honor of Prof. P. K. B. Nayar*. Trivandrum, India: University of Kerala.

Tracy, M. B. 1991. *Social Policies for the Elderly in the Third World*. New York: Greenwood Press.

Tracy, M. B. 1995. "Income Programs for the Elderly in Malaysia: A Policy Process Analysis." In Dixon, J. and Scheurell, R. P. eds., *International Perspectives on Social Security*. Westport, CT: Greenwood.

Tracy, M. and Adams, P. 1989. "Age at which Pensions are Awarded under Social Security: Patterns in Ten Industrial Countries." *International Social Security Review* 42(4): 447–61.

Tracy, M. B. and Papel, F. C. eds. 1991. *International Handbook on Social Insurance*. Westport, CT: Greenwood

Tracy, M. and Ward, R. 1986. "Trends In Old-age Pensions for Women: Benefit Levels in Ten Nations." *The Gerontologist* 26, December: 286–91.

Trattner, W. 1974. *From Poor Law to Welfare State*. New York: Free Press.

Trenk-Hinterberger, P. 1994. "The Range of Persons Covered by Social Security Schemes." In Maydell, B. von and Hohnerlein, E. M. eds., *The Transformation of Social Security Systems in Central and Eastern Europe*. Louvain: Peeters.

Triseliotis, J. 1977. *Social Welfare in Cyprus*. London: Zeno.

Tuavera, R. 1985. "Social Benefits in the Cook Islands." In *Social Security in the South Pacific*. Bangkok: International Labor Organization.

Tullock, G. and Eller, K. 1994. *Rent Seeking*. London: Edward Elgar.

Turner, J. A, and Beller, D. eds. 1990. *Trends in Pensions*. Washington, DC: US Government Printing Office, for the Department of Labor, Pension and Welfare Benefits Administration.

Turner, J. A, and Dailey, L. M. eds. 1991. *Pension Policy: An International Perspective*. Washington, DC: US Government Printing Office, for the Department of Labor, Pension and Welfare Benefits Administration.

Turner, J. [A.] and Wantanabe, N. 1995. *Private Pension Policies in Industrialized Countries*. Kalamazoo, Michigan: W. E. Upjohn Institute for Employment Research.

Tyabji, A. 1993. "Social Security in the Asian-Pacific Region." *Asian-Pacific Economic Literature* 7 (1): 53–72.

UK (United Kingdom) 1832. *Report of Commission on Poor Law*. London: Parliament.

UK 1942. *Report of the Inter-departmental Committee on Social Services and Allied Services* [Beveridge Report] (Cmnd 6404). London: His Majesty's Stationary Office.

UK 1998. *New Ambitions for Our Country: A New Contract for Welfare* (Cmd 38505). London: Her Majesty's Stationary Office for the Minister for Welfare Reform.

US (United States of America). Congress, Joint Economic Committee 1974. *How Income Supplements can Affect Work Behavior*. Washington, DC: US Government Printing Office

US HCFA (United States Healthcare Financing Administration) 1989. *International Comparisons of Healthcare Financing and Delivery: Data and Perspectives*. Washington, DC: US Government Printing Office.

US SSA (United States Social Security Administration) 1937–98. *Social Security Programs Throughout the World* [various biennial editions]. Washington DC: US Government Printing Office.

US SSA SSB (United States Social Security Administration *Social Security Bulletin*) 1991. "European Court of Justice Orders Equal Treatment in Awarding Pensions to Men and Women." 54 (2): 14–16.

Uttley, S. 1989. "New Zealand." In Dixon, J. and Scheurell R. P. eds., *Social Welfare in Developed Market Countries* . London: Routledge.

Uttley, S. 1993. "Adapting to Radical Innovation: Accident Compensation in New Zealand." *Policy Studies Review*. 12 (1 and 2): 144–58.

Veit-Wilson, J. H. 1992. "Muddle or Mendacity? The Beveridge Committee and the Poverty Line." *Journal of Social Policy*. 21 (2): 269–301.

Velthoven, B. van and Winden, F. A. A. M. van 1985. "Towards a Political-Economic Theory of Social Security." *European Economic Review*. 27: 263–89.

Verbon, H. 1988. *The Evolution of Public Pension Schemes* . Berlin: Springer-Verlag.

Vittas, D. and Iglesias, A. 1992. *The Rationale and Performance of Personal Pension Plans in Chile.* Washington, DC: World Bank.

Vivian, J. ed. 1995. *Adjustment and Social Sector Restructuring.* Newbury Park: Frank Cass, in conjunction with United Nations Research Institute for Social Development and the European Association of Development Research and Training Institutes.

Vogel, R. J. 1990. *Health Insurance in Sub-Saharan Africa: A Survey and Analysis* (Policy, Research, and External Affairs Working Paper Series 476). Washington, DC: World Bank, Africa Technical Department.

Voirin, M. 1992. "The Free Circulation of Individuals Between EEC Member States: Practical Implications for Social Security." *International Social Security Review* 45 (3): 55–70.

Voirin, M. 1993. "Social Security in Central and Eastern European Countries: Continuity and Change." *International Social Security Review* 46 (1): 27–66.

Voirin, M. 1995. "Private and Public Pension Schemes: Elements of a Comparative Approach." *International Social Security Review* 48 (3–4): 91–141.

Wadhawan, S. K. 1969. "Employees' Provident Fund Scheme — Development and Future Plans." *International Social Security Review* 22 (2): 251–57.

Wadhawan, S. K. 1972. "Development of Social Security in Asia and Oceania." *International Social Security Review* 25 (4): 395–424.

Walters, C. 1988. *Policies Affecting the Workforce Participation of Older Workers Overseas* (Social Security Review Discussion/Background Paper 24). Canberra, Australian Department of Social Security,

Waterman, F. and Brancoli, M. Raporteur 1986. *Interaction Between Prevention of Occupational Risks and Insurance Against Employment Accidents and Occupational Diseases: Report of the Permanent Committee on Insurance Employment Accidents and Occupational Diseases and the Permanent Committee on the Prevention of Occupational Risks to the International Social Security Association XXII General Assembly* (Report XVI, Montreal, 2–12 September). Geneva: International Social Security Association.

Watts, R. 1987. "Family Allowances in Canada and Australia 1940–1945: A Comparative Critical Case Study." *Journal of Social Policy* 16 (1): 19–48.

Weale, A. 1978. "Paternalism and Social Policy." *Journal of Social Policy* 7 (2): 157–72.

Weatherly, R. 1994. "From Entitlement to Contract: Reshaping the Welfare State in Australia." *Journal of Sociology and Social Welfare* 21 (3): 153–74.

Weaver, D. A. 1994. "The Work and Retirement Decisions of Older Women: A Literature Review." *Social Security Bulletin* 57 (1) Spring: 3–24.

Webb, S. and Webb, B. 1927. *English Local Government: English Poor Law History. Part 1, the Old Poor Law.* London: Longman.

Wedekind, R. 1985. "Social Security for Families with Young Mentally Handicapped Members: A Comparison Between the Federal Republic of Germany and Denmark." *International Social Security Review* 38 (3): 243–57.

Weimer, D. L. and Vining, A. R. 1992. *Policy Analysis: Concepts and Practice.* (2nd ed. Engelwood Cliffs, NJ: Prentice Hall.

Whiteford, P. and Bradshaw, J. 1994. "Benefits and Incentives for Lone Parents: A Comparative Analysis." *International Social Security Review* 47 (3–4): 69–91.

Whiteford, P. 1980. *Work Incentive Experiments in the United States and Canada*. Canberra: Australian Department of Social Security.

Whiteford, P. 1995. "The Use of Replacement Rates in International Comparisons of Benefit Systems." *International Social Security Review* 39 (2): 1–23.

Wicker, E. R. 1958. "Colonial Development and Welfare." *Social and Economic Studies* 7 (4): 170–92.

Wiktorow, A. 1992. "Soviet Union." In Dixon, J. and Macarov, D. eds., *Social Welfare in Socialist Countries* London: Routledge.

Wilcox, D. W. 1989. "Social Security Benefits, Consumption Expenditure, and the Lifecycle Hypothesis." *Journal of Political Economy* 97 (2): 288–304.

Wilensky, H. and Lebeau, C. N. 1965. *Industrial Society and Social Welfare*. London: Collier Macmillan.

Wilensky, H., Luebbert, G., Hahn, S. and Jamieson, A. 1985. *Comparative Social Policy: Theories, Methods and Findings* (Research Series 26). Berkeley, CA: University of California Institute of International Studies.

Williams, P. 1995. "At the Abyss." *Benefits Canada* 19 (2): 39–42.

Williamson, J. 1997. "A Critique of the Case for Privatizing Social Security." *The Gerontologist* 37 (5): 561–71.

Williamson, J. B. and Pampel, F. 1993. *Old-Age Security in Comparative Perspective*. New York: Oxford University Press.

Williamson, O. E. 1985. *The Economic Institutions of Capitalism: Firms, Markets, Rational Contracting*. New York: Free Press.

Wilson, D. 1979. *The Welfare State in Sweden*. London: Heinemann.

Wilson, T. ed. 1974. *Pensions, Inflation and Growth: A Comparative Study of the Elderly in the Welfare State*. London: Heinemann.

Wilson, T and Wilson, D. 1993. "Beveridge and the Reform of Social Security — Then and Now." *Government and Opposition* 28 (2): 353–71.

Wilson, T and Wilson, D. 1995. "Social Justice and the Reform of Social Security." *Social Policy and Administration* 29 (4): 335–44.

Wisman, J. D. 1978. "The Naturalistic Turn of Orthodox Economics: A Study of Methodological Misunderstanding." *Review of Social Economy* 36 (4): 62–39.

Wisman, J. D. 1979. "Legitimization, Ideology – Critique and Economics." *Social Research* 46 (2): 190–205.

Wisman, J. D. 1980. "Values and Modes of Rationality in Economic Science." *International Journal of Social Economics* 7 (3): 137–48.

Wisman, J. D. 1987. "Human Interest, Modes of Rationality and the Social Foundations of Economic Science." *International Journal of Social Economics* 14 (7 and 8): 88–98

Wolf, C. 1979. "A Theory of Nonmarket Failure." *Journal of Law and Economics* 22 (1): 107–39.

Wolfe, M. 1968. "Social Security and Development: The Latin American Experience." In Kasalow. E. M. ed., *The Role of Social Security in Economic Development* . Washington, DC: Department of Health, Education and Welfare.

Wolley, F., Vermaeten, A. and Madrill, J. 1996. "Ending Universality: The Case of Child Benefits." *Canadian Public Policy* 22 (1): 24–39.

Woodsworth, D. E. 1977. *Social Security and National Policy: Sweden, Yugoslavia and Japan*. Montreal and New York: McGill University Press.

World Bank 1994. *Averting the Old Age Crisis.* New York: Oxford University Press.

World Bank 1995a. *World Development Report, 1995: Workers in an Integrating World.* New York: Oxford University Press.

World Bank 1995b. *Social Indicators Report, 1995.* Baltimore: Johns Hopkins University Press.

World Bank 1995c. "Social Security Administration in Latin America." Unpublished paper, Washington, DC.

Wright, V. 1992. "The Administrative System and Market Regulation in Western Europe: Continuities, Exceptionalism and Convergence." *Rivista Trimestrale di Diritto Pubblico* (4): 1026–41.

Wright, V. 1994. "Reshaping the State: The Implications for Public Administration." *Western European Politics* 17 (3): 102–37.

Yakushev, L. P. 1991. "New Approaches to Social Security Provision in the USSR." *International Labor Review* 130 (3): 329–37.

Yee, L. D. S. 1994. "Provident Funds and Investment in Developing Countries in the Pacific." *International Social Security Review* 47 (1): 55–73.

Young, A. and Ashton, E, 1956. *British Social Work in the Nineteenth Century.* London: Routledge and Kegan Paul.

Yudin, P. 196–. *From Socialism to Communism* (Tr. Riordan, J.). Moscow: Progress Publishers.

Zacher, H. F. 1988. "Traditional Solidarity and Modern Social Security: Harmony or Conflict?" In Benda-Beckmann, F. von, Benda-Beckmann, K. von, Brun, O. B. and Hirz, F. eds., *Between Kinship and the State: Social Security and Law in Developing Countries.* Dordrecht: Foris.

Zeitzer, I. R. 1994. "Recent European Trends in Disability and Related Programs." *Social Security Bulletin* 57 (2): 21–26.

Zelenka, A. 1974. *Pension Systems in the Industrialized Countries,* Geneva: ILO.

Zschock, D. K. 1982. "General Review of Problems of Medical Care under Social Security in Developing Countries." *International Social Security Review* 34 (1): 3–16.

Zukowski, M. 1994. "Transformation of Economic Systems and Social Security in Central and Eastern Europe." In Maydell, B. von and Hohnerlein, E. M. eds., *The Transformation of Social Security Systems in Central and Eastern Europe.* Louvain: Peeters.

Index

About the Author

JOHN DIXON is Professor of Social Policy in the Department of Social Policy and Social Work at the University of Plymouth in the United Kingdom. Among his earlier publications are *Entering the Chinese Market*, with D. Newman (Quorum, 1998) and *Social Security Programs*, with R. Scheurell (Greenwood, 1995).

ISBN 0-275-96509-0

90000>

9 780275 965099

HARDCOVER BAR CODE

EAN